THE
SHRINE OF ST. PETER
and the Vatican Excavations

By

JOCELYN TOYNBEE

Professor of Classical Archaeology in the University of Cambridge

and

JOHN WARD PERKINS

Director of the British School at Rome

LONGMANS, GREEN AND CO

LONDON · NEW YORK · TORONTO

LONGMANS, GREEN AND CO LTD
6 & 7 CLIFFORD STREET LONDON W I
BOSTON HOUSE STRAND STREET CAPE TOWN
531 LITTLE COLLINS STREET MELBOURNE

LONGMANS GREEN AND CO INC
55 FIFTH AVENUE NEW YORK 3

LONGMANS, GREEN AND CO
20 CRANFIELD ROAD TORONTO 16

ORIENT LONGMANS LTD
CALCUTTA BOMBAY MADRAS
DELHI VIJAYAWADA DACCA

First published 1956

HERTFORDSHIRE
COUNTY LIBRARY

1089870

913·37 937.

B56-01997

PRINTED AND BOUND IN GREAT BRITAIN BY
HAZELL WATSON AND VINEY LTD
AYLESBURY AND LONDON

TO THE

VATICAN EXCAVATORS

PREFACE

THE idea of this book—an account for English readers of the recent excavations under St. Peter's—came first to one of us in the summer of 1952. Shortly afterwards a broadcast talk by the other suggested the possibility of a fruitful collaboration; and in the spring of 1953 the consent of the Vatican authorities was assured to the project of a joint work, which should be based (as any such work must be) on the findings of the official *Report* on the excavations, but which should at the same time present the results in the light of a critical and independent reading of the evidence. For this initial act of generosity and for the opportunity of studying the excavations at leisure, we wish to record our deep sense of indebtedness to the Vatican authorities, and in particular to the office of the Reverenda Fabbrica di San Pietro and to its Segretario Economo, S.E. Monsignor Primo Principi. It is thanks to the generosity of the same office that we are able to illustrate our work with a selection of the admirable photographs taken by the official Vatican photographer, Signor Renato Sansaini, thereby adding greatly to the value and intelligibility of our text. To the architect of the fabric, Ingegnere Francesco Vacchini, whose thankless task it is to satisfy the demands of enthusiasts like ourselves, we offer a word of special gratitude for all the courtesies extended to us in the course of our work.

For the plans and drawings (which are based on those in the official *Report* on the excavations, but have been redrawn to meet the special requirements of the present volume), we have been fortunate in being able to call on the help of the staff and students of the British School at Rome. Dr. G. U. S. Corbett is responsible for Figs. 17 and 18; Figs. 20 and 22, which first appeared in the *Journal of Roman Studies*, xlii, 1952, are the work of Mrs. Sheila Rizzello; Mr. I. Lacey, A.R.I.B.A., drew Fig. 4; Mr. John Graham, A.R.I.B.A., prepared the first draft of Figs. 2 and 3; and the final draft of these Figures, and the bulk of the remaining illustrations, are the work of Mr. Duncan Black, A.R.I.B.A., whose sympathetic pen and clear grasp of the technical questions involved have greatly simplified the task of presenting the results of a highly complex excavation. The drawings of Tombs B, F, and Z (Figs. 5, 6, and 7) are the work of Professor Apollonj-Ghetti, architect and surveyor to the excavations, who with great generosity has not only allowed us thereby to anticipate his own publication of the tombs in question (a publication which has been delayed by unforeseen circumstances), but has himself prepared the drawings in a form to suit our requirements. Our debt to him will be apparent to every reader, and we hope that this foretaste of his work will help to clear the way for his own fuller publication of the material at his disposal.

To all those of our friends who, in discussion, have helped to direct our inquiries into useful lines or to clarify doubtful points, we offer our grateful thanks. Professor Apollonj-Ghetti himself, Professor Axel Boëthius, Professor Fernand De Visscher, Mr. Hugh Last, and Padre José Ruysschaert are but five of the many who have helped us. Above all, we wish to express our very great indebtedness to Professor Enrico Josi and Professor Englebert Kirschbaum, S.J., to whose unfailing generosity and patience in allowing us to draw upon their knowledge of the excavations, of which they were in part in charge, our work owes much of any merit that it may have. The measure of our agreement with their conclusions will be evident to every reader; and where we have, on occasion, ventured to differ from their interpretation of the facts, we have done so in the knowledge that nobody will be happier than they to have provoked an honest difference of opinion, and to have made it possible for others to offer a modest contribution towards the solution of some of the problems left open by the work which they and their colleagues have so ably carried out.

JOCELYN TOYNBEE
JOHN WARD PERKINS

January, 1955.

BIBLIOGRAPHICAL NOTE

For convenience of reference the following publications are cited throughout in abbreviated form:

Calza   G. Calza, *La necropoli del porto di Roma nell' Isola Sacra*, 1940.

CIL   *Corpus Inscriptionum Latinarum.*

Eusebius, *HE*   Eusebius, *Historia Ecclesiastica.*

Ferrua   A. Ferrua, 'Lavori e scoperte nelle Grotte di San Pietro', *Bullettino della Commissione Archeologica Comunale di Roma*, lxx, 1942, pp. 96–106.

Guarducci   M. Guarducci, *Cristo e San Pietro in uno documento precostantiniano della necropoli Vaticana*, 1953.

Josi   E. Josi, 'Gli scavi nelle Sacre Grotte Vaticane', *Il Vaticano nel 1944*, 1944.

Liber Pontificalis   Ed. L. Duchesne, *Le Liber Pontificalis: texte, introduction et commentaire*, i, 1884–6; ii, 1888–92.

Lugli   G. Lugli, 'Scavo di un sepolcreto romano presso la Basilica di San Paolo', *Notizie degli Scavi*, 1919, pp. 285–354.

Mancini   G. Mancini, 'Scavo sotto la basilica di San Sebastiano sull' Appia Antica', *Notizie degli Scavi*, 1923, pp. 46–75, Pls. 9–16.

Pliny, *HN*   Pliny, *Historia Naturalis.*

Regionary   A. Nordh, *Libellus de Regionibus Urbis Romae*, 1949.
Catalogue

Report   *Esplorazioni sotto la confessione di San Pietro in Vaticano eseguite negli anni 1940–1949*: relazione a cura di B. M. Apollonj-Ghetti, A. Ferrua, S.J., E. Josi, E. Kirschbaum, S.J., prefazione di Mons. L. Kaas, Segretario-Economo della Rev. Fabbrica di San Pietro, appendice numismatica di C. Serafini, vol. i, testo; vol. ii, tavole, 1951.

Ruysschaert   J. Ruysschaert, 'Réflexions sur les fouilles Vaticanes, le rapport officiel et la critique, données archéologiques, données épigraphiques et littéraires', *Revue d'histoire ecclésiastique*, xlviii, 1953, 573–631; xlix, 1954, pp. 7–58.

SHA   Scriptores Historiae Augustae.

Tolotti   F. Tolotti, *Memorie degli Apostoli in Catacumbas: rilievo critico della Memoria e della Basilica Apostolorum al III miglio della Via Appia*, 1953.

CONTENTS

CONTENTS

PLATES

(*Between pages* 106–7)

INTRODUCTION

OF the many riddles hidden beneath the soil of Rome, none has aroused a deeper interest than that implied in the age-long tradition that the remains of St. Peter lie buried beneath the high altar of his great church in the Vatican. Since the sixteenth century it has been known that the church stands on the site of a Roman cemetery dating back to the days of the pagan Empire, and from time to time chance discoveries have revealed something of the wealth of ancient remains contained within this area. But until 1939 no systematic examination had ever taken place; and what little was known or could be guessed of the structures that preceded the present papal altar and Confessio was based largely on a literary tradition which we can now see to be, not only fragmentary, but on several fundamental points altogether misleading.

The immediate occasion for the excavations that were undertaken in the 'Sacre Grotte' or crypt of St. Peter's during, and in the years immediately following, the Second World War was the work carried out in 1939 to prepare a tomb for Pius XI, who had expressed the wish to be buried in the Grotte near the tomb of St. Pius X. This crypt, famous for its tombs of popes and princes, occupies nearly the full width of the nave above, and stretches eastwards from the Confessio to the line of the original east wall of the Renaissance church as it was first planned by Bramante. The floor of the church is here carried on vaulting, resting on two rows of piers, which divide the crypt into three equal aisles, running east and west; and the preparation of the tomb for Pius XI was made an opportunity for converting this crypt into a spacious lower church. It was in lowering the floor of the crypt, to provide more head-room for the lower church, that the discoveries were made which gave rise to the excavations. Barely 20 centimetres below the previous floor, the workmen came upon traces of the pavement of Constantine's church, Old St. Peter's, and, immediately below this level, a layer of graves and sarcophagi, in places two or three deep, which had been sunk through the floor of the old church. At one point in the south aisle they hit upon masonry almost directly below the surface; and this proved to be the upper part of the façade of a Roman mausoleum, seemingly complete except that the builders of Constantine's church had sliced off the pediment and the crown of the vault, and rammed the interior full of earth, as a preliminary to laying the pavement of their Basilica. Here was the confirmation of the Renaissance stories of pagan tombs, with their contents of carved sarcophagi, mosaics, and painted stuccoes largely intact; and Pius XII forthwith ordered as full and complete an excavation below the crypt as was compatible with the safety of the church. This excavation was, moreover, to include what none of the Pope's predecessors had ever sanctioned, a thorough, scientific examination of the whole region of the papal altar and Confessio down to virgin soil, to test the truth of the tradition of the Apostle's burial-place.

These excavations, which in addition to the light that they have thrown on the central problem of the Apostolic shrine, have revealed the remains of a Roman cemetery, untouched since it was buried from sight by Constantine's workmen, occupy an area measuring some 20 metres from north to south and 65 metres from east to west, and, at its deepest point (where the visitor today enters the excavations), nearly 9.90 metres (over 30 feet) below the pavement of the present church. They were made possible by the fact that the pavement is here carried on the vaulting of the crypt, the piers of which (many of them were found to rest on nothing more solid than the rammed earth within the tombs of the pagan cemetery) could be underpinned; but, even so, such an excavation, undertaken amid the foundations of the great Renaissance church, was a courageous enterprise, involving formidable engineering problems, which had to be resolved concurrently with the progress of the investigations. Hand in hand with the work of clearance, removing the earth with which the tombs were tightly packed, and demolishing, as far as possible, such later foundations as hindered access or masked the structure of the tombs, went the work of consolidation and reinforcement, underpinning and buttressing with modern walls and piers (each carefully stamped with the seal of the reigning Pope) the footings of the church above. A constant battle was waged with the Vatican's subterranean waters, the inveterate enemy of builders and explorers on the site, now conquered for the time being by the discovery and repair of a serious leak in one of the pipes laid long ago to drain those streams away. That, despite all, the work was brought to a successful conclusion, so that the long-forgotten city of the pagan dead is once more exposed to view, while the church above may fairly be said to be more securely founded than it was before the excavations were begun, is a tribute to the resource and skill both of the small group of archaeologists and engineers who directed the excavations, and of the team of 'Sanpietrini', the Vatican's hereditary workmen, who carried them out under their direction. There can be few achievements in the annals of archaeology that have had to overcome more formidable practical difficulties.

The excavations can never be thrown open to the general public. The space among the ancient tombs is too confined, the paintings, the mosaics, and the stucco-work that decorate them are too delicate and easy to damage. Only small, organized parties and individual scholars are permitted to visit the pagan cemetery and the actual remains of the earliest Apostolic shrine.* But all are free to visit the lower church and its monuments; and a good deal of what is here described can be seen and appreciated by any visitor who is prepared to relate the account of the excavations to the structure and monuments of the crypt and of the church above. The entrance to the lower church (formerly known as the 'Grotte Vecchie') is by a door in the south wall of the Basilica, opening off the Piazza dei Proto-martiri Romani, a little to the west of the former site of the Vatican obelisk. From this door a corridor leads northwards into the lower church, cutting through the partly exposed masonry of the three southern foundation-walls of the nave of Old St. Peter's, against the northernmost of which a stairway leads down to the excavations. On the left, as one enters, are three exhibition-rooms containing, amongst other exhibits, Antonio Pollaiuolo's magnificent bronze monument of Sixtus IV (1471–84) and the sorry fragments of Giotto's 'Navi-cella'; and from the south aisle of the lower church, when the lights are turned on in the excavations, one may catch, through gratings in the floor, vivid, if somewhat tantalizing, glimpses of the cemetery below—here a stretch of brick-built tomb-façade, here a richly painted sepulchral chamber with figured mosaic pavement, and here the interior of another mausoleum, bright with gaily coloured stucco-work. Along the walls of the lower church are ranged the

---

* Such permission can be obtained only through the office of the Reverenda Fabbrica di San Pietro.

tombs of popes and potentates, among them Otto II (d. 983), the only German emperor to be buried in Rome; Hadrian IV (Nicholas Breakspeare, the only English pope, 1154-9); Arnolfo di Cambio's beautiful effigy of Boniface VIII (1294-1303); Queen Christina of Sweden (d. 1689); 'James III of England' and his sons, the Young Pretender and Cardinal York; and Pius XI, the preparations for whose tomb were the occasion for the excavation. To the north, beside the exit, is a small museum, mainly of Christian sculptures of the late-classical and early-medieval periods. In it are some of the finest of the third- and fourth-century carved sarcophagi that have come to light at various times within the Vatican area.

The nave-altar of the lower church stands just to the east, and on a level with the floor, of the Open Confessio; and behind the altar at the end of the south aisle one can see the base-mouldings of the structure put up, on the design of Bramante, to protect the old high altar and the shrine during the construction of the new church. From the extreme western angles of the lower church there runs an elongated, horseshoe-shaped ambulatory with radiating chapels (the former 'Grotte Nuove'). The masonry of the curved inner wall of the western part of this ambulatory is that of the apse of Constantine's church, still standing to the height of the pavement of its Renaissance successor; and through successive doors opening off the ambulatory one can see (moving from east to west) the bases that once carried the 'barley-sugar' columns of the inner screen in front of the raised presbytery; the Open Confessio and the grille in front of the Niche of the Pallia, which occupies the heart of the primitive shrine; and, against the inner face of the Constantinian apse, the excavated stretch of the original Covered Confessio. At the western extremity of the ambulatory, a door cut through the masonry of the Constantinian apse gives access to the Cappella Clementina, fashioned in the seventeenth century out of the primitive chapel of the Confessio; and through the openwork gates one can see the chapel itself, the primitive altar in its gaudy eighteenth-century casing, and, immediately behind and above the altar, the marble facing, porphyry and *pavonazzetto*, of the back of the Constantinian shrine.

The privileged visitor can, of course, see more. Above all, he can visit the tombs of the pagan cemetery, which still have a freshness that carries him effortlessly across the sixteen hundred years since this cemetery was buried from sight. And he can enter the Cappella

Clementina; and from the confined space of narrow chambers opened up by the excavators to right and left of the chapel, he can see what is left of the north and south faces of the Constantinian shrine, and, caught up in a tangle of later masonry, the scanty remains of its predecessor. But here his advantage over the ordinary visitor is more apparent than real. Nobody can fail to be moved in the presence of these venerable relics; but just as photography is helpless to convey any satisfactory general picture of the early shrine, so the impression left on the visitor is one of the complexity and fragmentary character of what survives rather than any clear picture of the shrine as a whole. To understand the significance of these remains, one has to put oneself in the position of the excavators, and to piece together a mental picture of the whole from a number of scattered and visually unrelated scraps of evidence. For this the architect's plans and drawings are far more effective than either the camera or the human eye.

Preliminary reports on the Vatican excavations began to appear in Italian periodicals in 1941; and during the next ten years short accounts, some scholarly, others popular, of the whole or of parts of the Roman cemetery were published in most western European countries and in the United States. A number of these publications are listed in Note 13 to chapter 2. But the secret of what had been discovered beneath the papal altar was carefully kept until December 1951, when the great official *Report* by the excavators (see Bibliographical Note, p. ix) was given at last to an expectant, and perhaps unduly impatient, world. From the moment of the appearance of this *Report*, a stream of reviews and articles, ranging in tone from the laudatory to the severely critical, has flowed steadily and shows as yet no signs of abating. Fresh interpretations of the excavators' findings have been proffered; and some new discoveries, undetected by the excavators, have been claimed. The present writers have done their best to take account of the more important items in this very considerable literature up to the moment of going to press, and criticisms of the published opinions of some of the critics and of other writers on the subject will be found in the text and notes, and in Appendices B and C of this book.

The official *Report* is confined to discoveries made under and close to the Confessio of St. Peter's, and for that section of the excavations it is a definitive work. The purpose of the present book is very different—that of providing English readers with a comprehensive, connected, critical, and reasonably priced account of the whole of the area recently excavated on the Vatican Hill. The first part is concerned with all that we know of the Roman cemetery in this area—with the ancient topography of the district in which it developed, with the lay-out and chronology of its elaborate and costly house-tombs, with their architecture and art, with the social position and religious beliefs of those who owned them and were buried in them. As documents of Roman funerary practice and ideas about the after-life in the second and third centuries of our era, these tombs are outstanding; and for all that the focal point of the excavations was undoubtedly the Apostolic shrine, they have an interest and value that is quite independent of their relation to this shrine. Thus, in publishing the first serious and detailed study of this necropolis as an entity, the writers hope that they may have produced something that will be of real service to those who are, first and foremost, students of Graeco-Roman Antiquity.

St. Peter's shrine, with which the second part of the book directly deals, for all the intrinsic archaeological interest of the problem that it represents, obviously makes its widest appeal to those whose interests in it are religious, ecclesiastical, and historical. Here the writers' aim is to offer a straightforward and objective account of the facts as revealed by the excavations, and to present their own interpretation of those facts. For reasons that have already been made clear, the reader is forewarned against disappointment at finding no photographic views of the actual shrine among the plates: the conditions under which this part of the excavation took place were such as to preclude any but the most minutely detailed photographs; and for these (as for all such detailed documentation) the specialist must turn to the plates of the *Report*. Instead, the reader will find a number of text-figures. These are for the most part based on those in the *Report*, but have been redesigned and redrawn throughout to meet the particular requirements of the present text, to which they are an essential complement. So far as the illustration of so complex a site permits, they have been chosen and prepared with a view to simplicity and clarity of presentation and to the illustration of certain features of the excavation which, in the opinion of the writers, have as yet received inadequate attention.

In the concluding chapter and epilogue, the story of St. Peter's shrine and of its architectural and artistic setting is carried down into the Middle Ages. The third section of chapter 6 is devoted to the closely related cult-centre of St. Peter and St. Paul, established in the late-third century beside the Via Appia. It offers a new summary of the facts, in particular of those revealed by recent work, and a critical discussion of the theories current as to the purpose of this controversial monument.

It cannot be too strongly emphasized that this book makes no claim to be an exhaustive or definitive publication even of those parts of the Roman cemetery which are not covered by the official *Report*; such a publication is the right and responsibility of the Vatican excavators themselves. Instead, through the kindness of the excavators, three of the tombs in the eastern portion of the area, which find no place in the *Report*, have been selected for detailed scrutiny. The rest of the tombs are not catalogued systematically one by one, but are studied as parts of a larger whole. The chapters on the shrine are naturally based on the *Report*, supplemented and controlled, so far as is now possible, by personal observation. The primary source for this part of the excavation is, however, and must remain the *Report* itself, where the evidence—some of it, unavoidably, no longer accessible *in situ*—is set out with exemplary thoroughness and clarity. The present writers have, thanks to the facilities given to them by the Vatican authorities, studied on the spot everything that they describe, apart from those portions of the shrine itself and its immediate surroundings which the excavators were obliged, unhappily, to cover up again or to destroy in order to probe farther; and they have learnt much from private discussion of particular questions with some of the excavators. But they cannot, obviously, write with the knowledge and authority which belong only to those who have themselves conducted the excavations. The reader is asked to keep these inherent limitations of the book clearly before him.

The writers have had two main classes of readers in mind—the classical and archaeological specialist and the general reader. The former may not always have easy access to the *Report* (which, in view of its high price, is unlikely to circulate widely outside a limited number of learned libraries) or opportunity for studying the actual cemetery in detail; and it is for him that the notes are primarily, but by no means exclusively, intended. The latter may be interested in the subject from a variety of standpoints—religious, historical, architectural, artistic, and sociological. And since the term 'general reader' may be taken to include some who have not had a specifically classical or archaeological training, in their interests technical terminology is as far as possible avoided, Greek and Latin passages are accompanied by English translations, and Greek and Latin words and phrases, familiar to classical scholars, are explained. To write for two different categories of readers is to invite criticism from both. The writers can only express their hope that any shortcomings in this respect will be treated with indulgence.

Part One

THE VATICAN CEMETERY

I

THE VATICAN AREA IN CLASSICAL TIMES
(Fig. 1)

A ROMAN of the pagan Empire, miraculously projected through time and set down today near the Tiber, at the east end of the modern Via della Conciliazione, would have the greatest difficulty in recognizing his whereabouts. He might perhaps detect the familiar shape of the Mausoleum of Hadrian through the later trappings of Castel Sant'Angelo; and, as he turned westward towards St. Peter's, there would be much in the present-day setting the spirit of which he could both understand and appreciate—the spacious directness of the modern roadway, the arena-like piazza with its obelisk, fountains, and sweeping colonnades, the stately Corinthian façade of the narthex of St. Peter's, the gigantic, shining dome, on which his gaze would be riveted. But where would he find the old familiar landmarks of the Ager Vaticanus? Where would be the Mons, and where the Vallis? He might well conclude that they had vanished. Yet gradually, through the encrustation of majestic architecture, those homely, natural features of the region would unveil themselves before him. He would note how the ramp and steps at the goal of his level road mount steadily to gain the platform which gives access to the church; how the lofty mass of the palace piles itself up, tier upon tier, above him on the right, and how steeply the steps on the left of the central platform fall towards the entranceway which runs beneath the Arco delle Campane in the direction of the Sacristy. Penetrating through that archway he would see how the low-lying ground still fans out between the abrupt northern spur of the Janiculum on the east and the rapidly rising hillside which, on the west, enfolds the choir of the Basilica; and as he found his bearings, our Roman would realize that the palace and its grounds occupy the summit and the eastern slopes, the church the southern slopes, of the ancient Mons Vaticanus, and that the Sacristy and the

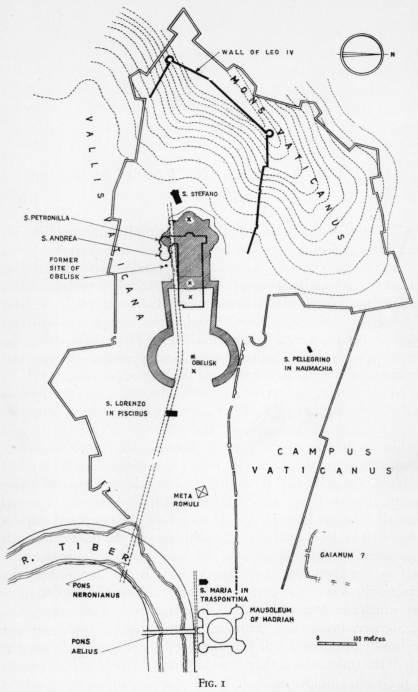

FIG. 1

The Vatican area, showing some of the main classical and early-Christian features. Shading indicates the present Church of St. Peter's and the Piazza San Pietro. Crosses mark the approximate find spots of pagan tombs outside the area recently excavated.

streets and buildings immediately east and south of it fill what was once the Vallis Vaticana.

In classical times the Ager Vaticanus formed the northern sector of the transtiberine region, the last of the fourteen administrative regions into which Augustus divided the city of Rome. Its most distinctive feature was a conspicuous hill, the Mons Vaticanus, descending sharply to a valley on the south and, on its east side, adjoining the river, to what was within living memory the flat, open ground of the Prati di Castello, the ancient Campus Vaticanus. These features can still be deciphered in the modern landscape, although they were far more strongly accented then than they are today. It was a thoroughly suburban, not to say rural, district, noted for its clay, from which earthenware vessels and bricks were made (and still are made), and for the wretched quality of the products of its vineyards.[1] Parts of it were certainly regarded as unhealthy, and references in literature to privately owned farms and estates in the area are rare.[2] There were, on the other hand, several large properties belonging to members of the imperial family. The elder Agrippina, or more probably her husband, Germanicus, laid out gardens near the Tiber (Horti Agrippinae), which passed later to her son, the Emperor Gaius, and eventually to Nero;[3] and although their precise limits have not been recorded, the natural inference to be drawn from passages in Pliny, Tacitus, and Suetonius[4] is that the Circus of Gaius and Nero in the Vallis Vaticana lay within this park. Other imperial gardens in the fourteenth region were the Horti Domitiae, which took their name from their first owner, who was probably Domitia Lepida, Nero's aunt, rather than her namesake, Domitia Longina, Domitian's Empress.[5] We know their general location from the fact that they contained the Mausoleum of Hadrian (Castel Sant'Angelo); and a lead pipe bearing the name of Crispus Passienus, the husband of Domitia Lepida, which came to light in 1889 on the site of the near-by Palace of Justice, may be a clue to their extent in this direction.[6] It is only to the north-west that we have any indication of the limits of Domitia's gardens. In this direction they probably adjoined the Gaianum, an open space mentioned in the fourth-century Regionary Catalogue and called after the Emperor Gaius, who used it for chariot-practices. It may be identical with the ruins shown to the north-west of the Castel Sant'Angelo in fifteenth-century 'prospects' of Rome; and numerous inscriptions set up in honour of charioteers have been found in the vicinity on the site of the Church of Santa Maria in Traspontina.[7] The Regionary Catalogue also lists two Naumachiae Vaticanae; and the remains of one of these artificial lakes, designed for staged naval combats, may have been discovered in 1949 some distance to the west of Hadrian's Mausoleum, on the north side of the Piazza Pio XII (the former Piazza Rusticucci).[8]

Of suburban temples in the Vatican district, with the possible but doubtful exception of a temple of Apollo (p. 21), we know of one only, the Phrygianum (Frigianum in the Regionary Catalogue) or shrine of Cybele, the Magna Mater Deum Phrygia. The main temple of this goddess in Rome was that erected on the Palatine after 204 B.C., when the Roman embassy brought from Pessinus in Asia Minor her image in the form of a black, pointed stone.[9] This Palatine temple was restored by Augustus,[10] and, according to the Regionary Catalogue (Reg. X), it was still standing in the late-fourth century. There was also a round temple of Cybele, adorned with paintings, which stood at the top of the Via Sacra.[11] But the Vatican sanctuary, although one of several, seems to have been a well-known and important cult-centre, to judge from the evidence of two inscriptions in which the Vatican is mentioned in the context, of the worship of Cybele, the one found at Lyon and dated to A.D. 160, the other at Kastel, near Mainz, dated to 236.[12] No less than nine inscriptions referring to the same cult have long been known from the immediate vicinity of St. Peter's, seven on marble altars found during the construction of the south façade, an eighth walled up in the old church, and a ninth, in Greek, found in the Mausoleum of Santa Petronilla (p. 11).[13] Two more were discovered in 1949, a fragmentary undated inscription of the same type found near the Church of San Lorenzo in Piscibus, and another complete altar of the cult, with an inscription of 374, in the Piazza San Pietro.[14] None of these texts came to light in its original position, but it is clear that the site of the shrine of the Magna Mater cannot lie far away. All the dated inscriptions in honour of the Phrygian goddess actually recorded as found in the Vatican area fall between the years 305 (CIL, vi. 1, 497)[15] and 390 (CIL, vi. 1, 512), and they show that her worship continued to flourish not far from St. Peter's shrine for some time after the Empire had become officially Christian.

Until the completion, in 134, of the bridge leading to the

Mausoleum of Hadrian (the Pons Aelius),[16] all communication between the Campus Martius and the Vatican was by the bridge which spanned the most westerly bend of the Tiber, at a point intermediate between two modern bridges, the Ponte Vittorio Emanuele and the Ponte Principe Amedeo Savoia Aosta. Some of the piers of this Roman bridge survive and are visible when the water is very low; and in the fourth century it seems to have already been in a ruinous condition, since the Regionary Catalogue does not cite it. The name by which it was later known—Pons Neronianus—is not recorded before the middle of the twelfth century; but the bridge itself must have existed in the days of Gaius and Nero to give access to the imperial gardens and, above all, to the Vatican Circus. There must also have been a road leading from the bridge to the Circus; and although we have no surviving mention of the Via Cornelia earlier than an inscription dating from the reign of Vespasian,[17] there is no reason why it should not have been in being under the Julio-Claudians. That a road of this name ran westwards, in the general direction of the hill on which St. Peter's subsequently stood, we know from its association with the Apostolic shrine in an early-medieval pilgrims' itinerary,[18] and traces of such a road have, in fact, been found to the east of the Piazza San Pietro, in the Borgo Santo Spirito, a few metres below the modern street-level and heading eastwards for the site of the Pons Neronianus.[19] From the level at which it was discovered this was probably the later, post-Constantinian, Via Cornelia. But there is also record of a substantial stretch of what may well be the early-imperial Via Cornelia, found at a depth of about 11·50 metres beneath the present surface, when foundations were being dug for the south-east corner of the existing Basilica.[20] That a highway did, in fact, run along the southern foot of the Vatican Hill as early, at least, as the first half of the second century can be inferred with reasonable certainty from the southward orientation of the pagan tombs beneath the south aisle of St. Peter's (p. 24). That this highway was the Via Cornelia is less certain (cf. Note 22); but for simplicity and convenience of reference the writers have retained throughout the identification proposed in the Report.

Closely associated with the Via Cornelia are the Via Aurelia and the Via Triumphalis, all three roads having been under the care of the same official in the reign of Antoninus Pius.[21] The earlier route of the Via Aurelia (the Via Aurelia Vetus) ran from the Pons Aemilius due west across the Janiculum: the later route (the Via Aurelia Nova) probably left the Tiber-bank at the Pons Neronianus and ran south-westwards across the northern spur of the Janiculum ridge;[22] while the Via Triumphalis probably ran north-westwards from the river at the Pons Neronianus across the level ground between the Vatican Hill and the Mausoleum of Hadrian.

Few features of Roman life are more familiar than the dwellings of the dead strung out along the highways on the outskirts of every settlement and city. The roads of the Vatican suburb were no exception. Nothing, indeed, would surprise a Roman *revenant* more than the total disappearance from sight of the hundreds of sepulchral monuments which once lined those roadsides, fitted in, wherever space was available, between the imperial pleasure-gardens, sports-grounds, clay-beds, brickworks, and vineyards. In the Middle Ages two notable tombs (long since demolished), known as the Meta Romuli and the Terebinthus respectively, still stood beside an ancient road which linked the Pons Aelius and the Mausoleum of Hadrian with the Via Cornelia.[23] Other burial-places were revealed near the now-vanished Porta Angelica in 1886, and on the site of the present Annona Vaticana in 1930; and a marble sepulchral altar was excavated in 1936 to the east of the obelisk in the Piazza San Pietro.[24] Turning to the site of the church itself, we learn from the reports of such writers as Antonio Bosio, Maffeo Vegio, Alfarano, and Grimaldi that many similar discoveries were made between the beginning of work on New St. Peter's in 1452 and the completion of the porticoes of the piazza by about 1667. Decorated pagan tombs came to light at such spots as those marked with a cross on the plan in Fig. 1 (all, it should be noted, on a line with the recently excavated mausolea), and were filled in again by the Renaissance builders after many of the sarcophagi and inscriptions which they contained had been removed, to find their way eventually to the gardens and museums of the city. But the two new, compact series of house-tombs (Figs. 2, 3), scientifically investigated, with their contents left intact, have now provided graphic and decisive proof that a great pagan necropolis underlay the Vatican Basilica. These tombs will be described in detail in chapters 2, 3, and 4. We must, however, consider here the contribution made by their discovery to our knowledge of the Vatican district during the classical period.

Until 1940 it was generally believed that the southern foundation-walls of the fourth-century church rested on the northern walls of the Circus of Gaius and Nero.[25] This Circus witnessed, according to Tacitus,[26] the torturing and slaughter of Christians by Nero in 64; and it was the traditional scene of St. Peter's martyrdom (chapter 5). Until 1940 it was also believed that the spot from which Sixtus V moved the obelisk in 1586 to the centre of the present Piazza San Pietro marked the line of the *spina*, or central wall, of the Circus; for Pliny states[27] that Gaius brought the obelisk, made by Nencoreus, son of Sesosis, from Egypt and placed it 'in the Circus of Gaius and Nero on the Vatican' (*in Vaticano Gai et Neronis principis circo*); and, as we know from any number of circus-scenes on works of Roman art, and from such actual examples as the obelisks set up by Augustus and Constantius II in the Circus Maximus, the *spina* was the normal position for obelisks in a Roman circus. Again, until 1940 it was believed that the Via Cornelia ran right under the Basilica, just to the south of the Apostle's shrine.

One of the major surprises, therefore, of the recent excavations has been the failure to find any trace either of the Circus or of the Via Cornelia beneath the church. The southern foundation-walls of Old St. Peter's came to light, built in alternating courses of brick and tufa, in a manner characteristic of the fourth century and unknown in the first; and so far from resting on first-century structures of any kind, they go straight down, in all three cases, to virgin soil. Furthermore, the southern row of mausolea obviously occupies the hitherto presumed line of the road (Fig. 2). Some of our old ideas of the topography of the Vatican region have therefore to be abandoned: Circus and road must have been located farther to the south. They cannot have been very far away. We have already noted reasons for holding that a Roman highway ran east and west near the southern foot of the Vatican Hill (p. 7); and, as regards the position of the Circus, the easternmost tomb investigated in the northern street of the necropolis (A in Fig. 3) yielded, most providentially, a highly important piece of evidence. It is an inscribed marble slab (*titulus*) inserted above the door of this second-century mausoleum, and it informs us that the occupant of the sepulchre, a certain Gaius Popilius Heracla, had given directions to his heirs to bury him near the Vatican Circus—*in Vatic(ano) ad circum*. The inscription is an extract from Heracla's will and is worth quoting in full, since it has considerable social and legal interest, in addition to its topographical significance. 'From the testament, written on three leaves, of Popilius Heracla. Gaius Popilius Heracla to his heirs, greeting. I ask you, my heirs, I order you, and I rely upon your good faith, to build me a tomb on the Vatican Hill near the Circus, next to the tomb of Ulpius Narcissus, at a cost of 6000 sesterces. For this purpose Novia Trophime will pay 3000 sesterces and her co-heir 3000. I wish my remains to be placed there and also those of my wife, Fadia Maxima, when her time comes to join me. I charge my freedmen and freedwomen with the right and duty of maintaining cult at that tomb. This applies also both to those whom I shall free by my will and to those whom I leave to be freed on certain conditions; and the same likewise applies to the freedmen and freedwomen of Novia Trophime and to all the descendants of the persons above mentioned. They are to enjoy the right of free access to the tomb for the purpose of making sacrifices there.'[28] Heracla was, perhaps, a circus-fan; or the reference to the Circus may be no more than a convenient way of describing the site of the plot that he had chosen for his tomb.

Where precisely in the Vatican area, to the south of the necropolis, Circus, road, and obelisk were located, we do not as yet know. It is reasonable to suppose that for a part of its way the road may have formed the northern boundary of Agrippina's gardens and provided access to the Circus; and in view of the lie of the ground, the Circus was probably laid out with its long axis running east and west. Whether its walls were of stone or of earth we cannot tell. It did not survive, one would suppose, the building of Old St. Peter's, and it finds no mention in the Regionary Catalogue. But it was clearly in use in the first half of the second century, in the time of Gaius Popilius Heracla; and if it is to the Circus rather than to the Gaianum (p. 5) that a passage in the life of the Emperor Elagabalus refers,[29] it was still in use nearly a century later (between 218 and 222). The passage in question records that the Emperor drove chariots drawn by four elephants *in Vaticano*, destroying some tombs for the purpose; and although speculation on the nature of the enlargement of the Circus on this occasion is idle until its actual site can be established with certainty, it is not unreasonable to suppose that it may have been set back a little way from the Via Cornelia, and that between it and the road, and to the west of the western boundary of the Horti Agrippinae, there may have been a line of tombs corresponding to, and facing, those of the newly excavated necropolis on the north side of the road, at the foot of the Vatican Hill. In this connection, there is one piece of evidence the full significance of which is not yet clear. When the Sacristy was added in the eighteenth century against the south-east angle of the south transept of the Renaissance Basilica, it took the place of a circular Roman mausoleum, which had been converted in the Middle Ages into the Church of Sant' Andrea, and was later known as the Church of Santa Maria della Febbre. It used to be supposed that this tomb dated from the later-fourth century, but its remains have now been revealed to be of the second century.[30] What is not yet clear is whether the pre-Constantinian Via Cornelia ran to the north or to the south of it. Of the two, the former seems to be more probable, if one relates the alignment of the newly excavated tombs to the position of the fragment of pre-Constantinian road found beneath the south-east angle of the present Basilica (Fig. 1), but, on the present evidence, one cannot be certain; and the whole history of previous speculation upon the problems of Vatican topography warns us of the dangers of trying to outrun the established facts.

Just to the west of Sant'Andrea there stood a second, and slightly smaller, circular tomb, the original date of which has not as yet been determined. In the early-fifth century it served for the burial of Maria, wife of Honorius, of Honorius himself, and possibly also of Theodosius II, if we can believe the story that his remains were moved in 451 from Constantinople to the Vatican Hill, to be buried *ad Apostolum Petrum*;[31] in 757 it became the Church of Santa Petronilla; and it was pulled down before Sant'Andrea, in the sixteenth century.

The obelisk raises a fresh set of difficulties, which the present excavations have done little to resolve. Until 1586, when it was moved by Domenico Fontana, on the orders of Sixtus V, to its present site in the middle of the Piazza San Pietro, it stood just to the south of the church, immediately to the east of the rotunda of Sant'Andrea. The site has not been excavated; but its exact position is known from a number of sixteenth-century drawings, prominent among them being those made by Marten van Heemskerck in 1533-4, which show it standing upon what appears to be the top of a truncated pyramidal base, almost immediately adjoining the walls of the rotunda.[32] We now know that this cannot have been the position of the *spina* of the Circus. Not only does the second-century rotunda lie right across the line, running from east to west, which the *spina* would have had to follow, but there would have been no room between the outer wall of the Circus and the recently excavated tombs for the road of which the remains were found when the south-east corner of the present church was built (p. 7).[33] Unless, therefore, the obelisk had already been moved in Antiquity (which seems unlikely), we are faced with two possibilities: either that this is not the obelisk of which Pliny speaks as having been placed in the Vatican Circus; or else that Pliny is using the phrase *in circo* in the less precise sense that it commonly bears in Roman topographical usage, whereby a district or a quarter takes its name from the most familiar monument in it, and that the obelisk was near, but not necessarily in, the Circus.[34] Until the site from which Fontana moved it has been excavated, it is probably wisest to be content with stating the problem and to leave the answer in suspense.

The essential responsibility for transforming the physical contours of the classical Ager Vaticanus into something that roughly corresponds with what we see today lies with the builder of Old St. Peter's, Constantine the Great. That Constantine himself planned and, to some extent at least, actually built that church is the well-known Christian tradition, and there seems to be no serious reason for questioning its authenticity (p. 195 f.). In order to obtain a level terrace on which to build his church, Constantine's engineers had to cut back the steep south-eastern slope of the Vatican Hill and to build out from it an enormous platform, an operation which involved the cutting and dumping of over a million cubic feet of earth, and which may be compared, on an enormous scale, with the construction of a tennis-court on a shelving bank. The area of the excavations is approximately that of the northern half of the projecting platform (with the exception of the eastern end, where the absence of vaulted supports for the pavement of the present church creates a serious practical obstacle to any further work); and within this area those tombs that stood in the way of the great longitudinal foundations of the nave of Constantine's church were ruthlessly demolished, and the remainder were packed with earth, their doors blocked, their superstructure dismantled, and the gaps between them linked with strengthening walls, to provide a solid, level basis for the pavement above. For all the care that was evidently taken to avoid unnecessary destruction—and even so his workmen do not seem to have hesitated to turn to their own use some of the materials recovered from the earlier buildings—this was drastic action and, in sponsoring it, the Emperor, even if he was not technically guilty of the criminal offence of *violatio sepulchri*, cannot have escaped the odium of putting out of action an extensive area of richly decorated and well-cared-for family-sepulchres.[35]   The application of the Roman law in such a case is disputed. If these operations were actually illegal, Constantine, as Pontifex Maximus, was in a position to carry through a measure mitigating, or dispensing himself from, the penalties for *violatio sepulchri*, which he would otherwise have incurred by building St. Peter's upon the site of the cemetery.[36] Alternatively, if it were only a question of his offending the owners of these family-tombs, and pagan sentiment generally, he may have been content with some pronouncement emphasizing the strict legality of demolishing the upper portions of the tombs and filling them with earth (*congestio terrarum*).[37] From the condition in which the tombs were found when excavated, it is clear that Constantine's builders took care to respect the dead themselves, carefully stacking in sarcophagi bones from those burials which they could not avoid disturbing; and the material from the dismantled upper parts of the tombs was carefully removed, not hurled down into the interiors, which were packed instead with clay from the Vatican hillside and with earth and rubble. But the fact remains that in building the Basilica just where he did build it, the Emperor had serious obstacles, moral no less than material, to overcome—obstacles which need not have been encountered had he chosen for it a site slightly farther to the south, on the level ground which marks the site of the Circus of Nero, the traditional scene of the Apostle's martyrdom. The fact that he did not do so argues conclusively that his choice was determined by the existence of another site, a cult-spot on the hillside (P in Fig. 3), where the excavators found the late-second-century niched construction to be described in detail in chapter 6. It is quite evident that, both in plan and in elevation, the position of the Basilica was determined by the desire to give this little shrine the place of honour as the central feature of the whole building; and it is not unnatural to infer from his insistence on it that Constantine believed it to mark the place where the bones of the Apostle then reposed.

To the evidence afforded by Constantine's choice of site we may now add that of an inscription found by the excavators in one of the tombs and since studied and published by Professor Margherita Guarducci.[38] In the central niche in the north wall of one of the tombs in the new cemetery, that of the Valerii (H in Fig. 3), she claims to have deciphered, beside a rough drawing in red lead (*minium*) of the head of St. Peter, an inscription, traced first in red and then in part retraced in charcoal: *Petrus roga Christus Iesus pro sanctis hominibus Chrestianis ad corpus tuum sepultis* ('Peter, pray Christ Jesus for the holy Christian men buried near your body'). Above this is a second head, still more rudely sketched in charcoal and flanked by an apparently meaningless flourish of black lines, which she reads as the letters CHR. This upper head she interprets as that of Christ surmounted by the heads and necks of a pair of phoenixes, symbolizing the death and resurrection of man's Immortal Redeemer; and, to right and left of it, she reads a complex of minute inscriptions, in part superimposed upon each other, some of them referring to the celestial bird, others alluding to events or states in the earthly and heavenly life of Christ and to the Three Persons of the Blessed Trinity. Here, indeed, if the primary inscription has been rightly read, we have (what Constantine's undertakings do not actually give us) explicit mention of the Apostle's body; and the inference to be drawn from it is that its writer believed St. Peter to be laid to rest not far from the spot at which his ungrammatical prayer was recorded.

To this inference is added a second. We know that in two of the pagan mausolea (F and Z in Fig. 3) there were Christian burials; and an originally pagan sarcophagus, found in the Tomb of the Valerii itself, may have been used as a Christian grave, to judge from the formulae employed in the inscription carved on its lid, commemorating a certain Valerinus Vasatulus (p. 91). It is the opinion of Professor Guarducci that in its last years the tomb passed into Christian hands (or was, accessible to Christians; *cf.* now Appendix D), and that the paintings and inscriptions belong to a time before Constantine's church was planned, at the very end of the third century and at the beginning of the fourth; they are at once a record of the prayers of the devout and 'a miniature theological compendium' for the benefit of Christians visiting the tomb.

In discussing these drawings and inscriptions, it is important to remember that there are two distinct problems involved. The one is that of the credibility of the reading; and since this contains a number of novel, not to say startling, features, and was not made generally accessible to interested scholars before many of these features had faded to complete illegibility, it will not be surprising if, despite the high reputation enjoyed by Professor Guarducci and by those privileged persons whom she cites as having read the inscriptions under her guidance, her reading is, nevertheless, submitted to searching criticism. This is a matter which the present writers are happy to leave to others more competent than themselves.[39] For the present volume it is the second problem that is by far the more important—what is the significance of these drawings and inscriptions for the history of the Vatican cemetery and of Constantine's Basilica? Assuming for the sake of argument the correctness of Professor Guarducci's reading, has she succeeded in demonstrating that these crude scribbles (solemn discussion of their 'style' and iconography should not be allowed to conceal that that is all they are) are necessarily earlier than the period of the dismantling of the tomb, and that they served any purpose more lasting than to record the prayers and aspirations of Christian workmen, or of others who may have had access to the tomb, during the considerable period of time that must have elapsed between the decision to dismantle the cemetery and its final disappearance below ground?

In the writers' opinion, she has not. Detailed discussion of the iconographic type of the portrait of Christ (if such it be) would be out of place in the present context; it is enough to remark that none of the arguments adduced for a date in the closing years of the third century would exclude the possibility of a date as late as, say, 320.[40] That the drawings and inscriptions are the work of two, possibly three, separate hands proves no more than that the tomb was accessible to pious scribblers for a certain period of time (as it certainly was during the work of dismantling the cemetery), and it need occasion no surprise that one of these thought fit to retrace some of the letters of one of the earlier texts; it is far from proving that the latter were already old and faded, or that the period of time involved must have stretched into decades. There are no compelling reasons for accepting a pre-Constantinian date, and at least one very good reason for doubting it. The Tomb of the Valerii was decorated with exquisite figured stucco reliefs, pagan in content (p. 82 ff.), which in view of their present condition must have been maintained in a fine state of preservation right down to the last. It is one thing to admit that individual Christians were buried in the tomb, one of them placed in a pagan coffin and recorded in a studiously non-committal epitaph: it is quite another to suggest that, so long as the tomb and its pagan ornament were kept in good order, anybody would have been allowed to get in and to scrawl the prayers and slogans of a persecuted cult on the walls of the central niche along-side the figure of the tomb's principal protecting deity.

These drawings, these inscriptions, were surely the work of persons who had access to the tombs of the cemetery during the period of many months, if not indeed of years, that must have intervened between the first work of demolition, to make way for the founda-tions of the outer walls and colonnades of the church, and the final packing with earth of the surviving tombs. An intermediate stage of this work was the construction of a network of lesser strengthen-ing foundations, to brace the surviving structures and to contain the loose fill in rigid compartments (pp. 12, 25, 198). One of these secondary foundations was built across the Tomb of the Valerii from the doorway to a point on the north wall overlapping the eastern half of the central niche; and it is, significantly, on the western half of the same partly dismantled niche that, with one possible exception, these drawings and inscriptions are found.[41] Later, when the fill within the tomb had already reached a level of nearly 6 feet above the pavement, another strengthening wall was built across the face of the western half of the tomb's north wall.[42] The filling was evi-dently done in stages. The lower head and the invocation *Petrus roga* were scribbled on the wall very possibly after the base of the niche had been destroyed and the main cross-wall built, but before any earth had been filled into the tomb. The upper head was added after the filling-in had been started (the crown of the head is at least 8 feet above the original pavement-level); and to this later phase belongs an inscription (which Professor Guarducci strangely omits to men-tion) scribbled in charcoal on one of the pilasters of the east wall of the tomb after the shaft of the stucco herm in front of it had been destroyed.

Seen in this perspective, the drawings and inscriptions take on a significance very different from that proposed by Professor Guarducci. They afford graphic and very human confirmation of what is already clear on other grounds, namely that Constantine's great church was built on a site that was closely associated in men's minds with the memory of St. Peter; and if the reading of the primary inscription could be accepted without reserve, the specific reference to the body of the Apostle would be a welcome addition to our knowledge of the nature of that association. Nevertheless, it is the construction of the church, and the material and moral difficulties that Constantine had to overcome to build it, that afford clearest proof of the importance that this particular site had for Christians in the early-fourth century.

The existence at that time of a belief that St. Peter was buried on the Vatican does not, of course, prove that his relics were really there then, or that they had ever been there. By then the lowest level beneath the primitive shrine had long been inaccessible (p. 160), and it is obviously arguable that an erroneous idea that it marked an actual burial could have grown up between its erection in the second half of the second century and Constantine's day. This is a point that must be considered in connection with the discussion of the nature and development of the primitive shrine (chapter 6). For the present, it is enough to have noted the fact of its existence and the significance of its siting for the history and topography of the Vatican in classical and post-classical times.

NOTES

1. Juvenal, *Sat.*, vi. 344: et Vaticano fragiles de monte patellas ('brittle dishes from the Vatican hill'). For the ancient brickfields, still in use, which lay alongside the Via Triumphalis, see S. B. Platner and T. Ashby, *A Topographical Dictionary of Ancient Rome*, 1929, p. 569. For Vatican wine, see Martial, *Epigr.*, vi. 92, 3: Vaticana bibis, bibis venenum ('drink Vatican, and you drink poison'); x. 45, 5: Vaticana bibas, si delectaris aceto ('if you like vinegar, drink Vatican'); xii. 48, 14: et Vaticani perfida vappa cadi ('the deceptive tastelessness of a jar of Vatican'); *cf.* Cicero, *De Leg. Agr.*, ii. 35, 96.

2. Tacitus, *Hist.*, ii. 93: infamibus Vaticani locis (of the troops of Vitellius encamped in the meadows beside the Tiber). For small private estates, see Aulus Gellius, *Noct. Att.*, xix. 7, 1: in agro Vaticano Iulius Paulus poeta . . . herediolum tenue possidebat ('Julius Paulus the poet . . . had a small family-estate in the Vatican district'); Symmachus, *Epp.*, vi. 58, 1: rus Vaticanum quod vestro praedio cohaeret accessimus ('. . . the Vatican countryside adjoining your estate'); vii. 21: urbanas turbas Vaticano in quantum licet rure declino ('as far as possible I escape the crowded city in the Vatican countryside').

3. *CIL*, vi. 2, 4346: Cydnus Ti. Germanici supra hortos. For these gardens, see P. Grimal, *Les jardins romains*, 1943, p. 147 ff. For their passage to Gaius, see Seneca, *De Ira*, iii. 18, 4: in xysto maternorum hortorum qui porticum a ripa separat ('in his mother's gardens, in a covered way between the portico and the river-bank'); Philo, *Leg. ad Gaium*, 181: δεξιωσάμενος γὰρ ἡμᾶς ἐν τῷ πρὸς Τιβέρει πεδίῳ τὸ πρῶτον—ἔτυχε δ' ἐκ τῶν μητρῴων ἐξιὼν κήπων ('[the Emperor Gaius] receiving us first of all on the level ground beside the Tiber, for he happened to be coming out of his mother's gardens'); and to Nero, see Tacitus, *Ann.*, xiv. 14; xv. 39, 44.

4. Pliny, *HN*, xvi. 201; xxxvi. 74; Tacitus, *loc. cit.*; Suetonius, *Div. Claud.*, 21.

5. Grimal, *op. cit.*, p. 150 ff.; for the perpetuation of the name into the third and fourth centuries, see SHA, *Vit. Aureliani*, 49, and the fourth-century Regionary Catalogue.

6. SHA, *Vit. Antonini*, 5: reliquias eius (*i.e.* of Hadrian) . . . in hortis Domitiae conlocavit. For the lead pipe of Crispus Passienus, see *Bullettino della Commissione Archeologica Comunale di Roma*, 1889, p. 173 ff.

7. The Gaianum is recorded by Cassius Dio, lix. 14. For the ruins north-west of Castel Sant'Angelo, see *Report*, i. p. 13. Inscriptions of charioteers are to be found in *CIL*, vi. 2, 10052–3; 10057–8; 10067; 4, 2, 33937; 33953.

8. *Report*, i. pp. 13–14. The general position of these Naumachiae is indicated by the site of the Church of S. Pellegrino in Naumachia (Fig. 1).

9. Livy, xxix. 37, 2; xxxvi. 36, 3.

10. *Res Gestae*, iv. 8.

11. Martial, *Epigr.*, 1. 70, 10: et Cybeles picto stat Corybante tholus ('where Cybele's dome with its painted Corybant stands').

12. *CIL*, xiii. 1, 1751: L(ucius) Aemilius Carpus IIIIII vir Aug(ustalis) item dendrophorus vires excepit et a Vaticano transtulit ('Lucius Aemilius Carpus, sevir Augustalis (*i.e.* member of a minor priestly order) and *dendrophorus*, renounced his manhood and transferred it from the Vatican [shrine]': at Lyon; the *dendrophori* were devotees of Cybele); *CIL*, xiii. 2, 1, 7281: in h(onorem) d(omus) d(ivinae) Deae Virtutis Bellon(a)e montem Vaticanum vetustate conlabsum restituerunt ('to the glory of the imperial house and in honour of the goddess Virtus Bellona they restored the Vatican Hill, which had fallen into decay': from Kastel; from this inscription it appears that the local shrine was called Mons Vaticanus).

13. *CIL*, vi. 1, 497–503 and 504 (St. Peter's); vi. 4, 2, 30780 (S. Petronilla).

14. *Report*, i. Fig. 2 (S. Lorenzo in Piscibus); Fig. 3 (Piazza San Pietro).

15. *CIL*, vi. 1, 505, 506, dating from 295, are not recorded as found on the Vatican.

16. Cassius Dio, lxix. 23; *CIL*, vi. 1, 973.

17. *Académie des Inscriptions et Belles-Lettres: Comptes-rendus*, 1925, p. 227 ff., recording an official responsible for the two roads Aurelia and Cornelia (curatori viarum Aureliae et Corneliae).

18. G. B. De Rossi, *La Roma sotterranea cristiana*, i. 1864, p. 141—Loci martyrum: Petrus in parte occidentali civitatis iuxta viam Corneliam ad miliarium primum in corpore requiescit ('Peter's body rests on the west side of the city, beside the Via Cornelia, at the first milestone').

19. *Report*, i. pp. 10–11, 26–7.

20. *Report*, i. p. 27.

21. *CIL*, xiv. 3610: curatori viar(um) Aureliae Veteris et Novae Corneliae et Triumphalis; *cf.* Note 17.

22. J. Carcopino (*Études d'histoire chrétienne*, 1953, p. 141 ff.) maintains that the road running to the south of the tombs was in fact the Via Aurelia Nova, and that the Via Cornelia ran across the Mons Vaticanus to the north of them. *Cf.* E. Kirschbaum, *Gregorianum*, xxix, 1948, p. 544 ff.; A. von Gerkan, 'Kritische Studien zu den Ausgrabungen unter des Peterskirche in Rom' (*Trierer Zeitschrift*, xx, 1953, p. 26 ff.).

23. *Report*, i. p. 17 ff. For the prolongation of the Via Cornelia to the Mausoleum of Hadrian, see Platner-Ashby, *op. cit.*, pp. 406, 562.

24. *Report*, i. p. 21 ff. (Porta Angelica); Figs. 6, 7, and p. 19 ff. (Annona Vaticana); p. 20 ff. (Piazza San Pietro).

25. The error dates back to the misinterpretation of these massive foundations (p. 197) by the observers of the Renaissance, notably by Grimaldi.

26. *Ann.*, xv. 44.

27. *HN*, xxxvi. 74; see Note 34.

28. *L'Année Épigraphique*, 1946, No. 136: ex codicillis triplicibus Popili/Heraclae/C(aius) Popilius Heracla heredib(us) salut(em)/vos heredes mei rogo iubeoque/fideique vestrae committo uti/monumentum mihi faciatis in Vatic-(ano)/ad circum iuxta monumentum Ulpi/Narcissi ex HS $\overline{VI}$ n(ummum) in quam rem/numerabit Novia Trophime HS $\overline{III}$ n(ummum)/et coheres eius HS $\overline{III}$ n(ummum) ibique reliquias/meas et Fadiae Maximae uxoris meae/si quid ei humanitus acciderit poni volo/cuius monumenti ius lego libertis liberta/busq(ue) meis et quos testamento manumisero/sive quem in statu libertatis reliqui et hoc amplius/Noviae Trophim(a)e libertis libertabusq(ue) eius/posterisque supra scriptorum et itum aditum am/bitum sacrificique faciendi causa ad id monu/(men)tum uti ei(s) liceat. For a photograph of the inscription, see E. Josi, 'Gli Scavi nelle Sacre Grotte Vaticane' (*Il Vaticano nel 1944*, 1944: offprint, p. 23).

For a commentary on legal points raised by this text see F. De Visscher, *L'Antiquité Classique*, xv. 1946, p. 117 ff.

29. SHA, *Vit. Eleg.*, 23: fertur (*i.e.* Elagabalus) . . . circenses exhibuisse . . .et elephantorum quadrigas in Vaticano agitasse, dirutis sepulcris quae obsistebant ('Elagabalus is said . . . to have given circus shows . . . and to have driven chariots drawn by four elephants in the Vatican, destroying tombs that were in the way').

30. *Report*, i. p. 26; ii. Pl. 2, *a*. Von Gerkan's assertion (*op. cit.*, p. 29) that one cannot distinguish the brickwork of the second and fourth centuries is not borne out by the excavations, which have afforded a copious series of the brickwork techniques used in the Vatican area from the second century onwards.

31. H. Koethe, *Mitteilungen des Deutschen Archäologischen Instituts: Römische Abteilung*, xlvi, 1931, pp. 9–26; M. Armellini, *Le chiese di Roma* (2nd ed., 1942), ii, pp. 913–15, 927–8, 933–6.

32. H. Egger, *Römische Veduten* (2nd ed., 1932) i, Pls. 33–6; *cf.* Pls. 20, 38, 41, 45 (anonymous sixteenth-century drawings) and Fig. 9, *a* (the plan of Dupérac, 1577, in the British Museum).

33. Von Gerkan's theory (*op. cit.*, Fig. 1) that there was no road between Circus and cemetery ignores both these remains and the problem of access to the Circus, which was certainly still a place of public entertainment when the tombs were going up (p. 9). Moreover, the analogy of all other known cemeteries of this sort and the development and lay-out of the Vatican cemetery itself (pp. 28, 30) alike attest the presence of a road immediately to the south of the excavations.

34. Our chief ancient authority is that passage in Pliny (*HN*, xxxvi. 74) in which, after describing the major obelisks of Egypt itself and the two brought to Rome by Augustus and set up respectively in the Campus Martius and on the central barrier (*spina*) of the Circus Maximus (Platner-Ashby, *op. cit.*, pp. 366–7), he states that 'there is a third in Rome in the Circus of the Emperors Gaius and Nero—it is the only one of all of them to have been broken during transport—which was made by [*i.e.* to the orders of] Nencoreus, son of Sesosis. There remains another obelisk of the same Nencoreus, a hundred cubits high, which he dedicated to the Sun on the instructions of an oracle after regaining his sight from blindness' (tertius est Romae in Vaticano Gai et Neronis principum circo—ex omnibus unus omnino fractus est in molitione—quem fecerat Sesosidis filius Nencoreus. eiusdem remanet et alius centum cubitorum quem post caecitatem visu reddito ex oraculo soli sacravit). The reading 'in molitione' is not certain but is that of the oldest and best manuscripts.

Three possible interpretations of this passage have to be considered:

(1) That the surviving Vatican obelisk is that described by Pliny, and that it stood in the Circus on the *spina*, which, as we know from the example of the Augustan obelisk in the Circus Maximus and of countless obelisk-shaped turning-points (*metae*) in classical representations of circuses elsewhere, would have been the natural place to put it. If so, we have to assume that it was moved in late Antiquity to the position which it occupied until 1586, presumably before the middle of the fourth century when the Regionary Catalogue mentions an obelisk 'in Vaticano' but omits all reference to the Circus. Against this we have to reckon that there is no record of its removal either in late Antiquity or in the Middle Ages; and, as we know from the literature (*e.g.* from Pliny

himself), to move an obelisk of this size was an undertaking that struck the imagination of Antiquity as forcibly as it did Fontana's contemporaries.

(2) That the surviving obelisk is not that described by Pliny as standing 'in circo', but is instead the obelisk mentioned by Pliny, in the passage quoted, as having been dedicated to the Sun by Nencoreus as a thank-offering for the recovery of his sight. On this hypothesis (C. Cecchelli, *Capitolium*, xxv. 3–4, 1950, p. 64 ff.) the Circus obelisk must have been overthrown when the Circus itself was abandoned or dismantled (at any rate, before the Regionary Catàlogue was compiled in the mid-fourth century) and still awaits discovery; whereas the surviving obelisk, as we know from the identical inscriptions carved near the foot of what were, in its original position, the east and west sloping faces, was dedicated by Gaius to the memory of his two imperial predecessors (divo Caesari divi Iulii f(ilio) Augusto/Ti(berio) Caesari divi Augusti f(ilio) Augusto/ sacrum: *CIL*, vi. 1, 882) and, as a funerary monument, it was respected by Constantine. This theory meets the known archaeological facts; but against it we have to set the strange failure of Pliny to mention the transport to Rome of this second obelisk; indeed, reading the passage in its context, the natural inter- pretation of his words (and particularly of the emphatic 'remanet') is that the second obelisk of Nencoreus, unlike its fellow, remained in Egypt. The hypo- thesis of a second obelisk is independent of the further, and altogether over- ingenious, suggestion put forward by Cecchelli (*op. cit.*) that the rotunda of Sant'Andrea is to be identified with the temple of Apollo mentioned by the *Liber Pontificalis* (ed. Duchesne, i. p. 118) as existing on the Vatican; and that Constantine respected the associated obelisk because he had transferred his allegiance from Apollo-Sol to Christus-Sol-Novus. Even less convincing is the suggestion put forward by Carcopino (*op. cit.*, p. 151 ff.) that the legend of a temple of Apollo arose from the misinterpretation of the Christus-Helios mosaic in Tomb M (p. 74), which in some way, according to him, remained accessible after the construction of the Basilica.

(3) That the surviving obelisk is indeed that described by Pliny, but that Pliny's phrase 'in Vaticano in circo' should be read in the less precise sense that it commonly bears in Roman topographical usage, whereby a district or a quarter takes its name from the most familiar monument in it. When Livy speaks of the temples of Juno and Diana 'in circo Flaminio' (xl. 52, 2–3), he does not mean that they stood within the Circus, but in its immediate neighbour- hood (in fact, they stood within the Porticus Octaviae, a hundred yards to the south of the Circus). Similarly, Pliny could well have described a funerary obelisk set up by the roadside near the Circus of Gaius and Nero (and very possibly, in view of the identity of the dedicator, in some clear architectural relationship to it) as being 'in circo'. In the context, it would have been less confusing if he had used a more explicit phrase, particularly in view of his reference, earlier in the same passage, to the obelisk of Augustus 'in circo maxi-

mo'; but this is a difficulty that has to be weighed against those that arise from either of the other two interpretations of the evidence.

For the later history of the obelisk, see Zucchetti, *Ecclesia*, 1950, p. 523 ff., in which he notes that it is rather shorter in proportion to its bulk than the other major obelisks of Rome, this being due possibly to reworking after the damage referred to by Pliny. The base illustrated by Van Heemskerck (Note 32) could be interpreted as a device to remedy this defect.

35. That the cemetery was still in active use, by pagans and Christians alike, at the time when the building of Old St. Peter's was projected is attested both by the generally excellent state of the pagan wall-paintings, stuccoes, mosaics, and carved sarcophagi (except for those that were unavoidably damaged by the church-builders; chapters 2 and 3), and by the fine quality of some of the later contents, notably the mid- or late-third-century vault-mosaics and wall-mosaics in Tomb M (p. 72 ff.). In several cases it can be shown that the owners of tombs continued to have access to them until work on the foundations of the church was well advanced (p. 198).

36. It is well known that under the later Empire dispensations were granted to town-councils for the use of grave-monuments and tombstones for strengthening town-defences in an emergency.

37. F. De Visscher, *Académie Royale de Belgique*; *Bulletin de la Classe des Lettres et des Sciences Morales et Politiques*, ser. V, xxxiv, 1948, p. 427; *Atti del Congresso Internazionale di Diritto Romano e Storia del Diritto* (*Verona* 1948), 1951, iii, pp. 187–8.

38. M. Guarducci, *Cristo e San Pietro in un documento precostantiniano della necropoli vaticana*, 1953 (cited hereafter as 'Guarducci'). The inscription and the two accompanying heads had been noted and photographed by the excavators, and referred to briefly by one of them, A. Ferrua, in *Il Messaggero* for 16 January 1952.

39. Among the terms read by Professor Guarducci are two that are new to lexicography—*dexiostasis* and *execaterostasis*, the latter interpreted as the Procession of the Holy Spirit from the Father and the Son and anticipating the famous *Filioque* clause. Most of the upper group of inscriptions are written in minute letters, from 1 to 5 millimetres high, and in some cases they are interpreted as being arranged in elaborate anagrammatical patterns, based on groups of common letters. When viewed by the present writers, through the courtesy of Professor Guarducci, in April 1953 (J.M.C.T.) and in January 1954 (J.B.W.P.), a great deal of what had been read by her early in 1953 had already faded into invisibility, and it would be presumption to comment in detail on the accuracy of a reading which one has had no opportunity of checking under better conditions. There are, however, two general queries that may legitimately be raised. The drawings and inscriptions have undoubtedly faded since they were first photographed in 1943 (Guarducci, Pl. 15) and in 1947 (*ibid.*, Pl. 16), and the

deterioration has been accelerated recently by the brilliant lighting to which
they have been subjected. Nevertheless, those parts of the complex that are
visible in the early photographs are still clearly visible. How is it that the rest
has faded so rapidly and completely? The other question is that of the extent
to which it is possible to distinguish the faded traces of lettering from the
accidental configurations on this much marked and damp-stained wall. The
danger is not that of reading too little but of reading too much. As regards the
inscription in large letters associated with the lower head (the only one of importance in the present context), the word *Petrus* can still be clearly read, and
it was almost certainly followed by the word *roga*; the rest is now so much
faded that one can do little more than say that there may well have been two or
three further lines of text, beginning with the words *pro s* . . . For criticism of
Professor Guarducci's methods of establishing the authenticity of the text that
she purports to read, see R. North, S.J., in *Verbum Domini* (Romae, Pontificium
Institutum Biblicum), xxxii, 1954, pp. 244–7: '. . . Expectatur adhuc demon-
stratio magis objectiva de actuali existentia inscriptionis talis qualis declaratur
inesse in pariete' ('We still await a more objective proof of the actual existence
of an inscription such as that which is stated to be found on the wall').

40. For a critical discussion of these arguments, see J. Ruysschaert, *Revue
d'histoire ecclésiastique*, xlix, 1954, pp. 8–18.

41. Only five words (and no drawings) are claimed to have been deciphered on the eastern side of the niche, to the right of the figure of Apollo
(Guarducci, Figs. 16, 17, and p. 61).

42. Guarducci, Pl. 14 *b*; *cf.* Pl. 6.

THE VATICAN CEMETERY—
I: LAY-OUT AND CHRONOLOGY;
THREE REPRESENTATIVE TOMBS

(Figs. 2, 3)

The Lay-out and Chronology of the Tombs

DESPITE the ancient, medieval, and Renaissance works of art that furnish the newly arranged lower Church of St. Peter and its approaches, they present an unmistakably twentieth-century aspect. We descend the stairs and slip through the narrow door, which gives access to the excavations (Figs. 2, 3)—a few seconds' journey—and at once we are back in the Rome of the second and third centuries of our era. We hardly notice the modern girders overhead or the modern piers planted here and there to support them. For we actually tread the ancient contours of the hillside, see the walls and façades of the tombs in much the same condition as that in which the Romans of the Empire saw them, and visualize with the mind's eye what had not been seen or imagined for nearly sixteen hundred years, the gabled roofs of those mausolea outlined against the open sky.

The entrance to the excavations is a narrow opening built into one of the great foundations of Constantine's church so that the work-men might move freely from one part of the site to another. As we step through this, we find ourselves face to face with the surviving northern portion of Tomb Z.[1] Like all the other tombs in this cemetery (except for the annex to R, which opens off a lateral alley-way), this tomb faced southwards, down the hill towards the Via Cornelia. But before pausing to inspect its details or to climb the modern steps which mount invitingly to the door of Mausoleum Φ on our right, we shall do well to make our way up the steep and narrow passage-way between the walls of Z and Φ and step into the street of tombs that runs east and west immediately behind them. It is here that one can get the best idea of the lay-out of the cemetery and the most vivid impression of what it once looked like.

Looking eastwards along this street we see, about 16 metres away, the modern wall that marks the eastern termination of the excavations. To the west (Pl. 4), about 10 metres away, the line of the street is blocked by the first of a series of transverse foundations built by Constantine's architects to give stability to the filling at the time when the cemetery was being dismantled. Through these foundations we can now pass by way of modern openings, cut to give access to the western section of the excavations. In Antiquity one would have had, instead, to turn left, right, and right again, skirting round the projecting forecourt of Tomb H (in front of which the enormous foundations of the south-east pier of the Renaissance dome now bar the way to any further excavation), to arrive at what nowadays appears to be a westward prolongation of the street already described. This appearance of continuity is deceptive. In Roman times the passage between Tombs L and V (opened by Constantine's workmen and enlarged by the excavators) was blocked by a bench-like tomb, extending from the angle of L to the north-west corner of V, and the tombs to the east and west respectively opened onto two irregular open spaces, to which the only access was from the south, passing on either side of Tomb V. From the western one of these two open spaces, which was later partly blocked by Constantine's foundations, we have now, as the Romans did, to turn left and make our way round the front of a projecting pair of Tombs, U and T, on the west side of which we find ourselves in an open rectangular area, bounded on the north by the now inaccessible Tomb S and on the west by another of the foundations put in by Constantine's architects (a similar Constantinian foundation, bounding the area on the south, has been partly demolished to provide access to the westernmost range of tombs). In Antiquity, the west side of this area lay a couple of metres farther back; and a modern opening in the Constantinian foundations leads us, up a steep step and through a travertine doorway on our right, into a narrow passage, which runs steeply uphill towards the north and ends in a flight of steps. At the far end of this passage, which rises sharply towards the modern roof (i.e. towards the level of the floor of the lower church), the steps are blocked by a low wall (Pl. 1);

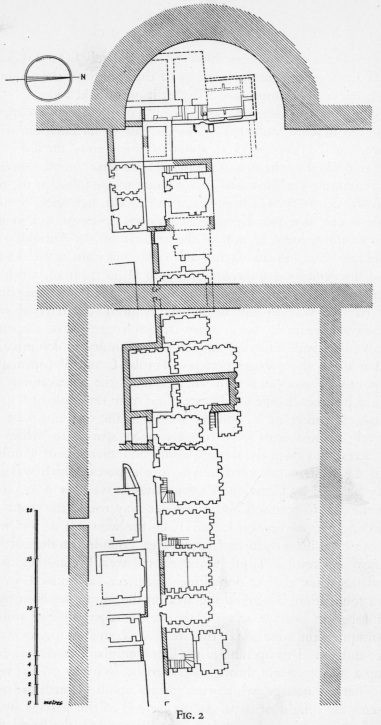

FIG. 2

The Vatican cemetery, as excavated. Shading indicates Constantinian foundations and partition-walls.

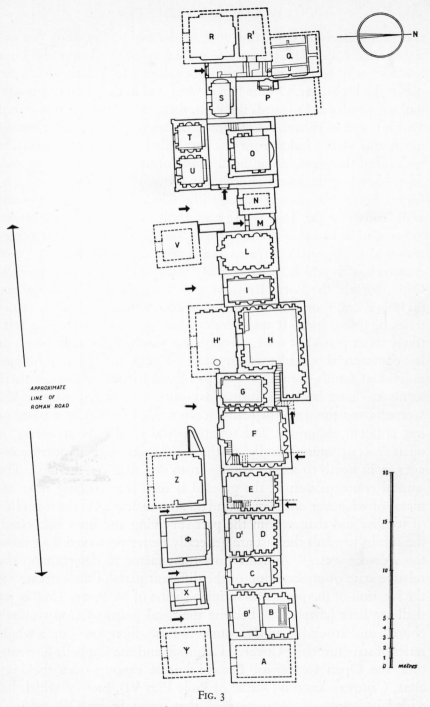

FIG. 3

The Vatican cemetery, restored. Arrows indicate entrances to tombs or groups of tombs.

and immediately beyond this wall, at the top of the steps, lies the altar of the Cappella Clementina, at the level of the lower church, a few feet only to the west of the spot where, in the church above, stands the high altar. On the left, as we stand in this sloping passage, looking northward towards the steps, there are the scanty remains of Tomb R and of its annex R[1]; and on our right a plain wall, running north and south, hides from us, embedded in its eastern face, the remains of the pre-Constantinian shrine of St. Peter (chapter 6) and, on the level of the lower church, the sixteenth-century Open Confessio. About the sloping passage (the Clivus) and its flanking east wall (known as the 'Red Wall') more will be said in a later context.

Such, in its broad outlines, is the lay-out of that part of the cemetery which has been excavated and is now accessible. It is a type of cemetery with which we are already familiar from the cemeteries at Ostia, outside the Porta Romana and alongside the Via Severiana, on Isola Sacra,[2] or in tantalizing fragments from the suburban cemeteries of Rome itself. It was developed, as we shall see, over a relatively short period of time, through the purchase, by individuals or by commercial speculators, of plots of land for the building of individual family-tombs or groups of tombs; and although there seems to have been no formal lay-out, the vicinity of the Via Cornelia and the need for ready access tended to impose a more or less uniform alignment and to group the tombs about streets or open spaces running parallel to the main road, with frequent passages from north to south, leading from one street to the next. The natural conformation of the ground is such that nothing now remains of whatever once lay behind (i.e. to the north of) the main line of tombs; and that, within the part surviving and now excavated, the tombs towards the east are generally better preserved than those towards the west.[3] Another important factor in determining the relative state of preservation of the different parts of the cemetery is the location of the pre-Constantinian shrine of St. Peter. This, as we shall see later (chapter 7), became the focal point of Constantine's church, and around it, in the course of time, there grew up a whole series of structures (the Covered Confessio and the Cappella Clementina, the Open Confessio, Bernini's great canopy over the high altar, Canova's kneeling statue of Pope Pius VI), each of which has added its quota of destruction to that wrought by Constantine's architects. Other large tracts of the cemetery have been completely obliterated by the foundations of Constantine's church and of its Renaissance successor; whereas to the east of the present excavations, where there is no doubt that further well-preserved tombs still await discovery, the fact that the pavement of the eastern half of the present-day church rests directly upon made-up ground, instead of upon the arched vaults of the crypt, imposes a serious obstacle to any further excavation.

Of the individual tombs within the cemetery, some have been called after their owners or other persons buried in them, whose names have been revealed by inscriptions that still survive; others bear titles based on some arresting feature of their ornament or structure. In the southern row, passing from west to east, are Z, the 'Tomb of the Egyptians' (p. 51 ff., Pl. 7); Φ, the family-tomb of the Marcii; X, an unnamed and now inaccessible painted tomb; and Ψ, an unnamed tomb, of which only the outer faces of the west and north walls have been cleared. In the northern row we proceed continuously from east to west. A, of which only the façade has been revealed, is the Tomb of Gaius Popilius Heracla (p. 9); B, with its forecourt B¹, is the Tomb of Fannia Redempta (p. 37 ff., Pls. 3, 6); C, the family-tomb of the Tullii; and D, with its forecourt D¹, the 'Reticulate Tomb', so-called from the character of its walling (p. 64). E is the family-tomb of the Aelii; F the family-tomb of the Caetennii (p. 44 ff., Pl. 2); and G, the roof of which is upheld by four modern pilasters, we may call, after its principal painting, the 'Tomb of the Steward' (p. 77 f., Pl. 16). The largest mausoleum of the whole series, H, with its forecourt H¹, is the family-tomb of the Valerii (p. 82 ff., Pls. 12, 13, 15, 31); next to it comes the 'Tomb of the Quadriga' (I) (Pl. 5), so called from the design of its mosaic pavement (p. 74 f.); and then L, a second family-tomb of the Caetennii, largely destroyed by the foundation-wall of the triumphal arch of Old St. Peter's. Beyond, up a narrow alley running north, is the miniature Mausoleum M, originally the pagan family-tomb of the Julii (p. 72 ff., Pl. 32), followed by the family-tomb of the Aebutii (N), of which it has been possible to clear only the façade (the interior was destroyed in the Renaissance by the foundations of the west wall of the nave of the crypt). Opposite L and M we pass on our left the north and west walls of the unnamed and unexcavated Mausoleum V; and in front of us the file of explored tombs doubles again, as we have seen. In the northern row is the

family-tomb of the Matuccii (O); while to the south of it lie the
twin mausolea, the 'Tomb of Lucifer and Hesperus' (U), so named
from the most interesting of its paintings (p. 79, Pl. 17), and the
Tomb of Trebellena Flacilla (T). Tomb S has no name and no
distinctive features; most of the interior was destroyed when the
foundations were dug for the south-east column of Bernini's great
bronze canopy over the high altar. R, with its accompanying courtyard R¹, is the Tomb of Flavius Agricola, whose epitaph and statue
reclining at a funerary banquet, were discovered by chance in
1626[4] on the spot now shown to be the site of this mausoleum and
soon afterwards destroyed; Q is an inhumation-area open to the sky
in ancient times.

We have now made a comprehensive, if cursory, survey of the
length and breadth of the Vatican cemetery, so far as it could be
excavated. When was this stretch of it laid out and in what order
were the tombs built?

There is no evidence for a precise, absolute dating of any of the
mausolea; but on general grounds there can be no doubt that most,
if not all, of them were built between about the year 125 and the
end of the second century. This is the period to which the
character of their brickwork belongs; and in almost every case
there is some element of the decoration (wall-paintings in particular) or of the fittings that can be dated to the period between
the middle of the second century and the early years of the third. It
was, moreover, the second and third centuries that witnessed the
gradual supersession of cremation by inhumation at Rome (p. 112 f.);
and both rites are represented in the Vatican cemetery in a way that
illustrates most graphically the whole gradual process of transition.
We can see this very clearly in the eastern half of the excavations.
One might have expected that the tombs nearer to the Via Cornelia
would have been the earlier and that the growth of the cemetery
would have been uphill, away from the road. Exactly the opposite,
however, seems to have been the case here, as in the Isola Sacra
cemetery at Ostia (Fig. 4).[5] Of the tombs in the northern row,
Tomb D contains only cremation-burials, and in the tombs on either
side of it cremations greatly outnumber inhumations. Across the
street, on the other hand, in the Tomb of the Marcii, inhumations
outnumber cremations; and in what is left of the 'Tomb of the
Egyptians' there are no cremations at all. In the course of time, as

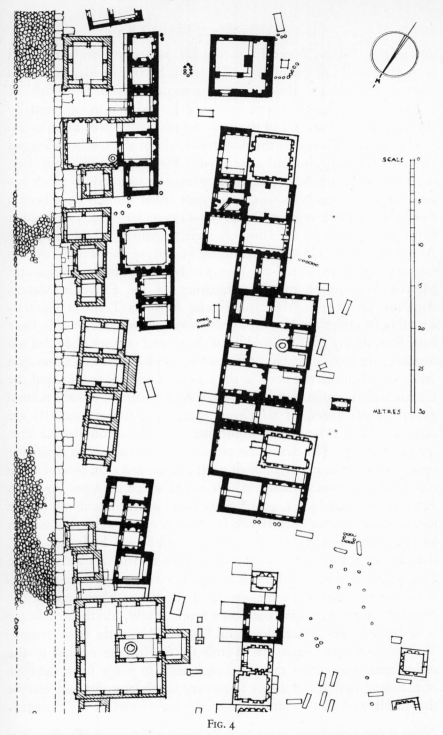

Fig. 4

Part of the classical cemetery at Isola Sacra, near Ostia. Plain outline indicates tombs of the early-second century; solid colour, those of the mid- and later-second century; hatching, those of the third century.

inhumation became general, we find the owners of tombs that had been built solely or mainly for cremations having to adapt them, as best they might, to the new requirements (Tomb B affords an excellent example of this process; p. 41); and it is in substantially altered form that several of the early tombs have come down to us.

The names of some of the persons to whom the tombs belonged are a useful indication of date. Gaius Popilius Heracla, the first occupant of Tomb A, instructed his executors to build his tomb beside that of Ulpius Narcissus, who must either himself have been a freedman of the Emperor Trajan (98–117) or have been descended from one; the Aelii of Tomb E were freedmen of the Emperor Antoninus Pius (138–61); freedmen buried in the Tomb of the Caetennii (F) bear the tell-tale names of Marcus Aurelius Filetus and Marcus Aurelius Hieron (*i.e.* freedmen of the Emperor Marcus Aurelius, 161–80); and the name Flavius Agricola (Tomb R) suggests a man born under the Flavian dynasty (69–96), who can hardly have been buried long after the middle of the second century.[6] In this last instance, we have valuable confirmatory evidence from a drain that was found beneath the floor of the Clivus. Tombs R and Q, and the Clivus and its eastern wall (the Red Wall), form a closely related group of structures, of which all except the first-named (R) are certainly of one build and constitute a single chronological unit (p. 59, Note 7). The drain, the purpose of which was to drain the open area Q, was partly built of tiles; and no less than five of these tiles bear an identical stamp, which can be dated between the years 147 and 161 (*CIL*, xv. 1, 401).* Since there is little likelihood of five identical tiles having been reused from some earlier structure, we can be reasonably certain that this group of tombs was built very little, if at all, after the death of Antoninus Pius in 161. As we shall see later (chapter 6, p. 140 ff.), this dating has very important implications for the history of the shrine of St. Peter. Elsewhere in the cemetery tile-stamps have only been found singly, and their evidence is of limited value, since tiles could be, and frequently were, reused. We do, however, learn that Tomb O, one of the earliest in the series, cannot be earlier than 123; and since, to judge from the type of masonry used, it is unlikely to be very much later, we may ascribe this tomb with some confidence to the later years of the Emperor

*Four of these stamps were discovered during the original excavations; the fifth came to light in 1954. *Cf. Report*, i. p. 102 f., Fig. 75.

Hadrian, who died in 138. That many of the tombs were still in use, or at least carefully maintained throughout the third century and into the early years of the fourth, is proved both by the subject-matter and style of the inscriptions, mosaics, and carved sarcophagi found within them, and by the good state of preservation of such of their ornament and contents as was not unavoidably damaged or destroyed by the church-builders. The survival of the cemetery into the fourth century is also attested by the discovery, in an urn in Tomb T, of a coin dating from the early years of the reign of Constantine.

Within these broad limits, the order in which the individual tombs were built can in many cases be determined by a careful study of their relation one to another. In the eastern half of the excavations the tombs of the northern row are all contiguous; and we can see that Tomb A is older than B (which was built up against it), B than C, C than D, D than E, and E than F. Tomb G, on the other hand, was earlier than either of its neighbours: it projects slightly forward from the common building-line of Tombs A–F, and its façade is slightly overlapped by the façade-cornice of F, whereas its own cornice has been cut back at the south-west angle by the builders of H, which also spreads itself into the vacant space behind G's north wall. The painted decoration of Tomb G is clearly by the same hand, or from the same workshop, as the original decoration of Tomb B (p. 42 f.), with which it must therefore be roughly contemporary. In the southern row, Tombs Ψ, X, Φ, and Z were all built detached from each other and from the tombs of the northern row. The suggestion (based on the predominance of inhumation over cremation, p. 30) that they are later than Tombs A–G does, however, find confirmation in the fact that, although built into the slope of a steep hillside, the careful masonry of their northern façades was clearly intended to be seen, and is finished to a level that corresponds very closely with that of the level street in front of Tombs A–G. To judge from the relative position of their foundations, Z is probably earlier than Φ.

In the western half of the excavations, the three earliest tombs appear to be I, L, and O. I is certainly earlier than H, since the west wall of H was built when the east wall of I was already standing, and the masonry of the forecourt (H¹) clasps its south-east corner. The junction of I and L is largely hidden by the masonry of an enormous

Constantinian foundation, which ran from north to south across the church at the junction of nave and transept; but a small hole cut in the masonry by the excavators does in fact seem to show that L was already standing when I was built; and since the lettering and style of the *titulus* of L corresponds very closely with that of the *tituli* of H and of F, it would appear that L, I, and H were built in fairly rapid succession, in that order. To the west of L the continuous line of tombs was originally interrupted by an alley-way, where once a small gully separated two projecting shoulders of the Vatican Hill; and we can only say that N appears to have been built when the ground-level had risen slightly above that of L and is therefore probably somewhat later; and that M, squeezed in between the two and blocking the alley-way, with no independent walls of its own, is certainly later than both. V was built after the bench-like tomb that formerly extended across the passage between V and L (p. 25) and was itself later than L; its carefully finished side- and rear-faces were clearly intended to be seen from the two small open spaces on either side of it. O, an elaborate tomb enclosed on two, and probably originally on three, sides within a precinct (which may also have served as a passage-way leading, up a flight of stairs, to the higher ground behind the tomb), is certainly one of the earliest tombs in the cemetery. N, the foundations of which are laid at a somewhat higher level, was built when the east wall of the precinct (destroyed in the sixteenth century) was already standing. S, too, is later than O (the junction of its east wall with the west precinct-wall of O is no longer accessible, but was examined by the excavators); and T and U, which were built as a pair, are later than both O and S, since their common back wall was built up against the south wall of the precinct of O, and their foundations override the outlet of a drain that was still in use when S was built. The Clivus and Q, which are of one build, are certainly later than S (the south end of the Red Wall is built up against the north-west corner of S), and probably later than R-R¹, which is probably itself also later than S.[7] In connection with this western group, we may note that, when T was built, its west wall was trenched into a large mound of earth, the removal of which at some later date has left a tell-tale scar in the otherwise regular masonry of the outer wall-face. This mound had not been there when S was built; and we can hardly doubt that it represents the spoil thrown out by the builders of an adjoining tomb

as they cut into the face of the hill to make a level platform on which
to build. One could not ask for a more graphic picture of the state
of the cemetery in the middle of the second century, as new tombs
crowded in to join the old; and, in the face of such haphazard trenching and dumping, we are reminded how very careful one has to be
in drawing any conclusions from the level within the accumulated
earth at which any particular object may have been found. As we
shall see later (chapter 6), questions of level play an important part
in the interpretation of the remains found on the site of the shrine of
St. Peter.

We may summarize this necessarily somewhat complicated
account of the growth of the cemetery by remarking that, so far
from embodying any rational plan of development, work seems to
have started in at least three separate places, with Tombs A, G, and O.
The eastern row of tombs, A–F, built to a common frontage in neat
succession from east to west, suggests the hand of a speculator, who
had bought a building-plot large enough to contain at least six
family-tombs (there may have been more to the east of A). But this
is an exception. Elsewhere the cemetery appears to have developed
almost haphazard in the spaces left between existing tombs. The
development was rapid. It is only at the western end that we can
measure it at all precisely, but here the interval between Tomb O
and Tomb Q cannot have been more than half a century at most
(after 123 and before 170), perhaps not more than twenty-five or
thirty years. The earlier tombs were set well back from the Via
Cornelia; but with this exception (which did not necessarily extend
to the rest of the cemetery, although the similar development of the
Isola Sacra cemetery suggests that it may well in fact have done so),
it is hard to detect any clear principle. Each tomb has to be studied
on its own merits and in relation to its own immediate neighbours.

The individual tombs of the Vatican cemetery were square or
oblong chambers, built of concrete faced externally with brick and
internally with rougher materials, with house-like façades, vaulted
roofs, and elaborate interior decoration. Most of them comprise a
single vaulted chamber; but in several there is an open forecourt set
either behind the façade, within the main building, or as a subsidiary
structure in front of it. Some remained free-standing, but by the
time the cemetery was fully developed the majority presented a more
or less continuous frontage to the streets and open spaces onto which

they opened. Tombs of this type were already well known before 1939 in the neighbourhood of Rome. Besides those of the Isola Sacra cemetery,[8] we may note the fine trio of second-century house-tombs found grouped together in a little semicircle under the Church of San Sebastiano on the Via Appia;[9] and many others of the same period, less fully preserved, had previously been revealed on the Via Ostiensis near St. Paul's-without-the-Walls,[10] or in scattered fragments from the great cemeteries that once lined the other roads out of Rome. But as documents of funerary art the Vatican tombs are unrivalled; and they fill out, with fresh and significant details, our picture of religious belief and practice among the Roman middle classes during a crucial epoch in the history of ancient eschatological thought (chapter 4).

To conclude this summary of the cemetery as a whole, we may note that it was not by any means limited to substantial mausolea of the type that now constitutes the greater part of the tombs visible within the excavated area. There were simple, early graves here and there on the slopes of the Vatican hillside before ever it was developed into a formal cemetery, as we now see it. In 'P', the area occupied by the later Petrine shrine (chapter 6), the later history of the site was such that some of these early graves survived and have been excavated; but the evidence of the ossuary attached to Z (p. 53) shows that they almost certainly had their counterpart elsewhere in the cemetery. Besides these humble graves, which had no visible structure above ground-level other than (presumably) some sort of gravestone, and which must very easily have been lost to sight, there were at least two upstanding tombs of a more substantial character, the bench-like tomb of masonry with a semicircular coping which once spanned the corridor between L and V (p. 25), and another similar tomb at right-angles to it;[11] and everywhere within the excavated area, the excavators found traces of later burials crowded into the open spaces between the mausolea, sometimes in substantial coffins, sometimes in tombs of masonry stacked one above the other against the existing walls.[12] These later graves have, for the most part, had to be cleared away either by Constantine's workmen or by the excavators to give access to the architecturally more significant and substantial mausolea of the second century, just as these mausolea themselves transformed and in part obliterated the early cemetery. But unless we bear these vanished tombs, both early and late, clearly in mind, we shall not get a true picture of the history and significance of those tombs which still survive.

This is no place for a systematic catalogue of every item of ornament or furnishing in each tomb taken in order. That must await the pens of the excavators themselves. Instead, we shall first illustrate and give a detailed account of three representative tombs—the Tomb of Fannia Redempta (B, B¹), the First Tomb of the Caetennii (F), and the 'Tomb of the Egyptians' (Z). In the following chapter (3), we shall review the surviving remains of the cemetery by categories— architecture and architectural ornament, the mosaics of wall, vault, and pavement, wall-paintings, stucco-work, sculpture, and other objects. Lastly (chapter 4) we shall discuss what can be known about the owners of the tombs, their social status, and their beliefs.[13]

The Tomb of Fannia Redempta
(Fig. 5; Pls. 3, 6)

Tomb B, the second tomb from the eastern end of the excavations in the northern row, is named after Fannia Redempta, the wife of Aurelius Hermes, a freedman of the two Augusti (that is, of the Emperors Diocletian and Maximian, 286–305). A bride at thirteen, she was forty-six years five months and seven days old when she died, after thirty-three years of successful married life (coniunx incomparabilis, her husband styles her).[14] Her epitaph is cut in irregular letters on a marble slab let into the side of her terra-cotta sarcophagus, which rests on an unopened grave-recess built up against the east wall of the inner chamber of this bipartite mausoleum.

The tomb is conventionally known as Fannia's; but it had already been standing nearly a century and a half when Fannia was buried in it. Originally it had been intended, primarily if not indeed exclusively, for cremation-burials.[15] It was built after A and before C; and it was one of three tombs within the cemetery that had an open forecourt in front of the burial-chamber proper; and it closely resembled Tomb D, in that the forecourt lay behind the façade and was an integral part of the main structure, whereas in H it formed a separate enclosure, in front of the main façade. To enter B, one stepped through a doorway of travertine set in a low brick façade. The excavators found this doorway blocked by Constantine's work-

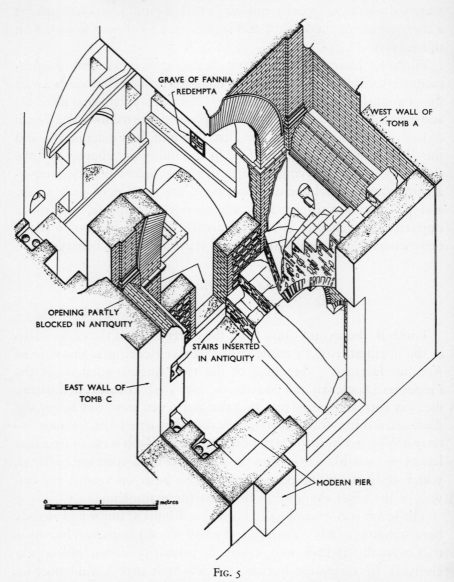

GRAVE OF FANNIA
REDEMPTA

WEST WALL OF
TOMB A

OPENING PARTLY
BLOCKED IN ANTIQUITY

STAIRS INSERTED
IN ANTIQUITY

EAST WALL OF
TOMB C

MODERN PIER

0   1   2 metres

FIG. 5

The Tomb of Fannia Redempta (Tomb B). The interior is shown as it appeared after the modifications undertaken in the third century. The detail of the façade (the lower part, of the second century; the upper part, Constantinian) is not shown. The staircase dates probably from the dismantlement of the tomb by Constantine's workmen. (*Drawing by B. M. Apollonj-Ghetti.*)

men, who had torn out the jambs and lintel and destroyed much of the façade, before adding fresh masonry to raise it to the level of those of the adjacent tombs. But two stretches of the original brick cornice can still be seen just above the level of the door; and to the east of the door there is the outline of the simple terra-cotta frame for an inscription or decorative panel, which was later removed and its place taken by a facing of small, carefully coursed tufa blocks. Comparison with Tomb D suggests that this was probably the original dedicatory inscription, for which there was no room in the normal position over the door. If so, it was perhaps removed in the third century, when the tomb was remodelled, and its place was taken by the inscription that stood over the inner door until removed by Constantine's workmen.

When the tomb was in use, one stepped down through the doorway into the open courtyard (B^1), some 3·70 metres wide and 2·50 metres from front to back. The flanking walls of this courtyard were some 2·60 metres high, and were capped with roll-topped brick copings (as in D^1; we may compare the similarly shaped travertine copings of H^1), and immediately behind and above them rose the walls of Tombs A and C, which were single-chamber structures, like most of the tombs in the Vatican cemetery. It is noticeable that the outer face of the coping of the west wall is cut off vertically in precisely the same way as that of the east wall, which was built up against the brickwork of the already existing Tomb A; the construction of Tomb C on the plot immediately adjacent to the west was evidently already foreseen when Tomb B was built. The south side of the forecourt, opposite the entrance, was almost entirely occupied by a high and wide brick archway, the soffit of which was continuous with the vault of the tomb-chamber (B), a cross-vaulted structure with short, lateral, barrel-vaulted wings, almost exactly the same size as the forecourt onto which it opened. On either side of the archway, immediately above the coping of the flanking walls of the forecourt, there is the lower part of a brick pilaster, which must have carried an entablature across the façade, above the arch.

When we enter B^1 we notice that six small round-headed niches for ash-urns are cut, in two superimposed tiers, in its west wall.[16] Six more niches are embedded in the east wall, but these have been largely obscured by a staircase, which is clearly a secondary feature. Somewhat similar, but original, stairs occur in the south-east angles

of Tombs E and F and in the eastern wing of Tomb H, all forming
a structural unity with the tombs to which they belong; and whether
they communicated with an east-west road, which ran across
the Mons Vaticanus, behind the cemetery (p. 19, Note 22), or
merely with open country, there can be little doubt that their purpose was to give access to the hillside which slopes up steeply to the
north of the tombs.[17] The staircase inserted into B¹, however, may
have served a different purpose; neither is there any trace of its
upward continuation against the well-preserved outer face of Tomb
A, nor is it easy to see how any such upper flight could have made
its way between the same wall and the tall inner façade of B. Again,
this staircase is of noticeably rough and flimsy construction, and
appears to have been built over a rough centering of earth. It seems
more probable, therefore, that it represents a final stage in the dismantling of the cemetery, when the street without was now already
blocked and partly filled in, and that its purpose was to allow the
owners of Tomb B, like several of their neighbours (p. 198), and
Constantine's workmen to have access to the tomb to the last
possible minute.

Whether or not this is the correct explanation of the staircase, there
is clear evidence that the mausoleum underwent radical reconditioni-
ing during the latter half of the third century. The original walls are
built of very neat, thin, rose-coloured bricks, with narrow layers of
fine mortar between each course (10 bricks to 35 centimetres in the
façade, 10 to 48 within the tomb); and the arch, with its long,
radiating tiles, framed by a narrow hood-mould of terra-cotta, is as
well proportioned as it is elegantly finished. But this arch between
B¹ and B, as we see it today, has been blocked by a very different type
of wall, faced with single courses of irregularly cut tufa blocks
alternating with single courses of bricks, all set in thick, coarse layers
of mortar (Pl. 3)—a type of masonry conventionally known as 'opus
listatum' and commonly held to have been typically and exclusively
used in late Antiquity. In this case it is obviously pre-Constantinian,
and we may note that its use in the Vatican cemetery for internal
wall-faces (although not for façades) goes back at least to the middle
of the second century (p. 269). Centred in this wall is a doorway
with travertine threshold and step, and neat brick imposts imitating
the earlier work; and over it is a tile-framed rectangular recess, let
into the body of the blocking-wall, from which someone, pre-

sumably a Constantinian builder, has ripped out the marble slab of a dedicatory inscription. Above this again, in the crown of the earlier arch, the excavators found the blocking-wall already dismantled in Antiquity. Perhaps it contained the marble framework of a window, which suffered the same fate as the inscription.

Did the tomb change hands when these changes were made? We do not know, although the evidence of the vanished inscription-panels suggests that perhaps it did. What is certain is that by the time they were carried out inhumation had superseded cremation, since the lowest portion of each of the lateral walls of the inner chamber is encased by a large tomb-recess, topped by a wide shelf; and it is on one of these shelves that the body of Fannia still reposes. The flat, painted surface of the lowest portion of the rear-wall may mask the recess for an earlier inhumation-burial, and an oblong tomb-shaft with travertine sides and rebated margin, sunk through the floor of the northern half of B, contains an open terra-cotta sarcophagus. It may once have been closed by a marble slab, which was removed by Constantine's workmen. The travertine tomb-shaft appears to represent an intermediate phase in the history of the tomb, prior to the final alterations, since it is itself clearly coeval with the rather coarse black-and-white mosaic pavement of the tomb-chamber, whereas the same pavement underlies, and is earlier than, the added tomb-recesses of the two lateral wings. The workmanship of this pavement, which shows two parrot-like birds confronted, with a vase between them and flanked by scroll-work, is very inferior to that of the original decoration of the tomb. Work of this quality is hard to date; but it could well belong to the early-third century, to which, on the evidence cited above, it must probably be assigned.

As in most of the tombs in the cemetery, the niches for cremation-burials in Tomb B are arranged symmetrically according to a uni-fied decorative scheme, which is divided into two zones by a shallow projecting plinth, about 95 centimetres above pavement-level. Above this plinth, in the centre of the rear-wall (Pl. 6), is a tall, semi-circular niche, roofed with a semi-dome, with two superimposed square niches on either side of it, and a similar square niche above it in the lunette formed by the cross-vaulted ceiling, which was low enough to be spared by the Constantinian church-builders. At either end of this wall is a small arched niche, at the level of the interspace between the two tiers of lateral square niches. In the original design, semi-engaged stucco colonnettes, arranged in pairs on either side of the central semicircular niche and of its flanking recesses, carried the frieze and tripartite pediment of an elaborate decorative entablature, composed of painted stucco upon a basis of projecting masonry. The removal of the stucco colonnettes, when the tomb was redecorated in the later-third century, accounts for the curiously detached effect of this entablature, the core of which remained, bracketed out from the wall-face, and was given a new and rather coarser coating of painted stucco. To get an impression of what the original scheme was like, we have to turn to a tomb such as F (p. 49), which has retained the greater part of its original ornament. The east and west walls were similarly decorated and underwent the same later modifications. Above the plinth (the top of which is level with that of the added grave-recesses) there was a central square niche, set within a projecting framework of stucco colonnettes and stucco-surfaced frieze and pediment. On either side of the central feature there was a smaller, arched niche. The smaller niches on all three walls were framed with tiny ornamental mouldings; and to complete the elaborate scheme of stucco-ornament, the capitals on the two inner faces of each jamb of the entrance-archway were decorated with alternate acanthus-leaves and lotus-leaves, set vertically in vigorous relief.

The all-over effect of the original second-century painted decoration on walls and ceilings is very restrained (Pl. 6).[18] Broad expanses of white background are laced with small polychrome motifs executed in a delicate, precise style recalling that of Japanese water-colour drawings. In the lunettes at the top of all three walls red deer step daintily along brown horizontal borders. Birds hover with light cords in their beaks, or, in oblong panels on the lateral walls, stand beside a slim-stemmed cylix. The lower part of all three walls, below the level of the projecting entablatures, has been largely redecorated at a later period; but to this same early phase belongs a series of painted yellow two-handled vases, set on the mouldings over the arched niches of the side-walls or painted at the back of each of the lower square niches of the rear-wall; and, in the central semi-circular niche of the rear-wall, revealed by the flaking off of later paint, an elegant peacock eyeing a wicker fruit-basket.

A cruciform design of five linked roundels occupies the vault. In the centre can be seen the faint traces of Helios driving his four-horsed chariot, whip in right hand and reins in left; and in the four smaller roundels there are the faded (and in one case wholly obliterated) busts of the Seasons. Along the groins of the vault, slender, flower-studded tendrils intertwine to form chains of elongated medallions; and other chains of small, gaily coloured discs (an unusual and distinctive motif, which is found again in Tomb G) are strung, like coins, between the two lateral Season roundels and the outer corners of the vault.

When the tomb was altered in the third century, the lunettes and the vault were left untouched, but the decorative scheme of the lower part of the walls was drastically modified. On the two side-walls, some of the original white ground and three of the four original painted vases survived; for the rest, the stucco colonnettes and mouldings were dismantled, and the surface of all three walls below the level of, and including, the surviving masonry core of the projecting entablatures were restuccoed and repainted. The new stucco is coarser than, and easily distinguishable from, the old, and the new painting, although vigorous and by no means ineffective, is quite different both in quality and in intention. In place of the delicate restraint of the earlier work, there are broad patches of colour, with sheets of imitation-marbling and impressionistic birds, beasts, and flowers. Along the rear-wall, just below the line of the old entablature, there is a cornice painted in false perspective; and below it two flanking panels of imitation-marbling and a third (now partly destroyed, revealing the earlier painting) within the central niche. A simple pattern of red lines on a white ground outlines the surviving architectural features of the earlier design; and in the spaces between these, on the two end-walls, flutter brilliantly plumaged red-and-blue birds. The eastern one of the two added grave-recesses is still sealed; but under the arch of the western one, which is open, revealing a plain terra-cotta sarcophagus, are sketched in vivid hues a goat, vases of flowers, naturalistic plants, and sea-monsters. Proof of the date of this redecoration is afforded by the presence of identical panels of imitation-marbling on the inner face of the inserted south wall, and by the continuity of the plaster between this and the redecorated parts of the earlier structure. To this same phase presumably belongs a ring of metal studs, which outlines the central medallion of the vault. These must have held a decorated disc of some perishable material, substituting for the chariot of Helios some device that was more in keeping with the beliefs of the later owners of the tomb.

The Tomb of Fannia was one of the first to be built within the area of the excavations, and it was maintained in good condition until the final abandonment of the area nearly two hundred years later. It gives us, in miniature, a cross-section of the story of the whole necropolis, of its architectural and artistic development, and of the evolution of its religious beliefs. To modern eyes, it is also one of the most intimate and immediately attractive of the tombs. One could not ask for a better introduction to the Vatican cemetery.

The First Tomb of the Caetennii
(Fig. 6; Pls. 2, 9–11, 14, 20, 21)

Tomb F was the first mausoleum to be cleared by the recent excavators. Its roof has gone; but its façade, which stands to a height of 4·50 metres, overtops those of all other tombs in the excavation and pierces the floor-level of the new lower church above. There, in the south aisle, a low, box-like structure encases the topmost surviving portion of this façade; and if the visitor is lucky and the lights are turned on below, he can crouch down, peep through the grating in the side of this protective box, and see something of the building which first gave away the secret of the Vatican necropolis.

Four inscriptions, still in place within the tomb, mention persons named Caetennius, members of an obviously wealthy and cultured family of the freedman-class (although themselves free-born), and their freedmen, buried with them in accordance with common Roman practice. In the centre, facing the entrance, stands an imposing altar-shaped base of marble with symmetrical acanthus-scrolls and half-palmettes on its rounded pediment, and a running floral border framing a dedication, cut in fine, bold lettering of the middle of the second century, *M(arco) Caetennio | Antigono | et Tulliae | Secundae | coniugi eius* (Pl. 20). A small, rectangular marble ash-chest with pointed pediment, now in a niche in the west wall, bears an inscribed panel centred in a laurel-garland slung from the horns of two ram-heads. Below the panel a couple of birds are feeding, while two tragic masks occupy the lower corners. The inscription, cut in much less regular letters, runs *D(is) M(anibus)/M(arco) Caetennio/ Tertio fecit/M(arcus) Caetennius/Chilo colibe/rto santissimo* [sic] (Pl. 21).

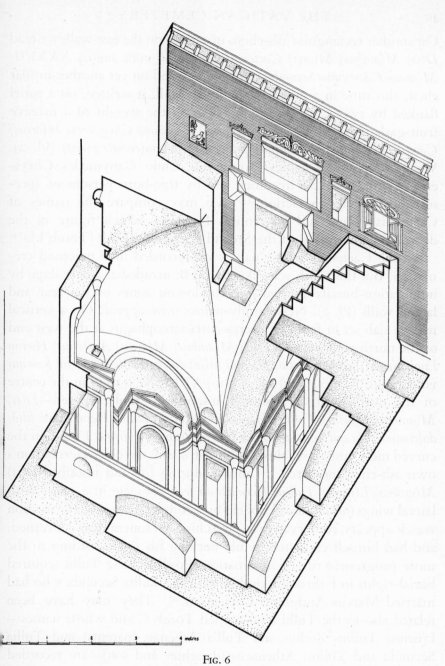

FIG. 6

The First Tomb of the Caetennii (Tomb F). Axonometric drawing, with vault and internal order restored to show the original architectural scheme. Later accretions are omitted. (*Drawing by B. M. Apollonj-Ghetti.*)

On another rectangular ash-chest, in a niche on the east wall, we read
D(is) M(anibus)/M(arci) Caetennii Ganymedis/vixit ann(is) XXXVII/
M(arcus) Caetennius Secundus/colliberto suo; and on yet another similar
chest, this time in a niche on the north wall, is written, on a panel
flanked by two Cupids straining beneath the weight of a massive
fruit-garland, D(is) M(anibus)/M(arco) Caetennio Chry/seroti M(arcus)
Caeten/nius Antigonus/iun(ior) patrono b(ene) m(erenti) f(ecit) (Pl. 2).
We note the Greek names—Antigonus, Chilo, Ganymedes, Chryseros—borne both by freedmen and by free-born persons of (presumably) servile extraction.[19] We may compare the names of
Caetennia Hygia and Caetennius Hymnus, which figure in the
dedicatory inscription of the Second Caetennii Tomb (Tomb L).[20]

All the Caetennii whose names are recorded in F practised cremation. But this tomb was, like Tomb B, invaded at a later stage by
inhumation-burials inserted into the lowest zones of the rear and
lateral walls (Pl. 2). New family-names now appear. On a vertical
marble slab set in front of a terra-cotta sarcophagus at the west end
of the north wall we read D(is) M(anibus)/M(arcus) Aur(elius) Hieron
Euokatus/M(arco) Aur(elio) Hieroni fil(io) dulcissimo/benemerenti fecit qui
vixit/an(nis) VI mens(ibus) duo dieb(us) XXVI. Next to it, in the centre
of the north wall, is a similar inscription similarly sited—D(is)
M(anibus)/L(ucius) Tullius Hermadion/L(ucio) Tullio Hermadioni filio/
dulcissimo fecit qui vixit/annis XVIIII m(ensibus) V diebus V; and in the
curved niche just above this second slab stands the elder Hermadion's
own ash-chest, prepared by himself during life and inscribed D(is)
M(anibus)/L(ucius) Tullius/Hermadi/on fecit/sibi vibus in a panel with
lateral wings (tabula ansata) upheld by a couple of Cupids. Hermadion
was, it appears, conservative so far as his own funeral was concerned,
and had himself cremated, while burying his son according to the
more progressive rite of inhumation. Possibly these Tullii acquired
burial-rights in F through kinship with the Tullia Secunda who had
married Marcus Antigonus Caetennius.[21] They may have been
related also to the Tullii who owned Tomb C and whose names—
L(ucius) Tullius Zethus and Tullia Athenais (parents) and Tullia
Secunda and Tullius Athenaeus (daughter and son)—are recorded
on the marble dedicatory inscription above its door.[22]

At a still later stage the grave of the younger Hermadion was
reused for a certain Siricius. In the top right-hand corner of the
marble slab his epitaph is scrawled, within a roughly incised ansate

tablet, in crude characters and odd Latinity—*Siricius/anorum* [sic] *XXV/mesorum* [sic] *V/uxor fecit Virgi/nio suo cum que* [sic] *bene vicxit a(nnis) VIIII.* Such an inscription could be Christian although it has no distinctively Christian features. But just below it, under the floor, is the burial of a woman who was certainly a Christian, Aemilia Gorgonia, whose marble tombstone bears the touching, if illiterate, epitaph composed by her devoted husband and recording her beauty and her chastity—*anima dulcis Gorgonia. mir(a)e i(n) specie et castitat[e]/ eius. Aemili(a)e Gorgoniae qu(a)e/vixit ann(is) XXVIII mens(ibus) II d(iebus) XXVIII/ dormit in pace/ coniugi dulcissim(a)e/feci.* The last six words are flanked by two doves, each perched on an olive-spray; and on the left side of the slab is incised a naïve little portrait of the deceased (?) drawing water (the living water of Eternal Life?) from a rectangular well.[23]

We have travelled a long way in the century and a half that separates the prim, correct formality of the second-century pagan epitaph of Marcus Caetennius Antigonus from the warm, spontaneous simplicity of this homely Christian grave. Seldom is a Roman tomb epigraphically richer than is the Mausoleum of the Caetennii, or more informative about the human personalities who made its history.

We turn now from the occupants of Tomb F to its structure and decoration. A single-chambered building, measuring 6 metres from east to west and 6·7 metres from north to south, it presents to the street a façade that is not only the tallest but also the most elaborate in the cemetery. The doorway was placed slightly to the west of the axis of the other decorative elements of the façade and of the central apse in the opposite (north) wall, in order to accommodate the staircase in the south-east angle of the interior, which was in this case certainly an original structural feature, not (as in B¹) a later addition. With its travertine threshold, imposts, and simply but strongly moulded lintel, it follows a stereotyped pattern, one that is already familiar from many of the tombs in the Isola Sacra cemetery and, to judge from the surviving examples (Tombs C, G, H, L, N, O, T, U),[24] was standard practice in the Vatican cemetery also. Such doorways were commonly edged with a slender terracotta beading; but here the architect has sought a more unusual effect, elaborating the beading into an intricate system of alternate ovoli and cavetti, which returns across the façade, at the level of the threshold, to form the crowning moulding of a shallow projecting plinth. This was balanced by an elaborate terra-cotta entablature, with a frieze, plain except for some feature (now destroyed) in a central panel, and a heavy console-cornice[25] (a gap in the centre of this marks the position of one of the many graves that were later dug down from the level of the floor of the Constantinian church). The crowning element of the cornice is unfortunately missing; similar tombs at Ostia were finished either with a pediment, triangular or (less commonly) curved, or with a plain horizontal cornice.[26]

It is, however, the five panels ranged in a horizontal line between the top of the door and the bottom of the entablature that lend an air of special distinction to this façade, breaking the austere simplicity of the plain brickwork surface. The central one of these, over and slightly to the right of the door, is framed with elegant terra-cotta mouldings, egg-and-dart and bead-and-reel, and crowned by an exquisite pedimental device, a curvilinear flower-and-palmette design rendered in low relief in terra-cotta (Pl. 11). It must originally have contained the dedicatory inscription of the tomb; but this was later removed and its place taken by a pair of small, rather roughly contrived windows, splayed and stuccoed on the inner side. Flanking this central panel are two smaller rectangular window-frames, bordered with terra-cotta dentil-mouldings and crowned by smaller versions of the motif over the central panel. The windows themselves are deeply splayed and admitted light through the narrow, vertical, slit-like openings in a pair of marble panels, similar to that which still survives, in position, in the façade of the adjoining Tomb E. The two outermost panels are terra-cotta reliefs, recessed into the surface of the wall. On the left, a portly quail stalks self-consciously past a tree (a myrtle or perhaps an olive) over a leafy branch of similar foliage (Pl. 9); the details are, very sparingly, picked out in darker colour. On the right, a columned building, with Ionic capitals and coffered ceiling (now unfortunately damaged), is built piecemeal into the brickwork after the manner of a terra-cotta mosaic (Pl. 10). The significance of these motifs is not immediately obvious. But the quail, like many another bird in a funerary context, may symbolize the soul of the departed in paradisal bliss; and the columned hall could represent the precinct of an aristocratic tomb-shrine or some royal dwelling in the kingdom of the dead. Exterior terra-cotta relief-work of this quality is relatively rare. And when we compare these refined productions with the simple frame-mouldings of the tombs at Isola Sacra,[27] and with the naïve, although spirited, terra-cotta pictures from business life and professional life that once enlivened their façades,[28] we have one measure of the distance in cultural and artistic standards which, by and large, separates the two cemeteries.

Except for a pair of round-headed cremation-niches in the north wall (only one of which survives, the other having been destroyed in Antiquity to make way for a later grave), the plinth, which is continuous along the east, north, and west walls, is occupied by arched grave-recesses for inhumation-burials. Above the plinth we find a more elaborate version of the system of curved and rectangular niches which we have already met, in simpler form, in Tomb B. A large, shallow apse with semi-dome dominates the north wall and frames a smaller curved niche, set in a projecting gabled structure with heavy projecting pediment of stuccoed masonry, and flanked by free-standing, vertically fluted columns of white stucco. Two tall, rectangular niches flank the apse. These are topped by the lower angles of a similar but larger and flatter pediment, which is thought of as broken by and supporting the archivolt of the apse; and each of the flanking niches was itself flanked by stucco columns similar to those of the curved niche of the central structure. Most of the lunette spanning the upper part of the north wall has been destroyed; and all the columns are now broken, showing how they were built up in stucco about a core of some perishable material bound with coarse twine to give it a firm seating.

Above the plinth along the west wall, there are two tall, curved niches, each crowned by a projecting, truncated-triangular pediment of stuccoed masonry, alternating with three rectangular niches, each of which is crowned by a similar, but rounded, pediment, and is divided into two superimposed compartments by a deep shelf, the outer surface of which, flush with the wall surface, is slightly convex. All of these niches are flanked by spirally fluted, free-standing columns of white stucco. The scheme of the east wall reproduces that of the west wall, but is slightly compressed to allow for the staircase in the south-east corner. Three small, superimposed, round-headed niches fill in the space left over at the south end of the west wall; others are set in the sides of the staircase and of the south wall; and seven more, three on the east and four on the west, are skyed at the top of the lunettes that span the lateral walls. A bracket high up on the south wall, over the entrance-door, may once have supported an ash-urn or a bust.

This elaborate architectural scheme was enlivened with figures in paint and stucco. In the semi-dome of the northern apse can be seen the faded traces of a painting showing Venus rising from the sea, attended by Tritons (an allegory of rebirth); and in the great lunette spanning the west wall are an ox and a ram in an idyllic landscape (symbols of paradise).[29] Tiny white stucco figures, worked in relief against a purple ground, adorn the convex panels that divide the two compartments of the rectangular niches in the lateral walls, and within the mouldings of the archivolt of the northern apse there is a frieze of miniature cranes and pygmies (an allegory of the contest of life and death) modelled in white stucco against a scarlet band. Similar figures probably once adorned the friezes of the engaged entablatures; but of these no trace now remains.

The vault was mostly destroyed when the tomb was dismantled; but the richness of the painted stucco ornament with which it was covered can be gauged from the fragments surviving from the lower angles of the cross-vault and of the short barrel-vault by which it was prolonged across the entrance (Pl. 14). It was coffered with square, oblong, and triangular panels, set in a rich framework of diminutive architectural mouldings—egg-and-dart, leaf-cymation, and repeated beads. Within some of the panels can be seen rosettes, leaf-sprays, dolphins, etc., standing out in white relief against backgrounds of purple, scarlet, and blue-green.

Unlike most of the tombs in the Vatican cemetery, which were carefully maintained to the last, F shows unmistakable signs of neglect in the period immediately before its dismantlement and burial. Almost the whole of the simple black-and-white mosaic pavement was lifted to make room for inhumation-burials, and carelessly replaced;[30] and the latest burials above ground, crowded roughly against the plinth or into the niches of the east wall, were contrived quite without regard for the niceties of the architectural scheme. Even so, damaged as it is, one cannot fail to be impressed by the brilliant polychrome effect of the inner decoration of Tomb F. It was a study in contrasts, with the simplicity of the floor (black and white), of the plinth (predominantly purple), and the upper part of

the walls (predominantly greenish-blue), serving to offset the richness of the ceiling and of the central zones of the three main walls.
The elaborate architectural scheme of the latter was further en-
hanced by the contrast between the gleaming white relief of the
stucco columns, entablatures, framing lines, and shells in the heads
of the curved niches, and the rich, flat tones of the Pompeian red of
the wall-spaces between the niches, and of the deep purple of the
angle-panels and of the inner faces of the rectangular niches. Although decorative schemes of this sort are found, in one form or
another, in most of the tombs in the Vatican cemetery, Tomb F
excels most of its fellows both in the scale of its architectural design
and in the wealth and quality of its painted and stucco ornament. To
judge from the remaining west wall and the west end of the north
wall of Tomb L (the Second Tomb of the Caetennii, not now
accessible), it is this tomb that comes closest, as we might expect, to
F; it shows the same scheme of apse and niches on a slightly reduced
scale and was almost certainly the work of the same architect.[31]
Tomb H is more grandiose, its white stucco figure-reliefs are more
ambitious in treatment and cover a wider range of subject-matter;
but in the studied avoidance of brilliant colours, and in the emphasis on
the quality of the stucco itself, it falls rather into a category by itself.
At Isola Sacra, too, many of the tombs have schemes of internal
decoration comparable to that of the First Tomb of the Caetennii;[32]
but none can rival it in quality. By any standard, it is an exceptional
example of its kind.

The 'Tomb of the Egyptians'
(Fig. 7; Pls. 7, 8, 22, 28)

Of the two mausolea now accessible in the southern row, Z, the
so-called 'Tomb of the Egyptians', in spite of being only in part
preserved, is the more important (Pl. 7). With the possible exception
of one or two cremation-niches in the destroyed southern part of
the tomb (as in the inner face of the south wall of the adjoining
Tomb Φ), it was built for inhumations alone; and although in this
case there may have been special religious reasons for the absence of
cremations (p. 55),[33] it seems likely on other grounds that Tomb Z
falls relatively late within the period covered by the excavated part
of the Vatican cemetery. When it was built, the ground behind

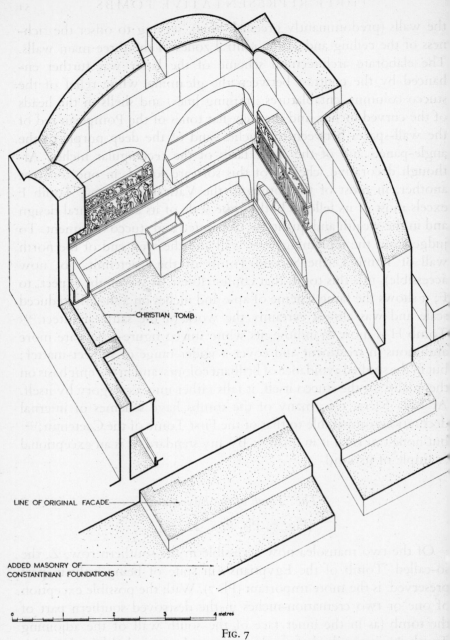

CHRISTIAN TOMB

LINE OF ORIGINAL FACADE

ADDED MASONRY OF
CONSTANTINIAN FOUNDATIONS

0   1   2   3   4 metres

FIG. 7

The 'Tomb of the Egyptians' (Tomb Z). The front half of the tomb (destroyed to make
way for one of the foundations of the Constantinian nave) is restored to show the
original plan. Later additions are omitted, except for the sarcophagi, which are shown as
found. (*Drawing by B. M. Apollonj-Ghetti.*)

already stood at the uniform, and partly artificial, level of the street fronting Tombs A–F; and the north façade, although less elegant than that of its neighbours, was clearly built to be seen. On the other hand, it is probably earlier than Φ. Along the exposed east flank, the line of its foundations slopes steeply downwards, following the irregular line of the surface of the hillside into which it was dug; whereas the foundations of the west wall of Φ, barely a metre away, are neatly trench-built, with a waterproofing that cuts deeply into the same surface-line at its northern end.[34] Z was itself waterproofed along the north face, towards the street; and the waterproofing extends to protect the north face of an irregular, chest-like structure of masonry built against the surviving northern part of the east face of the tomb. This structure, which is built of the same alternating courses of brick and tufa as the inner faces of the walls of the tomb itself, was found filled with human bones; and since the waterproofing must be pre-Constantinian (and may well be contemporary with the building of the tomb), the probable inference is that these are the remains of earlier burials, found and carefully reburied when the tomb was built. This conclusion is, as we shall see, not without relevance to the problem of the first shrine of St. Peter (p. 145 ff.).

When we enter the excavations, we are standing on the site of Tomb Z's southern half, destroyed by the most northerly of the three southern foundation-walls of the nave of Constantine's church. The low wall and steps immediately in front of us are modern; and the two small marble sarcophagi, flanking the steps, are not in their original positions. Of the tomb's façade we know nothing, and of its ceiling only the lower angles of the north-west and north-east pendentives of the shallow saucer-dome remain. The brickwork of the exterior of the north wall can be studied from the street. The masonry is rather coarse (10 bricks to 47 centimetres, with rather irregular jointing) and severely plain, and it lacks the elegant flat pilasters, with moulded bases, that adorn the three surviving exterior angles of its eastern neighbour, Tomb Φ. Inside, the north wall was cut by four arched tomb-recesses arranged like bunks in two superimposed tiers. No doubt four recesses similarly set out, occupied the east and west walls respectively, although now only two, one above the other, are left on each wall, at its northern end.

No prolonged study of the interior is needed to reveal two periods in the history of the mausoleum.[35] Originally the walls and pendentives were washed all over with flame-coloured paint, as a background for small figures and for other designs; and plain terra-cotta coffins of modest dimensions probably rested in some, at least, of the recesses. In the centre of the lunette above the top tier of recesses on each of the three surviving walls is painted a surprising figure, unique, so far as the present writers are aware, in west-Roman funerary archaeology—an Egyptian god: no Hellenized deity in western guise, such as Isis, Serapis, or Harpocrates, but a fully-fledged native divinity in national costume. Of this trio only the figure in the centre of the northern lunette can now be clearly distinguished (Pl. 8). The god stands to the left, with his right foot advanced beyond his left foot, trunk and shoulders frontal, head, legs, and feet in profile. His legs are bare from the knee downwards, and his bare feet rest on a dark-blue cushion decorated with two rows of stitched or woven zig-zags. Reaching to his knees is a bright-blue kilt, seen passing across the left thigh, ornamented with rosettes and horizontal lines in white, from which the surface-paint has now partly flaked away. Covering the right thigh is what should, in reality, be the overfold of the kilt, but which here appears as a separate apron of turquoise-blue with a stitched or woven vertical pattern of white rosettes between two white zig-zag borders. Very scanty traces are left of the bright-blue colouring of the deep belt, worn round the god's waist, which now almost merges with the flame-coloured background. Above the belt he wears a close-fitting bodice or jacket of turquoise-blue, adorned with scales outlined in white, the upper edge of which passes under the arm-pits, leaving the shoulders free; and a tail-like strip of the same colour and design thrusts down under and below the belt to cover the left buttock. The god's long, lean arms hang by his sides and he holds the two standard attributes of an Egyptian deity. Grasped in his right hand is a tall, slender wand, held vertically, the terminals of which (normally a double hook above and two inward-curving prongs below) are obscure. From his left hand depends the *ankh*, symbol of life, with its double-curved handle and cross-bar, below which there appear to be three short prongs, instead of the single prong projecting from the centre of the bar, which would have been correct. A broad, jewelled(?) collar passes across the shoulders below the base of the neck. The face is now very faint; but photographs taken shortly after discovery, when the colour was fresher, appear to show no human features, but a round eye like that of a bird and the pale outline, continuous with the line of the throat, of what seems to be a great hooked beak, resembling closely, if not exactly, the falcon-beak of Horus, the king-god, who restored Osiris to life. Horus, if such he is, has a bright-blue wig and a high headdress of dark blue, probably intended to represent his double crown, ornamented with two zones of diamonds also outlined in white.[36] On either side of the central figure are slung flower-garlands, and an animal stands towards the left in the lower left-hand corner of the lunette. The other motifs are now hard to define.

There can be little doubt that Tomb Z was built, in the first instance, for an Egyptian family resident in Rome and practising there some aspects of its native cult. This in itself would be sufficient to account for the absence of cremation-burials, since the Egyptians never burned their dead. That there were some influential Egyptians in the imperial city at this period we know from the story of the Egyptian priest Arnouphis, who accompanied Marcus Aurelius to his northern war and whose prayers were believed by some to have produced the celebrated 'Miracle of the Rain'.[37] To judge from the inaccuracies and misunderstandings shown in certain details of the figure of Horus(?), the paintings are probably the work of a Roman artist using models in a papyrus-roll or copy-book supplied by his Egyptian patron.

More conspicuous, if less intriguing, than these paintings are the ensigns of the tomb's second period—two luxurious sarcophagi of Greek marble, each crammed into one of the upper tomb-recesses, for which they give the uncomfortable impression of being just too large. The sarcophagus in the western recess on the north wall depicts the discovery of the sleeping Ariadne by Dionysus, an allegory of how the soul of the initiate will wake from the slumber of death to a life of union with its god (Pl. 22).[38] It may be dated on stylistic grounds to the closing years of the second century. Dionysus, clutching a Bacchic wand (*thyrsus*) and a wine-cup (*cantharus*), advances from the left in a car drawn by a lyre-playing Centaur, and is attended by his usual entourage of Satyrs, baby Satyr, Pan, Silenus, Maenads, Cupids, and panthers. A Satyr and a Cupid draw aside Ariadne's mantle; a Maenad clashes cymbals to rouse the sleeper; and on the right are three more Dionysiac revellers, a drunken *thyrsus*-bearing youth, clinging to a tree, and a couple of hoydenish

Maenads. The frieze on the vertical face of the lid, flanked by Satyr-masks, shows another rollicking revel-rout in low relief, among the participants in which are a Silenus on a donkey, Satyrs, Maenads, and a Bacchic youth offering sacrifice. Bacchic figures, now practically hidden by the walls of the recess, ornament the short sides. The sarcophagus, of Proconnesian marble, in the northern recess on the east wall is later in date, showing the panels of curved strigilations and lavish use of drilling in the treatment of the hair characteristic of about the beginning of the second quarter of the third century (Pl. 28). It, too, is Dionysiac, but much more restrained than its fellow, the revellers being confined to one central and two lateral panels, which alternate with the strigilated panels, on the front. In the middle stands Dionysus in a niche, with a fawn-skin (*nebris*) *thyrsus*, *cantharus*, and panther, while a sea-Centaur, blowing on a conch, tops each of the flanking pilasters. At the left end a half-draped Maenad, *thyrsus* in hand and with an overturned *cantharus* and a rearing panther at her feet, turns her back on us. At the right end a Satyr dances, holding a wine-skin and a child (either his own or the infant Dionysus); between his legs gambols a female panther. The vertical lid bears four frolicking sea-monsters—fish-tailed griffin, dragon, horse, and panther. They converge on the central panel, as though they were coming to fetch away the occupant, whose name was, for some reason, never inscribed there. Indeed, these beasts, like the sea-Centaurs in the panel below, symbolize, in the idiom of Dionysiac picture-language, the journey of the initiated soul across the ocean to the Islands of the Blessed, seat of the Bacchic paradise (p. 114); they are often seen conveying Nereids, Cupids, etc., across the waves. On each of the short sides of the sarcophagus a seated griffin, warder of the dead, guards the burial.

The eschatological hopes and ideas reflected on these sarcophagi are commonplaces of imperial-age Bacchic thought and representation; and it is highly probable that when they were placed in the tomb it had already passed into the hands of Roman practitioners of the Dionysiac mysteries.

Three more strigilated sarcophagi of the mid-third century can now be studied in Tomb Z. One of these is still in its original position. The terra-cotta coffin in the upper recess at the east end of the north wall is masked by a sarcophagus-front of Proconnesian marble, which shows a marine-procession, flanked by two Satyr-masks, in a frieze above the uninscribed *titulus*-panel,[39] and two crossed *cornucopiae*, symbols of other-world prosperity, beneath it. The two small sarcophagi flanking the modern steps were moved here from the Tomb of the Tullii (C) in which they were found, not, it seems, in their original positions, but apparently placed there by Constantine's builders. That on the west side, of Italian marble, with tiled and gabled lid, is inscribed *D(is) M(anibus) M(arci) Vlp(i) Pusinnionis Cupi[t]iani M(arcus) Vlp(ius) Pusinnio pater filio dulcissimo*, and figures a bust of the dead boy, wearing trabeate toga, in the central roundel.[40] The one opposite, of Greek marble, portrays in the centre of its lid the unfinished bust of the deceased backed by a curtain, symbol of apotheosis, with four sea-monsters advancing on him (or her?) from either end. At each end of the front is a mourning Cupid, on each short side a vigilant griffin.

The record of yet another episode in the story of the 'Tomb of the Egyptians' is not immediately obvious. In the lower tomb-recess on the west wall lies a humble, terra-cotta sarcophagus. Bending down, we see, painted in red on the stuccoed wall of the lunette above, the fragmentary funerary inscription of the Christian woman buried in it. It is very damaged, but contains the word *deposita*, a formula of which there does not seem to be any record from a pagan epitaph, and it is accompanied by a palm-branch and a dove.

Horus, Dionysus, Christ—each offering to their followers, if in and on very different terms, salvation and life abundant in the unseen world. This tomb paints for us a vivid picture of *praeparatio evangelii* in the pagan Empire.

NOTES

1. The letters by which the individual tombs are referred to (see Fig. 3) are those given by the excavators in the *Report*.

2. This cemetery, until the excavation of the Vatican cemetery the most complete surviving document of Roman middle-class funerary architecture, was well published and illustrated by its excavator, the late Guido Calza (*La Necropoli del Porto di Roma nell'Isola Sacra*, 1940; hereafter cited as 'Calza').

3. The upward slope from east to west is sharpest in the western half of the site, to the west of the natural gully (later blocked by Tomb M) between Tombs L and N. The fact that the building of M blocked the last means of access to the north suggests that this was the effective northern limit of the cemetery.

4. *CIL*, vi. 3, 17985a:

> Tibur mihi patria, Agricola sum vocitatus
> Flavius, idem ego sum discumbens, ut me videtis,
> sic et aput superos annis, quibus fata dedere,
> animulam colui nec defuit umqua Lyaeus.
> praecessitque prior Primitiva gratissima coniuncx
> Flavia et ipsa, cultrix deae Phariaes casta
> sedulaque et forma decore repleta,
> cum qua ter denos dulcissimos egerim annos.
> solaciumque sui generis Aurelium Primitivum
> tradidit, qui pietate sua coleret fastigia nostra,
> hospitiumque mihi secura servavit in aevum.
> amici, qui legitis, moneo, miscete Lyaeum
> et potate procul redimiti tempora flore
> et venereos coitus formosis ne denegate puellis;
> cetera post obitum terra consumit et ignis.

(Tibur is my native place, Flavius Agricola my name, yes, I'm the one you see reclining here, just as I did all the years of life fate granted me, taking good care of my little self and never going short of wine. Primitiva, my darling wife, passed away before me, a Flavian too, chaste worshipper of Isis, attentive to my needs, and graced with every beauty. Thirty blissful years we spent together; for my comfort she left me the fruit of her body, Aurelius Primitivus, to tend my house [or tomb?] with dutiful affection; and so, herself released from care, she has kept a dwelling-place for me for aye. Friends who read this, do my bidding. Mix the wine, drink deep, wreathed with flowers, and do not refuse to pretty girls the sweets of love. When death comes, earth and fire devour everything). See also Note 6.

5. See Calza, pp. 62–3. The Isola Sacra cemetery affords many parallels to the sort of development described here on p. 30 ff., and includes several instances of what appear to be plots bought up for commercial development (*cf.* p. 35).

6. The notes on the epitaph of Flavius Agricola in *CIL* (*loc. cit.*) run as follows: 'sub statua manu poculum tenenti eruta a.1626 inter augustissimi templi Vaticani ambitum FABR [Fabretti]; rep.d.14 Aug. 1626 Romae sub confessione basilicae D. Petri in basi statuae iacentis pateram manu tenentis una cum aliis statuarum fragmentis item nummis quibusdam Gallieni imperatoris. versus in loco tenebroso statim descripti sunt, deinde vero iussu summi pontificis calce illiti; statua ipsa occultata aut, ut perhibent nonnulli, in Tiberim proiecta est BARB [codex Barberinianus].' The Vatican excavators assign the statue and its inscription to the third century, on account of the coins of Gallienus stated to have been found with it (*Report*, i, p. 88). But the statue need not have been contemporary with the coins, which could easily have reached the tomb at a later date.

7. The excavators (*Report*, i, p. 104) claim that R, Q, and the Clivus are all contemporary. But A. von Gerkan (*Trierer Zeitschrift*, xxii, 1953, pp. 36–8) is probably right in arguing that R is structurally earlier than both Q and, in the form in which it has come down to us, the Clivus. The exposed face of the masonry of the east face of R and of R[1] shows that, when these were built, the ground-level immediately to the east rose more steeply than it did later, after the insertion of the concrete floor of the Clivus. The only evidence adduced by the excavators (*Report*, i, pp. 93–4) for the structural contemporaneity of R–R[1] and of Q is that where the steps of the Clivus abut on the face of the footings of R[1], these lack the customary waterproof facing, and must therefore have been built with the steps in mind. This argument, however, disregards the possibility that there had been some earlier feature (earlier steps?) at the point examined, and takes no account of the manifest difficulties of the builders of the Clivus in adapting the present steps to afford access to both R[1] and Q at the required levels. Moreover, the plan of Q certainly suggests that its builders were making use of an existing feature, the north wall of R[1].

These difficulties of interpretation are all resolved if we may regard R–R[1], although probably later than S, as having been built a few years before Q and, in its present form, the Clivus. The absolute chronology of Q and of the Red Wall is not affected. But we must envisage the Clivus coming into being as a passage-way left by the builders of R to afford access to R[1] and to whatever lay to the north of S, including possibly some of the early graves described in chapter 6. It was not until a few years later, with the building of Q and the Red Wall, that it assumed its definitive form.

8. See Note 2.

9. P. Styger, *Il monumento apostolico a San Sebastiano sulla Via Appia* (not dated), p. 15, Pls. 6–10; G. Mancini, 'Scavi sotto la basilica di S. Sebastiano sull'Appia Antica' (*Notizie degli Scavi*, 1923, pp. 46–75, Pls. 9–16; cited hereafter as 'Mancini'). Excellent picture-postcards showing the façades of the three tombs juxtaposed, and a detailed view of the façade of the Tomb of Marcus Clodius Hermes are taken from negatives by E. Richter, *Roma*, Nos. 323 and 325.

10. G. Lugli, 'Scavo di un sepolcreto romano presso la Basilica di S. Paolo' (*Notizie degli Scavi*, 1919, pp. 285–354; cited hereafter as 'Lugli').

11. *Cf.* the 'Tombe a Cassone' of the Isola Sacra cemetery, Calza, Figs. 13, 29, and pp. 76–80.

12. *E.g.*, *Report*, i, Figs. 43, 53 ii, Pls. 21. 2, 22. 2.

13. A detailed and definitive publication of Mausolea L to V is to be found in the *Report*. Among the partial and popular accounts of the tombs that have appeared are the following: (i) A. Ferrua, *Civiltà Cattolica*, 92-iii, 1941, pp. 358–65, 424–33; 94-iv, 1942, pp. 73–86, 228–41; *Bullettino della Commissione Archeologica Comunale di Roma*, lxx, 1942, p. 95 ff. (cited hereafter as 'Ferrua'); (ii) H. Fuhrmann, *Archäologischer Anzeiger*, lvi, 1941, col. 524 ff.; (iii) E. Josi,

'Gli scavi nelle Sacre Grotte Vaticane' (*Il Vaticano nel 1944*, 1944; offprint, cited hereafter as 'Josi'); (iv) *The Times*, 27 February 1946; (v) *Illustrated London News*, 7 September 1946; (vi) C. B. Welles, *American Journal of Archaeology*, li, 1947, pp. 284–5; (vii) E. Kirschbaum, *Gregorianum*, xxix, 1948, p. 544 ff.; (viii) R. T. O'Callaghan, *The Biblical Archaeologist*, xii, I, 1949, p. 1 ff.; (ix) H. Speier, *Wort und Wahrheit*, July 1949, p. 481 ff.; *Vermächtnis der antiken Kunst* (ed. R. Herbig), 1950, p. 199 ff.; (x) *Life*, 27 March 1950 (American edition); 19 April 1950 (international edition); (xi) J. Carcopino, *Études d'histoire chrétienne*, 1953, p. 134 ff.; (xii); O. Perler, *Die Mosaiken der Juliergruft im Vatikan*, 1953. Coloured picture-postcards are published in the Vatican City.

14. D(is) M(anibus)/Fanniae Redempta/e quae vixit ann(is) xx/xxvi mens(ibus) v dieb(us) vi/i Aurel(ius) Aug(ustorum) lib(ertus) Her/mes coniugi inc/omparabili cum/qua vixit ann(is) xx/xiii.

15. It is not impossible that the flanking walls of the inner tomb-chamber, replastered and repainted in the second period, originally contained arched inhumation-recesses. In D (to which B, although more elaborately decorated, bears a close resemblance) it is certain that there were none.

16. Six straight-headed niches, in two tiers, are cut in the eastern face of the surviving west wall of H¹, the forecourt of H. In D, the arrangement is slightly more elaborate.

17. Tombs that were otherwise similar to those of the Vatican cemetery occasionally had an upper storey or a terrace-roof, *e.g.* Isola Sacra, No. 29 (Calza, Figs. 18, 26–8 and pp. 75–7, 303–4); but the evidence that in the Vatican they served as a secondary means of access is cumulatively convincing. This is particularly clear in Tomb H, where the internal stairs (an original feature of the construction) rise steeply eastward behind the rear-wall of G, turn briefly north to skirt the projecting north-west angle of F, and then east again, to emerge at what was presumably the ancient ground-level in the angle between F and H. As the gaps in this row of southward-facing tombs were filled, access from the north would have become increasingly difficult.

18. Vatican coloured picture-postcards, Ser. V, 8–10.

19. A fifth inscription of these Caetennii, recorded by Ferrua (p. 100) but not seen by the present writers in the necropolis, contains another Greek name and reads—D(is) M(anibus)/Caetenniae Proclae/coniugi carissimae/quae vix(it) ann(is) XX/M(arcus) Aurelius Filetus/benemerenti titulu(m) posuit.

20. D(is) M(anibus)/Caetenniae/Hygiae/quae vixit ann(is) XXI d(iebus) XIII/M(arcus) Caetennius Hymnus/filiae pientissimae et/M(arcus) Caetennius Proculus/sorori karissimae/fecerunt et sibi et/libertis libertabusque/suis posterisque eorum/h(oc) m(onumentum) h(eredem) n(on) s(equetur) h(uic) m(onumento) d(olus) m(alus) a(besto).

21. Loose above the sarcophagus of the younger Hermadion are two fragmentary sepulchral inscriptions—(1) (D(is) M(anibus) A . . ./Tullia Tr . . ./

arissimo . . ./et A Valeri . . ./patrono be[nemerenti]/feceru[nt]; (2) [Dis]
M(anibus)/L(ucio) Octavio Corne[lia]/no filio dulcissim[o]/Cornelia Ammas/
mater pientissim[a]/fecit qui vixit an(nis)/XXIII mens(ibus) VI die/bus XI.

22. L(ucius) Tullius Zethus fecit/sibi et/Tulliae Athenaidi coniugi bene/
merenti et Tulliae Secundae et/Tullio Athenaeo filis, *etc.* The bases with epi-
aphs of the son and daughter are inside the tomb.

23. Guarducci, Fig. 11 and p. 25. A somewhat unusual feature of the well-
ead, presumably built of stone or marble, is its rectangular or square shape.
Most Roman well-heads in Mediterranean lands are circular; and round wells
re shown in catacomb-paintings depicting the Samaritan Woman, or the soul
f the departed Christian drawing Living Water (J. Wilpert, *Die Malereien der
Katakomben Roms,* 1903, Pls. 19; 29, 2; 54, 2). Some timber-lined well-shafts
ecently excavated in Roman London are, however, square in shape.

24. Tomb G presents a slightly elaborated version, with a pair of terra-
otta brackets supporting the lintel.

25. *Cf.* Isola Sacra, No. 80 (Calza, Fig. 16 and p. 339).

26. *Cf.* Isola Sacra, No. 54 (Calza, Fig. 9, flat entablature); Nos. 78, 79 (Calza,
ig. 16, triangular pediment); No. 80 (Calza, Fig. 16, curved pediment). The
riangular pediment is the normal solution, here and elsewhere.

27. Calza, Fig. 36.

28. Calza, Figs. 148–58.

29. Ferrua, p. 100, Fig. 5. For views of the interior of Tomb F, see Vatican
oloured picture-postcards, Ser. VI, 4–7.

30. A feature of the mosaic pavement is the series of libation-holes inset into
he border: small, square slabs of marble, pierced with a hole for the pouring
f offerings to the dead beneath. Compare the similar holes in the mosaic pavement of Tomb C. Of the black-and-white mosaic in C there survive a fragment
f a guilloche border and an area near the entrance showing a floral scroll
eopled with birds.

31. *Report,* i, Figs. 14, 15; ii, Pl. 4.

32. *E.g.* Calza, Pls. 1, 4, Figs. 45, 46, 47, 59, 69.

33. Inhumation-area Q also contained no cremations.

34. A section cut through what remains of the intervening levels would no
oubt settle the matter.

35. Vatican coloured picture-postcard, Ser. V, 6.

36. For representations of Horus in late-Egyptian art, with dress and attri-
utes closely resembling those of our figure, see: (1) S. Gabra, *Rapport sur les
ouilles d'Hermoupolis Ouest,* 1941, Pl. 13, 2: painting in 'funerary house' No. 21,
howing Thoth and Horus purifying the deceased, Horus wearing scale-bodice,
ilt with overfold of the same colour, and a 'tail' of another colour covering
he buttock (Graeco-Roman period); (2) A. Fakhry, *The Egyptian Deserts:
Bahria Oasis,* 1, 1942, p. 71, Fig. 31: painting of Horus with wand, *ankh,*

double crown, kilt, dark-coloured bodice and 'tail' (sixth cent. B.C.). For the standard type of Horus, see H. Bonnet, *Reallexikon der ägyptischen Religions-geschichte*, 1952, Fig. 78. The writers are much indebted to Professor J. Černy, Professor of Egyptology in the University of Oxford, and to Miss Rosalind Moss of the Griffith Institute, Oxford, for help with the elucidation of the dress and attributes of the Vatican figure.

37. Cassius Dio, lxxi, 8–10.

38. Josi, p. 10.

39. Here Cupids are shown some riding, others half-playfully attacking, friendly sea-monsters. The scene suggests the soul's struggle with death before its conveyance across the ocean to a happier world.

40. The sarcophagus of this boy's mother, also found stacked within the Tomb of the Tullii, is now in the early-Christian museum near the exit from the Sacre Grotte. The *titulus*, in the centre of the lid and supported by two Cupids, reads: D(is) M(anibus)/L(?) *Acestiae/Hedonetis†/coniugis/carissimae/M(arcus) Ulpius Pusinnio/maritus. To the left of it is an idyllic paradise-scene—a man, with an array of cups beside him, resting from enjoyment of the fruits of the vintage: a friend vainly tries to persuade him to take more; and the two oxen that draw the grape-laden wagon have lain down and patiently await their master's pleasure. On the right is the portrait-bust of Acestia, with a curtain held up behind her by another pair of Cupids. The whole of the front of the sarcophagus is filled with curved strigilations, apart from the extremities, each of which is occupied by a mourning Cupid (Ferrua, Fig. 4, *c*). This sarcophagus, and the two small pieces now in Tomb Z, were found stacked with bones, probably from burials which the Constantinian builders could not avoid disturbing.

*Luciae? or an error? A *praenomen* for a woman in the second century A.D. would be most abnormal.

†This would seem to be a somewhat unexpected form of the genitive of Hedone. A bilingual inscription from a marble sarcophagus found at Sinope in Asia Minor, gives the dative of the name Procope as Προκοπῇ in Greek and Procopeti in Latin (*Revue Archéologique*, 1916, p. 348). A similar dative, Aelianeti, occurs in an epitaph from Rome (H. Dessau, *Inscriptiones Latinae Selectae*, 8195). The writers owe both of these references to Miss J. M. Reynolds of Newnham College, Cambridge.

3

THE VATICAN CEMETERY—
II: ARCHITECTURE AND ART

THE basic features of the Vatican tombs have been already
summarized in the previous chapter, and three of them fully
described. It remains to complete, in this chapter, the general
architectural and artistic picture of the site.

Architecture and Architectural Ornament[1]

All the surviving tombs are rectangular in shape, and they range
in size from about 2 by 1·7 metres (M) to about 10 by 6 metres (H).
The majority are single, enclosed chambers, cross-vaulted or, in one
case (Z), roofed by what appears to have been a shallow domical
vault; barrel-vaults, common in the Isola Sacra cemetery, are represented only once, over the inner chamber of D. One of the tombs
(O) was originally built against the back-wall of a small, encircling
precinct, the western wing of which housed a staircase leading to
higher ground behind, and of which the eastern wing was later
blocked (possibly when M was built), converting the precinct into a
passage-way leading from the open space in front of M and N.
Another tomb (H), itself of normal construction, had an open
rectangular forecourt enclosed by a low wall in front of the main
façade; and in two others (B and D) the front half of the tomb itself
is open to the sky, constituting a similar forecourt within the main
structure, behind the façade. R, the façade of which faced south, had
an open courtyard (R¹) behind it, to the north. Owing to the slope
of the ground, the floor of this courtyard was at a considerably
higher level than that of the tomb itself, and it had to have a separate
entrance, opening off the Clivus, the passage-way between R and S;
but tomb and forecourt are certainly of one build; and since, like H¹,
the latter contained a small cistern below pavement-level, its function

was presumably the same as that of the more orthodox courtyards in front of Tombs B, D, and H. Q differed from all the other tombs in the cemetery in being entirely open to the sky, or covered, at best by a shallow impluviate roof around an open courtyard.

The exposed outer surfaces of the walls throughout the cemetery are faced with courses of slender bricks, neatly laid and set in fine mortar. The individual bricks are 28–35 millimetres thick and appear to come from two different brickyards or groups of brickyards those of H, L, V, Ψ, and the buildings opening off the Clivus (Q R¹) being yellowish-pink in colour, whereas the remainder are a deep, warm, reddish pink. The quality of the masonry in the façade. and in such features as the angle-pilasters is noticeably finer than in the side- or back-walls, being more carefully coursed and finely jointed;[2] and the effect of delicacy and refinement was heightened in Antiquity by washing the brick surfaces with a thin coat of crimson colour and picking out the joints with a thread of applied stucco (a well-preserved example of this pointing greets the visitor immediately on entering, at the south-west angle of Φ). The inner wall-surfaces of the tombs, which were never exposed but covered with stucco, were of altogether coarser masonry, sometimes of widely jointed brick (e.g. the inner face of the façade of G or the staircase in E), more often of the so-called 'opus listatum' (p. 40). The interior of D presents yet another style of walling, opus reticulatum, in which areas of network pattern formed by small, squared, facing-stones, set diamond-wise, alternate with horizontal courses of brickwork. This style was typical of the later-first century (e.g. in the last phase of Pompeii, destroyed in A.D. 79); and although it was still widely employed in the first half of the second century (its use in Hadrian's villa near Tivoli is a classic instance), it was evidently becoming old-fashioned by the time the Vatican cemetery was being developed. We meet it once again in the precinct-wall of O,[3] one of the earliest tombs within the excavated area, and itself, as we know from a tile-stamp found in it, either Hadrianic or later.

The doorways, which are of light-grey travertine and follow the stereotyped form already illustrated and discussed in the case of F (p. 47), stand out in bold and effective contrast to the dark, delicately coursed brickwork of the façades (Pl. 4). Some are still intact (A, C, F, L, N, O, and T), and that of L is inscribed in fr(onte) p(edes) XIIII (left) and in agr(o) p(edes) XIX (right), giving the dimensions of

the tomb, from east to west and from north to south respectively. [4]
Others were wholly or partially destroyed in Antiquity, presumably
by Constantine's workmen: B, D, E, G, H, M, R[1], S, and Φ have all
been robbed of some or all of their travertine components; and in
U the eastern impost has been displaced. The façades of Q, I, and Z
have been destroyed, doors and all; but the two imposts of I, inscribed in fr(onte) p(edes) XII and in a(gro) p(edes) XV, can be seen
reused in the Constantinian wall that replaces the façade of I.
Similar travertine doorways span the entrances to the Clivus, between R and S, and (in its later phase) to the passage-way-precinct in
front of O. All the doorways must once have had doors or metal
grilles, but these were no doubt removed when Constantine's workmen filled in the cemetery; the slots and the holes by which they
were secured can still be seen.

We have already noted (p. 53) the short roll of waterproofing
that protected the wall-bases of Z and Φ, where these were exposed
to the flood-water pouring off the hillside in stormy weather.
Drainage was then, as it still is today, a serious problem. We can see
this particularly clearly in the western part of the excavated area. Not
only is there similar waterproofing along the east wall of R and R[1],
where it faces onto the sloping Clivus (Pl. 1) and along the north
and east faces of Q, but both Q and S were provided with underground drains to carry the flood-water off to a lower part of the
hillside. A large, vertical duct built into the wall that blocks and
partly replaces the façade of D shows that Constantine's architects
had to face the same difficulty.

When we turn from construction to external architectural ornament, we find that the severe, box-like lines of the structure were
offset by simple crowning mouldings (as in B and D), or by more
elaborate façade-entablatures (as in F, p. 48) of moulded terra-cotta.
None of the entablatures is now complete, but enough remains of
several to give us an idea of the general effect. C, for example, still
preserves the greater part of a gay little frieze with an hour-glass
pattern, inlaid in black pumice-stone and red terra-cotta; G had a
frieze of seven rosettes, inlaid in brick; and immediately below the
architrave-moulding of the now largely destroyed façade-entablature
of Φ there was a frieze of delicate terra-cotta key-pattern. The
analogy of the Isola Sacra cemetery suggests that above cornice-
level many of the façades must have had pediments (e.g. H, with its

porch-like arrangement of frontal pilasters); but it is only in G that any part of such a pediment has survived. At the level of the door-sill, the crowning mouldings were balanced by a very simple base-moulding (that of F is exceptional in its elaboration); and in several of the tombs the severity of the main architectural lines was softened by the use of shallow, brick pilasters. H, the most pretentious and elaborate of the tombs, had four such pilasters, equally spaced across the façade, and O two, at the angles; in both, the moulded brick pilaster-bases survive, but the capitals are missing. Φ, a free-standing tomb, had pilasters at the four angles, and the fine foliate terra-cotta capital of one of these is still preserved. X, another free-standing tomb, the façade of which is not excavated, had pilasters at the two rear-angles.

Within this formal architectural setting, the façades were further enriched with inscriptions, windows, and decorative panels. That of F (p. 48) is the most elaborate of those excavated. But the less ambitious ornament of the other tombs should not pass unnoticed. The inscription-slabs were of marble and were set in terra-cotta frames of varying elaboration. That of C, for example, is deeply recessed, and the frame is crowned by a rich, projecting cornice. On either side of it was a small window, set within a plain terra-cotta frame, with a small pediment above; and the window itself con-sisted of a rectangular marble slab with a narrow, vertical loophole (both slabs are now missing), behind which the masonry was splayed in all directions to light the tomb. B and D did not require windows, being partly open to the sky, and the only ornament of the low façade, apart from the door and cornice, was a simple terra-cotta frame to the right of the door, which probably once contained the dedicatory inscription. E resembles C in having a symmetrical pair of small, pedimented windows, the western one of which still has its marble facing-slab in position. Above the door there is an elabor-ate terra-cotta frame, which may once have held an inscription but is now, as in F, a window. Elegant mouldings (astragal, egg-and-dart, fluting) ornament the recessed splays and, on either side, two flat terra-cotta pilasters support a projecting entablature and pedi-ment; these have well-modelled Corinthian capitals and the shafts are decorated in polychrome intarsia with bands of guilloche. The façade of G is largely hidden behind Constantinian masonry; but we can see that, below the pediment and entablature, there was a central terra-cotta frame (presumably for an inscription) and on either side of it two small window-frames which, like the door, had terra-cotta flanking consoles. H relied for effect on the more ambitious architectural scheme of the four shallow pilasters of its façade, which was relieved only by a marble panel over the door, on which the customary inscription was framed between two fluted pilasters, and by a pair of deep recesses set at lintel-height in the two outer intercolumniations. These two recesses (of which only the western one survives) can best be explained as having been designed to hold portrait-busts of marble or stucco, and this suggests that H and H[1] were planned as a single unit, since movable busts are unlikely to have been set in unprotected niches above an open street. The façade of I was destroyed by Constantine's architects, but L has preserved some interesting details. The flanking loophole-windows and, above them, two short strips of diamond-pattern terra-cotta intarsia, are here incorporated within the same marble slab as the inscriptions. The frame is decorated with upright fluting and segmented beading, and to right and left of it, flush with the surface of the brickwork, there is an inlaid terra-cotta *amphora*.[5] Above it, in the centre of the otherwise plain frieze, is an axe-symbol (*ascia*) in the same technique;[6] and near the extreme right-hand corner of the façade a square patch of later masonry may perhaps mark the position of a decorative panel removed in Antiquity. M had no room for more than a single panel over the door, with loophole-windows and an inscription cut, as in L, in the same marble slab; this was found and removed in the sixteenth century, and is now lost.[7] N has a marble inscription and two completely preserved windows grouped side-by-side above the door; the former is framed by an elaborate terra-cotta leaf-moulding, the latter by a simple beading with a small cornice above. Inset into the frieze, above the inscription, is a square tile with a circular hole cut in it to frame another small window. A plain moulded frame surrounds the marble dedicatory inscription of O; and each of its flanking windows is set in an ɪ-shaped frame of yellow tiles; it is one of the lower tiles in the eastern window that bears a tile-stamp of the year 123. Two similar but smaller windows are set high up in each of the lateral walls of Φ. The remaining tombs to the south and west of O are too much damaged to have preserved any decoration that they may once have had.

These embellishments relieve, but do not radically modify, the over-all impression of plain, business-like, functional architecture. For their external effect, these tombs relied rather on good materials and fine workmanship than on ornament. It is all the more startling, therefore, to find that the internal architectural schemes, glowing with colour and alive with ornament, are as exuberantly baroque as the outsides are severe. Above the relatively simple plinth, broken only by the shallow arches of the inhumation-recesses and by an occasional niche, elaborate combinations of apses, curved and rectangular niches, pediments, entablatures, and columns, all stuccoed and painted and sometimes engulfing the entire wall-surface, produce an effect which can best be compared with that of the stage-buildings (*scaenarum frontes*) of the contemporary Roman theatre. We have already discussed in the previous chapter (pp. 41 ff., 49 ff.,) two tombs, B and F, which illustrate this type of decoration, the one early and the other relatively late within the series. C, like B, was later stripped of its stucco ornament, but the original scheme was not unlike that of B; in the north wall a large, round-headed central niche flanked by two pairs of small square niches, one above the other, the whole crowned by a triple-pedimental entablature carried on four columns; and on the side-walls a similar scheme, with five instead of three intercolumniations. The schemes of T and U are identical: the entire back-wall of each is occupied by a plain rectangular recess, and in each of the lateral walls engaged columns carried an entablature (now destroyed) to frame three tall niches, one curved and two rectangular. In I, a large, round-headed niche, with a white stucco scallop-shell in the semi-dome, occupies the middle of the back- and two side-walls; and each of these central niches is framed in a projecting, gabled structure of stucco and flanked by a pair of plain rectangular niches. Above, there are substantial remains of the gaily coloured, coffered stucco ceiling, akin to the ceilings of C and F, with a red-white-and-blue 'Union Jack' design in the cross-vault and figured scroll-work of unusual delicacy along the groins (Pl. 5; *cf.* Pl. 14). G is more elaborate. Here the development of the stucco framework has been carried to its logical conclusion and forms a continuous entablature carried on free-standing columns round the three inner walls; the central niche in each wall resembles those of I, with the same stucco shells in the semi-domes; and the remaining intercolumniations contain the tall, vertical niches divided into two by convex-fronted partitions similar to those in F. E closely resembles F, but is on a smaller scale. As in G, the entablature is continuous; and in the middle of the rear-wall, over the central niche, it carries, enclosing and framing the pediment, an archivolt, within which the wall is recessed to form a shallow semi-dome, decorated with a white stucco scallop-shell. We may compare, and in detail contrast, this with F, where the development noted above is carried one stage further, by the breaking up of the continuous line of the entablature into projecting and re-entrant elements and the liberation of the central archivolt from the pediment beneath. Below the pediment in G, tall, curved niches alternate with pairs of superimposed rectangular niches, three in the north wall, five in the west, and in the east, below the supporting half-arch of the staircase, three. H, despite its more monumental character and restrained colour-scheme, falls within the same line of development. Its north and west walls have each three tall, round-headed niches alternating with tall, rectangular recesses, most of which are subdivided into two (as in F and G) by convex-fronted partitions. Instead of columns, the richly moulded plinth carried stucco herms, which in turn supported the continuous entablature. The east wall, south of the stairs, has one round-headed niche flanked by two pairs of rectangular recesses; and this scheme is repeated on the north wall of the western annexe, which is separated from the north wall of the main tomb by a large, rectangular, fluted stucco pilaster. The glory of this tomb is its stucco sculpture, both in the round and in relief; this will be described below (p. 82 ff.).

From the foregoing account, summary though it is, it will be seen that, for all their variety, the tombs of the Vatican cemetery represent stages in the evolution of a well-defined type of Roman mausoleum. It is only at the beginning and the end of the series that we find traces of something different. O, with its large, plain northern apse and lateral niches represents an earlier tradition, in which stucco played a more modest part. D was as conservative in its ornament as in its choice of burial-rite and of masonry; and in the simple gabled structures that occupy the middle of its rear-wall and of the north and south walls of its forecourt, D^1, we can see a rudimentary phase of the new style, a phase which had already been superseded in B and C. It was from the elaboration of these simple gabled structures to frame, at first groups of adjoining niches, and later whole wall-surfaces, that there evolved the decorative style of which F, with its deliberate disregard of the architectural function of its constituent elements, marks at once the culmination and the beginning of the dissolution. Apart from the three gabled structures and from a single horizontal line of fourteen small, round-headed recesses ranged symmetrically about them, the only ornament of D was a tiny moulding (now destroyed) at the level of the spring of the barrel-vault of the inner half of the tomb. There was no plinth. It was only with the introduction of inhumation that it became necessary to thicken the base of the wall in order to house the grave-recesses, and this, by providing a platform for the architectural development of the gabled structures of the zone above, was an important factor in determining the form of the subsequent development.[8] With the abandonment of cremation, inhumation-recesses invaded the upper parts also of the tombs, and there was no longer any place for the niches and elaborate, projecting orders that characterize most of the tombs in the Vatican cemetery. In Φ, there is still a projecting plinth, and the shallow upper recesses have little function save as frames for the paintings that ornament their walls. It is only in Z (which, whatever its absolute date, represents a later phase in the development of this type of mausoleum than the majority of its fellows)[9] that we see the logical outcome of the process. Here the upper wall-face, too, has been brought forward flush with the face of the plinth, from which it is divided only by a strongly projecting moulding. After the extravagant fantasies of the second century, we return once again to the functional simplicity from which we started.

In the details of their architecture and ornament, as in their architectural type, the tombs of the Vatican cemetery follow familiar lines. There is little for which we cannot find a parallel in kind, if not always in quality, in the Isola Sacra cemetery. The chief difference would seem to be that the lay-outs of the Vatican cemetery are more compact, no doubt because space was more limited and land-values higher,[10] and that the decorative details tend to be of a better quality (although it is in the strictly architectural detail that the difference is least apparent). Spacious precincts such as those of Isola Sacra Nos. 75 and 106-10 dwindled to the modest proportions of O or even become simple forecourts, either in front of the tomb (H) or, still more compact, behind the main frontage (B, D).[11] We miss the projecting benches that flank so many of the doors at Isola Sacra;[12] and a difference that can only be explained in terms of local architectural taste is the general use of cross-vaults in the Vatican and of barrel-vaults at Isola Sacra. The doorways, on the other hand, are almost identical in the two cemeteries;[13] and detailed parallels for all the Vatican window-types can be found at Isola Sacra.[14] Many of the Isola Sacra tombs have brick pilasters on their façades, and their pediments add an element that is missing from our picture of the Vatican cemetery.[15] Terra-cotta capitals and frames follow the same lines, but lack the richness and refinement of the best Vatican examples.[16] Polychrome intarsia, on the other hand, is equally developed in both.[17] It is in the interior schemes that the Isola Sacra cemetery most obviously falls short of the standards set by the tombs of the Vatican. Tombs such as Isola Sacra Nos. 19, 87, and 93[18] echo the achievements of their Vatican counterparts; but, even allowing for their ruined condition, it is clear that their ornament had not the same richness and refinement, nor their architectural schemes the same exuberance of invention.

Mosaics

Until comparatively recent times it was assumed that wall-mosaics and vault-mosaics, despite the clear allusions to be found to them in classical writers from the first century A.D. onwards,[19] were virtually unknown in the ancient world before the great church-building programme which Constantine inaugurated. Modern research, following C. Cecchelli's pioneer-essay, 'Origini del mosaico parietale cristiano',[20] has proved that view to be mistaken; and today we can muster a considerable body of evidence to show that the church-mosaics of the fourth century, such as that in the apse of Old St. Peter's (p. 212), were rooted in a long tradition stretching back through the third, second, and first centuries A.D., and probably even farther, into the late-Hellenistic period of the first and second centuries before our era. To this knowledge of pre-Constantinian wall-mosaics and vault-mosaics, pagan and Christian, the Vatican cemetery has made two notable additions.

As we climb the modern steps giving access to Mausoleum Φ, our eye is caught by a brightly coloured panel overhead, recessed into the brickwork facing of the façade, just to the west of the entrance. It is a polychrome *emblema*, or mosaic picture, in a plain terra-cotta frame, partly destroyed, but sufficiently preserved for its subject to be identified (Pl. 19). Like the large, sculptured sarcophagus within the tomb (p. 89 f.), the theme is drawn from the Dionysiac repertory and depicts the scene made famous by the Messenger's speech in the *Bacchae* of Euripides, the death of Pentheus at the hands of his mother Agave and other Theban women under the spell of Bacchic frenzy.[21] Pentheus has taken refuge in a pine-tree, of which the trunk and some of the branches survive, while of the king himself there remains only one foot, in a yellow-and-grey-striped shoe, seen in the fork of the branches. On the left are Agave and another woman, dressed as Bacchantes, with vine-wreaths, garments flying, and breast and legs partly exposed. In their right hands they hold respectively a dagger and a spear, while their left hands are raised to shake their victim from his perch. A third woman, now fragmentary, appears to be kneeling on the right; while a stout, striped tiger from the god's menagerie rears up against the tree-trunk. The marble tesserae are small and subtly shaped: the prevailing colours are buff, red, yellow, blue-grey, and dark green: there are definite signs of shading and plasticity in the modelling of the figures; and although the somewhat crude and clumsy drawing might suggest a date in the third century, it could well belong to the closing years of the second, the probable date of the tomb which it decorates. The lesson of the piece is the fate of those foolish souls who resist Dionysus.

But the Pentheus mosaic is, after all, but an isolated picture. More significant are the mosaics which once completely clothed the low vault and the north and lateral walls of Tomb M. From the subject-matter and the manner in which it is treated, these mosaics are not likely to be later than the middle of the third century, and they are, therefore, the earliest Christian vault-mosaics and wall-mosaics so far discovered.[22] The tomb was built, as we have seen (p. 29), by the pagan family of the Julii, probably towards the close of the second century. Its pagan beginnings are attested by a niche in the north wall, containing two cremation-burials, which was closed and plastered over at a later date, and by the pagan style of the dedicatory inscription, found and copied in 1574, but subsequently lost, which commemorated an infant, Julius Tarpeianus, who died at the age of one year nine months and twenty-seven days.[23] When the Julii became Christian or a new, Christian family obtained possession, the tomb was redecorated and three bodies were buried below the floor and another laid on the floor, against the east wall. The plain south wall was untouched; but the lower portions of the north, east, and west walls were painted with a rather dull dado of imitation-marble incrustation, executed in green and red lines on a white ground;[24] and the upper portions of the same three walls and the whole of the very slightly curving cross-vault were covered with the polychrome figured mosaics, worked in tesserae of opaque glass paste, which are, perhaps, the most important artistic document yet yielded by the Vatican cemetery.

On the ceiling, over a bright yellow background, spreads a luxuriant vine, realistically rendered in three shades of brilliant green. In the centre the vine frames an octagonal space with convex sides. Here a beardless male figure, with tunic, flying cloak, and nimbus, from behind which rays shoot upwards and sideways, stands in a chariot facing the spectator. His right hand is missing, but the arm is raised and his left hand supports a large globe. Of the chariot it-self and of its team, all that can now be seen is a pair of white, prancing horses with scarlet harness and, behind their legs, a single wheel (Pl. 32).[25] Of the actual tesserae, those composing the central group and the vine-scroll above and to the right of it, are still in position. But below and to the left of the octagon, and on the three walls, all the cubes have fallen from their places, leaving behind impressions of themselves in the top coat of plaster in which they had been bedded. To the art-historian this loss is a valuable gain, for it reveals that the design was first tinted in on the final surface, while still wet, to guide the hand of the mosaicist. These colours do not correspond with those of the tesserae, the background having been washed in buff and the vine-leaves and tendrils sketched in light brown with occasional splashes of green. In all of this, the tomb pro-vides a valuable record that the techniques of the later Christian mosaicist were rooted in pre-Constantinian practice. The craftsman presumably had before him a coloured cartoon, drawn to scale, of the whole design with which his field was to be decorated. He must then have built up the final plaster-bed, in which he was going to fix the tesserae, bit by bit upon the surfaces of vault and walls in areas each representing a day's work of tesserae-setting, painting on each area, as he went along, that part of the design to which it corresponded, before finally putting in the cubes.

The vine spreads down from the ceiling over the upper portions of the walls, and in it, on north, east, and west walls, are reserved lunette-like spaces, each containing a figure-scene. On the east wall is Jonah, falling legs-foremost from the ship into the mouth of the whale. His hands are outstretched as though in supplication, and two men stand in the ship beside the mast with hands upraised.[26] On the north (and most important) wall an angler, standing on what appears to be rocks, casts his line, on which he has caught a fish, while a second fish glides away.[27] Of the scene on the west wall just enough remains to show the head of the Good Shepherd with a sheep laid across His shoulders.[28] The last subject needs no comment. Jonah is a favourite theme with catacomb-painters and Christian sarcophagus-carvers of the third century; while the angler is the Fisher of Souls, familiar to us on such third-century Christian monuments as the well-known sarcophagus from La Gayole, in Provence.[29] Since, then, the wall-mosaics are unequivocally Christian in content, the charioteer, framed in the vine-scroll on the vault, with nimbus and rays about his head, can be none other than Christus-Helios—Christ the Sun, *Sol Salutis* and *Sol Iustitiae*. The eschatological beliefs that lay behind these mosaics will be discussed later (p. 116 f.). For the present, it is enough to note that here is a Christian world which, alongside the biblical scenes, is still ready to express its teaching through familiar pagan personifications and genremotifs.

For the study of the companion art of floor-mosaic, the Vatican cemetery has disappointingly little to offer. For this fact the introduction of inhumation and the resultant destruction (and in some cases replacement; *cf.* Tomb F, p. 50) of the original pavements may be partly to blame. Whatever the reason, it is a fact that, apart from the rather poor black-and-white example in Tomb B (p. 41) and the fragments of another like it in Tomb C (p. 61, Note 30), only one figured pavement of any pretensions, that which gives its name to Tomb I, the 'Tomb of the Quadriga', has so far come to light.[30] Another black-figure piece on a white ground, with confidently drawn interior white lines, it serves to throw into relief the brilliant colouring of walls and vault; and its subject is one beloved by mid-imperial sarcophagus-designers—the Rape of Persephone.[31] Pluto drives rapidly towards the left in a four-horse chariot. We can see his head, with shaggy hair and beard, his flying cloak, and his right hand extended to grasp the reins; but his prize, Persephone, pinned in the crook of his left arm, vanished when the north end of the pavement was damaged. Of the chariot only its wheels are shown; but the high-stepping horses, with tossing manes and aigrettes between the ears, like those of circus-racers, are complete. In front strides Hermes, wearing short cloak (*chlamys*), round, winged hat (*petasos*), and winged boots, brandishing a large serpent-staff (*caduceus*), and leading the right-hand outside horse by the bridle. He is Hermes Psychopompus, guide of souls, showing that the myth features here as an allegory of the rape of the soul from the body at death and of its passage to paradise. [32] In the lower part of the picture a flowery meadow, with two overturned baskets of plucked blossoms, recalls the setting of Persephone's abduction. The borders hold extracts from an 'animal-paradise'—coursing antelopes, boars(?), etc., and two rampant tigers converging on a two-handled vase—symbolic of the teeming life shared by the dead in the unseen world. The mosaic is a rare example of the treatment of the Persephone theme in this medium; and since it was laid subsequently to the inhumation-burials in the lateral grave-recesses, it must belong to the redecoration of the tomb in the early-third century (p. 78) rather than to the original construction a few decades earlier. It owes its preservation to the fact that this tomb, although well maintained down to the last, seems to have been very little used for later burials.

Wall-painting

In reviewing the wall-paintings of the necropolis, other than those already discussed in Tombs B, F, M, and Z, it will be convenient to visit the mausolea in order, beginning with those at the eastern end of the northern row, and returning along the southern row by way of T and U to Φ. In discussing the paintings and other works of art found in these tombs, we shall be considering them in two different, although related, aspects—as examples of the art and craftsmanship of their day, and as symbolic expressions of contemporary beliefs about death and the after-life. The latter aspect will be more fully treated in chapter 4 (*b*); but in anticipation of what will be said there, we may note one reservation that must be borne in mind in any discussion of Roman funerary symbolism; such discussion is almost bound to be expressed in terms more precise than the ordinary day-to-day usage of Antiquity might have seemed to warrant. In asserting that a certain motif probably had a particular meaning, one is claiming rather that it would probably have been so interpreted by a well-educated Roman observer. It does not follow that a great deal of the funerary symbolism of the Romans (as of many other peoples before and since) was not a matter of custom rather than of conscious device. Certain motifs were traditionally appropriate to the decoration of tombs and were part of the stock-in-trade of the individual contractors who decorated these tombs. Nevertheless, we may be sure that, whether or not the meaning was clearly before the observer, they were never felt to be merely ornament, but were part of the elaborate structure of funerary belief and practice which these tombs represent. At the risk of over-simplification, it is important always to keep in mind this aspect of Roman funerary art.

C, the Tomb of the Tullii, has little painting left, but three items should be noted. First, low down on the north wall, at the western corner, on the plinth, is the small figure of a charioteer (*auriga*) of 'the Greens', wearing a green coat and holding a palm-branch. He tells us of the soul's victory over death, as does also the second painting, that of a palm-tree in the central panel of this wall, immediately to the east of the *auriga*. Thirdly, on the walls and arched roofs of two superimposed niches on the east wall are showers of red roses on a white ground, a favourite symbol of the flowering of new life for the deceased in paradise, and one which features again and again, not only in the Vatican cemetery, but in other tombs of the period in the neighbourhood of Rome, notably in the Tomb of Marcus Clodius Hermes under the Church of San Sebastiano on the Via Appia,[33] and in the niches of the tombs at Isola Sacra.

Tomb D has less to detain us. In its painting as in its architecture it seems to have been the simplest and most severe of the tombs, and all that now remains is part of the plaster covering the lower walls of D and D^1, showing a white field divided into panels by fine red lines. E, on the other hand, has much more of interest to offer. On the north wall are painted a vase at the western end of the lunette below the vault, a green parrot embowered in roses in each of the two upper lateral niches, a torch-bearer in the right-hand niche below, and on the plinth more roses on the spandrels of the arched grave-recess. The same scatter of roses appears on the corresponding spandrels of both lateral walls and in small, arched niches on the west wall. On this wall again, in the tall, curved niche at its northern end, is an intriguing object, which hangs from a ribbon between a couple of green garlands. At first sight it suggests a string bag, stuffed with greengroceries, but is probably a pine-apple, with the two parts of what appears to be a double pipe (*tibia*) crossed behind it.[34] More imposing, if more familiar in content, is the painting in the western lunette, that of a pair of magnificent peacocks—well-known symbols of immortality, because the eyes of the tail when displayed were thought to represent the stars in the circle of the sky—which confront one another, on a white ground, from either side of a tall basket brimming with fruit and flowers.[35] In the lateral rectangular niches in the east wall are painted two vases, above, and two deer, below.

Tomb G was obviously decorated by the same hand or firm as that which was responsible for the earliest paintings in the Tomb of Fannia (p. 42 f.). Here, as there, we have the prevailing white ground on what is left of the vault and on the wall-lunettes above the niches and stucco entablatures, again laced with delicate, small-scale, polychrome motifs. There are similar finely outlined panels holding birds and flowers, the same chains of gaily coloured discs.[36] In the architectural scheme on the north wall a flower-basket and a shower of roses occupy the back-walls respectively of the two lower, rectangular flanking niches. The other rectangular niches on north, east, and west walls were sealed in Antiquity and plastered over, with paintings of birds, etc., on the plaster; and the south wall has its rose-strewn niches and, above the door, a dainty vase-like motif of pale blue, shooting up from a calyx of maple-red leaves. But the focal point of interest is the painting in the lunette of the north wall, directly above the central, triangular section of the tripartite stucco pediment, the painting which gives to G its name of the 'Tomb of the Steward' (Pl. 16).[37] An elderly, bearded man, wearing a mauve, brown-bordered tunic with long, wide sleeves is seated on the left on a backless seat. This seat has a thick, black cushion and straight, golden legs, elegantly turned, while to the right is a low, light table with green top and straight legs, recalling a modern card-table. In his left hand the bearded man holds an open scroll; and his right hand is raised, with fingers outstretched, as though he were computing, or emphasizing what he has to say to the small, clean-shaven, white-clad figure who stands before him farther to the right. This man's tunic is brown-bordered and fringed round its lower edge. He wears brown boots, holds in his left hand a dark-brown object, which may be a money-bag or ledger, and extends his right hand, making with it much the same gesture as that of his interlocutor. The meaning of the picture is clear. A master, or steward, is doing accounts with his slave. The standing figure is obviously not a child, but his scale is small compared with that of the other, who, when he rose from his seat, would tower, giant-like, above him. We may thus conclude that the mauve-clad person represents the dead owner of the tomb, drawn in 'heroic' proportions, because apotheosized, and busied with those mundane, professional tasks, steady devotion to which has earned him his happy after-life. As a document of religious belief, social life, costume, and domestic furniture, this lively little painting may be compared with the relief-panels of marble or terra-cotta, depicting the trade or craft of the deceased, which decorate so many of the tombs at Isola Sacra and at Ostia. The plastic, naturalistic style accords well enough with the probable date of the tomb, about the middle of the second century A.D. Above the scene a couple of mauve, crossed clubs dangle from a cord between two rope-like, highly stylized, yellow and sepia garlands.

Passing by Tomb H, where stucco-reliefs play the part of wall-painting (p. 82 ff.), we enter I, in which scant traces of earlier paintings are visible beneath the present early-third-century scheme. Here, in the white-ground lunettes above the stucco pediments, birds hold the field. Six small feathered creatures perch on scarlet borders in the northern lunette, while two large birds (presumably soul-birds), a peacock on the west and what appears to be a red-billed goose on the east, pace sedately through the rose-gardens of paradise.[38] Below the wall-spaces between the niches are divided into brilliant red and yellow panels, in two tiers, framed by purple bands; and on the red ground of the upper panels can be seen the faint traces of imposing figure-scenes. Towards the south end of the west wall is the ghost of a Victory; and, in the panels on the north and part of the east walls the story of Alcestis—Admetus leaning on a staff, Admetus consoling Alcestis faced with impending death, and, clearest of all, Hercules, lion-skin and club on shoulder, leading home by the hand the veiled Alcestis, delivered from the grave.[39] Even so will the souls of the departed, buried in this tomb, triumph over death. Parallels that spring to mind are the well-known Alcestis sarcophagus in the Vatican Museum and the short side of another piece in the Villa Faustina, Cannes, [40] figuring the same group as here in Tomb I; and, closest of all, the painting in Tomb 3 in the San Paolo necropolis, where Hercules's right arm is flung affectionately round the shoulders of Alcestis, who has just escaped through the doors of Hades. [41]

Of the original, possibly Hadrianic, decoration of O, the Tomb of the Matuccii, nothing is now visible. At some later date the walls were completely replastered and redecorated in a very simple scheme of purple-framed panels of green and yellow, which pay no attention to the two tiers of niches cut in the east and west walls. The walls of one of these niches, on the east wall of the tomb, are strewn with the usual roses. Near the north end of the west wall a wide entrance, blocked at a later stage to hold inhumation-burials, led into a narrow chamber under the stairs that flanked this mausoleum on its western side. Red and white roses and other blossoms beflowered the underside of the entrance-arch and the walls and ceiling of the chamber.

In T we return to figure-painting on a modest scale. Besides the familiar birds, rose-wreaths, and vases of flowers, [42] there are a grey dolphin on a red ground [43] and two Cupids bearing a garland on the north wall; a red panther chasing a red deer—symbol of pursuing death—in the western grave-recess; [44] and a head of Dionysus, crowned with ivy and framed by tendrils, on which birds are perching, in the central niche in each of the lateral walls. The lateral niches of the twin Tomb U repeat the trite motifs of roses, birds, and flower-baskets. The lunettes of its grave-recesses figure flying birds (north), a peacock flanked by trees (east), [45] and a cock(?) and serpent (west). But in the central niches of the lateral walls, painted in grey on a deep-red background, are the two attractive cosmic figures after whom the tomb is called, Lucifer and Hesperus, the morning and the evening star, personified as naked boys and symbolizing the dawn and eve of human life, or rebirth after death; they occupy, strangely enough, the west and east (instead of the east and west) walls respectively. Lucifer (Pl. 17) [46] climbs the heavens on a prancing mount. His cloak flutters behind him and his flaming torch is held erect; there is a nimbus about his head and his star shines out above his brow. Hesperus plunges headlong with torch reversed. [47]

The walls of Tomb Φ, with its two tiers of grave-recesses on north, east, and west, are, like those of Z, washed all over with a flame-coloured background, against which are painted figure-scenes in white, suggestive of low reliefs in stucco.[48] Of those on the lower tier, only one can now be distinguished: it shows a man running with outstretched hands towards a peacock. In the lunettes above is portrayed a succession of mythological pictures—the Judgment of Paris, an allegory of the soul that chooses beauty and wins thereby immortality,[49] the Bacchic rout discovering the sleeping Ariadne (p. 55), and a group of four figures, three dancing and one seated, the meaning of which is obscure. The rest is faded. More arresting than any other painted figures in this cemetery are the two nimbus-crowned Sileni who brood over the tomb from the spandrels between the upper recesses on the lateral walls (Pl. 18).[50] Each wears a billowing cloak, and holds, besides a *cantharus*, a tambourine (*tympanum*) in one case, a *thyrsus* in the other. The legs of each are lost in a calyx of acanthus-leaves, from which flowery branches, harbouring birds, spring to right and left to follow the curved arch of the recess below. These mysterious beings cap the Dionysiac themes of the Pentheus mosaic (p. 72) and of the great carved sarcophagus in the centre of the tomb (p. 89 f.). The only traces of cremation here are two niches in the south wall, the upper one of which is showered over, on roof and walls, with the never-failing roses.

Funerary painting of this sort depended for the clear expression of its ideas on the very familiarity of its symbolism, and it is inevitable that the Vatican tomb-painters should have followed along many of the beaten tracks. Despite this, they have presented us with some highly interesting and unusual subjects; and if we compare their work with that of their contemporaries at Isola Sacra,[51] we cannot fail to be struck by the high general level both of taste and of technical accomplishment which the paintings of the Vatican cemetery represent.

Figured Stucco-work

Of all the minor forms of sculpture practised in the Roman age, none is more attractive than the art of modelling, in relief and in the round, in fine, white stucco. Decorative stucco-work was cheaper and easier to produce than carving in stone or marble, soft and delicate in texture, and equally elegant whether left white or gaily painted; and, although capable of restrained expression, it lent itself particularly to the baroque exuberance of ornament that characterizes several phases of imperial art. We find it at all levels of society, from the imperial residences downwards, in public as well as in private buildings;[52] but as an effective substitute for richer materials, it appealed above all to the tastes and purses of comfortably-off and cultivated middle-class families. In domestic architecture it was a useful alternative or accessory to wall-painting; it is sufficient to recall such familiar examples as the pure-white vault-decoration of a rich late-republican or early-imperial house near the Villa Farnesina in Trastevere, now in the Museo Nazionale Romano; the handsome pairs of large white griffins, framed in acanthus scroll-work against a vivid-red ground, in the late-republican 'Casa dei Grifi' under the Flavian palace on the Palatine; and the frieze, depicting the story of the Iliad in white figures on a bright-blue background, found in a shrine in the 'Casa del Cryptoportico' or 'Casa Omerica' in the Via dell'Abbondanza at Pompeii.[53] From the houses of the living the craft passed, by a natural transition, to those of the dead, to mausolea; and although, from the perishable nature of the material, only a minute fraction of the vast output of the Roman firms of plasterers has come down to us, it is tombs, wholly or relatively undisturbed since ancient times, or such forgotten subterranean shrines as the Basilica near the Porta Maggiore, that have yielded the bulk of our surviving material.[54] The Vatican cemetery is no exception; and both from the quantity and from the quality of the stucco-work represented it must now be reckoned a *locus classicus* for the study of this delightful and all too scantily represented art.

Some, indeed, of the stucco-work discovered in this cemetery is of a very modest and unambitious character. Such are the miniature figures already noted in F (p. 50), on the purple, convex panels of the lateral walls, and in the red archivolt-frieze over the northern apse. These have their counterparts on the west wall of E, where tiny white stucco figures fill the frieze below the tripartite pediment, against a background that is divided symmetrically into three panels, two purple and one red; and on the east and west walls of G, where there is a similar frieze on a red ground. In G again, the restored triangular pediment of the north wall, just below the painted group of the steward (p. 77 f.), contains a white mask of Oceanus against a white or faded-blue ground;[55] and in I, in addition to the remains of rectangular figured panels with grape-vines in the field of the vault and of bands of delicate, figured scroll-work along the groins (both belonging to a redecoration of the tomb undertaken, it would

seem, not long after its original construction), there is a handsome
decorative panel in the lunette of the north wall with a fanciful,
ribbon-decked, white candelabrum in the centre, flanked by a pair
of large, swan-like birds, the whole set in an oblong frame against
a purple ground.[56] Among the scanty remains of Tomb R is the
fragment of a panel carrying large-scale floral sprays, part, it would
appear, of a once imposing frieze.[57] On the square pilasters at the
northern angle of Tomb C there are small red and purple panels
figuring miniature Cupids and rosettes.

In all this there is nothing out of the ordinary. But when we
enter H we begin to turn the pages of a new chapter in the history
of Roman-age funerary stuccoes.[58] The tomb was founded, as its
dedicatory inscription informs us, by a certain Gaius Valerius Herma
for himself and for his wife Flavia Olympias, his daughter Valeria
Maxima, and his son Gaius Valerius Olympianus, and for his
freedmen, freedwomen, and their descendants.[59] The Greek names
suggest that the family was of originally servile origin. But it had,
by this time, risen to a level of affluence and of literary and artistic
culture exceeding (to judge from their tangible expression in this
tomb) that of any other persons buried in the excavated portion or
the Vatican cemetery. Two inscriptions inside the tomb tell us a
little more about the family. The young Gaius Valerius Olympianus
died at the age of four;[60] and one of Herma's freedmen, Gaius
Valerius Eutychas, put up a tombstone to his wife Dynaten *permissu
C(aii) Valerii Hermaes patroni optimi.*[61] H, like most of the Vatican
tombs, was built for both burial-rites; above the plinth there are
cremation-niches and recesses, in the floors of which can be seen
holes for ash-urns, and below, in the plinth itself, larger arched
recesses for inhumations. But our present concern is with the large-
scale figured decoration, in predominantly white stucco, which
enriches every niche and recess in the upper zone and is unparalleled
for scale and complexity in any Roman tomb hitherto excavated.

Each of the tall, curved niches in the north, east, and west walls
(eight in all), and each of the two full-length, rectangular niches that
flank the principal curved niche (that opposite the main entrance in
the north wall), is occupied by a single, statuesque figure in high
relief. These figures range in height from 1·05 to 1·45 metres; all
stand on pedestals, and, with three exceptions, they are topped by
relief-work in the lunette-shaped semi-domes of their niches. The

three central figures on the north wall, however, have no such reliefs above them. They are taller than the rest—their heads reach up almost to the tops of the niches, and whereas the other figures are, all but one, obviously those of human beings, these must be figures of divinities.

When Constantine's builders drove a foundation-wall (now removed) right across the mausoleum from the entrance on the south to the centre of the rear-wall on the north, they almost completely destroyed the figure in the principal curved niche in the latter, leaving little but the scar of his form on the background. But enough of this remains to reveal a slim, youthful male figure, naked save for a short cloak (*chlamys*), which is looped across the elbows and falls down on either side of him. His left arm is extended towards our right, and parts of the wings of a bird perched on his left hand still survive in relief; of his right arm nothing survives below the elbow, and all that we can say is that it was probably in some way or other bent back across the body. The general type of the figure suggests Apollo, with whom birds, the raven and the vulture, for example, are commonly associated,[62] presiding over the dead as healer, purifier, and saviour. For Professor Guarducci's suggestion that this is Apollo-Harpocrates there is no sure evidence. The figure to the west of this central figure is indubitably Minerva, with helmet and shield, conqueress of death,[63] patroness of the arts, and embodiment of the wisdom and learning on which, it seems (p. 84), the male Valerii prided themselves, and which served as their passport to immortality. In the tall, rectangular niche on the east is another goddess, with veil, cloak spread out behind her, and tunic falling in a long, straight fold in front of her. The last item suggests that she might be Isis in the guise of *regina manium*, Queen of the Dead;[64] and since there was found in the tomb an exquisite gilded stucco head of a young boy, dating from the late-second century (a portrait, perhaps, of Gaius Valerius Olympianus), with the Isiac curl on the right side, it may be that some of the Valerii were devotees of Isis.[65] The curved niche in the projecting eastern annexe shows a figure with bat-wings, holding a reversed drinking-horn in his right hand and a small torch in his left. The bat-wings indicate that he is the god Hypnos, symbol of the sleep of death; and in the lunette above him two winged Cupids, with hair dressed in the style favoured by Commodus's Empress, Crispina, uphold a golden *cornucopiae* brimming with poppy-seeds, below which is a golden spray of Persephone's pomegranate.[66]

The figures in the other six full-length niches are all human, and all, in the present writers' opinion, portray deceased members of the Valerii family. The heads are in every case either destroyed or badly damaged, but their bodies are for the most part well preserved. To the west of Minerva is a man holding a scroll, to the east of the Isis figure, another man; both are half-draped to indicate heroic guise. In the lunettes above these two persons are a pair of reclining cosmic figures in low, delicate relief. On the west is Tellus, Mother-Earth, facing to the right and propped against a rock under a tree. She is naked save for a cloak (*himation*) flung across her knees, she holds a *cornucopiae* heavily loaded with fruit, and on her head she wears a luscious garland of fruit and corn-ears (Pl. 12). Her companion-figure on the east, reclining to the left, is the bearded Oceanus, stretched out on his cloak upon a rock. He holds a rudder (or an oar) and an anchor, and crab-claws sprout from his shaggy, weed-like hair (Pl. 13). In the curved niche in the east wall of the tomb, south of the annexe, stands a man wearing a long tunic and cloak. In his left hand he displays an open tablet or scroll, on which we can read the letters MAE. If, as seems very likely, these letters were originally preceded by HER, we should have here the portrait of the founder of the mausoleum, Gaius Valerius Herma. In the lunette above his head are what appears to be a dish (*patera*) and the writing-materials of a man of letters—wax diptych and pens (*stili*).[67] In each of the lateral niches of the wall opposite, the west wall, is the stately, dignified figure of a heavily draped woman, standing fully to front. We feel tempted to equate these figures with Flavia Olympias, wife of Herma, and her daughter, Valeria Maxima. In the lunettes above them are toilet-articles and other feminine objects—mirrors, jewel-casket or cosmetic-box, perfume-bottle, distaff, and spindle—for their use beyond the grave and as symbols of their worldly duties and status.

The bearded man, wrapped in tunic and cloak, who occupies the central niche in the west wall, between the two women, was clearly a very important person, since his niche equals in width that of the Apollo and is larger than that occupied by any other human figure (Pl. 15). But human he is, as his boots and tunic make plain. He is veiled for sacrifice and pours a libation from a dish held in his right hand, while with his left hand he clutches a fold of his cloak. The upper part of his face has vanished; but most of his beard remains and is undoubtedly trimmed in the style affected by Marcus Aurelius in such portraits as his bronze equestrian statue on the Capitol. The present writers are, however, unable to accept Professor Guarducci's suggestion that this figure represents the divinized Emperor himself. The resemblance of his beard to that of Marcus is no argument, since the royal style of trimming hair and beard was regularly copied by a sovereign's contemporaries. Professor Guarducci quotes a passage from the *Vita Marci* in the *Historia Augusta*, in which it is stated that, after his death, statues of the divinized Emperor were set up in private houses, and were still to be seen, in the writer's own day, in many houses alongside figures of the household-gods, the *di Penates*.[68] But nothing is said about this practice being applied to tombs; and, if it had been, we should expect to have found traces of it in quite a number of Roman family-tombs of this class and period. Moreover, the objects in the lunette above are not imperial insignia but, as in the case of the figure identified with Gaius Valerius Herma, the emblems of a man of letters—scroll, book-box and pen-case. To claim that these indicate 'the philosopher on the throne' is to be guilty of anachronism. It is posterity that acclaims Marcus Aurelius first and foremost as the author of the Meditations; to his contemporaries, as still to Cassius Dio and to the author of the *Vita Marci*, he was primarily a statesman and a soldier, and it was as such that he earned his apotheosis; his writing and his philosophy were the by-products of his private life. This is an essentially priestly figure; and we notice, furthermore, that his veil does not cling close round the head, as is normal with sacrificing figures, but is raised as if supported by some form of flat-topped head-dress underneath it. It could well be that under the veil, causing it to assume this peculiar line, is some such sacerdotal crown as that worn by the Archigallus, the high priest of Cybele, at Isola Sacra[69]—not, of course, in this case that of a professional Archigallus, but that of the priest of some other deity. If so, this figure would be that of a learned priest-ancestor, the grandfather or even the father, of Gaius Valerius Herma, perhaps the founder of the family of the free Valerii, buried elsewhere (since he is not mentioned in the dedicatory inscription), but portrayed and honoured in the splendid mausoleum which Herma had grown rich enough to build.

Besides the full-length figures in relief, there were also free-standing portrait-busts in stucco representing, presumably, other members of the family. It is perhaps to one of these that a fragmentary, bearded stucco head, found loose in the tomb (Pl. 31), belongs. The style and coiffure—close-cropped, curly beard and lank, straight locks on the brow (p. 95)—are those of the second half of the second century. The lightly incised line marking the iris of the eye and the realistic rendering of 'crow's feet' and furrows are other distinctive features.

We do not know in whose honour the veiled man was pouring his libation, whether in honour of one of the deities figured in the tomb or of the dead themselves. But the setting of all the human persons featured here is unmistakably Dionysiac. On the back-wall of every one of the twenty square-headed recesses, which (as in F) alternate with the full-length niches, is modelled in very delicate and low relief a member of the Bacchic revel-rout, swiftly advancing to right or left. There are crouching and running Satyrs, the latter sometimes carrying golden throwing-stick (*pedum*) and *nebris*, Maenads clashing cymbals, playing on double pipe, dancing, or rushing along with torch or *thyrsus*, Pans striding rapidly with pan-pipe, dish, or *amphora*. [70] These wild, ecstatic, hurrying creatures, done in a technique that is really closer to drawing than to sculpture, offer a vivid contrast to the staid, motionless, plastically rounded figures of the dead Valerii and to the still, statuesque, frontally presented gods and goddesses. Bacchic, too, are the heads, modelled virtually in the round, that crown the tall, slender herms set between the recesses and niches. Jutting out from the surface of the walls as supports for the cornice, in place of the more familiar colonnettes, they have suffered many casualties at the hands of Constantine's workmen; but enough survive to give us some idea of their type and quality. Some were Satyr-heads, with intense, semi-bestial expressions, moustaches, tufted beards at the tip of the chin, and hair brushed up in a tangled mat above the brow (Pl. 31) or plastered in lank locks over the crown. Others are statuesque figures, with formally curled hair and beards, which resemble nothing in classical sculpture so much as they do the saints flanking the portal of some Romanesque cathedral. Coming, as they do, from a metropolitan Roman workshop, they are among the strangest and most thought-provoking finds of recent years.

All these stuccoed figures seem to have been predominantly

white, with bright splashes, here and there, of polychrome and gilding. The tomb, when intact, must have presented an exceptionally rich and varied spectacle; and among known Roman mausolea it is unique. Indeed, the herm-heads and the full-length portraits of men and gods are examples of large-scale, stucco figure-sculpture, in high relief and in the round, for which few parallels can be cited in Italy and the western provinces. There is the large, coloured figure of Serapis in high relief, enthroned in a niche, in the courtyard of the 'Insula del Serapide' at Ostia; and we have, also at Ostia, the large relief-figures, probably of the fourth century, from the baths north-east of the theatre.[71] The figures, dated c. 400, in the Platonia under San Sebastiano on the Via Appia are almost Byzantine.[72] For comparable heads in the round we have to travel to the southern shores of the Mediterranean, to Sousse in Tunisia, to Sabratha in Tripolitania, and to Egypt.[73]

In conclusion, we may note that, quite apart from their artistic value, as representatives of a craft of which all too little has survived, the stuccoes from these tombs throw interesting light on the way the stucco-workers went about their task. In at least one instance (Tomb I) the colonnettes were built up about a core of the same interlocking terra-cotta tubes as were frequently used architecturally for small drainage-ducts or to form the basis of a light barrel-vault. Elsewhere the colonnettes were built up about a vertical shaft of some perishable material which was wound with twine or wicker to give a good grip to the stucco coating. The larger relief-figures, as we can see very clearly in Tomb H, were first sketched in outline with a fine point on the smooth surface of the plaster, and then built up around a core of coarser material. Many of the smaller figures, on the other hand, were barely keyed into the underlying surface, and in some cases the latter can be shown to have been already dry and painted before the figures were applied. In some of the tombs (e.g. in B and F) it is clear that the stucco-work had fallen into disrepair or had been replaced in other materials before the cemetery was abandoned. Elsewhere, however, so far as the damage done by Constantine's workmen allows us to judge, it was well maintained to the last; and although some of the more elaborate architectural fancies represented in the cemetery went out of fashion after the second century, the examples cited in the previous paragraphs are enough to show that the craft was still alive and vigorous in late

Antiquity, as indeed it remained, in parts at any rate of Italy, throughout the Middle Ages.

Sculpture

Of classical sculpture proper—that is, of marble carving—the most conspicuous and best-preserved examples from, and still on, the site of the cemetery are the sarcophagi. The pagan pieces, of which the group in Tomb Z has already been described (p. 55 ff.), are all pre-Constantinian, and were found during the recent excavations in or between the mausolea, where most of them remain, apart from two small ones now removed to the museum of Christian sculpture near the exit from the present lower church (p. xviii). The Christian sarcophagi fall into two categories. There are the chance-finds (such as the famous piece of Junius Bassus dated to 359)[74] made within the Vatican zone at various times prior to 1939 and now displayed in the museum. And there are the pieces brought to light by the excavators, which had been sunk through the floor of Old St. Peter's into the area of the filled-in tombs or into that of the foundations of the church just to the north of them. Most of these are now housed in the museum or in the lower church; but one very large sarcophagus of Greek marble, firmly embedded in a foundation-wall of the church and the east wall of R and R¹, can be seen in position, at right-angles to the Clivus and immediately to the west of its steps (Pl. 1).[75]

The fifteen sarcophagi chosen for mention here are representative pieces, which illustrate the history of this branch of funerary relief-sculpture from the mid-second to the mid-fourth century. They include all but a few of the post-1939 finds. Nine of them date from the third century, when inhumation was almost universally practised in the capital. Two are of the second century; and the four fourth-century pieces are Christian and post-date the Constantinian Basilica.

The style and technique—absence of drilling and of undercutting—of the earliest piece suggest that it was carved in the reign of Hadrian. Made of Greek marble for a baby, with corners rounded on the inside and furnished with a tiny head-rest, it is one of the most touching infants' coffins that have survived from ancient times. Along the upper edge of the front, above a trio of plump Cupids shouldering two great garlands of fruit, we read, no name, but the pathetic statement (in well-cut lettering) *mensibus VI diebus X*. The tragedy deepens when we turn to the short sides, on each of which a grief-stricken parent is represented. The father (on our left), bearded and wearing a tunic and soft leather shoes, is seated on a straight-legged stool, chin on hand and a pensive, almost dazed, expression on his face. The mother (on our right), muffled in a thick mantle drawn over the head, is weeping on a round, wicker(?) seat,[76] her face pillowed in the palm of her right hand. The design on the front is a stock one; but the lateral figures look like portraits, carved *ad hoc*, of this homely but endearing couple.[77] The lid and the bones have vanished, and the piece stands in the street, backed against the north wall of Ψ, where it was placed by the Constantinian builders; we do not know from which tomb it came.

The other second-century sarcophagus, the Bacchus and Ariadne piece from Tomb Z, has been described already (p. 55 f.) and need not detain us here (Pl. 22). It displays the deep undercutting, lavish use of the drill, and smooth, soapy surface characteristic of carving under Commodus.

Of the third-century pieces, all but one bear the panels of curved fluting, or strigilations, so much favoured by sarcophagus-decorators of the period and carried on by some into the mid-fourth century. A sarcophagus of Greek marble, excavated in R but now lodged in the space between the side-walls of X and Ψ, can be dated to the early decades of the third century by the coin of Septimius Severus found inside it, along with the skeletons of an adult and a child. In the central panel on the front, between the strigilated areas, stand Meleager, victim of the Calydonian boar, and his beloved, the Arcadian princess Atalanta, the group being an allegory of the parting caused by death. At either end of the front is a flat, fluted pilaster, and a marine procession occupies the lid.[78] The magnificent Dionysiac sarcophagus, of Proconnesian marble, which stands in the centre of Φ on a pavement of *opus sectile* (a patch-work of yellow, white, and grey marbles), can be dated to about the time of Alexander Severus (222–35) by the portraits, on the lid, of its owners, Quintus Marcius Hermes and his wife Marcia Thrasonis, named in the central, neatly cut inscription,[79] the panel for which is supported by two youthful Satyrs. Husband and wife (Pls. 24, 25) are each backed by a curtain, held up by a couple of Cupids and Victories respectively and probably symbolizing the vault of the sky, where the souls of both have gone to dwell. Marcius Hermes has short, clipped beard, neat hair, and slightly Semitic features, and he holds a scroll, possibly his will or the scroll of destiny. Marcia Thrasonis's hair is dressed in a style recalling that of the mother of Alexander Severus, Julia Mamaea. She holds a pomegranate and has the realistic, pinched-in cheeks of an elderly woman. Close inspection shows that these vivid portraits had been carved from the life (since the piece was bought before the couple's death) by a very skilful hand on the blanks left for the faces by the craftsman who cut the rest of the lid-design. On the front, the work of another clever artist, are three excellently modelled, plastic and naturalistic, but deeply undercut, figure-groups in the centre and at the ends, with strigilated areas between them (Pls. 26, 27).[80] In the middle is Dionysus, flushed with wine and supported by a Satyr and a Pan; on the right a Satyr dances with an infant in his arms; and on the left a dancing Maenad, with puffed cheeks, plays vigorously upon a double pipe. The lacy, black-and-white effect of the ornament above the arch under which Dionysus stands is noteworthy.

We have already studied in Tomb Z (p. 56) another, less imposing, Dionysiac piece, very similar in content to the sarcophagus of the Marcii, but with frolicking sea-beasts on its lid (Pl. 28). It is interesting to note how closely the general decorative scheme of this pagan piece is followed by a Christian sarcophagus, of Italian marble, now in the museum (Pl. 29). Since this was found by the excavators under the floor of Old St. Peter's,[81] it must date from near the middle of the fourth century; and its arrangement—a figure standing with outspread hands in the position of an 'Orante' in the centre between two strigilated areas, with pilasters at the angles—can indeed be paralleled on other fourth-century pieces.[82] The 'Orante' here, a graceful, veiled woman, wears, moreover, typical fourth-century dress, with rich necklace and wide, hanging sleeves. Her hands are extended laterally across a couple of flanking palm-trees, symbols of victory over death;[83] and on the ground at her feet is a small, square box, with hand-strap and lock, presumably to hold scrolls of the Scriptures.[84] But what is startling, at first sight, is the likeness between the lid-motifs of the third-century pagan and fourth-century Christian pieces—the appearance on the latter of a no less engaging, if soberer, version of the pagan sea-procession, made up of eight portly dolphins rolling along in double file through the waves, from which two tridents, emblems of Neptune, are emerging. The dolphin-procession (without the tridents) does, in fact, recur on some other Christian pieces, such as the 'marriage'-sarcophagus found in the Catacomb of Praetextatus and now in the Lateran Christian Museum.[85] But the new Vatican example affords as clear an illustration as any of the close association between pagan and Christian sarcophagus-workshops in late-antique times, of the persistence of third-century decorative schemes into the fourth century, and of the readiness of Christians in the third and fourth centuries to adopt and 'baptize' the other-worldly imagery of their pagan contemporaries.

To return to the third century, a cock-fight, symbol of the 'battle of life', beneath the central medallion-portrait of the deceased gives a special interest to an otherwise undistinguished piece of Italian marble, in the Tomb of the Tullii. A favourite mid-third-century type of sarcophagus with curved ends and strigilations flanked by two groups of a lion devouring a fawn (symbol of death's ravening power) is exemplified by a piece, in Greek marble, found in the Tomb of the Valerii and now standing outside it, in H¹. It was dedicated to their father by three brothers.[86] On the lid are hunting-scenes, allegories of the soul's defeat of death and evil or depicting the pleasant pastimes of paradise. Similar scenes, but lacking the strigilations, can be seen on another mid-third-century piece, also of Greek marble, which also was found in the Tomb of the Valerii and now stands outside it. The front is covered by a single, deeply drilled and undercut relief, that of a lion-hunt, with the deceased (the face is clearly a portrait) in the centre as chief protagonist, mounted on a rearing horse, supported by Virtus, and in the act of spearing a ferocious lion, which bounds towards him. On the left half of the lid the spoils of the chase are coming home on an ox-waggon; and on the right-hand half is the unfinished bust of the dead man, scroll in hand, with a curtain upheld by two Cupids behind him and an attendant peacock.[87] All these motifs, peacock included, are pagan. But on the ansate tablet in the centre of the lid, and continued along its lower border, is an inscription, cut in very rude letters, which may be Christian in character. It reads—*D(is) M(anibus)/Valerinus/Vasatulus/vixit annis/XXI m(ensibus) IIII d(iebus) X/h(oris) III Valeria Flo/rentia coius [= coniunx]/fecit marito/suo anime/ benemerenti d(e)p(ositio) eius VII idus sep(te)m(bres)*.[88] The phrase *anime benemerenti* could be pagan, although very common, of course, in Christian epitaphs;[89] but *depositio* is, so far as we know (p. 57), an exclusively Christian formula. We seem, then, to have here an instance of the practice, known elsewhere, of the use of a pagan sarcophagus for a Christian burial.

An attractive and unusual little piece, of Italian marble with curved ends, now in the museum, was found in Tomb R. On the front a central column, flanked by curved strigilations, holds the middle of the field, while to right and left are two figure-groups carved on panels sunk into the thickness of the marble wall of the coffin. Each group shows a girl seated with a standing attendant. The girl on the right sits on a thickly cushioned folding chair, with a sun-dial on a base beside her; the object once held in her extended hands has vanished, but her attendant holds a scroll. Her counterpart on the left is ensconced in a high-backed basket-chair; she grasps a *plectrum*, ready to strike the lyre partly supported by the little figure beside her.[90] It is possible that both girls represent the same person (the deceased) pursuing two of her accomplishments; and the moral of the picture is that devotion to the arts and sciences wins for the soul a blessed hereafter.[91] Trophies of arms cut in low relief on the rounded ends symbolize victory over death.

Standing in the street, where it had been placed by Constantine's workmen against the north wall of X, is the Proconnesian marble sarcophagus of Marcia Felicitas, purchased for her by her sister, Marcia Urbica.[92] On the front, the bust of Marcia Felicitas herself appears in high relief in the central medallion, below which is a pair of gaping tragic masks. She holds a scroll, perhaps her will or the scroll of destiny, and her hair is dressed in the style favoured both by Otacilia, wife of Philip the Arabian (244–9), and by Salonina, wife of Gallienus (253–68) (Pl. 23). At the curved ends stand to the front, each with his horse, the Dioscuri, symbols of the hemispheres, who guard the tomb and escort the soul to paradise;[93] and on the lid, to right and left of the inscription, the Four Seasons, in the guise of Cupids, recline among fruit-laden baskets and vases, reminding us of life abundant in the unseen world and of the endless cycle of eternity.[94] The portrait is very good; but the figures are clumsy and ill-proportioned. Art is beginning to decline; and a still further deterioration can be traced on the sarcophagus, also of Proconnesian marble, which contained the body of Ostoria Chelidon (the social implications of which we shall consider later; p. 106). Roughly executed full-length figures of husband and wife, each backed by a curtain, occupy the ends of the front, and on the lid the beloved marine procession is mainly rendered by deeply incised lines—a lazy substitute for true relief.[95]

One effect, if a relatively minor one, of the Peace of the Church inaugurated in 312 was a renaissance of art in general, and of sculpture in particular, under the influence of a liberated and rapidly expanding Christianity. In sarcophagus-carving many of the old traditions of the third century were reinvigorated, including the scheme of lateral panels separated by areas of carved strigilations. We have already studied an instance of this in the sarcophagus depicting an 'Orante' flanked by palm-trees (p. 90); and the same arrangement occurs on the large sarcophagus still in position beside the Clivus.[96] Here a very favourite fourth-century marriage-motif —busts of husband and wife in a medallion—with an idyllic scene below, a herdsman milking a goat,[97] fills the centre, while statuesque figures of St. Peter and St. Paul stand at the extremities. Of the characteristically Constantinian, and later, narrative-type of Christian sarcophagus, with an 'Orante' in the centre and Old and New Testament episodes deployed on either side,[98] a fine example in Italian marble, now in the museum, was found sunk through the floor of Old St. Peter's in the Constantinian filling just outside Tomb N and on a level with its dedicatory inscription.[99] The stories of Jonah and of the 'Three Children' in the fiery furnace occupy the lid.

But for novelties in iconography on the fourth-century Christian sarcophagi yielded by the Vatican necropolis we must turn to a lid also found beneath the pavement of the Constantinian church and now set up to the left of the altar at the west end of the north aisle of the lower church.[100] On either side of the empty inscription-panel, upheld by a couple of Victories, run biblical scenes, from the Old and New Testaments. The carving on the left figures two episodes from the story of Joseph, a theme hitherto unknown in the repertory of early-Christian sarcophagus-decorators. We see Joseph lifted from the pit by his brethren and sold to the merchants; and the purchase of corn by Joseph's brethren in Egypt in the presence of Joseph, who stands beside a corn-measure in front of the masonry walls of a granary, while one brother is already making off with a loaded sack. The narrative runs in chronological order from right to left, instead of from left to right. On the opposite side of the central panel the Three Magi, each with his Phrygian cap and camel, are bringing their gifts on flat dishes to the Holy Child, the first gold, the second frankincense in a squat jar with a stopper, the third myrrh, which is contained in two phials laid horizontally on the dish. The gold consists of a thick, bejewelled collar, fashioned to resemble a laurel-wreath, which the Child has snatched from the first, now empty, dish and is holding aloft with evident delight. The Virgin, veiled and cloaked, is enthroned in a high-backed, draped chair; and behind it, overshadowing this happy nursery-scene, stands a plain cross, prophetic of the Sacrifice to come—a cross, as yet unique in a scene of adoration and perhaps the earliest direct representation of the cross in Christian pictorial art so far known.[101] The lid is cut from a slab of Proconnesian marble with ugly, dark-grey streaks—a slab such as would probably not have been selected for relief-work in an earlier and more fastidious age. But the style and technique of the carving are, for the time, remarkable. The composition is well-spaced and well-balanced; the movement of the figures naturalistic, vigorous, and varied; the modelling careful, generous, and plastic. The piece has been convincingly dated to c. 340;[102] and it may rank as a little masterpiece of mid-fourth-century Christian sculpture.

As a storehouse of sculptured sarcophagi, the Vatican necropolis can more than hold its own with Isola Sacra, even if it has produced no reclining figure in high relief to compare with that of the Archigallus now in the Museum at Ostia.[103] But as a source of sculpture in the round it falls far short of the sea-port cemetery, with its rich series of portraits, idealized heads, genre-groups and genre-figures.[104] For the almost total absence of such monuments in the Vatican tombs the responsibility probably lies with Constantine's builders, who may well have received orders to clear away such movable objects (the extraction of which would not constitute violatio sepulchri), either to preserve them as works of art or to secure unimpeded space for the tight-packed fillings. That some large-scale marble portraits, either wholly or virtually in the round, were among the furnishing of the mausolea we know from two life-size heads in Greek marble, one male, the other female, found in the filling of H¹, high up, above the level of the dedicatory inscription over the door of H. Whether they originally stood in H or H¹ we do not know. It is likely that both belonged to full-length portrait-statues, and both are slightly flattened behind, as though they had been attached to backgrounds.

The style of the male head[105] is that of the late-second century. Furrows, folds, and creases on the flesh are naturalistically indicated, and the irises of the eyes are marked by lightly incised circles, the pupils by deep drill-holes. The hair and beard are also deeply drilled, but avoid the prickly nervousness of some late-Antonine portraits, where black and white are violently contrasted. The combination of lank locks on the brow and stubbly beard and the realistic treatment recall the stucco bearded head from the Tomb of the Valerii (p. 86, Pl. 31), although the latter clearly represents a different person, and the head of the Roman general in the scene on a late-Antonine sarcophagus in the Vatican Museum showing the submission of barbarians.[106]

The female portrait[107] is a lovely, but somewhat baffling, object (Pl. 30). It shows the deceased in the traditional attitude of Pudicitia (Modesty), with mantle veiling the hair. The delicate turn and inclination of the head, the elegance of the hand and wrist, the softly rounded contours of the cheeks, and the sensitive curve of the mouth have a grace and charm comparable to those found in women's portraits of the mid-to-late second century. But the schematic treatment of the hair, forehead, eyebrows, and large, lightly marked, wide-open eyes suggests that the period of execution was the late-third or early-fourth century, when the coronal of plaits on the crown of the head, once favoured by Faustina Major and her contemporaries, was again in fashion.[108] The nearest parallel is the Pudicitia portrait-statue found in 1939 at Ostia in the 'Collegio degli Augustali', which is convincingly assigned by R. Calza to the early-fourth century.[109] If this dating of the Vatican lady were correct, it would indicate that a high artistic and cultural standard was maintained by some, at least, of the owners of the cemetery on the eve of its obliteration; and it would illustrate the tenacious hold of classical naturalism on late-antique art in the West.

Miscellaneous Objects

Of small, miscellaneous works of art from the necropolis there are only two to be described. Both were found in niches in the west wall of the Tomb of the Aelii, and both are receptacles for ashes, exquisitely cut in yellow alabaster.[110] The smaller is a chalice, with widely spreading mouth, slender foot, and two handles set low on the body of the vase. The second, and larger, takes the form of a graceful flagon (*oenochoe*) with a single handle, foliate-shaped above and meeting the body of the vessel in a Medusa-head of superb workmanship. The Medusa, once an earth-goddess and goddess of fertility, later protectress of the dead, is well known, in both her life-giving and in her apotropaic function, as one of the most familiar themes in Roman-age funerary decoration.

NOTES

1. Of the tombs referred to in this section, the following items have been illustrated in the *Report* or in the books and articles listed on p. 59 f., Note 13.

(a) *Decorated Façades*

C (D, E, and F visible beyond)	*Report*, ii, Pl. 1, *b*; *Josi*, p. 16.
F (E visible beyond)	*Report*, i, colour-plate A; *Life*, 10 April 1950, Fig. 2; Vatican coloured picture-postcard, Ser. V, 7.
H inscription-slab	Guarducci, Pl. 2.
L façade	*Report*, i, Fig. 17; ii, Pls. 3, *a*, 5, *a*.
inscription-slab and frame	*Report*, ii, Pl. 3, *b*.
N façade	*Report*, i, Fig. 19; ii, Pl. 6, *b*.
inscription-slab and frame	*Report*, i, Pl. 9, *a*.
O façade	*Report*, ii, Pl. 13, *a*.
inscription-slab and frame	*Report*, ii, Pl. 9, *b*.
Φ terra-cotta capital	*Report*, i, Fig. 9.

(b) *Internal Decorative Schemes*

E	Vatican coloured picture-postcard, Ser. V, 11.
F	*Report*, ii, Pl. 2, *b*; *Life*, 10 April 1950, Figs. 6, 7; Vatican coloured picture-postcards, Ser. VI, 4, 5.
H	Guarducci, Pls. 3, 6.
I	Vatican coloured picture-postcard, Ser. VI, 10.
L	*Report*, i, Figs. 14, 15; ii, Pl. 4, *a*, *b*.
M (other than mosaics)	*Report*, i, Figs. 20, 21; ii, Pl. 10.
O	*Report*, i, Fig. 26; ii, Pl. 15, *a*.
R	*Report*, ii, Pl. 24, *a*, *b*.

S   *Report*, ii, Pl. 22.

T   *Report*, i, Figs. 36, 38–40, colour-plate E; ii, Pls. 16, *b*, 18, *a*.

U   *Report*, i, Fig. 41, colour-plate D; ii, Pls. 17, 19, *a*.

2. In the façades the average height of 10 courses ranges from 30–1 (H, L, T) to 35–6 centimetres (A, O, R); and in the secondary walls from 40–1 (T, U) to 47–8 centimetres (G, I, O). The surviving back- and side-walls of V are of unusually fine masonry, 10 courses to 28 centimetres. The junctions of the different qualities of masonry are effected by means of quoin-like panels at the angles, similar to those used in framing wall-surfaces of *opus reticulatum* (*e.g. Report*, i, Fig. 20; *cf.* Fig. 30). See also Appendix C, p. 268 ff.

3. *Report*, ii, Pls. 13, *b*; 14, *a*, *b*. In the Isola Sacra cemetery, *opus reticulatum* remained in common use well into the middle of the second century.

4. *Report*, i, Fig. 17. *Cf.* Tomb 7 of the San Paolo cemetery (Lugli, Fig. 11 and p. 314).

5. *Cf.* the *amphora* painted on the lower part of a wall of Tomb 9 in the San Paolo cemetery (Lugli, Fig. 14). In funerary contexts the *amphora* may symbolize either the purification of the deceased by water or the wine of eternal life enjoyed by him or her in paradise.

6. *Report*, i, Fig. 17; ii, Pl. 3, *a*. For discussions of the *ascia*, or axe-symbol, frequently found in tombs, on sarcophagi, and on gravestones, see F. Cumont, *Recherches sur le symbolisme funéraire des romains*, 1942, p. 298, Note 3; also H. Wuilleumier in *Revue de l'Histoire des Religions*, cxxix, 1944, ii, pp. 40–83; J.-J. Hatt, *La tombe gallo-romaine*, 1951, pp. 85–107; P.-L. Couchond and A. Audin, 'Requiem aeternam . . . L'Ascia, instrument et symbole de l'inhumation' (*Revue de l'Histoire des Religions*, cxlii, 1952, pp. 36–66). The two last-named authors conclude: 'L'ascia n'implique pas un espoire mystique dans la vie éternelle [the theory of H. Wuilleumier]. Seulement la garantie, fondée sur un rite matériel, d'un repos définitif. Comme l'a bien vu M. Hatt, cette materialité du rite explique seule la formule *sub ascia dedicavit*'. An *ascia* in terra-cotta inlay occurs in the pediment above the entrance to one of the San Sebastiano house-tombs (Mancini, Pl. 9; see also p. 173). It may be noted here that each of these three tombs has lateral loophole-windows, in two cases cut through, in one case flanking, the *titulus*-slab.

7. *Report*, i, pp. 39–40.

8. We may contrast the tombs of the Isola Sacra cemetery, which echo the superficial forms but not the functional logic of the metropolitan models; it is in only a few tombs of the late-second century (Nos. 19, 87, and 93) that the upper wall-face is actually set back from that of the plinth.

9. Tombs of this type belong to the latest phase of the Isola Sacra cemetery, during the late-second and early-third centuries; Calza, p. 40.

10. To judge from the evidence of inscriptions, the size of the tombs in the Vatican cemetery was well up to average by metropolitan standards. The writers owe this observation to Miss L. R. Taylor.

11. Isola Sacra, No. 75, Calza, Figs. 22, 25; Nos. 106–10, Calza, p. 369 ff. Open forecourts in front of the main façade (as Vatican H[1]) are common at Isola Sacra (e.g. Nos. 54, 87, 93–5), both as part of the original structure and as later additions; whereas there is only one case (No. 92) of an internal forecourt, as in Vatican B and D.

12. Calza, Figs. 16, 21, and p. 69. There is a single bench in D, against the west wall of the forecourt.

13. Calza, Figs. 16, 22, 32, 33, and pp. 84–5. Cf. the doorways in the trio of tombs under San Sebastiano (Mancini, Pl. 9); and in the San Paolo cemetery (Lugli, Figs. 1, 4, 5, 10, 11, 19, 30).

14. Calza, Figs. 16, 22, 25, 35, 36, and pp. 87–8.

15. Pilasters: Calza, Figs. 6, 8, 18, 26, 33, and pp. 85–7; although found at all periods, they are noticeably commoner in the latest (early-third-century) phase of the cemetery. Pediments, see p. 61, Note 26.

16. Calza, Fig. 26 (capitals); Figs. 12, 20, 36 (moulded frames).

17. Calza, Figs. 32, 34, 37. Still more elaborate examples can be seen at Ostia itself, in the cemetery outside the Porta Romana.

18. Calza, Figs. 11, 45, 47; Pl. 4.

19. Pliny, HN, xxxvi. 189. Cf. Statius, Silvae, i. 5, 42–3; Seneca, Epist., 86, 6; SHA, Vit. Pescenn. Nig., 6; Vit. Trig. Tyr., 25; CIL, viii. 1, 1323.

20. Architettura ed Arti Decorative, 1923, pp. 12–21.

21. The subject can hardly be the 'Hunt of the Amazons', as stated in Life for 10 April 1950 (international edition, p. 40, Fig. 14) and by Josi, p. 7. For coloured reproductions see Life, loc. cit., Fig. 14; Vatican coloured picture-postcard, Ser. V, 1.

22. For a full discussion of the iconography of these mosaics in relation to Scripture, the Liturgy, the writings of the Fathers, Christian sculpture and painting of the third century, and to comparable motifs in contemporary pagan art, see O. Perler, Die Mosaiken der Juliergruft im Vatikan, 1953.

23. D(is) M(anibus)/Iulio Tarpeiano/vixit ann(is) I me(n)s(ibus)/VIIII diebus XXVII/Iulia Palatina et/Maximus parentes/fec(erunt) lib(ertis) libert(abus) pos/terisq(ue) eorum/h(oc) m(onumentum) h(eres) n(on) s(equetur).

24. Report, ii, Pl. 10; i, Figs. 20, 21.

25. For excellent coloured reproductions, see Report, i, Pls. B and C; Vatican coloured picture-postcards, Ser. VI, 11, 12. The hole in the vault was already there in 1574, when the tomb was first discovered (so Alfarano, cited in Report, i, p. 39), and it may well have been made by Constantine's workmen; it must have been on one of these earlier occasions that the missing tesserae were removed. If there were indeed four horses, as one would expect, the missing pair must have

been uncomfortably crowded, with the fourth horse just showing behind the third.

26. *Report*, ii, Pl. 12, *b*.

27. *Report*, ii, Pl. 12, *a*.

28. *Report*, i, Fig. 22.

29. J. Wilpert, *I sarcofagi cristiani antichi*, i, Pl. 1, 3: F. Gerke, *Die christlichen Sarkophage der vorkonstantinischen Zeit*, 1940, Pl. 52, 1; 54, 2.

30. *American Journal of Archaeology*, li, 1947, Pl. 70; Vatican coloured picture-postcard, Ser. VI, 10.

31. C. Robert, *Die antiken Sarkophag-Reliefs*, iii. 3, 1919, Pls. 119–31.

32. *Cf.* (1) the well-known painting, now in the Museo Nazionale Romano delle Terme, found in the Tomb of the Octavii on the Via Triumphalis and dating from the early-third century: it shows the soul of the six-year-old Octavia Paulina being carried off by Cupid in a chariot, drawn by a pair of doves and preceded by Hermes Psychopompus, to the gardens of paradise, where the souls of other children, some with the butterfly-wings of Psyche, one in the guise of Minerva, are plucking red roses around a statue of Hekate (*Notizie degli Scavi*, 1922, p. 432 ff., Fig. 3, Pl. 2; F. Wirth, *Römische Wand-malerei*, 1934, Pl. 38); (2) the painting from the syncretistic Tomb of Vibia on the Via Appia, inscribed *abreptio Vibies et descensio* and depicting Pluto in a quadriga to right, holding Vibia in his arms and preceded by Hermes Psychopompus (S. Reinach, *Répertoire de peintures grecques et romaines*, 1922, p. 18, No. 6; Cumont, *op. cit.* (Note 6), Fig. 17; *CIL*, vi. 1, 142*b*).

33. Mancini, Pls. 11, 1; 13, 1, 2. *Cf.* the tombs excavated in 1710 in the Vigna Moroni on the Via Appia, now destroyed, but drawn in the Corsini Codex (M. H. Swindler, *Ancient Painting*, 1929, Fig. 609 and p. 397); and the *colum-baria* found recently on the Via Portuense in Rome (*Bollettino d'Arte*, xxxviii, 1953, Fig. 4 on p. 161). For the Feast of Roses (*Rosalia* or *Rosaria*) in commemora-tion of the dead, see Pauly-Wissowa, *Real-Encyclopädie*, 2nd Ser., I, 1, 1914, col. 1111 ff.

34. Vatican coloured picture-postcard, Ser. VI, 1.

35. Josi, p. 3.

36. Vatican coloured picture-postcard, Ser. VI, 8; *cf.* Pls. 3 and 6.

37. Vatican coloured picture-postcards, Ser. VI, 8, 9.

38. Vatican coloured picture-postcard, Ser. VI, 10.

39. *American Journal of Archaeology*, li, 1947, Pl. 69.

40. Robert, *op. cit.*, iii, 1, 1897, Pl. 7, 26 (Vatican), and p. 28, Fig. 22, *b* (Villa Faustina, Cannes). *Cf. ibid.*, Pl. 7, 31 (Rome, Villa Albani).

41. Lugli, Fig. 6.

42. *Report*, i, Fig. 39.

43. *Report*, Fig. 40.

44. *Report*, ii, Pl. 17, *a*.

45. *Report*, ii, Pl. 17, *b*.

46. For a coloured reproduction see *Report*, i, Pl. E.

47. *Report*, ii, Pl. 19, *a*.

48. Vatican coloured picture-postcards, Ser. V, 2, 3.

49. Ferrua, Fig. 9.

50. *Ibid.*, Pl. 2.

51. Calza, Figs. 45–78, Pls. 4, 5.

52. Palaces: *e.g.* a first-century cryptoporticus on the Palatine, E. L. Wadsworth, *Memoirs of the American Academy in Rome*, iv, 1924, pp. 44–5, Pl. 11 Domitian's villa at Castel Gandolfo, *ibid.*, pp. 49–55, Pls. 13–15, 1; and th tantalizing surviving fragments of the elaborate stucco ceilings of Hadrian villa at Tivoli, *ibid.*, pp. 61–3, Pl. 17. Public buildings: *e.g.* the Stabian an Forum Baths at Pompeii, *Art Bulletin*, xiii, 1931, p. 457; the temple of Isis a Pompeii, *Papers of the British School at Rome*, xviii, 1950, p. 10, Pl. 6, 1; th Colosseum, Wadsworth, *op. cit.*, pp. 41–3, Pl. 10, 2–3.

53. Farnesina stuccoes: Wadsworth, *op. cit.*, pp. 23–34, Pls. 1–9. 'Casa d Grifi': E. Rizzo, *Monumenti della pittura antica scoperti in Italia: le pitture del 'Casa dei Grifi' (Palatino)*, 1936, Fig. 16, Pls. B and 4. Pompeii, 'Casa Omerica' V. Spinazzola, *Pompei alla luce degli scavi nuovi di Via dell'Abbondanza (ani 1910–23)*, 1953, ii, Figs. 869–900, Pls. 33, 35 (coloured); *cf.* Pl. 34 (coloured the stucco figure-work on the vault of the shrine.

54. Tombs: two of the tombs under San Sebastiano on the Via Appi Mancini, pp. 46–75, Pls. 15, 16, Wadsworth, *op. cit.*, pp. 64–8, Pls. 18, 19 Tomb of the Valerii, Via Latina, *ibid.*, pp. 69–72, Pls. 20–4; Tomb of th Pancratii, Via Latina, *ibid.*, pp. 73–8, Pls. 23–35; *columbarium*, Via Portuense *Bollettino d'Arte*, xxxviii, 1953, pp. 165–7 and Figs. 10–13; No. 95 at Isol Sacra, with a frieze depicting the Labours of Hercules, a favourite sepulchr allegory of apotheosis earned by a life of labour (p. 110 f.), Calza, Fig. 43. For th Underground Basilica near the Porta Maggiore, see *Monumenti Antichi*, xxx 1926, cols. 601–848, Pls. 2–43; Wadsworth, *op. cit.*, pp. 79–87, Pls. 36–49, 1.

55. Vatican coloured picture-postcard, Ser. VI, 8.

56. Vatican coloured picture-postcard, Ser. VI, 10.

57. *Report*, ii, Pl. 24, *a*.

58. For a full account of this mausoleum, see the publication by M. Guarducc cited on p. 22, Note 38, in which the following items are illustrated:

Pl. 2—dedicatory inscription.

Pl. 3—interior of the tomb, looking north-east, towards the annexe.

Pl. 4—detail of one of the stucco herms; also illustrated by Josi, p. 9.

Pl. 5—central figure of the east wall, identified as Herma.

Pl. 6—general view of the north wall.

Pl. 7—figures identified as Isis and Hypnos.

Pl. 8—gilded stucco head of a child.

Pl. 9—central figure of the north wall, identified as Apollo.

Pl. 12—central figure of the west wall, identified as Marcus Aurelius; *cf.* Fig. 5; also illustrated by Josi, p. 9.

Figs. 3, 4—lunettes with figures of Tellus and Oceanus.

Fig. 7—lunette above the figure identified as Marcus Aurelius.

The stuccoes are to be the subject of a separate and more detailed study by G. Mustilli, now in preparation.

59. C(aius) Valerius Herma fecit et/Flaviae T(iti) f(iliae) Olympiadi co(n)iugi et/Valeriae Maximae filiae et C(aio) Valerio/Olympiano filio et suis libertis/ libertabusque posterisq(ue) eorum. A similar inscription, obviously removed from this tomb, was found reused in the fourth-century grave ε in 'P' (p. 210). It reads: D(is) M(anibus)/C(aius) Valerius Herma dum/vivo mihi feci et/ Flaviae T(iti) f(iliae) Olympiadi co(n)iugi (*Report*, i, pp. 113–14; Guarducci, Note 2); it may have stood beside the entrance to the forecourt, H¹, or in the central inhumation-recess in the north wall of H, and was presumably removed when the Constantinian partition-wall was built (pp. 16, 83).

60. D(is) M(anibus) C(aio) Valerio Olympiano qui vixit/annos IIII menses V dies XIII/C(aius) Valerius Herma pater. There are, in addition, two *graffiti* scribbled by members of the family or household of the Valerii on the plaster of the south wall of the tomb, just inside the door.

61. D(is) M(anibus)/Dynateni C(aius) Valerius Eutychas/co(n)iugi bene-merenti fecit/permissu C(ai) Valeri/Hermaes patroni optimi.

62. W. H. Roscher, *Ausführliches Lexikon der griechischen und römischen Mythologie* i, col. 444.

63. For the funerary role of Minerva, see her appearance on lead coffins from Britain, Syria, and Palestine (*e.g. Archaeologia*, xvii, 1814, pp. 333–4, Pl. 25, 2; *Berytus*, vi, 1939–40, Pl. 7, No. 3; *Syria*, xv, 1934, Pl. 44, 11; and on circular silver plaques attached to a sarcophagus from Emesa, Syria (*Syria*, xxx, 1953, p. 16, Pl. 7, 1).

64. Apuleius, *Metamorph*, xi, 5; *cf.* Guarducci, p. 9.

65. Guarducci, p. 8 and Note 5. Even if the goddess were Isis, the identifica-tion would not prove the central figure to be Apollo-Harpocrates; the third figure, Minerva, has no specifically Isiac connections.

66. Josi, p. 10.

67. The round, dish-like object might be an inkstand.

68. SHA, *Vit. Marci*, 18.

69. Calza, Figs. 110, 111.

70. Ferrua, Fig. 8, illustrates characteristic examples of Satyrs and Maenads.

71. Serapis: G. Calza, *Ostia: nuovi scavi (Itinerari dei musei e monumenti d'Italia*, Ia), 1947, p. 11. Relief-figures: *Art Bulletin*, xiii, 1931, p. 458.

72. *Art Bulletin, loc. cit.*

73. Sousse: *Archäologischer Anzeiger*, 1907, col. 168, Fig. 2: portrait-head of an

African. Sabratha: *Antiquity*, March 1949, Pl. 10, *c*: portrait-head of a woman Egypt: O. Rubensohn, *Hellenistiches Silbergerät in antiken Gipsabgüssen*, 1911 Pls. 16, 17 (portrait-heads and heads of Athena); C. C. Edgar, *Catalogue généra des antiquités égyptiennes du Musée du Caire: Greek Sculpture*, 1903, p. 69. Nos 27603, 27604, Pl. 32 (busts of Serapis and Isis).

74. F. Gerke, *Der Sarkophag des Iunius Bassus*, 1936.

75. Another very large post-Constantinian sarcophagus was found in the earth-packing at the level of the ceiling of H and now stands in the centre of tha tomb. It is strigilated and bears on the front the unfinished busts of a married pair in a medallion, and it has crossed shields incised on each of its short side (Guarducci, Pl. 3).

76. A woman plaiting a funerary garland is shown seated on a similar round wicker seat at either end of the front of a 'Noah's Ark' Christian sarcophagus a Trier (E. Espérandieu, *Recueil général des bas-reliefs, statues et bustes de la Gaul romaine*, vi, 1915, No. 4989, with figure). The writers owe this reference to Mis J. Liversidge of Cambridge.

77. Josi, p. 22.

78. *Report*, i, p. 86; ii, Pls. 26, *b*, 27, *a*.

79. Q(uintus) Marcius/Hermes sibi/et Marciae/Thrasonidi/dignissimae coniugi vibis/posuit.

80. Josi, p. 11.

81. *Ibid.*, p. 4. *Cf.* the similarly schemed Christian piece from under the pavement of Old St. Peter's: *ibid.*, pp. 3, 4.

82. *E.g.* Wilpert, *op. cit.*, i, Pl. 63, 1–3; note especially the Villa Alban 'Orante' sarcophagus, No. 3 on this plate.

83. *Cf.* Wilpert, *op. cit.*, i, Pl. 92, 1.

84. *Cf.* again the Villa Albani 'Orante' sarcophagus, where the tops of six scrolls are emerging from a similar box.

85. Wilpert, *op. cit.*, i, Pl. 70, 4. *Cf. ibid.*, i. Pls. 36, 1; 140, 2; ii, Pls. 244, 2 257, 5; 263, 4; iii, Pls. 278, 1; 280, 2, 8. For possibly Christian examples, see A Rumpf, *Die antiken Sarkophag-Reliefs*, v, 1, 1939, p. 79, Figs. 119, 120, 121 p. 90, Fig. 146; p. 91, Figs. 147, 148; pl. 58, 307. *Cf.* the funerary relief, now in the Lateran Christian Museum, of the Christian sarcophagus-decorator Eutropos, which shows a lid (for a sarcophagus with curved ends) with two file of dolphins converging on the central inscription-panel (*ibid.*, p. 100, Fig. 154) *Ibid.*, p. 92, Fig. 320 figures a probably pagan piece; *ibid.*, Pl. 20, 57, a certainly pagan piece, with the dolphin-procession. This collection of examples suggest that the dolphin-procession was, on the whole, more popular with Christian than with pagan carvers. For lids of Christian sarcophagi with the sea-lions, sea-bulls, etc., so popular with the pagans, see Wilpert, *op. cit.*, i, Pl. 19, 6; ii, Pls 251, 1; 252, 1, 3; iii, Pl. 280, 3, 4. 6, 7.

86. D(is) M(anibus)/T(ito) Caesenio Severi/ano benemerenti/Caesenii/
Faustinus Pompe/ianus et Rufinus/patri incomparabi/li.

87. Josi, p. 10; Guarducci, p. 23, Fig. 9. Oddly enough, the blank head on the
lid shows signs, below the left ear, of a female coiffure roughly blocked out.

88. Guarducci, Fig. 10 and pp. 22–5.

89. For pagan examples of the use of *anima* in such contexts, see H. Dessau,
Inscriptiones Latinae Selectae, 1768, 7988, 8006, 8426, 8482, 9440, 9441; for Christian, E. Diehl, *Inscriptiones Latinae Christianae Veteres*, iii, 1931, pp. 483–4.

90. *Report*, ii, Pl. 29. For a variant of our left-hand group on a Christian
sarcophagus (Corsini sarcophagus), see Wilpert, *op. cit.*, i, Pl. 69, 3.

91. For an especially vivid illustration of the idea of immortality won through
musical skill, see the sarcophagus of Julia Tyrannia at Arles, on which are
depicted the instruments of the dead woman's *disciplina*—her water-organ,
lyre, *plectrum*, guitar, syrinx, and music-case (Espérandieu, *op. cit.*, i, 1907, No.
181, with figures). Such representations suggest that music played a more
honourable part in Roman education and culture than Quintilian's words in
Inst. Or., I, xii, 14 might lead us to expect.

92. D(is) M(anibus) S(acrum)/Marciae Fel/icitati Marcia/Urbica sorori/
carissimae.

93. Cumont, *op. cit.* (Note 6), p. 64 ff.

94. Josi, p. 10.

95. *Ibid.*, p. 7.

96. *Report*, i, Figs. 54, 58 and p. 81; ii, Pls. 27, *b*; 28.

97. *Cf.* Wilpert, *op. cit.*, i, Pls. 70, 4; 81, 1; 134, 3.

98. *E.g.*, *ibid.*, i, Pls. 99, 1, 5; 109, 7; 112, 2; 113, 1, 2, 3; 115, 1, 2; 122, 2;
123, 3; 126, 1, 2; 127, 1, 2; 143, 1; 151, 2; 152, 1, 5; 158, 1; ii, Pls. 205, 5; 207,
2; 220, 2.

99. *Report*, i, pp. 37–8; ii, Pls. 7, 8.

100. L. de Bruyne, 'Importante coperchio di sarcofago cristiano scoperto
nelle Grotte Vaticane' (*Rivista di Archeologia Cristiana*, xxi, 1944–5, p. 249 ff.).

101. For de Bruyne's interpretation of the so-called 'cross' at Herculaneum as
the scar of a wooden wall-bracket, see *ibid.*, p. 281 ff. *Cf.* p. 124, Note 42. The
symbol on the left-hand pilaster on the left-hand short side of the Brescia ivory
casket, if rightly interpreted as a cross, would appear to anticipate that on the
Vatican sarcophagus by several decades (R. Delbrück, *Probleme der Lispanothek
in Brescia*, 1952, pp. 43–5, Pl. 2). But Delbrück's early dating (c. A.D. 320) of
the casket is far from certain: it could be as late as the fifth century.

102. *Ibid.*, p. 275.

103. Calza, Figs. 108, 109; for other sarcophagi from Isola Sacra, see *ibid.*,
Figs. 94–107, 112–20.

104. *Ibid.*, Figs. 121–5, 144–5, 147 (portraits); Figs. 130–1, 133–4, 138–43
(idealized heads); Figs. 126–9, 132, 135–7, 146 (genre-groups and genre-figures).

105. *Fasti Archaeologici*, iv, 1949 (1951), No. 5286, Fig. 138.

106. E. Strong, *La scultura romana*, 1923–6, Pl. 52.

107. *Fasti Archaeologici*, iv, 1949 (1951), No. 5286, Fig. 139.

108. *E.g.* R. Delbrück, *Spätantike Kaiserporträts*, 1933, Pls. 11 (coin-portrait of Constantia), 66, 67 (bust of Fausta(?) in the Louvre), 72 (bust of unknown woman at Strasbourg).

109. R. Calza, 'Statua iconica femminile da Ostia' (*Bollettino d'Arte*, xxxv, 1950, p. 201 ff., Figs. 1–4).

110. Vatican coloured picture-postcards, Ser. V, 11, 12, and VI, 2; *Life, loc. cit.*, Fig. 9; Josi, p. 5. A third may await discovery in one of the unopened niches.

4

THE VATICAN CEMETERY—
III: THE OWNERS AND OCCUPANTS—
THEIR SOCIAL POSITION AND BELIEFS

(a) Social position

IT is one of the most remarkable social phenomena of the imperial age that the professional grades and artisan-classes of the capital seem to have been recruited very largely, in some cases most exclusively, from persons who either had themselves been born in slavery or were the descendants of slaves who had been freed and founded free families. The majority of these families, as their names betray, were originally of Greek-speaking extraction; and even if we allow for such practices as the giving of Greek names to slaves from other parts of the Empire—it was normal for a Greek slave after liberation to retain his slave-name as a third name (cognomen)—the immigration to the capital of free-born merchants and artisans, and the assumption by westerners of Greek names for reasons of professional prestige (as a ballet-dancer might assume a Russian name or a hairdresser a French name), it is quite clear that in the second and third centuries a very high proportion of the well-to-do middle classes in Rome was of eastern Mediterranean stock, and that a substantial percentage of this number was of servile origin.[1]

We must obviously beware of generalizing about the state of affairs in the Empire as a whole from the evidence afforded by such highly cosmopolitan centres as Rome and Ostia. But there is no doubt that this is the over-all picture of Roman metropolitan society reflected in the Vatican tombs. Of the background and circumstances of the owners of these tombs we learn a little from their portraits, as in the case of Quintus Marcius Hermes and his wife in Tomb Φ (p. 89 f., Pls. 24, 25), and of the steward in Tomb G (p. 77 f., Pl. 16). But, as might be expected, it is inscriptions from the excavated area that form the primary source of our knowledge; and these record the names of 105 individuals, 67 men and boys and 38 women and girls, buried in or connected with the cemetery. A list of these names numbered in alphabetical order, with notes and references, will be found in Appendix A, p. 254 ff.; while all the epigraphical texts that have not been already quoted in previous chapters are collected, and arranged according to the tombs in which they came to light, in a note to the present chapter.[2] The architecture and works of art surveyed in chapters 2 and 3 are the measure of these people's wealth, education, and tastes. But it is the texts that tell us of their social status, racial background, and something of the range of their professions and trades.

The general impression left by such a study is that few, if any, of the persons commemorated belonged to free families of genuinely Roman race. Some of them, no doubt, were actually free-born. Such, for instance, was probably the case with Quintus Marcius Hermes (No. 51), with Gaius Popilius Heracla (No. 69), with Gaius Valerius Herma and his wife and children (Nos. 37, 88, 94, 95), and with the builders of the Tombs of the Tullii (C) and Caetennii (F, L). None of these is described as *libertus* or *liberta*. But freedmen do not always reveal their status; and their tell-tale Greek *cognomina* suggest that their immediate forebears, at any rate, had been slaves or freedmen. It is, however, likely that the Greek-named Ostorius Euhodianus (No. 62), who reached a higher rank than that of any other person mentioned in this portion of the cemetery, that of a consul designate, came of a family that had been free for several generations. His daughter, Ostoria Chelidon, received a particularly sumptuous burial. Inside her coffin her embalmed body was found intact, wrapped in purple, covered with a fine veil of gold, and adorned with a golden bracelet weighing 75 grammes.[3] Among the other Greek-named individuals who are not specifically styled freedmen some may well have been born in slavery.

Twenty-two persons on our list are known to be freedmen or freedwomen by categorical statement or virtually certain inference. Conspicuous among these are the Aelii Tyranni, two of whom (Nos. 7, 80) were imperial freedmen in state-employ, as was also Fannia Redempta's husband, Aurelius Hermes (No. 14). One member of the family of the Aelii, Urbanus (No. 85), whose memorial-slab was erected after his father had been freed, is described as an

Plate 1

View of the Clivus, looking north

Plate 2

Plate 3

Inner façade of the Tomb of Fannia

Plate 4

View of the street, from Tomb D, looking west

Plate 5

Interior of Tomb I: the north wall

Plate 6

Interior of the inner chamber of the Tomb of Fannia: the north wal

Plate 7

Interior of the Tomb of the Egyptians

Plate 8

Painting of an Egyptian god in the Tomb of the Egyptians

Plate 9

Terra-cotta relief, showing a quail, on the façade of the First
Tomb of the Caetennii

Plate 10

Plate 11

Terra-cotta decoration of a window in the façade of the First Tomb of the Caetennii

Plate 12

Stucco relief of Tellus in a lunette in the Tomb of the Valerii

Plate 13

Stucco relief of Oceanus in a lunette in the Tomb of the Valerii

Plate 14

Fragment of the painted stucco vaulting of the First Tomb of the
Caetennii

Plate 15

Niche, showing the stucco figure of a veiled man, in the Tomb
of the Valerii

Plate 16

Plate 17

Painting of Lucifer in Tomb U

Plate 18

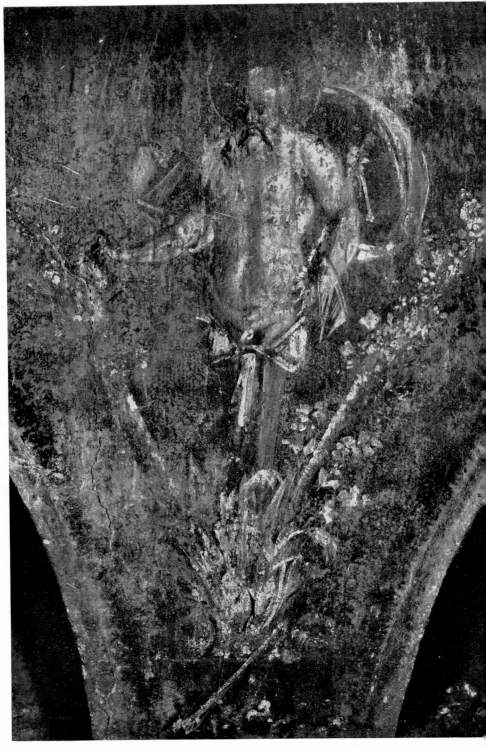

Painting of a Silenus in the Tomb of the Marcii

Plate 19

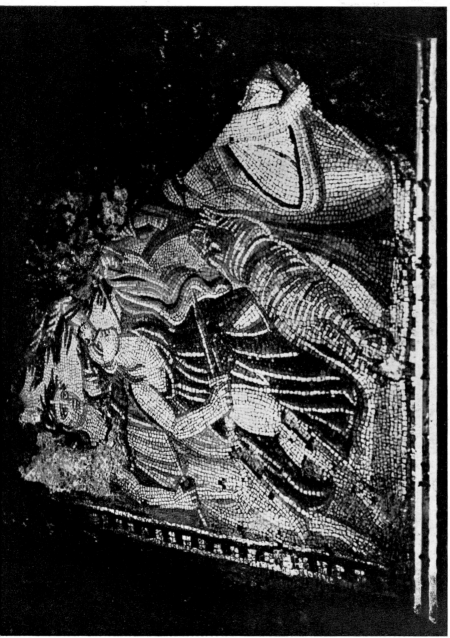

Mosaic, showing the death of Pentheus, on the façade of the Tomb of the Marcii

Plate 20

Inscribed base, commemorating Marcus Caetennius Antigonus
and Tullia Secunda, in the First Tomb of the Caetennii

Plate 21

Inscribed ash-chest, commemorating Marcus Caetennius Tertius,
in the First Tomb of the Caetennii

Plate 22

Detail of a sarcophagus showing Dionysus and Ariadne, in the
Tomb of the Egyptians

Plate 23

Detail of the sarcophagus of Marcia Felicitas

Plate 24

Plate 25

Portrait of Marcia Thrasonis on the sarcophagus in the Tomb of the Marcii

Plate 26

Detail, showing a Maenad, of the sarcophagus in the
Tomb of the Marcii

Plate 27

Detail, showing Dionysus and a Satyr, of the sarcophagus in the
Tomb of the Marcii

Plate 28

Dionysiac sarcophagus in the Tomb of the Egyptians

Plate 29

Christian sarcophagus in the museum under St. Peter's

Plate 30

Marble head of a woman found near the Tomb of the Valerii

Plate 31

(*i*)

(*ii*)

Stucco heads of a Satyr (*i*), and of a man (*ii*)
in the Tomb of the Valerii

Plate 32

Christus-Helios in the vault-mosaic of Tomb M.

imperial slave. Several freedmen and freedwomen are recorded as possessing freedmen and freedwomen of their own (Note 2, ix. xvii).

The Greek *cognomina* borne by 55 persons in this cemetery form a richly varied collection—Ammas, Andria, Antigonus, Athenais, Athenaeus, Berenice, Charito, Chelidon, Chilo, Chryseros, Demetrius, Diodorus, Dynaten, Entimus, Euhodianus, Euokatus, Eutychas, Eutyches, Filetus, Ganymedes, Gigas, Gorgonia, Hedone(?), Heracla, Herma, Hermaiscus, Hermadion, Hermes, Hieron, Hygia, Hymnus, Iolaus, Isidorus, Megiste, Narcissus, Olympianus, Olympias, Onesimus, Pallas, Philumenus, Spatale, Stratonice, Theonice, Thrasonis, Trophime, Tyrannus, Zethus, and Zmaragdus. There may have been individual exceptions, but in the context there can be no doubt that the majority of these people were wholly or partially descended from Greek-speaking forebears. On the other hand, the Latin *cognomina* borne by 50 of the persons mentioned offer no certain proof that their owners were of originally free Roman stock. Two of the members of the freedman-family of the Aelii (Nos. 4 and 6) bear Latin *cognomina*, and Marcus Caetennius Secundus (No. 30), Marcus Caetennius Tertius (No. 31), and Restitutus (No. 70) were certainly freedmen. Titus Julius Priscianus (No. 44),[4] the son of Onesimus,[5] was probably a Greek slave who had been given his freedom by a member of the family of the Julii. The second name (*nomen*), Ulpius, borne by the two Pusinniones (Nos. 83, 84), suggests that their family had been freed under Trajan; and such Latin names as Felicitas (No. 48), Primitivus and Primitiva (Nos. 16, 38), Redempta (No. 36), Successus (Nos. 66, 67, 68), and Victoria (No. 41) smack of servile extraction. Moreover, Greek and Latin names appear side by side in single families—as, for example, in those of the Aelii, Tullii, and Valerii. Brothers and sisters were given Greek and Latin *cognomina* indifferently, a practice which would in the course of time have tended to obliterate traces of foreign origin; and, as is to be expected, husbands with Greek names married wives with Latin names, and vice versa.

Of the professions and trades followed by the owners of these tombs the Vatican cemetery tells us far less than does the cemetery at Isola Sacra, where not only are there a great many inscriptions, but where it was also the custom to enliven the façades of tombs with rough but vivid terra-cotta reliefs depicting the business-life of those

who built them. The owners of the Vatican tombs were less concerned to commemorate their means of livelihood, and the record is
relatively scanty. Ostorius Euhodianus was the only individual, so
far as we know, who climbed to senatorial heights (Note 2, xx). His
son-in-law, Vibius Iolaus, was *a memoria imp(eratoris) Augusti*; that is,
a secretary employed in the drafting and dispatching of state-papers,
a position of trust and influence (Note 2, xx). Among the Aelii the
imperial freedman Titus Aelius Tyrannus was *a comm(entariis)
prov(inciae) Belgicae*, occupying some post in the public archives or
finance-bureau of the northernmost of the Gallic provinces (Note
2, vii); while Urbanus, son of the elder Tyrannus, who was born an
imperial slave, *Aug(usti) verna*, and died before his father had won
his freedom, was *adiutor tabulari(orum) rationis patrimoni*, assistant
accountant in the department of the 'privy purse' (Note 2, viii). We
do not know the nature of the civil-service post held by Aurelius
Hermes (chapter 2, Note 14); and an unkind fortune has failed to
preserve for us the epitaph of the steward in Tomb G (p. 77 f., Pl. 16).
We know the latter's profession, but are ignorant both of his name
and of the capacity in which he followed his calling, whether on his
own account or in imperial, or other, service. Again, we cannot tell
whether the writing-materials rendered in stucco above the heads of
two of the family-portraits in the Tomb of the Valerii (p. 84 f.) mean
that these people were professional writers and men of letters, or that
they merely devoted their leisure-moments to literary pursuits.
There are only two inscriptions that refer specifically to trade.
Matuccius Entimus and Matuccius Zmaragdus were *lintearii*, linen-
dealers or linen-weavers (Note 2, xvii); and the wife of Cnaeus
Coelius Masculus dealt in olive-oil and wine from the Spanish
province of Baetica.[6] So far as the evidence allows us to generalize,
it seems that in the Vatican cemetery we are moving less in commercial and manufacturing circles than among the lower clerical and
administrative grades of the public services.

Three inscriptions throw some light upon the arrangements sometimes made with regard to the ownership of tombs or of individual
burial-sites inside them. Tomb N was built by Marcus Aebutius
Charito; but while it was building, or when it was just finished,
Volusius Successus and his wife, Volusia Megiste, bought half of it for
their son, Quintus Clodius Romanus (Note 2, xvi). In C, we hear of
the mother of Tullia Secunda ceding part of her daughter's burial-

place to Passullena Secundina, perhaps a relation (Note 2, i); and in the Tomb of the Valerii, Valerius Philumenus and Valeria Galatia gave Titus Pompeius Successus a *locus* in the tomb in which he might bury his son and their friend, the free-born Titus Pompeius Successus junior (Note 2, xiv).

(b) Beliefs

The first four centuries of our era, within which the Vatican cemetery falls, are more fully documented, both by surviving objects and by the written word, than any other period in the history of ancient religious thought. This was an age in which materialism, a race for wealth, position, and the maximum of creature-comfort, were curiously combined with an intense preoccupation with the unseen world stretching beyond the frontiers of mundane existence and knowledge. It was a time of ever-deepening conviction (in all but the most rarefied philosophic and sceptical circles) that the terror and power of death could be conquered, and that a life richer, happier, and more divinely ordered than that experienced here was attainable hereafter, under certain conditions, by the souls of the departed. This mainly optimistic attitude to death was, of course, very different both from the pessimistic view familiar in the literature and art of classical Greece and from the negative, colourless picture of the fortunes of the dead current in early Rome. Relics of former notions did, indeed, linger on far into the Empire. But, broadly speaking, thought about death and after-life was undergoing something little short of a revolution; and it is to this rapidly changing climate of ideas that the Vatican tombs bear eloquent testimony.[7]

The root of this change lay in the increasingly individualistic outlook of the age, which engendered the belief that something so autonomous, complex, and subtly developed as the human personality must be endowed with a more than fleetingly vital and temporarily individual significance. By the first century B.C. the traditional Greek view of the soul's future state as a shadowy, emasculated half-life was virtually outmoded, except as a literary convention; and the earlier Greek conception of the aim of the mysteries as a shedding of individuality, as a welcome reabsorption of the individual into an insentient, universal life-force, had begun to be replaced by trust in the efficacy of those rites as passports to an immortality personally and consciously experienced.[8] Similarly, the primitive Roman notion of the dead as *di manes*, divine, but a mere collectivity of unindividualized spirits, by the opening of our era survived only in the conventional phraseology of funerary inscriptions. The ubiquitous formula *D(is) M(anibus)*, or *D(is) M(anibus) S(acrum)*, followed by the personal name, or names, of the deceased individual in the genitive or dative case, is a contradiction in terms that would have been impossible so long as the words retained their original significance. Even the most intellectualized theories of astral apotheosis, whereby the soul was held to rejoin at death the pure, fiery element from which it ultimately came,[9] were rapidly transposed by Roman thinkers into a more humane and personal key. This is vividly apparent in Cicero's *Somnium Scipionis*, where the starry being Africanus is described as dwelling among the blessed dead in the Milky Way—*ea vita via est in caelum et in hunc coetum eorum qui iam vixerunt et corpore laxati illum incolunt locum quem vides (erat autem is splendidissimo candore inter flammas circus elucens), quem vos . . . orbem lacteum nuncupatis* ('such a life is the road to heaven, to the company of those whose earthly life is done and who are freed from the body and live in that place which you see (it was the circle—or he was the star—that blazed with most brilliant light among the fires) and which you call the Milky Way') (*S.S.*, iii. 6 = *De Rep.*, vi. 16). But he still retains his recognizable shape—*se ostendit ea forma quae mihi ex imagine eius quam ex ipso erat notior* ('he appeared in that shape which was better known to me from his portrait than from his person') (*S.S.*, i. 4 = *De Rep.*, vi. 10)—and takes an eager interest in the fortunes of his descendant Aemilianus. The same insistence on the continuing identity of bodily form and on lively concern for mundane pursuits and family affairs conditions Virgil's picture of the heroes in Elysium.

Closely linked with belief that the dead remember with affection their ties with living friends is the strong moral accent in Roman eschatological thinking and imagery. Physical and mental tortures are reserved in Homer (*Odyssey*, xi. 576–600) and in Virgil (*Aeneid*, vi. 548–627) for legendary criminals of superhuman stature. But the general view by the beginning of the Empire was that all men must expect a reckoning and judgment after death, and that a life well spent, with duties successfully performed, had a bearing on the state of the soul thereafter. A vivid instance of this is the address to Lucius Aemilius Paullus, censor of 22 B.C., composed by Propertius for Paullus's dead wife, Cornelia, daughter of Scribonia. Cornelia's soul, on trial, catalogues her virtues and good works;[10] and, in their own way, the genre-scenes from daily life on countless funerary monuments are no less eloquent. Useful toil and cultural accomplishments alike merit personal immortality. Among the stuccoes of the Underground Basilica by the Porta Maggiore, scenes of the school-room and gymnasium denote the training and testing of souls in this life (p. 100, Note 54). On the Igel Monument, near Trier, scenes from the business-activities of the Secundini figure side by side with the 'labours' of Perseus and Achilles and the apotheosis of Hercules.[11] The same thoughts lie behind the whole series of biographical sarcophagi, with episodes from the lives of generals, statesmen, philosophers, poets, musicians, and even of specially gifted children.[12] So, too, in the Vatican cemetery, the painting of the steward in G (p. 77 f., Pl. 16), and the portraits of a musical and learned girl on the small, curved sarcophagus from R (p. 92), have more than merely commemorative or biographical implications.

This view of the meaning of mundane pursuits and labours as figured in funerary art is not incompatible with the evidence of epitaphs alluding to such topics. Many of these, it is true, treat toil and care as burdens from which death brings release.[13] But so does 'blessed are the dead which die in the Lord . . . they rest from their labours', in a context in which the trials of this world are regarded as reaping rewards in the next.

Behind all funerary portraits of late-Hellenistic and Roman times, such as those just cited from Tombs G and R, such as the stucco ancestor-portraits in the Tomb of the Valerii (p. 84 f., Pl. 31) and the heads from marble portrait-statues found in the filling outside it (p. 94 f., Pl. 30), lies belief that the face reflects the individual soul surviving as a personal entity. The sculptured, modelled, or painted features are, indeed, the embodiment in visual form of the moral being who has earned his place in paradise; and this best explains a very familiar aspect of Roman sepulchral iconography—the concentration on head or bust at the rest of the body's expense. Brilliant examples of it in the Vatican cemetery are the faces of Quintus Marcius Hermes and his wife on the lid of their sarcophagus (Pls. 24, 25) and the medallion-portrait (*imago clipeata*) of Marcia Felicitas, who gazes at us as from a burnished shield or looking-glass fixed in the front of her coffin (Pl. 23). Such gripping, vivid realism would have little meaning in the tomb apart from an assurance that the characters and qualities mirrored in those features live on.[14]

No pointer to growth of belief in individual survival is more insistent than the superseding of cremation by inhumation during the second and third centuries. Here the Vatican cemetery adds its own important witness to what may best be described as a significant change of emphasis in Roman after-life ideas at this period, a change already, of course, well known and much studied from the evidence of earlier discoveries. As we should expect, the new rite won its way slowly and gradually. The art of sarcophagus-carving, it is true, flowered with some suddenness during the reign of Hadrian.[15] But the continued co-existence of both rites from the middle of the second century onwards is revealed both by the architecture and furniture of the tombs and by such chance-allusions as that contained in the words *cetera post obitum terra consumit et ignis*, the last line of Flavius Agricola's epitaph (p. 58, Note 4; the whole epitaph suggests an attitude more earth-bound, more in accordance with the doctrines of Epicurus, than that adopted by most of Agricola's contemporaries). By the middle of the third century, however, if not earlier, inhumation had probably become the normal practice in Rome and Italy and other central areas. The view that pure fashion or merely ostentatious taste for elaborate and expensively decorated coffins could have wrought a change in so fundamental a matter as that of burial-custom is not convincing;[16] on the other hand, contemporary paganism gives no hint of any dogma of bodily resurrection (p. 117 and Note 36); and the abandonment of cremation was too general to owe anything to Jewish habit and too early to be due to Christian influences. The explanation has, therefore, to be sought elsewhere. In the end, it must be admitted, interred bones and burnt bones come to much the same thing. Grave-goods, implying some belief in personal survival, accompany cremations, as well as inhumation-burials; just as holes and pipes for libations, enabling dead and living to share in one communion-feast, are found with both, and in this very cemetery.[17] But inhumation is a gentler and more respectful way of laying to rest the mortal frame, which has been, no trammelling prison-house to be thankfully discarded,[18] but the temple and mirror of the immortal soul and lasting individuality.

The change of rite may well have expressed a vague, perhaps, but deepening intuition of the human body's meaning and purpose *sub specie aeternitatis*, which the Christian doctrines of the Incarnation and Resurrection of the Body were to clinch and clarify.

Pagan speculation about the other-world was, indeed, still passing through a groping and experimental stage. The general trends of its thought are clear; but when we ask where the soul was to spend its eternity, the answers returned are confused and various. Often the dead are conceived of as still close at hand, resting securely in the kindly bosom of maternal Earth (*cf.* Pl. 12), the *grata humus* (Note 10), who rewards her deserving children. Hence the familiar, reiterated prayer of the epitaphs *s(it) t(ibi) t(erra) l(evis)*— 'may the earth rest light upon you'. Hence, too, the thought of immortality as union with the Earth-goddess—*cinis sum cinis terra est terra dea est/ergo ego mortua non sum* ('I am ash, ash is earth, earth is divine; therefore I am not dead');[19] and the notion of bones or ashes giving birth to flowers blowing on the grave—*hic iacet Optatus pietatis nobilis infans/cui precor ut cineres sint ia sintque rosae,/terraque quae mater nunc est sibi sit levis oro,/namque gravis nulli vita fuit pueri* ('here lies Optatus, a child noble and dutiful; I pray that his ashes may become violets and roses, and that the earth, whose child he now is, rest light upon him, as he in his life weighed heavy on no man').[20] Ideas of this kind may partly have inspired the superabundant wealth of fruits, plants, and flowers which we have noted, time and again, painted or modelled on the inner walls of the Vatican tombs or carved on their occupants' sarcophagi. But there is no reason to hold that such thoughts denied individual survival or involved a 'renunciation of personality'.[21] The epitaphs, in quoting or addressing the dead in the first or second persons, imply the continuance of his or her identity; and the rich floral ornament of the tombs is intimately linked with unmistakable symbols and allegories of the paradisal bliss into which the individual soul will enter. Another epitaph warns the traveller, resting beside a rustic tomb, not to be startled if the dead man dwelling there should suddenly accost him—[*hic ia*]*cet; et viridi requiesce, viator, in herba,/*[*ne*]*u fuge, si tecum coeperat umbra loqui* ('here he lies; and you too, wayfarer, rest upon the green grass, and fly not if his shade address you');[22] and even to the worldly Flavius Agricola, Tomb R, in the closely built-up suburban cemetery, is his eternal home—*hospitium . . . in aevum*, kept secure for him by the dutiful son whom his wife has bequeathed to him (p. 58, Note 4). In fact, the Vatican house-tombs, and their counterparts elsewhere, so simple without, so richly decked and colourful within, were surely regarded as places in which the dead, in some sense or at some times, resided.[23] Hidden away behind stout doors and seen only by members of the owners' families on anniversaries and feast-days, when sacrifices, ceremonial meals, and ritual washings took place,[24] all this luxuriant internal ornament and art must have been designed as much to delight the dead as to gratify and to instruct the survivors. The souls of the former, visiting, perhaps intermittently, the tombs where their relics reposed, could be made to feel at home there by renderings in paint, stone, or stucco of the useful and familiar objects—the toilet-articles, the tools, the writing-materials, which once had served them;[25] and still more emphatically be reminded, by the wealth of after-life imagery, of the blessed lands where now they dwelt.

It is, indeed, upon the distant, other-world dwellings and occupations of the dead that the pictorial language of the tombs insists most vigorously. As to the whereabouts of those habitations, Roman paganism offered several rival and conflicting theories. To some, as to Virgil (in part), to Apuleius,[26] to those who commissioned reliefs and mosaics of the Rape of Persephone (p. 74 f.) and such paintings as the *descensio*-scene in Vibia's mausoleum (p. 99, Note 32), the next world was sited deep in the bowels of the earth, like the Hades of ancient tradition.[27] Others placed it in the sky, in the hemispheres,[28] of which, as we have seen (p. 92), the Dioscuri were representatives, in the atmosphere, whither souls were borne by purifying winds, or in the moon.[29] Others, again, threw open to all human souls the harbours of the Blessed Isles across the ocean (*cf.* Pl. 13), reserved in the literary tradition only for heroes, and, like the Vatican carvers and painters and their fellows, delighted to picture the homeward journey of the happy dead, carried safely across the waves on the backs of friendly, frolicsome sea-lions, sea-bulls, sea-horses, sea-dragons, sea-griffins, Tritons, sea-Centaurs, and other ocean-born creatures, or of gently rolling, steadily voyaging dolphins (pp. 56, 90 f., Pls. 28, 29).

But however variously the pagan paradise might be localized, the life which the elect enjoyed there was envisaged in a commonly repeated pattern of images. Souls, in the shape of Cupids, Psyches, and other children, more often still in the guise of birds of brilliant plumage, play, feed, or wander in gardens of laden vines or glowing flowers, or feast eyes and appetites on luscious fruits bursting from horns of plenty, vases, and baskets. Sheep, goats, and oxen in idyllic landscapes (p. 50) tell of the peace and security of heaven; wild animals, merrily sporting, as in the border of the Persephone pavement (p. 75), symbolize its teeming life. Pictures of sleep (p. 83) or heavenly banquets (cf. p. 58, Note 4) promise rest and refreshment after the labours of this world;[30] and in union with the gods there is ecstasy such as wine induces (p. 86). It is surely to such Elysia, peopled by sentient, individual souls, and not to a losing of the personality in the pure life-essence of Earth,[31] that the gorgeously painted gardens of sepulchral art, and the constant references to fruits and flowers in the epitaphs, are bearing testimony. References in epigraphy to the passage of the seasons[32] and the frieze of sculptured Seasons on the lid of Marcia Felicitas's sarcophagus (p. 92) need not allude merely to the literal passing and repassing of the earthly year above the grave. They speak to us, rather, of that unceasing cycle of eternal life the gates of which death will fling open.

For the optimistic pagan, soaked as he might be in all this reassuring imagery, death was still a dreaded and awe-inspiring event. There was the grief felt at parting from parents, children, brothers, sisters, and friends, of which the Vatican tombs alone give ample evidence. There was the violent sundering (abreptio) of soul from body to be experienced. Nothing human can escape death's cruel clutches, his yawning and all-devouring jaws (p. 91). Nevertheless, for the virtuous or initiated soul, even this grim barrier reared between man and paradise could be broken down and turned into a means of positive triumph. Death could be 'swallowed up in victory'; and, in the pictorial language of Roman funerary art, trophies of arms (p. 92), the slaying of savage foes or ravening beasts (p. 91), Victories (p. 89), victorious charioteers (p. 76), palm-trees (cf. Pl. 28), and palm-branches[33] announce the final overthrow of man's last enemy.

Yet this deliverance could not be won by man unaided. He needed a divine patron or saviour; and of these there were many in latter-day paganism. No less than seven of them are figured in the excavated sector of our cemetery. There are Hermes, the kindly guide of souls (p. 75); Hercules, who braved all the terrors of hell and

brought back Alcestis, soul and body, from the grave (p. 78 f.);
Minerva, who gave men victory over death and wisdom to bring
them to immortality (p. 83); Apollo, healer, purifier, and master of
the Muses (p. 83); Isis, if Isis she be, in the Tomb of the Valerii (p.
83)—Isis, who promised her convert, Lucius, that, from his place
in paradise, he should see and adore her, even in the subterranean
hemisphere of Hades, shining through the darkness and reigning in
the inmost halls of night;[34] and the Egyptian Horus (if he be rightly
identified), king and deliverer of the dead, penetrating westwards,
in all his strange, un-Roman panoply, to Rome itself (p. 54 f., Pl. 8).
Most eagerly followed and most powerful of all these pagan saviours
was Horus's Graeco-Roman doublet, Dionysus, who punished un-
believers (p. 72, Pl. 19), but rewarded his devotees, coming with his
ecstatic train in all the glory of his triumph to rouse the soul of the
initiate (Ariadne) from the sleep of death to mystic marriage with
himself in paradise (p. 55, Pl. 22).[35]

In the last resort, these pagan gods and heroes, however humanely
and graciously pictured, were but symbols or projections of natural
faculties and forces, rooted neither in time nor in history. Whether
they had ever really walked this earth, no one inquired. The violent
death and restoration to life that some of these, and other, pagan
saviours were held to have experienced appealed to men's hearts.
Yet they were basically no more than allegories of winter-death and
spring-time renewal. But in the smallest of the Vatican mausolea,
M (p. 72 ff., Pl. 32), a Roman family expressed its faith in a very
different Divine Saviour, Who had lived at a known date and in a
certain place, Whom men had seen and handled, Who had shared
men's pains and sorrows, and had conquered death by suffering it
Himself; Whose death and resurrection were attested by eye-
witnesses and recorded soon afterwards in written documents. The
message of this faith—that God had become incarnate in a Man—
was wholly new[35a]. Yet it proclaimed itself the heir of Israel; and by
its readiness to use and adapt the after-life imagery of Graeco-Roman
paganism it showed its understanding of the latter's speculations,
problems, and hopes. On the walls and ceiling of this tomb the vine
of Dionysus has become the True Vine of Christ, in which the vital
sap of the heavenly plant is diffused through all its branches. On the
north wall the human soul, typified by a fish and plunged in the
waters of Baptism, is drawn forth by the Angler, washed and reborn

nto a new, divine life of Grace—a positive conception of restoration
o a supernatural plane of which the pagan world seems to have had
10 inkling; on the east wall death engulfs the Christian as the whale
levoured Jonah, but only to yield him up again, alive and vic-
orious, at the bodily resurrection—another belief unknown to the
pagan mysteries (p. 112);[36] and on the west wall the Good Shep-
1erd bears off the rescued soul to peace and everlasting union with
Himself in Heaven.[37] In the centre of the vault the theme of triumph
over death reaches its climax in the figure of the risen and ascending
Christ, the new Sol Invictus, Christus-Helios, radiant with Easter
ight.

Into this quiet and majestic scene, poised above the tomb, are
gathered many familiar pagan art-types of the sun-god in his
chariot, and of the apotheosis of emperor or hero. Our thoughts at
once turn to the second-century Helios, girt by the Seasons, on the
ceiling of Fannia's mausoleum (p. 42 f., Pl. 6), symbol of a pagan
paradise sited in the sky; to the saluting, globe-bearing figure of Sol
Invictus, constantly repeated on coins, sculptures, silver-ware, etc.,[38]
of the third and fourth centuries; to such episodes as that of the
deified Emperor mounting skywards on the relief from Ephesus, now
n Vienna;[39] and of Hercules on the Igel Monument, drawn into
heaven by the hand of his patroness Athena.[40] To the Christian
beholder, the Vatican mosaic breathes another spirit. The Chariot-
er's right hand is raised in strength and power, but in His greeting
here is also benediction; the globe round which the fingers of His
eft hand are curving spells unlimited, but spiritual, dominion—
*egnum veritatis et vitae, regnum sanctitatis et gratiae, regnum iustitiae,
moris, et pacis*;[41] and it may be no accident that the rays to right and
eft of His nimbus trace strongly accented horizontal lines, forcibly
uggesting the transverse bar of a cross, the banner of His and of the
Christian's victory.[42] In all of this the Christian message was new.
But the forms in which it was expressed were, like those used by
ews under the Empire,[43] borrowed, to a very large extent, from
he familiar circle of contemporary pagan symbolism; and it was
heir very familiarity that gave them meaning and made them ready
nstruments for the propagation of the new faith. In the mosaics of
his tiny mausoleum we see a microcosm of the whole dramatic
istory of Christ's peaceful penetration of the pagan Empire.

NOTES

1. For a full discussion of this question see Tenney Frank, 'Race Mixture in the Roman Empire' (*American Historical Review*, xxi, 1916, pp. 689–708) *Economic History of Rome*, 2nd ed., 1927, pp. 202–18; *An Economic Survey of Ancient Rome*, v, 1940, pp. 218–36; H. J. Loane, 'Industry and Commerce in the City of Rome (50 B.C.–A.D. 200)' (*The Johns Hopkins University Studies in Historical and Political Science*, lvi, 2, 1938). Frank's theories have been criticized by M. L. Gordon, 'The Nationality of Slaves under the Early Roman Empire (*Journal of Roman Studies*, xiv, 1924, pp. 93–111); and by W. L. Westermann *s.v.* 'Sklaverei' in Pauly-Wissowa, *Real-Encyclopädie*, Supp. vi, 1935, col 1003 ff. See also A. M. Duff, *Freedmen in the Early Roman Empire*, 1928, *passim*

The best recent study is that of H. Thylander, 'Etude sur l'épigraphie latine (*Acta Instituti Romani Regni Sueciae*, Ser. V, 1952). Thylander reinforces Frank' conclusions, which he considers to be, if anything, over-conservative. It was the usual practice of the Romans to give Latin names by choice to their slaves, no Greek names, which must normally be regarded as evidence of origin, proxi mate or ultimate, in Greek-speaking lands. The Greek names borne by Nero' German guardsmen were a freak of that philhellenic enthusiast, unparallele in other reigns.

2. i. (Tomb C) D(is) M(anibus)/Tulliae [*sic*] Secunda/filiae [*sic*] hic sita/est Passullenae Secu/ndinae mater/cessit D(is) M(anibus)/T(itus) Tullius Athenaeus filius hic situs est.

ii. (Tomb D) D(is) M(anibus)/Aeliae/Strato/nices Iu/nius Rufi/nus con/iugi

iii. (Tomb D) D(is) M(anibus)/Q(uinto) Iunio/Rufino/v(ixit) an(nis) XXI parentes.

iv. (Tomb D) D(is) M(anibus)/Iuniae/Spatal(a)e/coniugi/Iul(ius) Euty/ches.

v. (Tomb D) Iulio/Eutyche/ti/v(ivus) f(ecit) sibi.

vi. (Tomb D) D(is) M(anibus)/T(iti) Iulii Prisciani/fili(i) pientissimi/v(ixi a(nnis) XIII m(ensibus) VIIII/M M̄ (see Note 5) Onesimus/pater fec(it).

vii. (Tomb E) T(ito) Aelio Aug(usti) lib(erto) Tyranno/qui fuit a comm (entariis) prov(inciae) Belgicae/coniugi dulcissimo/Aelia Andria uxor et/Aelia Valerianus socer/et Restitutus fctt [= fecerunt] collib(erto).

viii. (Tomb E) D(is) M(anibus) Urbano Aug(usti) vern(ae)/adiutori tabula (orum) rationis patrimoni vixit annis XXI m(ensibus) VII d(iebus) XXX Tyrannus Aug(usti) lib(ertus)/et Aelia Urbana parentes filio karissimo.

ix. (Tomb E) D(is) M(anibus)/Aeliae Saturninae vixit ann(is) XXXV mens(ibus) II Aelia Aug(usti) lib(erta) Urbana/libertae karissimae.

x. (Tomb E) D(is) M(anibus) S(acrum)/Aeliae Urbanae/matri karissima Tyrannus filius.

xi. (Tomb E) D(is) M(anibus)/Aureli Gigantis/et Papiriae/Profuturae/ei Iulius/Hermadion amicis.

xii. (Tomb E) D(is) M(anibus)/Statia Kara vix(it)/ann(is) XXXV Iul(ia) Victo/ria mater inf(elix) f(iliae) dulcis(simae).

xiii. (Tomb H) D(is) M(anibus)/Valeriae Theonices/coniugi karissimae et/de se benemerenti fecit/Q(uintus) Aninius Liberalis.

xiv. (Tomb H) D(is) M(anibus)/Tito Pompeio T(iti) f(ilio) Successo iun(iori)/ qui vixit annis decemno/vem me(n)sibus duobus die uno fi/lio carissimo dulcissimo T(itus) Pompeius Succ(essus) pater/cui locum obt(ulerunt) Valerii Philumenus et Galatia amico benemerenti.

xv. (Tomb H¹) D(is) M(anibus)/Pompeiae Maritim(a)e/matri/T(itus) Pomp- (eius) Proculus Suces(sus)/b(ene)m(erenti) fecit; on a strigilated sarcophagus with curved ends.

xvi. (Tomb N) D(is) M(anibus)/M(arcus) Aebutius Charito/fecit sibi et libertis/ libertabusque suis/posterisque eorum/D(is) M(anibus)/C(aii) Clodi Romani q(ui) vix(it) a(nnis) XIX m(ense) I d(iebus) XXI L(ucius) Volusius Suces/sus et Volusia Megiste/filio dulcissimo emerunt in parte dimidia et sibi posterisq(ue)/ suis lib(ertis) lib(ertabus)q(ue) p(osterisque) eorum h(uic) m(onumento) d(olus) m(alus) a(besto): Report, ii, Pl. 9, a.

xvii. (Tomb O) T(ito) Matuccio Pallanti patrono/optimo fecerunt/Matuccii II Entimus et Zmara/gdus lineari et sibi liberis/que suis posterisque eorum/et libertis libertabusque/suis: Report, ii, Pl. 9, b.

xviii. (Tomb O) D(is) M(anibus)/T(ito) Ma[t]uccio Deme/trio q[u]i vix/it ann(is)/XXIIII . . . T(itus) Ma/tucciu[s Herm]a/iscus co[lliber]/tu[s]. Under this inscription is a roundel pierced by four holes through which libations could be poured on the ashes of the dead: Report, i, p. 49, Note 1.

xix. (Tomb T) D(is) M(anibus) Trebellenae/Flaccillae/Valeria Taccina/ matri dulcissim(ae) fecit.

xx. (Behind Tomb Z) D(is) M(anibus)/Ostoriae Che/lidonis c(arissimae? or -larissimae?) f(eminae)/Ostorii Euho/diani consulis/designati/filiae in/compara/ bilis castita/tis et amoris/erga maritum/exempli femi/nae Vib(ius) Iolaus/a memoria/imp(eratoris) Augusti/uxori.

We have no evidence that the two pagan inscriptions in honour of L(ucius) Clodius Tineius Pupienus Bassus and L(ucius) Caesonius Manlius Bassus respectively, found reused in Christian graves under the floor of the Basilica, came from this cemetery (Ferrua, Fig. 1 and p. 96).

3. Josi, p. 5.

4. The second i of Iulii bears an accent (apex).

5. Whether the M M̄ before Onesimus represent praenomen and nomen (Marcus Manlius(?)), or some other abbreviations, is uncertain. M̄ would be very abnormal as the abbreviation of a nomen. A. E. Gordon, Supralineate Abbrevia- tions in Latin Inscriptions, 1948, p. 83, gives examples of praenomina (e.g. Marcus and Manius) so abbreviated, but none of a nomen with supralineate abbreviation.

6. The fragmentary marble inscription recording the names of Nos. 102 and

103 now stands on end just inside the entrance to Tomb T; it was found loose during the excavations and its original position is unknown. The surviving text reads:

. . . ne]gotiatric(i) olear(iae) ex provinc(ia) Baetic(a) item vini

. . .]ate incomparabili Cn(aeo) Coelio Masculo patri piis[simo . . .] Coelia Mascellina parentibus fecit.

Cf. H. Dessau, *Inscriptiones Latinae Selectae*, 7488, mentioning a 'negotiatrix frumentaria et legumenaria [*sic*].'

From the same cemetery, but not found in these excavations, is an inscription (*CIL*, vi. 1, 1101) referring to a curiously assorted group of *argentarii* (in the context, money-changers), *exceptores* (scribes), and *negotiantes vini Supernat-(enses) et Arimini(enses)* (dealers in wine from the Adriatic coast, with head-quarters at Rimini). This inscription, found in 1611, is a dedication of the year 251 to the Caesar Herennius Etruscus. Another inscription, containing part of a burial-assignment to three *argentarii* and a large number of *exceptores*, is incorporated in the altar of the Confessio (p. 217; *Report*, i, Fig. 130).

7. Among pioneer-studies of Roman eschatological ideas is Mrs. Arthur Strong's *Apotheosis and After Life*, 1915. The fundamental modern works on the subject are those of Franz Cumont—*Recherches sur le symbolisme funéraire des Romains*, 1942; *La stèle du danseur d'Antibes et son décor végétal: étude sur le symbolisme funéraire des plantes*, 1942; *Lux Perpetua*, 1949. See also K. Lehmann-Hartleben and E. C. Olsen, *Dionysiac Sarcophagi in Baltimore*, 1942, and I. A. Richmond, *Archaeology, and the After-Life in Pagan and Christian Imagery*, 1950.

8. In the *Frogs*, 324 ff., Aristophanes transfers to the lower world the song of the initiates who carried the statue of Iacchus from Athens to Eleusis at the Eleusinia. The passage can hardly be regarded as certain evidence for belief in personal immortality for Dionysiac *mystai* in fifth-century B.C. Athens, as is suggested by H. I. Bell in *Cults and Creeds in Graeco-Roman Egypt*, 1953, p. 8.

9. Virgil, *Aen.*, vi, 746-7: . . . purumque relinquit aetherium sensum atque aurai simplicis ignem ('. . . leaves clear the ethereal sense and the flame of pure spirit').

10. Propertius, iv. 11. See especially the concluding lines, 99–102:

> causa perorata est. flentes me surgite, testes,
> dum pretium vitae grata rependit humus.
> moribus et caelum patuit: sim digna merendo
> cuius honoratis ossa vehantur avis.

('The case for my defence is done. Stand up, my witnesses, and weep for me, while kindly earth requites my life's deserts. To virtue even heaven's gates are unbarred: may I be found worthy, that my bones may be borne to join my honoured ancestors'.)

11. H. Dragendorff and E. Krüger, *Das Grabmal von Igel*, 1924.

12. For culture as a road to immortality, see Cumont, *Recherches*, etc., chapter iv: les Muses.

13. *E.g. CIL*, v, i. 3415; viii, 1, 2401; ix, 60. Contrast the view of Richmond, *op. cit.*, p. 39.

14. A remarkable piece of evidence for the respect, if not awe, inspired by a portrait as reflecting, and in a sense perpetuating on earth, the spirit of the person figured, comes from the Romano-British villa at Lullingstone in Kent. Two large portrait-busts of private individuals in marble, apparently abandoned in the villa when it was deserted towards the end of the second century, were found and set up and venerated in an underground room, by the new owners, who reoccupied the place during the second half of the third century. These new-comers are unlikely to have had any family-connection with their predecessors, still less to have known personally the originals of the portraits. See *Archaeologia Cantiana*, lxiii, 1950 (1951), pp. 35–43, Pls. 2–4.

15. J. M. C. Toynbee, *The Hadrianic School*, 1934, p. 161 ff.

16. A. D. Nock, 'Cremation and Burial in the Roman Empire' (*Harvard Theological Review*, xxv, 1932, p. 321 ff.).

17. For an instance of this practice in association with a cremation, see that in O (Note 2, xviii). For its association with a burial, see the graves beneath the floor of F (p. 61, Note 30) and the child's grave (γ) in P (p. 145, Figs. 11, 13).

18. As in *Somnium Scipionis*, 3, 2 = *De Rep.*, vi. 14—immo vero . . . hi vivunt qui e corporum vinculis tanquam e carcere evolaverunt ('they live indeed who have escaped from the fetters of the body as from prison').

19. *CIL*, vi. 4, 29609.

20. *CIL*, ix. 3184.

21. As inferred by Richmond, *op. cit.*, pp. 25–8.

22. *CIL*, xi. 2, 5357.

23. *Cf.* Cumont, *Lux Perpetua*, pp. 13–28.

24. A cistern, possibly used for rites of purification, was discovered under courtyard R¹, adjoining Tomb R (*Report*, i, Fig. 54), and another in the forecourt, H¹, of Tomb H. Ovens for cooking, couches for reclining at funerary banquets, and wells are common at Isola Sacra (Calza, p. 56). There is a similar couch in the forecourt of Tomb D; but otherwise this practice (for which see also p. 172) has left no tangible trace in the Vatican cemetery.

25. A notable instance of the attempt to provide a homelike atmosphere for the dead is furnished by the famous Simpelveld sarcophagus now at Leiden (E. Espérandieu, *Recueil général des bas-reliefs, statues et bustes de la Gaule romaine*, xi, 1938, pp. 107–9, No. 7795, with figures; Cumont, *Lux Perpetua*, Pl. 1), on the inner walls of which is carved a veritable 'Dutch interior' showing the dead lady's furniture and possessions in the minutest detail. Here there can be no question of mere commemoration, or of ostentation on the part of the deceased's survivors, since all this elaborate carving would never have been seen

by mortal eye once the burial had taken place. Curiously enough, the human relics inside the coffin had been cremated (*Académie des Inscriptions et Belles-Lettres : Comptes rendus*, 1931, p. 351 ff.).

26. *Metamorph*, xi. 6.

27. *Cf.* Cumont, *Lux Perpetua*, pp. 55–77.

28. *Cf.* Cumont, *Recherches*, etc., chapter i.

29. *Cf. ibid.*, chapters ii and iii.

30. *Cf. ibid.*, chapter v.

31. As held by Richmond, *op. cit.*, p. 26.

32. F. Bücheler, *Carmina Latina Epigraphica*, 1, 1895, No. 439:

> ver tibi contribuat sua munera florea grata
> et tibi grata comis nutet aestiva voluptas
> reddat et autumnus Bacchi tibi munera semper
> ac leve hiberni tempus tellure dicetur.

('May spring bestow on you her welcome offerings of flowers, and bounteous summer nod to you her gracious tresses; may autumn ever bring you Bacchus's gifts, and earth ordain for you a gentle winter.')

33. Palm-branches accompany two of the sepulchral inscriptions in D (Note 2, ii, iii) and the epitaphs of Tullia Secunda and Titus Tullius Athenaeus in C (Note 2, i).

34. Apuleius, *Metamorph.*, xi. 6—vives autem beatus, vives in mea tutela gloriosus, et cum spatium saeculi tui permensus ad inferos demearis, ibi quoque in ipso subterraneo semirutundo me, quam vides, Acherontis tenebris interlucentem Stygiisque penetralibus regnantem, campos Elysios incolens ipse, tibi propitiam frequens adorabis. ('Thou shalt live happy, thou shalt live full of glory under my protection; and when, this space of life accomplished, thou shalt descend to the Underworld, there too, in the hemisphere beneath the earth, thou shalt find me whom thou seest now, shining out amidst the gloom of Hades and ruling in the halls of darkness; thou shalt dwell in the Elysian Fields and shalt ever adore me, thy protectress.')

35. For elaborations of these themes, see Lehmann-Hartleben and Olsen, *op. cit.*, *passim*, and Richmond, *op. cit.*, pp. 29–38.

35a. The theory of ancient ruler-worship, that a man, by virtue of becoming ruler, 'made manifest' in a specific human shape some god of mythology, was wholly different from the Christian doctrine of the Incarnation.

36. *Cf.* M. P. Nilsson, *Harvard Theological Review*, xlvi, 1953, p. 184.

37. The essential feature of the art-motif of the Good Shepherd, an animal carried across the shoulders of its bearer, was known in archaic and classical Greek art, as the familiar figures of the Moschophorus and Hermes Criophorus show. Among early-imperial examples of the type, possibly based on Hellenistic prototypes, the following may be cited: (1) a glass disc from a house at Pompeii showing a naked Cupid with a lamb on his shoulders (*Notizie degli Scavi*, 1908,

p. 35, Fig. 5); (2) the painting of Spring as a girl with a lamb on her shoulders from the 'House of Ganymede' at Pompeii (G. M. A. Hanfmann, *The Season Sarcophagus at Dumbarton Oaks*, 1951, Fig. 89); (3) the male figure of Spring carrying a goat in the second-century A.D. paintings from the Tomb of the Nasones near Rome (P. S. Bartoli, J.P. Bellori, M.A. La Chausse, *Picturae Antiquae Cryptarum Romanarum et Sepulcri Nasonum*, 1791, Pls. 21, 22). In imperial sculpture the motif naturally occurs more often on Christian sarcophagi of the third and fourth centuries. But when it appears in pastoral scenes on pieces in mixed pagan and Christian contexts, as in the cemetery at Isola Sacra (Calza, Figs. 117–20, and pp. 216–18), we cannot be sure that it is of Christian origin. In fact the earliest sculptural instance of it in Roman art is the personification of Winter on the lid of an unequivocally pagan Antonine sarcophagus in the Vatican (E. Strong, *La scultura romana*, 1923–6, Pl. 52); the motif occurs again on the early-third-century Phaethon sarcophagus in Tortona Cathedral (C. Robert, *Die antiken Sarkophag-Reliefs*, iii. 3, 1919, Pl. 115, 350, *c*); and there is nothing to suggest that the Season sarcophagi, on which Winter figures in this guise, were not completely pagan (*e.g.* Hanfmann, *op. cit.*, Figs. 55, 59, 75, 77; *cf.* a recent find from Carthage published in *Fasti Archaeologici*, iv, 1949 (1951), No. 3438, Fig. 58, and a piece from Henchir Romana in the Bardo Museum at Tunis, Room VIII, No. 1476). Finally, we may note the same representation of Winter on the probably late-fourth-century Parabiago *patera* (see Note 38). It seems likely that Romano-Christian artists (or their patrons) adapted to their own use a well-established pagan art-motif under the inspiration of Luke 15:5 and John 10: 11–16. A late-fifth-century version of this theme in a context that is not specifically Christian occurs in the mosaic of the great palace at Constantinople (G. Brett, W. J. Macaulay, R. B. K. Stevenson, *The Great Palace of the Byzantine Emperors*, 1947, Pl. 46).

38. Coins: H. Mattingly and E. A. Sydenham, *The Roman Imperial Coinage*, V, ii, 1933, Pls. 1, No. 13; 2, No. 9; 5, Nos. 1, 9, 10. Sculpture: on the east attic of the Arch of Constantine: E. Strong, *La scultura romana*, 1923–6, Fig. 203; H. P. L'Orange and A. von Gerkan, *Der spätantike Bildschmuck des Konstantins-bogens*, 1939, Pl. 38*a*. Silver-ware: the silver-gilt *patera* from Parabiago, now in the Brera Gallery at Milan: A. Levi, *La patera d'argento di Parabiago* (*R. Istituto d'Archeologia e Storia dell'Arte: Opere d'Arte*, v), 1935, and E. Strong, *The Burlington Magazine*, lxxii, 1938, Fig. on p. 92 and p. 96, by both of whom the piece is wrongly attributed to the second century. For the correct, fourth-century, dating see A. Alföldi, *Die Kontorniaten*, 1942, Pl. 71, 1 and pp. 69–70.

39. E. Strong, *La scultura romana*, 1923–6, Pl. 50. For the Hadrianic dating of the series of reliefs to which this belongs, see F. von Lorenz, *Mitteilungen des Deutschen Archäologischen Instituts: Römische Abteilung*, xlviii, 1933, pp. 309–10.

40. Dragendorff and Krüger, *op. cit.*, Pl. 8.

41. 'A kingdom of truth and life, a kingdom of holiness and grace, a kingdom

of justice, love and peace' (from the Preface of the Mass for the Feast of Christ the King).

42. If this impression is not deceptive, we have here a remarkable and, it appears, unparalleled instance of the association of a cross, or at least a hint of a cross, with Christ in mid-third-century art. *Cf.* p. 103, Note 101.

43. E. R. Goodenough, *Jewish Symbols in the Graeco-Roman Period*, 1953.

Part Two

THE SHRINE OF ST. PETER

5

THE PETRINE TRADITION

THE primacy of the Roman Pontiff as St. Peter's successor is an article of faith proposed for acceptance by the teaching authority of the Roman Catholic Church; and it is the commonly received opinion within the Church that this implies belief that the Apostle lived, at least for a time, and died in Rome, after transmitting his primacy to his successors in the Roman see. These facts have regrettably, but inevitably, been sufficient to involve the whole question of St. Peter's residence and death in Rome in controversy; and although this book is in no way concerned with the doctrinal context of the belief, it is clear that some survey of the historical arguments supporting it is essential to the study of our subject—the material relics of the Apostle's shrine beneath the papal altar of the Vatican Basilica. The word 'shrine' precisely expresses what has, in fact, been found—the place where St. Peter was venerated from at least the third quarter of the second century; and it does not exclude the possibility that that place was a 'tomb-shrine' marking the site of his burial. But it should, at the outset, be plainly stated that the question of St. Peter's presence and death in Rome and that of the identification of his grave are separate questions. It goes without saying that, if it could be proved that St. Peter was never in Rome, it would be vain to argue whether a particular spot on the Vatican Hill does, or does not, represent his tomb. Conversely, the fact that absolute certainty about his grave-site is, in the view of the present writers, not at the moment attainable does not in any way affect belief in his close association with the Church in Rome.

The discovery of the pre-Constantinian Vatican shrine erected, as we shall see later (p. 141), c. 170, at the latest, represents the great historical achievement of the recent excavations below the Confessio. It gives us, for the first time, archaeological evidence that the cult of the Apostle on the Vatican, and hence the tradition of his residence and martyrdom in Rome, can be traced back to little more than a century, if as much, after the reputed date of his death. The Roman tradition seems to have been accepted without question in Antiquity.[1] The powers claimed by the bishops of Rome as successors of St. Peter were at times disputed, but the fact of the succession passed unchallenged. Any attempt to explain away the tradition by reference to political or ecclesiastical rivalries has, at the same time, to explain the circumstances in which such a story could have been invented and propagated within a period of time which is little, if at all, more than the lifetime of persons who had known St. Peter. There is the same difficulty in accepting the notion that the whole story of St. Peter's one-time presence in Rome, of his leadership of the Roman Church, and of his martyrdom under Nero just outside the imperial city, arose solely from a mistaken interpretation of Babylon as Rome in 1 Peter 5: 13, an interpretation for which (on such a hypothesis) there was no foundation of fact. There is, actually, good reason for believing this interpretation to be the original and right one (p. 132). But, even if it were not, we should still have to hold that by the middle of the second century the Roman Church had so completely lost all record of its earlier history, less than a century before, that it was able to build up, and to secure the acceptance of, a complete legend about St. Peter's activities and end which was based on the faulty exegesis of a single word in Scripture. Indeed, if we accept the earliest of the literary allusions (p. 130 f.) to St. Peter's death in Rome, we should have to place the birth of the supposed error within a few decades of the date at which the first epistle of St. Peter is generally agreed to have been composed (62–4).[2] The written evidence prior to the third century may be scanty, scattered, and undetailed; but it is credible and consistent and, cumulatively, far from negligible.

A salient feature of all the post-biblical references, one which they share with the proto-Christian art of the third and fourth centuries and with the Catholic liturgy, is the coupling of St. Peter with St. Paul. This emerges very clearly from the latest of the documents that concern us, a description by a Roman priest, Gaius, of the 'trophies', or martyr-shrines, of St. Peter and St. Paul on the Vatican Hill and beside the Via Ostiensis respectively. Gaius was active in the pontificate of St. Zephyrinus (199–217), and his words, preserved in

Eusebius (*HE*, ii. 25, 6, 7), are therefore first-class evidence of the state of affairs that obtained in Rome by the end of the second century. 'I can show you,' he wrote in controversy with the Montanist Proclus, 'the trophies (τρόπαια) of the Apostles. For if you go to the Vatican or to the Ostian Way, there you will find the trophies of those who founded this Church.'[2a] The archaeological connotations of this passage will be considered in the next chapter (p. 154 ff.). What concerns us at the moment is the allusion to the two Apostles as fellow-founders of the Roman Church and fellow-martyrs, and to the existence of their shrines near the city as well-established Christian landmarks.

To St. Paul, at any rate, the title of 'founder' of the Roman Church was obviously applied in the general sense of his being one of its Apostolic leaders and an Apostolic pillar of its faith, since it is clear both from Acts and from Romans 15: 20–2 that he did not literally found the first Christian community in the city. Whether the 'other man', on whose foundations in Rome St. Paul was unwilling to build, was St. Peter we have, of course, no means of knowing. St. Peter would not appear to have been in Rome at the time (57–9?) when St. Paul wrote Romans, since no salutation is sent to him. Nor is St. Peter's name included among those who send greetings from Rome in Colossians (59–63?) and 2 Timothy (62–3?). The dates of all three letters are very uncertain. But St. Peter could have paid his first visit to the city, and then have left it for a while, before the writing of Romans; and he might well have been away on visits to Christian communities elsewhere at the moments at which the two other letters were penned. Indeed, the charge to 'confirm his brethren' (Luke 22: 32) would have made travelling on such 'visitations' an essential feature of his ministry.[3]

If the term 'founded' is used in a general, non-literal sense of St. Paul's relation to the Church in Rome, the same is true of the term 'planted' as applied to St. Peter's activity in the Church in Corinth (a certainly Pauline foundation) by Dionysius, bishop of Corinth, in *c.* 170. In his letter to the Romans, quoted by Eusebius (*HE*, ii. 25, 8), Dionysius says that St. Peter and St. Paul both 'planted' and taught at Corinth; and it would seem to be implied by 1 Corinthians 1: 12 that St. Peter paid at least one Apostolic visit to that city. But for our present purposes the interest of Dionysius's letter lies in its further statement that St. Peter and St. Paul had also 'planted' in

Rome, that they had taught together in Italy, and had suffered martyrdom at the same time (or on the same occasion). Whether by ὁ αὐτὸς καιρός is meant the same day, or same year, or same period of persecution, we cannot say.

Our next literary allusion to St. Peter and St. Paul in Rome is in the letter sent to the Romans by St. Ignatius of Antioch at some date during the second century.[4] The natural inference to be drawn from the words addressed by the writer to his correspondents in chapter 4—'I do not command you as Peter and Paul did (οὐχ ὡς Πέτρος καὶ Παῦλος διατάσσομαι ὑμῖν)'—is that the two Apostles were singled out for mention as having exercised authority in the Roman Church within living memory.

The earliest non-biblical passage that concerns us is contained in chapters 5 and 6 of St. Clement of Rome's letter to the Corinthians. The date most generally accepted for this letter is the close of the first century,[5] 'that is, not much more than thirty years after the Apostles' deaths; and in view of its great importance this passage is worth quoting in full. 'But let us pass over examples from ancient days and come to those champions who lived very near to our own time (τοὺς ἔγγιστα γενομένους ἀθλητάς). Let us take the noble examples that belong to our own generation (τῆς γενεᾶς ἡμῶν). By reason of jealousy and envy the greatest and most righteous pillars [of the Church] were persecuted and contended even unto death (οἱ μέγιστοι καὶ δικαιότατοι στῦλοι ἐδιώχθησαν καὶ ἕως θανάτου ἤθλησαν). Let us place before our eyes the good Apostles. There was Peter, who by reason of unrighteous jealousy endured not one or two but many hardships, and so, having borne his witness, departed to his appointed place of glory (καὶ οὕτω μαρτυρήσας ἐπορεύθη, etc.). By reason of jealousy and strife Paul pointed out the way to winning the prize of endurance. After he had been seven times in bonds, had been driven into exile, had been stoned, had been herald (κῆρυξ = preacher) to the East and to the West, he won a noble reward for his faith, having taught the whole world and reached the extreme West. And having borne his witness in the presence of the rulers, so he departed from this world (καὶ μαρτυρήσας ἐπὶ τῶν ἡγουμένων, οὕτως ἀπηλλάγη τοῦ κόσμου) and went (ἐπορεύθη) into the holy place, famed as a pattern of endurance.[6] With these men of holy lives were gathered a great multitude of the elect, who, through many outrages and tortures, being the victims of jealousy, became a great example among us (ἐν ἡμῖν). By reason of jealousy women, being persecuted, after they had suffered cruel and unholy insults, reached in their race the goal of faith and won a noble reward, feeble though they were in body.'

St. Clement was writing from Rome; and the most natural interpretation of his words is that, in singling out St. Peter and St. Paul as Apostolic exemplars, he was, like St. Ignatius after him, appealing to examples personally associated with his own Church, as well as personally known in Corinth; and that, in referring to the Apostles' unnamed fellow-victims 'among us (ἐν ἡμῖν)', he was alluding to those members of the Roman Christian community who had fallen victim to the Neronian persecution. St. Clement's terminology closely corresponds with that employed by Tacitus in his famous description (*Ann.*, xv. 44) of the anti-Christian 'pogrom' in Rome in 64.

The use of the word μαρτυρεῖν does not, by itself, necessarily imply at this early age that a Christian's witness to his faith was sealed with his blood. But the word μάρτυς was already used in this special sense of St. Stephen in Acts 22: 20; and the context of the Clementine sentences is surely decisively in favour of interpreting μαρτυρήσας, applied in so emphatic a position to each Apostle in turn, as denoting martyrdom. Moreover, ἀθλητής ('champion' or 'athlete') appears frequently in early-Christian literature and inscriptions with the meaning of 'martyr' in the strict sense.[7] It is highly improbable that the ends in which the 'contending' of these 'athletes' and 'pillars' culminated was, not execution, but natural death. That St. Clement believed St. Peter and St. Paul to have suffered martyrdom in Rome under Nero is, in fact, the most reasonable deduction to be made from this passage.

We must conclude our survey with a brief discussion of the biblical evidence for two parts of the Petrine tradition—the manner of the Apostle's death and his residence in Rome.

The manner, but not the place, of St. Peter's death is well known to be recorded by implication in the final chapter of St. John's Gospel (21: 18, 19), written towards the close of the first century. The writer recounts the prophecy made by Christ to the Apostle after the Resurrection—'When thou shalt be old thou shalt stretch out thy hands and another shall gird thee and carry thee whither thou wouldest not'; and he adds his own parenthetical comment—

'And this He said, signifying the manner of death by which he was to glorify God (σημαίνων ποίῳ θανάτῳ δοξάσει τὸν θεόν)'—a comment which implies that St. Peter's martyrdom by crucifixion, regarded by the writer as having fulfilled the prophecy, was a fact familiar to his readers. 'Stretch out the hands' was a recognized Roman phrase for crucifixion.[8] Obviously the comment, not the prophecy, was interpolated after the event.

For biblical evidence of St. Peter's presence in Rome we have to turn to the passage already mentioned (p. 128), the earliest in our series of early-Christian documents, 1 Peter 5: 13. That St. Peter was in fact the author of this letter is agreed by all Catholic, and by the majority of modern Protestant, scholars. The case for the document's authenticity is set out, for instance, by the Dean of Winchester, the Very Rev. E. G. Selwyn, in the introduction (p. 7 ff.) to his *The First Epistle of St. Peter* (1946); and another recent Protestant writer, Oscar Cullmann, while leaving the actual authorship of St. Peter as an open question, accepts the epistle, in his *Peter: Disciple— Apostle—Martyr* (1953, p. 82 ff.), as a very early document, written at least by one who was acquainted with the Apostle and his movements. That 'Babylon' in the final salutation—'The Church in Babylon greets you (ἀσπάζεται ὑμᾶς ἡ ἐν Βαβυλῶνι συνεκλεκτή)' — is equivalent to 'Rome' was almost universally held until the Reformation; and in modern times this interpretation is accepted, not only by Catholic commentators, but by the great bulk of Protestant scholars, including the two just cited. That the Mesopotamian Babylon was intended is extremely unlikely. We know from Josephus (*Ant. Iud.*, xviii, 9) that the Jewish community in Babylon (with which a Jewish-Christian group would have been classed) was virtually destroyed during the principate of Gaius; we have no knowledge of any Christian Church there in the first century; and St. Thomas is the only Apostle associated in later Christian tradition with those eastern regions. It is still less probable that St. Peter was writing from the Egyptian Babylon, a Roman military station mentioned by Strabo (xvii. 1, 30, 807) and Josephus (*op. cit.*, ii. 15, 1) and situated near the modern Cairo. On the other hand, we know from the canonical Apocalypse 17: 5, etc., from the Apocalypse of Baruch 11: 1 (ed. R. H. Charles, 1896, p. 18; ed. R. Graffin, *Patrologia Syriaca*, i, 2, 1907, cols. 1084–5), and from the Sybilline Oracles, v, 159 (ed. J. Geffcken, 1902, pp. 111–12) that 'Babylon' was an early-Christian and Jewish *soubriquet* for 'Rome'. Historical considerations do, in fact, all point to the strong probability that St. Peter's first epistle was written in Rome, either at his own dictation to a secretary, or by someone using his name to convey his teaching and message from Rome to the Christians of Asia Minor; and that the Apostle was therefore in the city during the early sixties.[9]

To sum up, we may say that the passages, which we have been reviewing, indicate, if not by completely explicit statement, at least by their implications and the natural inferences to be drawn from them, that all the essential points in those parts of the Petrine tradition which concern us here were known to the Christian world of the late-first and second centuries. These passages occur in documents which are now generally agreed to be genuine and trustworthy records of the period. It may be doubted whether the date, authorship, and reliability of the documents would ever have been called into question were it not for the bearing which they have upon the controversial issue of St. Peter's residence and martyrdom in Rome; and if the passages are indeed authentic and are to be accepted in the sense which they seem most naturally to bear, the onus of proof rests squarely on those who claim that the whole Petrine tradition was an invention of the Roman Church at some date before the middle of the second century. The evidence of these texts, taken in conjunction with the new discovery of the mid-second-century Vatican shrine and with the absence of any rival tradition, justifies us in accepting the Roman tradition as being far more likely to be factual than legendary; and it offers a legitimate basis for discussing, without *petitio principii*, the archaeological problem of where on the outskirts of Rome the two Apostles could have been buried.

NOTES

1. The Waldenses, the first Protestants, who would accept nothing that was not explicitly stated in the Scriptures, seem to have been the first to query the Roman Petrine tradition, possibly as early as the twelfth century. In 1326 it was again questioned by Marsilius of Padua. *Cf.* O. Cullmann, *Peter: Disciple—Apostle—Martyr*, 1953, pp. 71–2.

2. *E.g.* E. G. Selwyn, *The First Epistle of St. Peter*, 1946, p. 56 ff.

2a. See also Josi, Appendix C, p. 267.

3. The infant Church was obviously surrounded by a hostile world, by a hostile Jewish world in particular; and it has been suggested to one of the present

writers by Miss E. M. Chrystal (Fellow and Director of Studies in Theology at Newnham College, Cambridge) that the absence of any mention of St. Peter in the Pauline salutations to and from Rome may have been due to security-reasons. It might well have been held prudent to keep the whereabouts of this Jewish-Christian leader secret.

4. H. Grégoire, *Les persécutions dans l'empire romain*, 1951, p. 102 ff., assigns Ignatius's letters to the time of Marcus Aurelius.

5. *E.g.* by J. B. Lightfoot, *The Apostolic Fathers*, Part I, *S. Clement of Rome*, Vol. i, 1890; R. Knopf in H. Lietzmann's *Handbuch zum Neuen Testament*, Ergänzungs-Band: *Die Apostolischen Väter*, i, 1920; K. Bihlmeyer, *Die Apostolischen Väter*, Teil i, 1924; J. A. Kleist, *The Epistles of St. Clement of Rome and St. Ignatius of Antioch*, 1946. The letter is actually written, not in Clement's own name, but in that of the Roman Church. Yet there would seem to be no valid reason for doubting the ancient tradition that Clement did, in fact, send it. In his letter to Pope Soter, written *c.* 170, Dionysius of Corinth stated that 'Clement's letter' to Corinth was read aloud in the Corinthian Church on Sundays (Eusebius, *HE*, iv. 23); and Irenaeus, bishop of Lyons, gave an account, *c.* 180, of the contents of this very letter and described it as having been sent 'under Clement' (*Adv. Haer.*, iii, 3, 3 = Migne, *Patrologia Graeca*, cols. 849–50).

6. That οὕτω should be taken, not with μαρτυρήσας ('having thus borne his witness'), but with ἐπορεύθη ('and so, having borne his witness, he went') in St. Peter's case is clear from the parallel passage referring to St. Paul, where οὕτως goes with ἀπηλλάγη and ἐπορεύθη ('and having borne his witness, so he departed . . . and went').

7. *Journal of Roman Studies*, x, 1920, pp. 52–3.

8. *E.g.* Plautus, *Miles Gloriosus*, ii. 4, 359–60: credo ego istoc exemplo tibi esse pereundum extra portam/dispessis manibus, patibulum quom habebis.

9. P. 128 and Note 2.

6

THE PRE-CONSTANTINIAN SHRINE*

(Figs. 8, 9)

(a) The Mid-second-century Shrine and its Antecedents

WHEN Constantine built his great church over a part of the Vatican cemetery, the factor that limited his choice of site and compelled him to build on ground that presented very serious difficulties, both moral and material, was the presence within the cemetery of a structure which, at all costs, had to appear at a particular point within the finished building. The precise character of that structure, its purpose, what went before it, and what was its history during the century and a half between its construction and its incorporation within Constantine's church—all these are matters that may be discussed. But the fact of its existence immediately beneath the high altar of the present church has been established beyond question; and although there are earlier features underlying it, it forms the obvious point of departure for any discussion of the whole complex sequence of remains revealed by the recent excavations.

There are two reasons in particular why these remains should be difficult to interpret. The one is Constantine's choice of this particular spot to be the focal-point of his church, in elevation as well as in plan. In order that the structure of the earlier shrine might stand up above the pavement of the church immediately in front of the apse, the level of that pavement had to be fixed at a height that involved the demolition of all the immediately adjoining buildings; only to the south and east did the slope of the ground preserve the lower part of the standing walls, whereas any buildings that there may once have been to the north or west, beyond the immediate periphery of the shrine, were destroyed, foundations and all. The

* In referring to the graves that immediately surround the shrine the writers have used for convenience, the letters of the Greek alphabet assigned to them by the excavators (*cf.* Note 6).

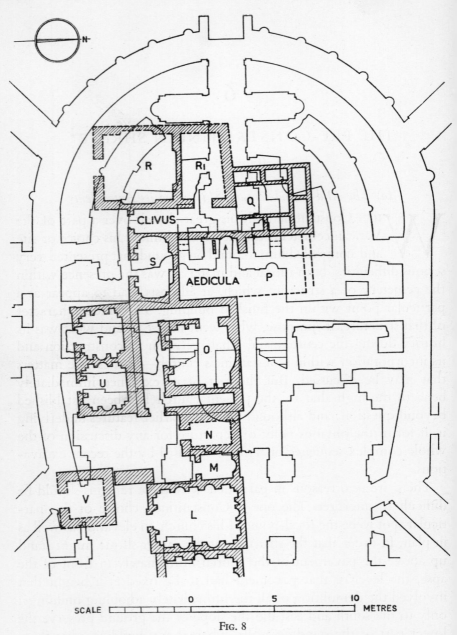

Fig. 8

The western part of the classical cemetery, shown in relation to the structures of the lower church.

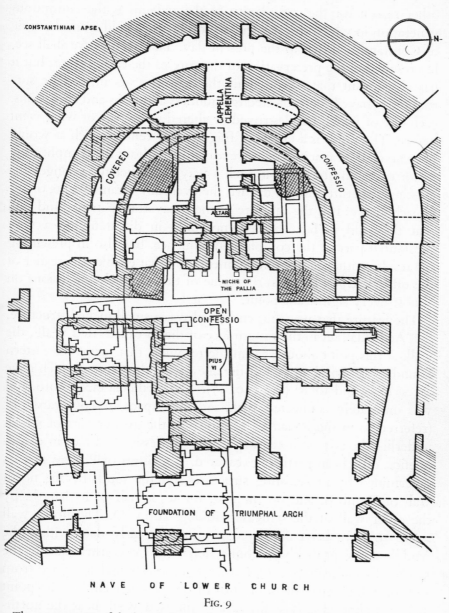

FIG. 9

The western part of the lower church, shown in relation to the tombs of the classical cemetery. The areas of cross-hatching represent the foundations of Bernini's canopy.

other reason for the complexity of the remains is the continuous veneration in which this particular spot has been held from the time of Constantine down to the present day. That fact, as we shall see, has resulted in the preservation of the core of the early shrine; but it has also meant that, throughout the centuries, its immediate surroundings have been subjected to countless additions and alterations, each one of which has destroyed or altered some part of what went before. The result is a tangle of fragmentary remains such as would have taxed the capacities of any excavator, without the complicating factor of having to work in such a way as neither to endanger the existing structures nor to disturb the everyday arrangements of the church above. It is the measure of the excavators' patience and skill that they did in fact succeed, not only in disentangling a very substantial part of the complicated sequence, but also in presenting the results with a clarity of documentation that enables the reader of the official *Report* to assess the value of the authors' conclusions on almost every significant point.[1]

The feature that was thus enshrined was a small niched structure, the 'Aedicula', set in the eastern face of the so-called 'Red Wall', the wall, at this point about 45 centimetres wide, that forms the eastern boundary of Tomb Q and of the alley-way, the Clivus, which gave access to Q and to R[1] (Figs. 10, 17). The Aedicula faced onto, and was intimately connected with, an open space or courtyard, 'P' (referred to in the *Report* as 'Campo P'), the greater part of which underlies the sixteenth-century Open Confessio, and has, in consequence, only been partially excavated. The limits of P were in part determined by pre-existing structures, on the south by the north wall of Tomb S, and on the east, for some half of its length, by the outer wall of the staircase flanking Tomb O. The north wall seems to have been destroyed at quite an early date within the Middle Ages, probably in connection with the construction of the Covered Confessio (p. 216), but its position can be determined from the surviving traces of the return of the plaster facing at the point where it abutted against the face of the Red Wall, near the northeast angle of Tomb Q. The northern part of the east wall has not been traced; but it is a reasonable assumption that it was carried northwards from the north-west angle of O, delimiting a roughly rectangular area, a little more than 7 metres from north to south by nearly 4 metres from east to west. The entrance to this area, which

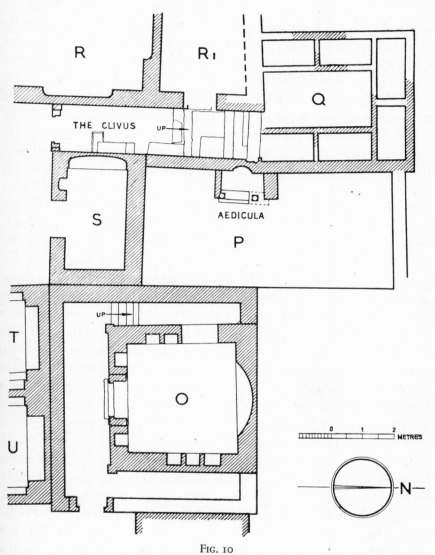

FIG. 10

The second-century shrine and the adjoining tombs.

was open to the sky and does not seem at first to have had any formal paving, must have been either from the north or, rather more probably, in view of the lie of the ground, from the east, behind and above Tomb O; how steep the slope was can be gauged from the fact that the floor of P and of the Aedicula, which was almost exactly level with that of the tessellated pavement of Q, was over 3 metres above that of O (Fig. 13).[2]

The Aedicula stood facing onto this open courtyard, P, at a point near the middle of the west wall, where a slight projecting bend in this wall marks the junction between the Clivus and Tomb Q. It consisted essentially of three superimposed niches cut or recessed into the body of the Red Wall, and of certain other features, now much damaged, which projected forward from the face of the wall to frame the upper two niches, the only two that were visible above ground (Figs. 15, 16, 17). The lowest niche, N^1, was below pavement-level, and it appears to have been cut roughly out of the foundations of the Red Wall when these were already complete, and when the part of them that backed onto Tomb Q had already received a thick waterproof coating, designed to protect the tomb-recesses within from the infiltration of damp. The upper two niches, on the other hand, N^2 and N^3, were constructed at the same time as the wall into which they are recessed. Both are now so fragmentary, and their remains so boxed about by other venerable structures (N^2 by the 'Niche of the Pallia' (p. 223), which bites rather more deeply into the Red Wall, destroying such of the curved surface of N^2 as was not already buried below floor-level; N^3 by the early-medieval high altar (p. 219) and by its twelfth-century successor) that a number of points of detail are uncertain; but, by opening up the Red Wall from the back, *i.e.* from the Cappella Clementina, the excavators were able to examine closely the structure of the surviving northern shoulder of the lower niche, N^2, and in their considered opinion the brick-work of the angle was not a later addition to the Red Wall, but was built with it; and they further state that the travertine slab separating N^2 from N^3 (p. 141) was similarly an original feature, not a later addition. Unless we are to dispute this clear and factual account,[3] it would seem, therefore, to have been proved that the niche below ground, N^1, was in some sense an afterthought, cut out of the already existing structure of the foundations of the Red Wall; but that the two niches above ground, N^2 and N^3, were built as an integral part of the wall that rested on these foundations and that they were contemporary with it. Since it is clearly established that the Red Wall, although a relatively late feature within the sequence of tombs in this part of the cemetery, can have been built very little, if at all, after the death of Antoninus Pius in 161 (p. 32), the construction of the Aedicula can be dated with considerable confidence to the period c. 160, or to the years immediately following.

N² was 1·40 metres high and 0·72 metres wide; and, although somewhat irregular in shape, it was carefully built. N³ was wider, about 1·12 metres, and it was separated from N² by a travertine slab, 11 centimetres thick,[4] of which the two broken ends (t¹ and t²) survive in position, embedded in (and of one build with) the Red Wall, at a level that corresponds approximately with the shoulders of the semi-dome of the later Niche of the Pallia (p. 223). This slab projected about 1 metre forward from the face of the Red Wall, and at the two outer angles it rested on a pair of marble colonnettes (the shaft and base of one of these were found still in their original position; both capitals have gone, and the northern colonnette was moved in Antiquity, p. 163), which stood in turn on a threshold-like travertine slab, approximately at the level of the floor of P. The upper part of N³, and any superstructure that the Aedicula may once have had, were destroyed by the builders of the early-medieval high altar (the horizontal layer of tiles shown in the accompanying illustrations belongs probably to this later period, not to the original structure), and the only other surviving feature of note is a small, rectangular, window-like opening (later blocked) in the middle of the back-wall of N³, a puzzling feature for which no really satisfactory explanation has yet been put forward.

Discussion of the purpose and meaning of the Aedicula must be deferred until we have given some account of the remains of whatever preceded it on the same site. For its finished appearance in Antiquity we are dependent on conjecture. The excavators have very wisely kept such conjecture to a minimum, restoring only a simple pediment above N³ and shallow flanking pilasters to carry it. It may well in fact have been more elaborate. It would have been very natural to have treated this niche as the niches of the majority of the tombs of the Vatican cemetery are treated, with a projecting pediment carried on free-standing stucco colonnettes over an arched recess (Fig. 17). Such a treatment would have been more satisfying

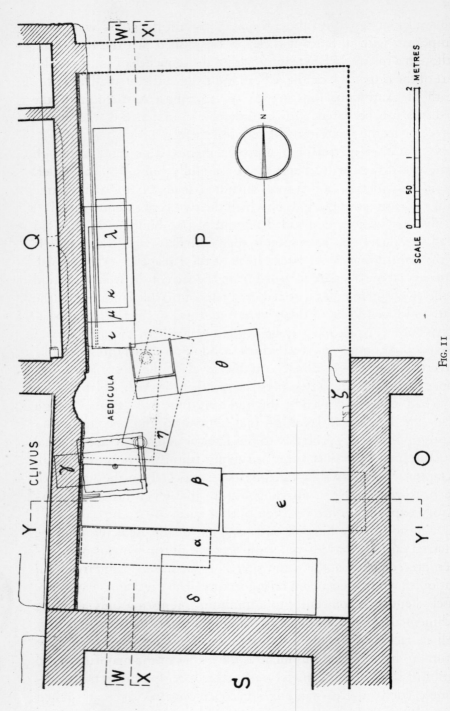

FIG. 11

Plan, below pavement-level, of the pre-Constantinian shrine and of the underlying graves. W–W¹, X–X¹ and Y–Y¹ indicate the approximate

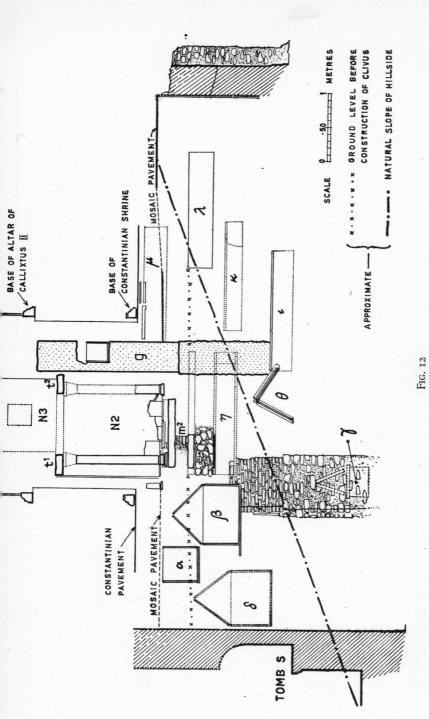

FIG. 12

South-north cross-section (X–X¹) of the pre-Constantinian shrine and of the underlying graves. Note that the earlier levels (which are schematic) apply only to this section-line, since the original hillside also sloped sharply upwards from the east to the west (*cf.* Fig. 13). Five of the graves shown (δ, ι, κ, λ, μ) lie just off the section-line. For the slope of the natural hillside, see p. 183, Note 9.

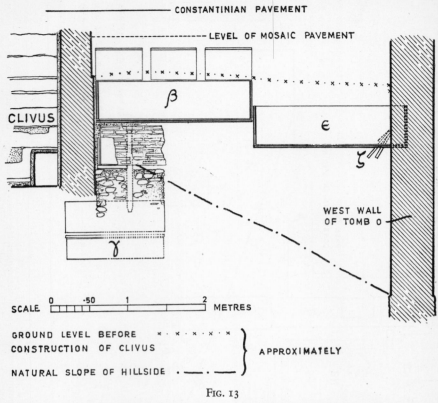

FIG. 13

West–east cross-section (Y–Y¹) of the graves immediately underlying the pre-Constantinian shrine. Note that the surface of the original hillside also sloped sharply upwards
from south to north (*cf.* Fig. 12). Grave ζ, which is included to show the relative depth,
lies over a metre to the north of the section-line. For the slope of the natural hillside,
see p. 183, Note 9.

aesthetically, and it would have been thoroughly in keeping with
what we know of contemporary architecture. It remains, however,
a matter of pure conjecture; and it is upon what actually survives
that the nature and purpose of the Aedicula must be judged.

When the Red Wall, and with it the Aedicula, was built, at a date
which can be determined approximately as between A.D. 160 and
170 (p. 32), the site already had quite a long history behind it. How
long, and of what exactly that history consisted, are matters that
have to be established on the basis of the facts revealed by the
excavations; and since their interpretation depends not merely upon
the nature of the remains uncovered, but also, and essentially, upon
the relation of these remains one to another, it will be necessary to

describe them in some detail before attempting any interpretation of the whole complex picture.

The essential fact that has emerged from the excavations is that, for some considerable time before the establishment of the Aedicula and of its accompanying courtyard P, this part of the Vatican cemetery had been in use as a graveyard for burials of an altogether simpler and less costly type than those described in chapters 1 to 4. Unlike the big family-mausolea, these early graves were simple in-humations, single bodies or small groups of bodies, each occupying little more than the space needed for an extended burial and marked at the surface (we may presume, although the markers have not survived) by some headstone or similar monument. Graves of this sort, the poor man's version of the inhumation-recess in the mauso-leum of a well-to-do family, are a regular feature of the larger Roman cemeteries (one can see them best at Isola Sacra);[5] and although they have no place in the wealthier, more closely built-up parts of one of these cities of the dead, there are indications that the builders of at least one of the large mausolea of the Vatican cemetery, Z (p. 53), came upon similar scattered burials, dating from an earlier, less en-cumbered phase in the development of the cemetery, and had to make special arrangements to deal with the bodies found therein. Except for the fact that at this early date cremation was the rule and inhumation the exception, these early burials on the site of the Aedicula and of P are what one might expect to find on excavating any early-imperial Roman roadside cemetery.

The earliest of these graves, Grave γ,[6] is also the most elaborate (Figs. 11–13). It is a child's tomb, of which the foot underlies the foundations of the Red Wall and the head projects into P, on an alignment that is slightly north of east and somewhat oblique to that of the Red Wall and of the other related structures. The terra-cotta coffin was protected above by pairs of large flat tiles, laid gable-wise, and for some two-thirds of its length, towards the head, it was en-cased within a rectangular mass of masonry, which housed a vertical tube for the pouring of libations to the dead beneath. The upper part of this masonry mass, which was faced in brick as a basis for marble veneer and was originally visible above ground, rises just in front of the foundations of the Red Wall, immediately to the south of, and overlapped by, the Aedicula, and it has been truncated by later burials. When it was built, the ground-level, marked by a change of build and by a well-defined foundation-offset, was about 1·25 metres below that indicated by the foundation-offset on the east side of the Red Wall, and nearly 1·70 metres below that of the floor of P and of the Aedicula.

Very little, if at all, later than Grave γ is another grave, θ, which lies slightly to the north and east of it, on the same slightly oblique alignment (Figs. 11, 12). This was a very simple burial, of a type familiar from the poorer graves at Isola Sacra, in which the body was laid in the bare earth, protected only by pairs of large flat tiles and of flanged roof-tiles, set gable-wise over it. The crown of the protecting gable is some 1·30 metres below the floor of P and about 40 centimetres above the offset footing of Grave γ; and if we allow for the relative position of the two tombs in relation to the steep north-west-to-south-east slope of the ground, and assume that the protecting tiles were, at any rate, lightly covered with earth, the two graves would appear to have been dug at approximately the same phase in the development of the site, before any substantial amount of earth had been dumped on the natural surface of the hillside. One of the tiles of Grave θ bears a maker's stamp, from which we learn the important fact that it cannot be earlier (but could, in certain circumstances, be later) than approximately the reign of Vespasian (A.D. 69–79).[7]

Later again than either γ or θ, but still earlier than the Aedicula, is another grave, η, which ran at an angle oblique both to the Red Wall and to the two earlier graves, across the west end of θ and the north-east corner of the superstructure of γ (Figs. 11, 12). The north end of this grave was destroyed in Antiquity, but the excavators found the south end still in position, and this shows that the coffin consisted of a chest, built up of tiles, which was protected above by a layer of mortared brick and rubble and the whole covered by a marble slab. The top of this marble slab, which presumably marks the surface-level at the moment when this grave was dug, is barely 20 centimetres below the bottom of the travertine sill of the Aedicula, which thus rested almost directly upon it.

Two other early graves require brief mention. The one is a poor burial, ζ (Figs. 11, 13), of the same general type as Grave θ, but built up against, and therefore later than, the west wall of Tomb O; from its position relative to O and S and to the other graves, it must belong to approximately the same phase of the development of the site as η.

The other, Grave ι, lies up against the east face of the foundations of the Red Wall, immediately to the north of the Aedicula. The burial, which is unusually deep (about 1·50 metres below the floor of P), seems to have been made while the Red Wall was actually building, since the flat tiles that cover it rest against the wall-face and are sealed in place by its waterproof rendering (Figs. 11, 12).[8]

The date and significance of these early tombs has been much discussed, and such discussion has almost inevitably been coloured by the very different views that may be taken of their relation to the Aedicula and of the significance of the Aedicula itself. It may be useful therefore, at this point, to ask how one would have interpreted the evidence afforded by these early tombs had it been presented in another context, without the troublesome connotations introduced by the building of the Aedicula and by the later development of the site.

In the first place, it is quite clear that the whole character of the site was determined by the configuration of the ground. The natural slope of the Vatican hillside was far steeper here than at any other point within the excavated area, with a two-fold slope—eastwards towards the re-entrant gully that was later to serve as an alley-way between Tombs L and N, until it was closed by the building of M (p. 34), and southwards towards the main valley up which ran the Via Cornelia. It was into the curving face of this slope that the earliest graves were dug (the oblique alignment of γ and θ probably reflects the natural lie of the ground); and it was into the same slope that the several mausolea had to be trenched and terraced, an operation which must have involved the cutting and dumping of large quantities of earth. We can in fact see the scar of one such dump against the west face of Tomb T (p. 34); and it is assuredly to another such operation, and not to the gradual accumulation of earth washed down the slope by winter rains, that we must attribute the raising of the ground immediately to the west of Tomb O and to the north of Tomb S to a level of over 2 metres above that within the tombs themselves. This raising of the level within what was to become P took place after the building of Tombs O and S, but before the building of the Red Wall, and therefore of Tomb Q; that is to say, at some date between approximately the years 140 and 160; whereas, of the graves, it is clear that γ and θ were dug from the original surface, η and ζ from the new, raised surface.[9]

This interpretation of the relation between graves and mausolea and, in particular, the interpretation of the difference in levels between Graves γ and θ, on the one hand, and Grave η, on the other, as the result of a single man-made deposit, rather than (as is often assumed) of the gradual accumulation of soil through natural agencies, is of great importance when we try to assign a date to the individual graves. Once even the possibility of such an interpretation is admitted, it becomes impossible to argue, with the excavators, that Graves γ and θ *must* be very much earlier than the building of the Red Wall and of P. They *may* very well be so; but all that the stratigraphic evidence proves is that they are certainly earlier than the middle of the second century and, in the case of θ, later than the date of the early-Flavian tile used in it.

Another fact of importance for the interpretation of these early graves is that they are all inhumations. This does not, in itself, prove that they were Christian; indeed, one of them, γ, is almost certainly not.[10] But as late as the beginning of the second century, as one can see from the mausolea of the Vatican cemetery, cremation was still the normal rite in Rome; and the absence of cremations from this corner of the cemetery may reasonably be interpreted as an indication that, like the original owners of Tomb Z (p. 55), the persons buried here were influenced by some special beliefs, which affected their burial-customs. There is nothing to prove that the occupants of Graves η, θ, and ζ were not pagans; but in view of the later history of the site, after the middle of the second century, there is much to be said for the suggestion that some or all of them may have been Christians. That the builders of the adjoining Tomb Q were Christians, as has been suggested (Appendix B, p. 265), is more doubtful. Apart from the fact that it contains only inhumation-burials, there is nothing whatever to indicate the beliefs of its occupants; and, as Tomb Z (p. 55) reminds us, Christians and Jews were by no means unique in this respect in the second half of the second century. While admitting the possibility that Q may be Christian, it would be unwise, in default of more positive evidence, to base any arguments as to the nature and purpose of the Aedicula upon such a hypothesis.

We may summarize the conclusions of the preceding paragraphs as follows. There are four graves that certainly antedate the building of the Red Wall and of P, and of these two (γ and θ) may be as early

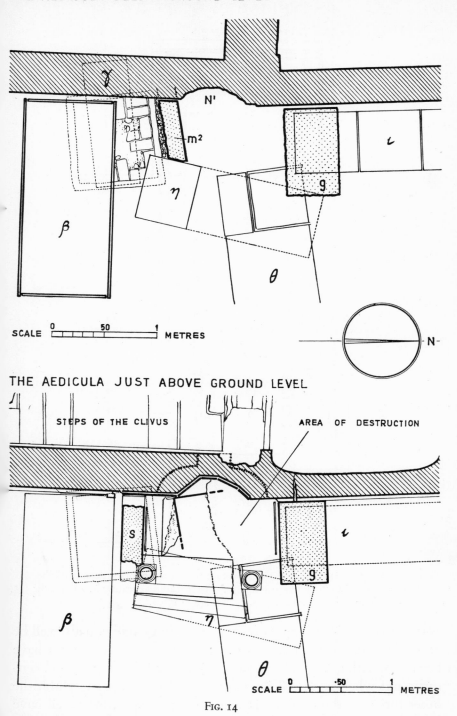

THE AEDICULA JUST ABOVE GROUND LEVEL

STEPS OF THE CLIVUS

AREA OF DESTRUCTION

SCALE 0   ·50   1   METRES

FIG. 14

The surviving pre-Constantinian remains of the Aedicula: (*above*) plan below ground level; (*below*) plan immediately above ground level (the outlines of the underlying graves are included for purposes of reference).

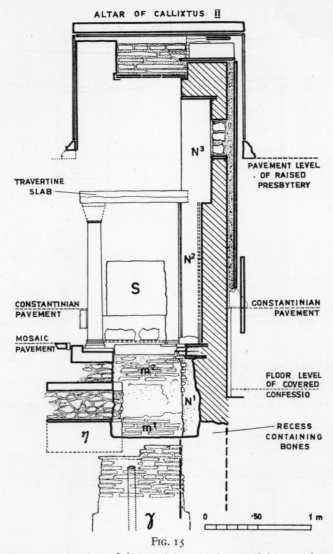

FIG. 15

East–west cross-section of the surviving pre-Constantinian remains of the Aedicula, shown in relation to some of the later features encasing it. All details of the Niche of the Pallia (*cf.* Figs. 23, 24) are omitted.

as the second half of the first century A.D., but could equally well be of any date down to about 140; the other two (η and ζ) must have been dug within a decade or two of the middle of the second century; and whereas one of the four (γ) is that of a pagan child, the other three are those of adults who, in the context, may well have been (but were not necessarily) Christians.

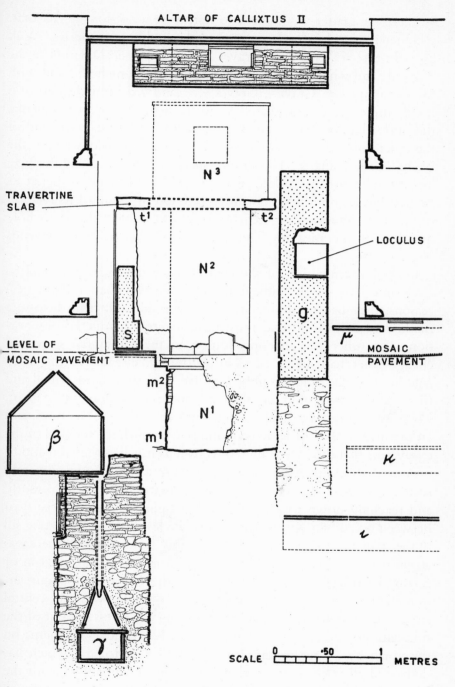

FIG. 16

As Fig. 15, but from south to north (W–W¹ in Fig. 11).

There the matter would have to rest, were it not for the fact that, whether by accident or by intention, the building of the Red Wall brought three of these early graves into close physical relation to the Aedicula and what lay beneath it. Together with niche N^1 and with the contemporary Grave ι, Graves γ, η, and θ delimit the site of a small empty space immediately beneath the centre of the Aedicula, the 'little chamber' that was discovered by H. Grisar at the end of the nineteenth century, in the course of his explorations below the Niche of the Pallia.[11] This empty space, whatever its significance, lies at the heart of what later was certainly the Petrine shrine, at its deepest level; and it is on our interpretation of it and of its relation to the early graves and to the later structures above it that the whole question of the meaning and purpose of the Aedicula depends (Figs. 14–16).

In their examination of the central space the excavators had to overcome two serious difficulties. The one was that, for practical reasons, they had to approach it from the side and from below, a method of excavation that must have severely hampered observation. The other was that in addition to the substantial structural changes that had taken place in Antiquity, already in the early Middle Ages the whole central area had been thoroughly rifled and the northern half of it smashed beyond recognition (pp. 226–9). These facts must be held to account for certain obscurities and ambiguities in the official Report; and it says much for the skill of the excavators that they were able to recover as much as they did and to present it so clearly. We have to envisage a small, approximately rectangular space, measuring about 1·20 metres from north to south, and reaching down to a level ('fondo originario' in the Report) of between 60 and 80 centimetres below the level of the travertine sill of the Aedicula; and below the floor of this 'little chamber' there was an unspecified depth of what the excavators describe as filled-in or accumulated earth ('terra di riporto' in the Report) containing innumerable coins of all ages and countries.[12] On the west, the central space was bounded by N^1, an irregular, curved recess cut out of the foundations of the Red Wall and obviously secondary to them; on the north by a later footing (that of Wall g, p. 162 ff.), which has destroyed all trace of any earlier feature in this direction, with the possible exception of a rough, slightly projecting core of masonry on the north flank of N^1, which is interpreted by the excavators as the stump of a destroyed retaining-wall that once delimited the central space on this side; on the east by what survives of the upper part of Grave η, with its protecting cover of masonry and its marble slab, and by a fill of disturbed earth where η has been destroyed; and on the south, by two small, superimposed retaining-walls, m^1 and m^2, of which the lower one, m^1, is cut by and is earlier than the foundations of the Red Wall, whereas m^2 is built up against, and is therefore structurally later than, the same foundations. Both were built up against a backing of earth on their south side; and on the exposed north face of m^1 there were sparse traces of what may have been a very fine, red-surfaced, white stucco. These two walls, m^1 and m^2, both follow the same oblique alignment as the two earliest graves, γ and θ;[13] and whereas m^2 is clearly a part of the same building as the superstructure of the Aedicula and owes its alignment to the fact of being built on m^1, it is evident that m^1 must in some way or another have been related to the early graves. The excavators interpret it as all that survives of a revetment that once ran round the four sides of what later became the central space, in order to protect whatever once occupied that space from the encroachment of the rising earth. An alternative explanation is that it served a similar purpose in respect of γ. Neither interpretation is altogether free of difficulties, and the surviving evidence is hardly sufficient to justify further discussion.

With the construction of the Aedicula we are on firmer ground. Despite the havoc wrought by the builders of Wall g and by later pilferers, enough remains to show that the central space was closed over, but (as the votive coins indicate) it was closed in such a way as to allow access from above.[14] Whether there was a removable lid or some form of fixed grating, we cannot say. But there are the remains of a substantial seating for a closure-slab built into the Red Wall along the south side of the central space (over m^2) and at the south-west angle; and it is a singular and significant fact that this seating is aligned, not on the axis of the Aedicula, but on that of the early graves and of m^1 and m^2. The difference, which is as much as 10 degrees, cannot possibly be accidental; and it shows that, in at least one important respect, the builders of the Aedicula were concerned to present a visible record of a state of affairs that had otherwise been altogether suppressed, even at the expense of the obvious requirements of monumental symmetry.

Finally, we have to note that at this point the bottom of the foundations of the Red Wall rises sharply, only to drop again to a deeper level along the east wall of Tomb Q.[15] At the same point, at the base of N¹ and at the level corresponding roughly with the floor of the central space, there is, in the top of the arched-up foundations, a fissure which forms a narrow recess reaching under and through the foundations of the Red Wall; and in the earth below, and at the back of, this recess the excavators found a number of reburied bones, which they state categorically to be human. For reasons that are by no means clear, no detailed report has yet been issued about these bones, and all the information that we have about them at present is the further statement by one of the excavators that a preliminary examination has shown them to be those of a person of advanced age and powerful physique; the sex, it seems, cannot be determined, and the skull is missing.[16] Meanwhile, it is obvious that, despite the absence of a scientific record, the implications of such a discovery made in such a place must be taken into account, however tentatively, in any critical discussion of this site (p. 158 ff.).

Such are the facts revealed by excavation, and it is in the light of these facts that we have to interpret the literary evidence for the death of St. Peter, for the disposal of his body, and for the history of what was later universally believed to be the site of his tomb.

That the Aedicula is none other than the 'trophy' (τρόπαιον) of St. Peter, seen on the Vatican Hill by the priest Gaius somewhere about the year 200 and cited by him as an object familiar to contemporary Roman Christians (p. 128 f.), seems to be accepted by all responsible scholars.[17] Whether, at this date and in such a context, the word τρόπαιον (literally, a monument of victory or triumph) indicated a burial-place, the tangible memorial of the Christian victory through martyrdom, or whether it could have been used more widely of any place in which the Apostle was commemorated, without necessarily implying an actual grave, is on the other hand disputed;[18] and in the present state of knowledge it would certainly be unwise to press the claims of either interpretation on purely philological grounds. That Eusebius believed Gaius to be speaking of a tomb-monument seems clear enough; and for our purposes it is sufficient to note that it is a natural, if not indeed the most natural, interpretation of the passage. The 'trophy' of St. Paul on the Via

Ostiensis (where is now the church of St. Paul's-without-the-Walls) certainly marks a spot other than that traditionally associated with his martyrdom, at Tre Fontane, over 2 kilometres distant; and the two 'trophies' are cited together as comparable to, and effectively counterbalancing, the tombs of Philip and of his daughters, which the Christians of Hierapolis in Asia Minor claimed to possess. In either case, whatever the precise meaning of the word τρόπαιον, it can hardly be doubted that the monument revealed by the excavations is the same as that seen by Gaius; and that to a Roman writing at the very end of the second century or in the early years of the third, it was the outstanding tangible memorial of St. Peter's mission and death in Rome.

Such a monument must have been built with the authority of one of the popes; and it is possible that the record of this fact is preserved in the *Liber Pontificalis*, which dates in its present form from the sixth century, but preserves a great deal of authentic earlier material. The statement that Pope Anacletus 'built and set in order a memorial-shrine to the blessed Peter, where the bishops might be buried' (*memoriam beati Petri construxit et composuit ubi episcopi reconderentur*)[19] can hardly be accepted as it stands, since Anacletus lived at the end of the first century and there is no trace of the construction of such a shrine at so early a date. It has, however, been pointed out that the name Anacletus could easily have been confused with that of Anicetus, the traditional dates of whose pontificate, *c.* 155–65, accord very well with the date, *c.* 150–70, suggested for the shrine by the archaeological evidence.[20] We cannot be sure, but the identification is plausible and fits the known facts.

What did the 'trophy' mark? One suggestion that has been put forward,[21] and one that deserves serious consideration, is that it stands on the site of the gardens of Nero and marks the reputed site of the Apostle's execution. The excavation has revealed no certain traces of a grave beneath the Aedicula; nor indeed can there be any certainty that St. Peter's body was ever recovered from the executioners for burial by the Christian community. In the normal course of events, the body of one who was an alien (*peregrinus*), and in the eyes of the law a common felon, might well have been hurled into the Tiber. If a special request for it had been lodged with the Roman authorities, it would have been legally recoverable; the action of Joseph of Arimathaea constitutes an obvious precedent. But under the conditions of the Neronian persecution, as described by Tacitus,[22] when 'admission' (presumably of adherence to the Church) was sufficient ground for arrest, it may reasonably be argued that such a request would have been altogether too dangerous to the petitioner; and that there would, moreover, not have been the same interest in the preservation of bodily relics at this early date as there was later, when belief in the imminent end of the world had faded and the cult of martyrs had begun to make its appearance. The possibility, therefore, that St. Peter's body was, in fact, not recovered for burial is a real one. But the evidence of Tacitus's narrative, with its highly coloured references to the 'vast multitude' (*multitudo ingens*) of believers and to their sufferings, can hardly be used to exclude the alternative possibility that, for example, some influential and well-placed sympathizer might have obtained the body from the executioners unofficially, without formal appeal to authority; and if so, the further possibility that the shrine on the Vatican Hill marks the real or reputed grave of the Apostle is one that has to be considered on its own merits.

The suggestion that the 'trophy' is a monument marking the traditional site of St. Peter's execution presents certain difficulties. The one is topographical. Tacitus tells us that for the torturing and death of the Christian victims of the persecution of 64, Nero offered his own gardens and gave a circus-spectacle, in which he himself took part in the dress of a charioteer (*Ann.*, xv. 44: *hortos suos ei spectaculo Nero obtulerat et circense ludicrum edebat*). It is not clear from Tacitus's words whether the entire spectacle was limited to the Circus, which lay within the gardens and must certainly have been the scene of most of the atrocities described, or whether any part of it was staged elsewhere within the gardens. The Circus itself certainly lay in the Vallis Vaticana, to the south of the public road, which would have been a very natural boundary to the whole estate; and, had the gardens in fact extended northwards, across this road, it is not easy to see how, as imperial property,[23] any part of them could have relapsed into the derelict condition suggested by such humble roadside burials as Graves γ, θ, and η: it is clear from the epitaph of Heracla (p. 9 f.) that the Circus, at any rate, was maintained as a place of public entertainment. It is far from certain, therefore, that any part of the spectacle can have taken place on the Vatican hillside, on the site occupied later by the Vatican cemetery. A more serious objection, however, to the identification of the 'trophy' as a memorial marking the site of St. Peter's crucifixion is the character of the monument itself. It is evident that to the builders of the Aedicula it was a matter of great importance to mark precisely that particular spot, and not one so much as 50 centimetres to the right or to the left. Not only did the form of the sealing-slab over the central space below ground draw attention to the exact location and orientation of that space, but the position of the whole monument within the Red Wall, at the junction of the Clivus and of Tomb Q, is so awkward that it can only have been due to a strong feeling that it had to mark this particular spot, and no other.[24] Such an insistence, in the face of practical difficulties, on a minutely exact location implies something far more tangible than a mere tradition that here, or hereabouts, was the scene of St. Peter's martyrdom; it assuredly implies that the Aedicula replaces something that stood here before, which (on this hypothesis) can only have been an earlier monument to the same event.

Is such an earlier monument, marking the site of execution, historically credible? Does it not attribute to the Christians of the late-first or early-second century an attitude of mind to the holy places of the Church (as distinct from the corporeal relics of its martyrs) that is hardly attested before the third century and does not seem to have taken monumental shape before the fourth? And, even if we accept the plausibility of such a monument at such a date, is there not good reason to doubt whether, lacking the sanction accorded by Roman law and sentiment to a grave, a memorial in honour of a condemned and executed member of a proscribed cult could have been put up and maintained in full view of a public highway; whether, as the cemetery developed around it, it would have been accorded the respect that was evidently accorded to the predecessor (whatever it may have been) of the Aedicula; or whether the second-century Christian community would have felt so strongly about its exact location as not to be prepared to shift the site of its successor the 50 odd centimetres necessary to built it against, rather than into, the Red Wall?[25]

A final objection to the hypothesis of a pre-existing monument marking the supposed place of St. Peter's execution is that it takes no account of what is surely the most singular feature of the remains revealed by the excavators, namely the difference between the relation of Niche N^1 to the foundations of the Red Wall and that of Niches N^2 and N^3 to the wall itself. That the Aedicula is an integral part of the upstanding structure of the Red Wall we cannot doubt; and yet the niche below ground, N^1, is evidently a structural after-thought, cut out of the foundations of the Red Wall after they had been built. Since it is physically impossible that N^1 should have been cut after the building of the Aedicula, this can only mean that there was a change of plan between the cutting and laying of the founda-tions and the building of the wall above; and, in view of the in-sistence of the builders of the Aedicula on marking this particular spot and no other, the reason for the change of plan can only be that the foundations had revealed something that was, in detail at any rate, unexpected. The simple and natural explanation of these facts is that that something was a body, which the Christian community of the time believed to be that of St. Peter; and that the arching-up of the foundations at this point (p. 154)[26] is due to the discovery of that body by the workmen engaged in digging the foundation-trench and their efforts to avoid disturbing it.

The body, if such it was, would have lain in the angle between the two earliest graves, γ and θ, with one end of the grave beneath the site of the Aedicula, the other end projecting beyond the line of the Red Wall. The burial must have been a very simple one to have left no material trace, probably no more than a trench in the bare earth covered by a few tiles; and, if so, it is more likely to have been later than, and to have conformed to, the far more substantial Grave γ, beside which it lay, than to have itself dictated the position and alignment of γ. On the other hand, its position in relation to γ and θ would most naturally suggest that it was earlier than the latter. In either case, it would have belonged to this early group of graves, dug before the raising of the ground-level in what was later to become P; and the actual grave would, therefore, have been at least a metre below surface-level at the time of the construction of the Red Wall. We do not know how such a grave would be marked. It is not impossible to imagine circumstances in which there would be no formal marker, or in which an original marker might have be-come displaced or buried. Alternatively, there may well have been some sort of gravestone or surface-monument; and it would have been a simple operation for anybody interested in the maintenance of the grave to have removed and replaced this at a new surface-level. By the time the Red Wall was built it is clear that all three graves lay well below surface-level; and although the builders of the Red Wall, whether by design or accident, contrived to avoid disturbing the buried superstructure of γ, it was only the depth of the actual terra-cotta coffin that saved that part of it which projected across the line of their foundations from interference. The same circumstances would have operated in the case of a body buried alongside it to the north, except that in this case, owing to the relative shallowness of the grave and the rise in the natural surface-level, the risk of disturbance would have been far greater.

That the Christian community of the mid-second century did in fact believe St. Peter to be buried in approximately this spot, and that the builders of the Red Wall, in trenching for their foundations, did hit upon one end of a deeply buried grave, which was promptly identified as that of St. Peter, is a hypothesis that would explain a great deal that is otherwise puzzling in the archaeological record. The proprietors of the Clivus and of Tomb Q would have been as anxious as the members of the Christian community to avoid the troublesome formalities (including an animal sacrifice) involved in moving the remains for reburial.[27] The workmen had already carried the foundations of the wall as far as possible over, rather than through, the grave, by leaving it as an 'island' of earth, on either side of which these foundations descended to a deeper level. Now, by agreement between the interested parties (if not, indeed, already by the workmen at the moment of discovery), that part of the skeleton which had already been disturbed by the initial trenching was hurriedly reburied in the same place, under the foundations of the wall (p. 154); and the original plan was modified to allow the incorporation of a funerary monument, the Aedicula, directly over what remained of the original grave.

This or any other attempt to reconstruct the fortunes of the skeleton to which the bones in the recess under the foundations of the wall belonged can only be provisional, pending an authoritative report stating the number of bones found, their nature, and the parts of the body from which they come (cf. Note 16). This is a fact that cannot be too strongly emphasized. Nevertheless, on the evidence at present available, it is difficult to see where these bones, assuming them to be human, can have come from if they did not come from a grave on the site of what later became the central space. The bones buried in Graves γ, θ, and ζ were found still in position;[28] and although Grave η was subsequently damaged and the bones within it dispersed (very probably in the ninth century, p. 228), it was certainly still intact when the Aedicula was built (the whole weight of the colonnettes and of the travertine sill rested on the marble covering-slab); and with the construction of the Aedicula there can have been no further access to the recess.

The hypothesis of a pre-existing grave does, in fact, account for a number of features that cannot easily be explained otherwise. It explains the sudden rise and fall of the foundations; it explains the difference between the relation of Niche N^1 to the foundations of the Red Wall and that of Niches N^2 and N^3 to the wall itself; and, above all, it explains the insistence of the Christian community on marking this exact spot and no other. It does not, of course, follow that because the builders of the Aedicula believed this to be the grave of St. Peter, the body so commemorated was necessarily that of the Apostle. All that the archaeological evidence permits us to say for certain is that any such burial must have taken place some time before the middle of the second century, possibly (but by no means certainly) as early as the first century; and that it would have stood in what, in the context, may reasonably be interpreted as a significant relationship to at least two other early inhumation-burials. These are the archaeologically established facts in the light of which we have to interpret the action of the Christian community in building the Aedicula where and how they did. On the one hand, it may be argued that there is serious doubt whether the Apostle's body was ever recovered for burial; and that, even if it were recovered and buried, it is unlikely that there would have remained, a century later, any very clear record of the place of its burial; a grave, and particularly a humble grave like this, could all too easily have dropped out of sight and memory. On the other hand, although one cannot absolutely exclude the 'invention' of an unnamed body, localizing a previously vague tradition of St. Peter's burial on the Vatican Hill, the actions of the builders of the Aedicula do seem clearly to imply something more precise; and, if St. Peter's body was in fact recovered for burial, there is no reason to suggest that its position would not have been marked in the usual Roman manner, any more than we are entitled to assume that the grave found by the builders of the Aedicula had no identifying feature over it. We may sum up

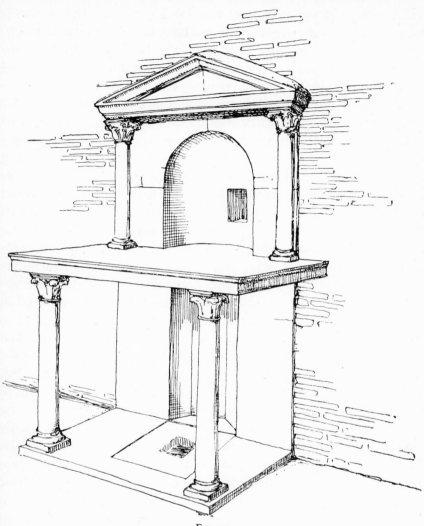

FIG. 17

Restored view of the second-century shrine (the Aedicula) as originally planned and built. The pediment, the round head to the upper niche, the upper pair of colonnettes, and the precise form of the opening in the sealing-slab are conjectural. (*Drawing by G. U. S. Corbett.*)

this discussion of the evidence revealed by the recent excavations as follows: although it is not certain that the Aedicula marks the site of an earlier grave, the hypothesis that it did so explains much that is otherwise obscure; and although there is nothing to prove that this grave was that of St. Peter, nothing in the archaeological evidence is inconsistent with such an identification.

In conclusion, we may note that, architecturally, the Aedicula belongs to a familiar category of niched funerary monuments (Fig. 17). Gabled niches of this sort were normally part of a larger tomb-structure, and as such are a commonplace of the funerary architecture of the first and second centuries that we meet in such cemeteries as those under San Sebastiano and at Isola Sacra, and in the Vatican cemetery itself. They could, however, on occasion be used independently. An example, which is instructive both for its resemblances to, and for its difference from, the Vatican Aedicula, is the Tomb of Sabinus Taurius at Isola Sacra.[29] This is a small grave-monument built up against an adjoining mausoleum, and consists of a pedimented, column-flanked niche, containing a representation of the dead boy standing at the open doors of his tomb, and below this a smaller recess, which held the ash-urn and was sealed by the commemorative inscription (Fig. 18). Architecturally, the main difference between the two monuments is in the character and development of the lower recess, and this is presumably to be explained in terms of the special function that the Vatican shrine was designed to fulfil. It would be wrong to attribute to the second century ideas that were not current until the third or fourth about the sanctity of the remains of martyrs and the veneration due to them. Nevertheless, it is evident, from the care that was taken to provide some form of access to the part below ground, that the Aedicula was something more in the eyes of its builders than a mere grave; and it is hardly surprising, therefore, that it should have contained unusual features. For the present, we can only guess at the purpose of such elements as the table-like slab separating the upper from the lower niche;[30] we must be content to note that they exist and that they do serve to distinguish this monument from more commonplace examples of contemporary funerary architecture.

(b) The Shrine from the Late-Second to the Early-Fourth Century

At some date which cannot have been very long after the initial construction of the Red Wall, this wall developed a serious crack near the south-east angle of Tomb Q, presumably as a result of the weakening of both wall and foundations by the incorporation of the Aedicula. To remedy this, it was found necessary to build against its eastern face a substantial buttressing-wall, g, 47 centimetres thick and projecting 85 centimetres into P, with foundations cutting right

FIG. 18

The Tomb of Sabinus Taurius at Isola Sacra. (*Drawing by G. U. S. Corbett.*)

down through the underlying levels to a depth of over a metre below the then surface;[31] and to make room for this buttress, the northern edge of the travertine slab of the Aedicula had to be cut back some 20 centimetres, and the northern colonnette shifted an equivalent distance southwards, breaking the symmetry of the original monument (Figs. 14, 15, 16,). The insertion of *g* must also have involved certain modifications to the sealing-slab dividing Niches N¹ and N², and in particular to its northern seating, but the later destruction of the greater part of the northern half of the monument

(p. 227) has destroyed all clear trace of this work. In partial compensation, the lower part of the Red Wall immediately adjoining the central niche on either side was now faced with slabs of white marble.

After the addition of the buttress, the Aedicula must have presented a very makeshift appearance, and it was presumably to remedy this that there was added on the south side of the niche a second projecting wall, S (Figs. 14, 15, 16), to balance the first. This second wall is only about 20 centimetres thick, and that it was added after g is clearly shown by the fact that, where it abuts on the Red Wall, it is built up against the added white-marble facing. To the same phase must belong the addition of a facing of grey marble to the inner faces of the two flanking walls (S and g) and to the curved face of Niche N^2, and the insertion of what was probably a low barrier or railing, running across the front of the monument at ground-level and slotted into the bases of the two supporting colonnettes. At this stage, too, the original, oblique orientation of the sealing-slab was adjusted to conform to the axis of the Red Wall; and with this change there disappeared from sight the last surface-indication of the phase that had preceded the building of the Red Wall and of the Aedicula.

Later again, the floor of courtyard P was paved with a tessellated paving of coarse, white-marble cubes, edged with a band of dark green (Figs. 12, 13). The level of this pavement, the first formal paving of the courtyard of which any trace survives (there is a substantial stretch still in position at the north-west corner of P, beneath the Constantinian pavement), was some 6 centimetres above that of the original floor, and, to match it, the original travertine threshold supporting the colonnettes of the Aedicula was capped with a marble slab. At some stage, probably but not certainly before the laying of the pavement, two burials, $\varkappa$ and λ, were made in terracotta coffins close against the Red Wall to the north of the Aedicula (Figs. 11, 12).

There are, thus, traces of at least three modifications to the original scheme of the Aedicula before the major rebuilding undertaken by Constantine. There is nothing to indicate the date of any of the changes, which could equally well have followed rapidly upon each other and upon the initial construction of the monument or have been spread over the century and a half between its construction and the building of the Basilica. They are not in themselves sufficient to furnish an answer to the question discussed in the following section (pp. 167–82), whether or not the body of St. Peter, or any part of it, was removed for safety to the Via Appia during the Valerianic persecution in A.D. 258. The space below the Aedicula was so damaged by later intruders that it is quite impossible to say exactly what it contained, and in what form; still less whether that something was at any time removed and later replaced. What is, however, quite evident is that, whatever at any particular moment the shrine may have contained, it was carefully and continuously maintained from the day it was built until Constantine gave it the central place in his great new Basilica.

The most telling evidence for this continuity of cult is that afforded by a series of *graffiti*, prayers and invocations scratched by visiting Christians on the plaster of the north face of the added buttressing-wall, *g*. These *graffiti*, which are so thick on the wall that in places there are two or three superimposed layers, await detailed publication; but their general character is already clear from the preliminary account given by the excavators in the pages of the *Report*.[32] With one exception they are in Latin, and they are not invocations of St. Peter, as probably in the Tomb of the Valerii (p. 14) and certainly under the church of San Sebastiano on the Via Appia (p. 171), but names or the simple prayers of pilgrims for the spiritual well-being of their relatives or friends, living or dead—LEONTA; SEVERA; VRSIANE; SIMPLICI VIVATE IN ✶; NICASI VIBAS IN ✶; VICTOR CVM SUI(S) GAVDENTIA VIBATIS IN ✶; IN ✶ VENEROSA VEA; VERVS BONI-FATIA VENEROSA VEA; these are typical examples.

The date of these *graffiti* is sufficiently indicated by the frequent use of the Chi-Rho monogram, ✶, used in its earlier form as an epigraphic abbreviation for the name of Christ rather than, as later, as an independent symbol, the badge of the triumphant Christian faith. They must have been cut within a decade or two of the turn of the third and fourth centuries, and they belong therefore to the latest phase of the Aedicula as an independent monument, before its incorporation within Constantine's church. The single exception to the group is a *graffito* that is not included in the official *Report*, but is referred to elsewhere by the individual excavators. It is written in Greek and is cut in the plaster of the Red Wall, and it seems that it is earlier than the rest and invokes the Apostle by name.[33]

These *graffiti* confirm (if indeed confirmation is needed, in view of Constantine's actions a few years later) that the shrine remained an object of veneration and a place of pilgrimage throughout the latter part of the third century and into the early years of the fourth. What, with a single and probably early exception, they strangely fail to do is to mention St. Peter by name. To conclude from this, in the face of all the other evidence, that the Aedicula was quite unconnected with St. Peter is as wrong-headed as, pending the study and full publication of the texts, any detailed conclusion is premature. Nor does the silence of these texts in itself afford conclusive proof that, at the time when they were scratched on the walls, St. Peter's body must have been elsewhere.[34] One may argue that invocations of a martyr by name are by no means the invariable rule, and that the object of veneration on the Vatican hillside was too well known to require specific mention.[35] Nevertheless, in an age when the cult of martyrs was daily growing in popularity, and in a medium that was so essentially personal, the absence of any specific allusion to St. Peter is an unexpected fact, and it is one that has to be taken into account in any discussion of the relationship between the Vatican shrine and the late-third-century shrine of St. Peter and St. Paul on the Via Appia.

There is one feature of the later history of the Aedicula for which no satisfactory explanation has been put forward.[36] This is a *loculus*, or box-like receptacle, made up of thin slabs of marble let into the northern face of the buttressing-wall, *g*, about 80 centimetres above ground-level (Fig. 16). It is later than the *graffiti*, which it cuts through, but earlier than the Constantinian shrine, by the north wall of which it was sealed into place; and when found it had already been rifled and contained only a few scraps of metal (including a medieval coin minted at Limoges), traces of organic matter, and some fragments of bone mixed with earth. The suggestion[37] that this *loculus* was cut by Constantine to receive the relics of St. Peter, retranslated to the Vatican after a temporary sojourn beside the Via Appia, disregards the cardinal fact that the focus of Constantine's shrine remained exactly what it had been before—the centre of the Aedicula. Even if we assume that he had, in fact, to retranslate the relics, it is inconceivable that he would have placed them anywhere but at the central point of the shrine itself, which was at the same time the central point of the whole great Basilica built around it. About the *loculus*, we must be content to say that it must have been cut to contain some object which the builders of the Constantinian shrine wished to preserve, in perpetuity, in close association with the remains of St. Peter. What that object was we shall probably never know.

(c) The Cult-centre of St. Peter and St. Paul beneath the Church of San Sebastiano by the Via Appia

No discussion of the Vatican shrine and of the early history of the remains of St. Peter would be complete without some reference to two other early shrines, that of St. Paul, about a mile outside the walls of Rome, beside the Via Ostiensis, and that in which St. Peter and St. Paul were jointly commemorated, near the third milestone of the Via Appia, on the site of what later became the Church of San Sebastiano.

Of these, the former is still covered by the Church of St. Paul's-without-the-Walls, and there is not much that we can say for certain about its early history. All that we do know suggests that this was closely analogous to that of the Vatican shrine. What the second-century Christian community rightly or wrongly believed to be the grave of St. Paul lay near, but not actually on, the traditional scene of the martyrdom (at Tre Fontane, 2 kilometres to the south), within a busy roadside cemetery. A line of tombs belonging to this cemetery has been excavated just to the north of the church;[38] and although no scientific excavation has ever taken place within the church, there is a well-authenticated record of the discovery in the middle of the nineteenth century of walls built in characteristic late-first-century or early-second-century masonry, immediately adjoining the traditional site of the Apostle's grave, beneath the high altar; and these walls must, in the context, almost certainly have belonged to similar tombs.[39] At the end of the second century the site was marked by a 'trophy', of which Gaius speaks in terms identical with those used of the 'trophy' of St. Peter on the Vatican Hill (p. 128); and, with the triumph of Constantine, it became, like St. Peter's, the site of a monumental church in honour of the Apostle.[40] For reasons that are probably rightly explained as primarily practical and topographical in character, the Constantinian church was small by comparison with its sister foundation; and some fifty years later it was replaced by the new, and far larger, church which still stands on the site, and which, despite the ravages of earthquake, fire, and man, is still one of the most impressive monuments that have come down to us from Roman Antiquity.[41]

The earliest visible feature is a slab, inscribed *Paulo apostolo mart(yri)* and pierced by a vertical shaft. This slab beneath the high altar presumably corresponds in function to the slab which from the fourth century onwards sealed the deepest levels of the Petrine shrine (p. 202 f.);[42] but, with the example of St. Peter's before us, we can be sure that, without full and scientifically conducted excavation, we lack the essential basis for detailed speculation about whatever went before. For the present we must be content to note that there was this important shrine of St. Paul beside the Via Ostiensis, and that, if we allow for the divergences imposed by the differing natures of the two sites, it seems to have undergone much the same stages of development as the sister-shrine on the Vatican Hill. Its excavation could hardly fail to throw light upon some of the dark places in the early history of St. Peter's.

With the shrine of St. Peter and St. Paul on the Via Appia we are on firmer ground. The literary record is scanty and confused; but the site has been thoroughly excavated, and it is not so much the facts that are in dispute as their interpretation; and since, despite all the obscurities, it is quite certain that the history of this shrine is, in some way or another, intimately connected with that of St. Peter on the Vatican Hill, we are bound to give some account of the much-debated problem whether, at any stage between their martyrdom and the establishment of their respective churches by Constantine, the bodies of St. Peter and St. Paul found a temporary home *ad Catacumbas*,[43] on the site of what is now the Church of San Sebastiano.[44]

The literary record is tantalizingly vague. We have the well-known opening lines of the metrical inscription of Pope Damasus (366–84), which was seen near the site and recorded by a seventh-century pilgrim:

> *hic habitasse prius sanctos cognoscere debes*
> *nomina quisque Petri pariter Paulique requiris*

('Here you should know that the saints once dwelt, you who are seeking the names of both Peter and Paul').[45] But whether it was in life or after death that the Apostles 'dwelt' there is not made clear. That the feast of St. Peter and St. Paul (29 June) was celebrated in the

ourth century on the Via Appia, as well as on the Vatican and by the
Via Ostiensis, we know from a variety of sources, including the
hymn of St. Ambrose in honour of the two Apostles:

> *trinis celebratur viis*
> *festum sacrorum martyrum.*[46]

But it is not until the sixth century that we get a clear statement of
what was then believed to be the reason for the duplication of
shrines in the case of each Apostle. Gregory the Great, writing to the
Byzantine Empress Constantina, records a tradition, current in his
day, that the bodies of the Apostles received temporary burial *ad
Catacumbas* 'at the actual time of their martyrdom' (*eo tempore quo
passi sunt*), before being transferred to their permanent resting-places
on the Vatican and by the Via Ostiensis;[47] and it is presumably to
the same period, shortly after their martyrdom, that we should refer
the statement in the *Liber Pontificalis* that their bodies were taken to
the Vatican and the Ostian Way from the Catacombs.[48] No doubt
their graves were already being shown there to pilgrims, as we find
them a century later in the Salzburg 'Pilgrim's Itinerary': 'Next you
will proceed along the Via Appia to Saint Sebastian the martyr,
whose body lies in the crypt. There, too, are the tombs of the
Apostles Peter and Paul, where they lay for forty years; and at the
west end of the church you go down by steps to where Saint
Quirinus, pope and martyr, rests.'[49]

This tradition may go back to a much earlier date. It was, however, not the only story current in Antiquity; and by the sixth century the Church had rationalized too much of what was obscure in
her earlier history for us to place over-much reliance on such testimony. In earlier documents we find a mention of the shrine in
association with the year 258 (*Tusco et Basso consulibus*, in Roman
reckoning). This association first appears in a corrupt entry in the
'Chronograph of 354' or 'Calendar of Philocalus', the Christian
supplement to which incorporates two lists, the *Depositio Martyrum*
and the *Depositio Episcoporum*, which must have been compiled, with
a greater or lesser degree of editing, from the traditional records of
the early Church.[50] The entry makes nonsense as it stands: *III Kal.
Iul.* (= 29 June) *Petri in Catacumbas et Pauli Ostense*; and on the
analogy of the fuller, although still not entirely satisfactory, entry
in the so-called Hieronymian Martyrology, which dates from the

early-fifth century and must derive from some closely related source, it is usually emended to read *III Kal. Iul. Petri in Vaticano Pauli vero in Via Ostiensi utriusque in Catacumbas Tusco et Basso consulibus* ('29 June [the martyr-feast] of Peter on the Vatican, and of Paul on the Via Ostiensis, and of both at the Catacombs, A.D. 258').[51] It was on the basis of these entries, so emended, that Duchesne— linking the date 258 with the shrine at the Catacombs only and concluding that it refers to the inauguration of this last-mentioned cult-centre and not to that of the feast-day itself (p. 181)—put forward the theory, still widely (although by no means universally) accepted, that at the time of the Valerianic persecution of the Church in 258, the bodies of the two Apostles were removed from their graves on the Vatican Hill and by the Via Ostiensis, and were taken for safety to the Via Appia; and that they were not returned to their rightful tombs until the reign of Constantine, or until the churches newly erected in their honour were completed.[52]

The ancient tradition of an association between the Apostles and the San Sebastiano site received sensational confirmation in 1915, when A. de Waal and P. Styger excavated under the church a group of buildings, now known as the Memoria of St. Peter and St. Paul, the walls of which were found to be covered with *graffiti* mentioning the two Apostles by name.[53] This group of buildings, which dates from the second half of the third century, lay in a cemetery-district to the south of the Via Appia. On the north side it was bounded by a continuous line of northward-facing *columbaria* (small mausolea for cremation-burials), which go back to the second half of the first century A.D.; and on the west by a somewhat enigmatic building, the so-called Villa, with wall-paintings, including the well-known harbour-scene,[54] which probably served as a place of reunion for the users of the cemetery (that it was built as a residence within an already established cemetery is most improbable). Towards the south the ground fell away sharply beyond a retaining-wall, of which all but the south-western corner was destroyed when the church was built. The north-eastern corner of the area so enclosed consisted of a large room, the so-called Triclia (literally, 'drinking-place'), equipped with a bench and a kitchen,[55] and decorated with rustic wall-paintings. This room overlooked, but does not seem to have communicated directly with, a paved courtyard, flanked on the north and west by covered porticoes. The angle between the two porticoes was occupied by a room to which there does not seem to have been any direct access at this period (this section of the Memoria occupies part of an earlier building); and immediately to the south of this, against the north wall of the west portico, there was a niche-like structure, decorated partly with mosaic and partly with marble veneer, which has been variously interpreted as a niche for a statue, a domestic shrine (*lararium*), a throne, or a table for offerings (*mensa martyrum*)[55a] Opening off the south side of the courtyard, near the west corner, there was a square mausoleum, with an open porch and an apse, in which were found a number of burials; and in the middle of the courtyard, opposite the Triclia, steps led down to a water-tank cut in the rock nearly 10 metres below. The entrance to the Memoria was on the east side, immediately to the south of the Triclia, where a flight of steps led down from what must have been a side-road or lane leading off the main Via Appia.

The walls of this building, both of Triclia and of courtyard alike, were covered with *graffiti*, scratched on the plaster by visiting pilgrims, who were obviously humble and sometimes illiterate persons. Thirty-three of these *graffiti* were read *in situ* on the walls, while fragments of one hundred and seventy-nine others were found scattered around in the earth, and one similar *graffito* came to light in the so-called Villa. For the most part the *graffiti* consist of simple prayers invoking the aid of the Apostles; *Petre et Paule in mente nos habeatis, Petre et Paule subvenite Primo peccatori, Petre et Paule conservate Vincentium, Paule et Petre petite pro Victore, Paule et Petre petite pro nobis omnibus* ('Peter and Paul'—or 'Paul and Peter'—'have us in mind', 'help Primus, a sinner', 'preserve Vincentius', 'pray for Victor', 'pray for us all') are representative examples. Some are written in Greek, most of them in Latin, and one or two are in Latin written in Greek characters (presumably by persons who spoke Latin but wrote only in Greek)—Παυλε ετ Πετρε ιν μεντε νος αβετε, i.e. *Paule et Petre in mente nos habete* ('Paul and Peter, have us in mind'). Some of them mention *refrigeria*; examples are: *Petro et Paulo Tomius Coelius refrigerium feci, at (= ad) Paulum et Petrum refrigeravi, Dalmatius votum is promisit refrigerium, XIIII Kal. Apriles refrigeravi Parthenius in Deo et nos in Deo omnes, . . . refrigerav[imus] . . . [f]elicissimus cum s[uis]* ('I, Tomius Coelius, partook of* a refreshment-

---

* The precise meaning of the verbs in these texts is uncertain; they might signify 'held' or 'offered'.

meal for Peter and Paul', 'I partook of a refreshment-meal near Peter and Paul', 'Dalmatius promised and vowed a refreshment-meal', 'On 16 April I, Parthenius, partook of a refreshment-meal in God, and all of us in God' (the last clause was added by a different hand), 'We partook of a refreshment-meal, . . . the most happy with his friends'). In normal Christian usage *refrigerium* means the 'refreshment' of celestial bliss. Here, however, it must have the very different, and in Christian practice seemingly unique, meaning of an actual meal, eaten in honour of the dead. In this sense, the *refrigerium* was a pagan custom, a ceremonial meal eaten in commemoration of, and shared with, the dead, normally at or near the tomb, something distinct both in origin and in intent from the familiar communal feasts that were held by Christians in commemoration of martyrs and the departed generally during the third and fourth centuries (*cf.* p. 209). It is obviously far from easy to read the minds of those who produced these scribblings. Nevertheless, we seem to have here an instance of that assimilation of Christian to pagan thought and practice which must often have taken place at lower levels, but which the Church as such cannot have countenanced.[56] At all events, the purpose of the Triclia, with its kitchen and its water-tank, was evidently to provide a setting for these ceremonial meals, in a place which Christians of the later-third century believed to be associated in some special way with the names of St. Peter and St. Paul.

What was the nature of that association? And when was this cult-centre established? In order to understand the full significance of these questions, we have first to glance briefly at the previous history of the site.

The Church of San Sebastiano stands on the northern edge of, and at the west end partly overlaps, what was once a valley with steeply sloping sides or cliffs, into the face of which had been cut a subterranean quarry for *pozzolana*, the dark, volcanic deposit used by the Romans for making concrete. This quarry, which dates from the first century A.D., if not earlier, lies directly below the courtyard of the Memoria and the southern part of the nave of Constantine's church (p. 178); and from it steps led down to a water-tank about 3 metres below the floor of the quarry and nearly 14 metres below the level of the floor of the church (to be distinguished from the similar water-tank cut to serve the cemetery in the next period and, later, the Memoria). When the quarry was exhausted, its empty galleries and passages began to serve for burials. One of these was that of a freedman (or, conceivably, the son of a freedman) of the Emperor Trajan (98–117), named Marcus Ulpius Calocerus, and the quarry-cemetery must have been in use, therefore, as late as the beginning of the second century. Soon afterwards, however, part of the roof collapsed; the rest was demolished and the debris levelled to form a sunken, oval courtyard (the *Piazzuola*); and facing onto this courtyard at the north-west end, built partly above ground and partly into the hillside, was a group of painted and stuccoed mausolea, with pedimented, brick façades, of the same general type as those in the Vatican cemetery—the Tomb of Marcus Clodius Hermes, the easternmost; next to it, the 'Tomb of the Innocentii'; and on the west, facing eastwards, the 'Tomb of the Axe', so-called from the axe-symbol (*ascia*, p. 67) incorporated into the brickwork of the façade.[57] The lower chambers of these tombs, reached by stairs, occupied three of the surviving tunnels of the quarry and incorporated the early burials already established in them; and their contiguous façades, giving access directly to the upper chambers, enclosed the north-western end of the oval courtyard. The actual work of construction took place from east to west, but all three tombs are part of a single, closely interrelated complex, planned and built at the same time as the cemetery was established in its new form round the oval courtyard; and from the style of the brickwork, and from parts, at any rate, of the internal decoration, the whole can be dated to about the middle or third quarter of the second century, contemporary, that is to say, with many of the later tombs in the excavated part of the Vatican cemetery. To the east and south of the trio of mausolea were other groups of burials, cut into the rock-face of the oval courtyard; in the middle, steps led down to a rock-cut water-tank; and on the hilltop, at the level of the *columbaria*, the whole site was enclosed within an irregular rectangular precinct, delimited to the north by the back-wall of the *columbaria*, and on the other three sides by walls of basalt, of which those to the west and south, at any rate, are almost certainly contemporary with the establishment of the oval courtyard, enclosing and demarcating the limits of a property which was now for the first time visible, if not directly accessible, from above.[58]

With the establishment of the precinct, there was a natural tendency to transfer some of the ritual observances connected with the

cult of the dead to the less crowded space above the tombs. This, a
any rate, is the most probable explanation of the so-called Sigma,
curved chamber, with an encircling bench, the remains of which ca
be seen underlying the courtyard of the Memoria, directly over th
central chamber of the Tomb of Clodius Hermes.[59] The floor of th
Sigma was of a waterproof concrete; and traces of a corresponding
floor have been identified farther to the west, suggesting that ther
may have been a similar chamber over the other two tombs. If so
about the turn of the second and third centuries it was replaced b
a more substantial, barrel-vaulted structure, which stood against th
west wall of the precinct, adjoining the Villa, immediately over th
'Tomb of the Axe' and a part of the 'Tomb of the Innocentii'. In fron
of it, a vertical shaft allowed water to be drawn directly from th
water-tank that served the oval courtyard; and the interior of th
chamber was decorated with paintings, including what is sometime
interpreted as a *baetylus*, a ritual stone, but is more probably a grea
ritual club associated with the cult of Diana, as in the well-know
painting in the 'House of Livia' on the Palatine.[60]

Before the end of the second century there is no definite trace c
Christianity. Very soon afterwards, however, Christian burials be
gin to appear among the rock-cut graves of the oval courtyard;[6
and about the year 200, or shortly after, the attic-like superstructur
over the pedimented façade of the Tomb of Clodius Hermes w:
decorated with a series of Christian scenes. On the left is a pastor:
scene, including the figures of the Good Shepherd with a sheep o
His shoulders and a second shepherd running to meet Him with ou
stretched hands—a version of the Parable of the Lost Sheep. On th
right is depicted the miraculous Feeding of the Multitude by th
Lake of Genesaret: the crowds are placed at five or six tables, c
which can be seen the loaves and fishes; and to the right agai
Christ Himself, instead of standing, rod in hand, to perform th
miracle, as in the catacomb-versions of the episode, moves slowl
away from the banquet accompanied by four companions. Th
central scene of the series is poorly preserved, but seems to hav
shown a crowd of people listening to a teacher. The treatment
these scenes is more purely narrative and less symbolic than in th
catacomb-paintings; and this deviation from the normal renderii
suggests the possibility (p. 179) that this group of paintings may ha
been executed for some non-Catholic Christian sect.[62]

Towards the end of the period during which the oval courtyard was in use, the level of the floor rose rapidly, the result presumably of the excavation of new galleries and grave-recesses within a very restricted area. By the time that the ground in front of the mausolea had risen 1·5 metres, it became necessary to build steps down to the doorways of the two that were still in active use—that of Clodius Hermes and that of the Innocentii. These steps were sheltered by wooden porches, the timbers of which break into the Christian paintings described in the preceding paragraph. This, however, was only a temporary expedient. Soon afterwards the whole sunken area was deliberately filled in up to the level of the surrounding precinct, and the three mausolea were completely and finally buried. It must have been just before this final raising of the level that the central one was used by the members of a burial-club, the 'Innocentii', whose club-names, painted in Greek characters on the plaster sealing of their graves, were borrowed from those of the senatorial emperors of 238–44—*duobus Gordianis Innocentiorum, Gordiano Innocentiorum,* and *Popenio Balbeino Innocentiorum.* Cut into the plaster of another chamber of the same tomb was a Christian *graffito*—ΙΤΧΘΥΣ, combining the familiar Ichthus-monogram of primitive Christianity with the Tau-cross.

Such, in outline, is the history of the site before the constitution of the Memoria; and we can see that, unlike the subsequent church, which overrode and obliterated all previous landmarks, the Memoria was shaped and conditioned at every turn by what had gone before. The line of the outer wall of the Triclia was that of the previous boundary-wall. To the north the courtyard was bounded by the line of *columbaria,* and to the west and south by the precinct-walls of the original cemetery-enclosure, on the western one of which now stood the outer wall of the so-called Villa. Against this wall, the west portico occupied the southern half of the barrel-vaulted cult-chamber. The flight of steps leading down to the water-tank prolongs the line of a flight of steps that had already been cut to serve the graves opening off the oval courtyard. Only the square mausoleum was an entirely new feature, and that had to be established on the one side of the Memoria which was still open ground, built out on the shelving bank towards the south.

The use of the Memoria, no less than its outward form, was conditioned by its antecedents. How the ground passed into Christian

hands we do not know. There had been, as we have seen, a considerable Christian element using this part of the cemetery by the
Appian Way, side by side with pagans, in the immediately preceding period; and Roman law was concerned with the fact of
burial, not (under normal conditions) with the beliefs of those buried.
The Vatican cemetery affords several striking instances of the passage
of a tomb from one cult to another (e.g. Tomb M, p. 72, and the
'Tomb of the Egyptians', pp. 51–7); and the fact that the area
covered by the Memoria now fell into Christian hands has very
little bearing on its earlier history. What is more important is that,
despite the filling-in of the earlier graves (a good instance of the
common and legitimate practice of *congestio terrarum*, p. 13), Roman
law and sentiment alike would have forbidden the use of the ground
for any but a funerary or commemorative purpose. Any such suggestion as that put forward by Lanciani, for example,[63] that the
Triclia was a wayside tavern, which came to be used by Christians
because of some vague traditional association of the site with the
Apostles, disregards the elementary fact that the Memoria is situated
in the heart of a busy cemetery-area and over the site of a number of
recent burials. The property on which the Memoria was built had
been clearly and precisely delimited as a funerary area ever since the
building of the basalt enclosure-walls, a century before, and the title
would have carried equally clear and precise obligations.

That the purpose of the Memoria was the commemoration of a
temporary burial of the Apostles *ad Catacumbas* immediately after
their martyrdom is a theory that finds little support from the
excavations. It is true that this thesis has recently been presented,
plausibly and in great detail, by Tolotti,[64] who maintains that an
empty grave-recess in the smaller of the two stucco-vaulted chambers in the lowest level of the 'Tomb of the Axe' is none other than
the temporary resting-place of the Apostles after their martyrdom,
and that the whole subsequent evolution of the site was dictated by
the requirements of the cult developed about this hallowed spot; not
only was the primitive quarry-cemetery deliberately slighted to
provide a more decorous setting for this grave within the framework
of the oval courtyard, with its accompanying mausolea; but this
in turn was filled in, to preserve intact the actual grave, after
the regular commemorative observances had been transferred, in
accordance with contemporary practice, to a cult-chamber above

ground—the barrel-vaulted chamber in the north-west corner of
the Memoria precinct. With the establishment of the Memoria in its
final form, this chamber in its turn gave place to the marble-en-
cased niche, which is explained as a *mensa martyrum* marking the
approximate position of the empty grave, now buried far beneath.
The reason for the initial choice of site for the grave Tolotti believes
to have been the residence of the Apostles near by during their
lifetime (a residence perhaps commemorated in later tradition, p.
179), and he goes so far as to claim that the earlier of the two water-
tanks, buried when the quarry was abandoned, was cut to serve them
as a baptismal basin.

The extravagance of this last claim must not be allowed to obscure
the real value of Tolotti's contribution to the study of this baffling
site. But the basic thesis is untenable. There is absolutely no trace of
Christian interest, let alone of special veneration, within the 'Tomb of
the Axe', although the grave-recess itself was still accessible at a
time when Christians were already active, and left their mark, elsewhere in the cemetery; and the unequivocally pagan paintings of
the barrel-vaulted cult-chamber are inconceivable as the decoration
of a commemorative shrine built in honour of the Apostles at the
turn of the second and third centuries, and still in use fifty years
later. That there is a thread of continuity in the development of the
cemetery, Tolotti is right to emphasize; but it is a continuity imposed
by Roman funerary custom and law, not by a specifically Christian
tradition. The abandonment of the primitive quarry-cemetery is
amply explained by the partial collapse of the former, a collapse
which (as Tolotti rightly observes) was followed immediately by the
establishment of the oval courtyard under conditions which allowed
the incorporation, intact, of substantial parts of the earlier cemetery,
some of it certainly pagan;[65] and the demonstrably crowded state
of its successor, after a hundred years of continuous use, is in itself
quite sufficient to explain its suppression in favour of a more convenient and dignified lay-out within the framework of the funerary
precinct that was already established and in active use at surface-
level. One cannot exclude the possibility of other, specifically
Christian, considerations; but they are not needed to explain the
transition from the quarry-cemetery to the Memoria, and they have
left no tangible evidence.

The date of the establishment of the Memoria can be fixed within fairly close limits. It cannot be earlier (but could be considerably later) than the latest attested burials in the oval courtyard, those of the Innocentii (p. 175), who assumed the names under which they were buried between the years 238 and 244. On the other hand, the church is now generally accepted as a Constantinian foundation (the earliest dated burial subsequent to its erection is of the year 349)[66] and the complete absence of the Constantinian monogram from the large series of *graffiti* cut on the walls of the Memoria strongly suggests that this was already in active use before the end of the third century.[66a] These facts indicate a date for the constitution of the Memoria between the 'sixties and 'eighties of the third century, with a possible margin of ten or fifteen years either way. It will be noted that the date given by the *Depositio Martyrum*, 258, falls somewhat early, but still within the possible limits of the bracket so established; and if this date has any basis in fact, it would not be unreasonable to suppose that the establishment of the Memoria occurred in 258, or possibly a few years later, as the result of events that took place in 258.

What can these events have been? One recent suggestion, put forward by Dom Mohlberg,[67] is that this date saw the establishment here of a shrine by the followers of Novatian, the rigorist rival of Pope Cornelius (251–3). The unusual character of the paintings on the Tomb of Clodius Hermes suggests that this tomb may have been used by the members of some non-Catholic sect; and in this context mention may also be made of the use in the *graffiti* in the Triclia of *refrigerium* in a sense rarely, if ever, found in Christian epigraphy and literature (*cf.* p. 172 and Note 56) and of the presence there of a funerary kitchen paralleled in pagan tombs (*cf.* p. 172 and Note 55); while the omission of the name of Pope Cornelius from the *Depositio Episcoporum* may indicate that it and its companion-document, the *Depositio Martyrum*, were edited by Novatianist sympathizers. The Novatianists (who accepted the decrees of the Council of Nicaea) were not formally treated as heretics and suppressed until the early-fifth century, and they would, therefore, have been in a position to own property and to build both the Memoria and the subsequent church (the original name of which was Basilica Apostolorum)[68] as a centre for the veneration of Rome's principal martyrs, in rivalry to the Catholic shrines on the Vatican and beside the Via Ostiensis. On this theory, the shrine must have passed later into Catholic hands, either when the Novatianists were suppressed or (more probably, in view of the interest shown in the site by Pope Damasus) on some unrecorded occasion before the middle of the fourth century (perhaps at the time of the building of the Constantinian church, which, indeed, completely destroyed the upper part of the former Memoria and rendered the rest of it inaccessible to worshippers); and in time the cult of the Apostles, whose remains were venerated at the two great official shrines, came to be superseded by that of St. Sebastian, who was buried in the crypt below the church.

The theory is ingenious. It must be remembered, however, that the Novatianist character of the *Depositio Episcoporum* and the *Deposition Martyrum* is far from certain; the omission of Pope Cornelius from the former may indicate no more than that he died, not as a martyr in Rome, but as an exile at Centumcellae; and if these lists were Novatianist, then the entry *hunc Silanum martyrem Novati furati sunt* must, as Dom Mohlberg himself notes, be regarded as a later, anti-Novatianist addition.[69] Moreover, the link between the former occupants of the Tomb of Clodius Hermes (the paintings on which were suppressed in its final phase) and the owners of the Memoria is decidedly slender; and we have, in any case, so little comparative material from the catacombs that is demonstrably as early as these paintings that even their attribution to a non-Catholic sect is not certain. Nor can we be sure that the *graffiti* in the Triclia were the work of schismatics. Finally, in order to account for the continuation in Catholic hands of what had begun as a schismatical cult-centre (whether Novatianist or other), we should have to postulate the existence, by the middle of the fourth century, of some tradition, common to Catholics and schismatics alike, but almost certainly not founded on fact, that the Apostles had either lived on this site in their lifetime or been temporarily buried there at the time of their martyrdom. The Memoria may be, as Dom Mohlberg suggests, a Novatianist shrine; but the case is very far from proved.

Is it possible, then, that the Church of San Sebastiano is, as Duchesne suggested long before the excavation of the Memoria, the site of the temporary resting-place of the Apostles, brought there for safety in 258 on the occasion of the Valerianic persecution, which had broken out in the August of the previous year?[70] This is a question to which scholars are no nearer giving an agreed answer than they were half a century ago. Against the theory of translation, it is pointed out that no trace of any Apostolic tomb has been found within the Memoria; and that the Vatican excavations have yielded no clear evidence either of an initial translation or of a subsequent re-establishment of the relics by Constantine; that it would, in any case, have been senseless to have moved St. Peter's remains for secrecy and safety from the relative quiet of the Vatican cemetery to a spot adjoining the busiest highway leading out of the city, only a few hundred yards from an imperial police-post, the *statio frumentariorum*, near the Tomb of Caecilia Metella;[71] and that the whole of this district is likely to have been under police-observation and dangerous, since large Christian cemeteries, to which access for public worship was forbidden, had already developed there, at no great distance from the site of the Memoria; that the Roman law against *violatio sepulcri*, besides making the removal of the remains illegal, would have given them ample protection in their original position— even a felon's permanent grave would have been safeguarded as (in Roman legal terminology) *locus pro religioso*, if not as *locus pleno iure religiosus*.[72] None of these arguments is, in itself, conclusive. It was not the accessibility of the sites that the Church had to fear, so much as the fact that the two 'trophies' must have been well known to the imperial authorities; and in this respect the position of the Memoria, newly constituted in a private cemetery area and well set back from the main road, might have had much to commend it. Despite the severity of the regulations governing *violatio sepulcri*, there is a great deal of evidence (*e.g.* the frequent reuse of sarcophagi and the very insistence of tomb-owners on the sanctions against misappropriation) to show that the sacrosanctity of the tomb was in practice all too often disregarded; and although there is no record of the official violation of martyrs' relics, the Christian community might not unreasonably have feared the same imperial high-handedness as that which fifty years later Constantine showed in his treatment of the Vatican cemetery, and may well have preferred to be wise before the event. And we have to remember that it would not have been a question of the removal of a massive sarcophagus (as has often been assumed or implied in the past), but of something far smaller, which might have left little or no tangible evidence either of its presence or of its removal; a reliquary small enough to be contained within the central space below the Vatican 'trophy' would have been readily transportable, provided that it could have been extracted secretly; and it could have been housed, for example, on or in the niched structure to the west of the Memoria, or immediately behind it in the inaccessible chamber at the north-west corner of the courtyard—a position which falls significantly on the axis of the Constantinian church, just in front of the apse, where later stood the memorial to the two Apostles. Such a translation might, moreover, have served to satisfy the needs of the Christian community at a time when its clergy were denied access to the existing cemeteries and martyr-shrines for purposes of public cult;[73] and it would provide a reason for the celebration there of *refrigeria*, which normally, if not invariably, took place in or near a tomb.[74]

It is one thing, however, to show that a third-century translation of the remains of the Apostles is by no means as improbable an event as many of its critics have maintained. It is quite another thing to demonstrate that such a translation did, in fact, take place, in the face of what must always be the most serious argument that this theory has to encounter—the failure of the surviving literary sources to make any specific mention of such an event. Furthermore, it must be borne in mind that the famous entry in the Calendar of Philocalus (if correctly emended) is capable of another interpretation. It tells us that in the fourth century the liturgical feast of St. Peter and St. Paul was celebrated at three cult-centres on 29 June. But the date 258 may have nothing to do with the third of those centres, that by the Via Appia; it may be the year in which the Roman Church inaugurated the feast-day. By the mid-third century the cult of the martyrs was developing in the West; we know that the Christians continued to meet for public worship in defiance of Valerian's decree forbidding it; and a time of persecution would be a natural moment for Roman Christians to devise a special commemoration (*dies solemnis*) of their martyr-founders.

The origin of the cult of the Apostles by the Via Appia remains, in fact, an unsolved problem; and here the excavations under St. Peter's have proved no more conclusive than those under San Sebastiano. Nevertheless, this and other recent work has thrown some light upon our question; and it may be useful, in conclusion, to consider to what extent such work has advanced us towards discovering an answer to it. In the first place, it is now quite certain that there was a continuity of popular veneration of the shrine on the Vatican Hill. Of that the *graffiti* on the flank of the Aedicula (p. 165) afford clear and positive proof; although, in their failure to mention St. Peter by name they contrast strangely with the vividly personal invocations of the two Apostles in the Memoria. The excavations have yielded no evidence, one way or the other, to show whether any relics preserved within the hollow space below the Aedicula were or were not removed in the late-third century (p. 165). On the other hand, if the bones found at the base of N¹ (p. 154) do indeed represent some part of a burial disturbed by the builders of the Red Wall and identified by the Christian community as those of St. Peter, then any later translation of the remains can only have been partial.

Such a partial translation, foreshadowing the later Christian practice of distributing relics,[75] cannot be proved; and it raises a number of points which, in the view of some scholars, renders it improbable. But it does suggest a straightforward reason for the establishment of the Memoria. This Memoria we now know was set up within the precinct of a large, and presumably privately owned, mausoleum (that this mausoleum itself ever housed the remains of the Apostles seems to be excluded by the scant respect paid to it by the builders of the church); and we know that the owners of this precinct were the heirs to a cemetery established nearly two centuries before, a cemetery in which Christians had played an important but by no means predominant part. It is within such a setting that we have to explain the evidence for the Memoria of the Apostles *ad Catacumbas*. We do not yet know whether conditions at the shrine of St. Paul by the Via Ostiensis were such as to favour a partial translation of relics in his case. Perhaps excavations beneath the high altar of St. Paul's-without-the-Walls will one day furnish the conclusive answer that still eludes us.

NOTES

1. For a detailed account of how the digging was conducted and of the finds made, the specialist will consult the text and detailed illustrations of the *Report*. For such a study this book is no substitute. Unless otherwise indicated, the facts here set out will be found to be documented in the *Report*; the interpretation given to them is that of the present writers.

2. *Report*, i, Figs. 32 and 81. The later tessellated pavement of P, which is 5–6 centimetres above that of the original floor of the Aedicula, is some 3·15 metres above the floor of the interior of Tomb O, and 3·45 metres above the offset of its foundations at the south-west angle. It is not improbable that the

staircase within the precinct of O, originally designed to give access to O from the north, was later made available to the owners of P as a means of access to P from the south, after the blocking of the alley-way between Tombs L and N by the construction of Tomb M (p. 34). This would help to explain the alterations of the outer doorway of O (which would thereafter have corresponded in function to the doorway closing the Clivus leading up to Q and R¹) and the blocking of the original east wing of O's outer precinct.

3. As do P. Lemerle, *Revue historique*, ccviii, 1952, p. 205 ff., and A. von Gerkan, *Evangelisch-Lutherische Kirchenzeitung*, vi, November 1952, p. 379 ff. It is the great merit of the excavators that they have presented their conclusions and the facts on which they are based in a form which allows their conclusions to be examined critically; but unless one is prepared to rely on their statements of observed fact (and in the writers' experience their observations are very reliable), further discussion would seem to be useless.

4. Marrou's theory (Cabrol–Leclerq–Marrou, *Dictionnaire d'archéologie chrétienne et de liturgie*, xv. 2, 1953, *s.v.* 'Vaticanum', 3342) that t^1 and t^2 are the two lateral members of a canopy-like structure that was open in the middle and closed in front by a third member, parallel to the Red Wall, takes no account of the broken state of the inner faces of t^1 and t^2, which shows that both of them originally extended inwards. The function suggested for such a structure, as 'une sorte de clôture à hauteur de homme, délimitant, interdisant, solemnisant l'espace d'un lieu saint', would have been served more efficiently by a balustrade at ground-level.

5. Calza, Figs. 9, 10, and p. 80; although mainly grouped on the outskirts of the cemetery, there is also a considerable scatter of individual graves between the larger mausolea, and these scattered graves must there, as in the Vatican, have constituted a considerable problem as the cemetery developed and became more crowded.

6. The nomenclature of the tombs, by the letters of the Greek alphabet, follows that given in the official *Report*.

7. *Report*, i, Fig. 84 = *CIL*, xv. i, 1273: *Stat(ius) Marcius Demetrius f(ecit)*. A single tile, such as this, might easily have been reused from some earlier building, and cannot in itself, therefore, be used to prove that this grave is of Flavian date.

8. It is hard to believe, with Ruysschaert (see Bibliographical Note), pp. 29–30, that Grave *ι*, a flimsy tile-covered structure, can antedate the Red Wall and that the Red Wall could possibly have been built without disturbing it.

9. From the levels given in the *Report* (see particularly Figs. 81 and 82) for the floors of Tombs O, Q, and S, and for the foundation-offsets of the west wall of O and the north wall of S (the change of build marks the point at which, when the tomb was built, the wall-surface became visible above ground), one may calculate the natural north-west-to-south-east slope at this point as not less

than 1 in 3. On such a slope there could have been no natural accumulation of rain-washed soil before the construction of S. On the other hand, the fact that at its south end the foundation of the Red Wall is 1·50 metres higher on the east side than on the west, can only mean that when the Clivus was built it had to be trenched into ground that already stood at the higher level indicated by Grave η. The successive surface-levels are illustrated schematically in Figs. 12 and 13; it must be emphasized that, on the available data, the positions given can only be approximate and take no account of possible minor irregularities in the terrain due to terracing or dumping. It does not follow that these slopes were maintained over any considerable area; indeed, there is evidence (e.g. the level of the waterproofing of the north wall of Q and the stairs in E and H) to suggest that there may have been more level ground above and to the north of the tombs. Instead of a uniformly sloping hillside, we have to envisage the northern row of tombs as built into a steep bank, which was interrupted here and there (e.g. at M) by natural gullies. One can see the same sort of country today anywhere in the Campagna.

10. The excavators (Report, i, p. 113 and Note 1) suggest that Grave γ may be Christian. But none of the Christian parallels cited for the familiar pagan practice (cf. Tombs C and F in the Vatican cemetery, p. 61, Note 30) of providing a pipe for the pouring of libations on the bones beneath is earlier than the third century, nor do any of them have the altar-like superstructure.

11. Analecta Romana, i, 1899, pp. 274–97.

12. Report, i, pp. 122, 225 ff. Of the 231 recognizable Roman coins, 6 were minted before the construction of the Aedicula, 77 range from Marcus Aurelius to Maxentius, 148 are of Constantine or later. The post-Roman coin-series continues down to the fourteenth century. 'Fondo attuale', which figures in the illustrations of the Report without explanation in the text, appears to be the level to which the excavations were carried; it has no significance for the interpretation of the ancient remains.

13. θ (like ι) was, of course, already buried far below the floor of the central space.

14. This point is curiously omitted from consideration by the excavators, and their restored view of the Aedicula (Report, i, Pl. G) shows a solid slab between N^1 and N^2. In view of the heavy rainfall in Rome in the winter months, it seems probable that the means of access was some sort of removable lid.

15. Report, i, p. 120. Cf. Ruysschaert, pp. 596–7.

16. Report, i, Fig. 87 (in which some of the bones have been drawn forward to the mouth of the recess) and p. 120; E. Kirschbaum, Stimmen der Zeit, September 1952, p. 406. In view of the importance of every scrap of evidence from a site of this complexity, it seems strange that no authoritative medical analysis of these bones has been published either in the official Report or during the four years that have elapsed since that work appeared.

17. The theory of H. Grégoire (*La Nouvelle Clio*, iv, 1952, p. 398 ff.) that the late-second-century Christians localized the grave of St. Peter in the Tomb of the Valerii (pp. 14 ff., 82 ff.), and that this tomb, despite its unequivocally pagan stucco ornament, is to be identified with the 'trophy' of Gaius, need hardly be taken seriously.

18. For the view that the 'trophy' is a memorial-shrine unaccompanied by any burial, see A. M. Schneider, *Theologische Literaturzeitung*, lxxvii, June 1952, p. 322 ff.; A. von Gerkan, *Evangelisch-Lutherische Kirchenzeitung*, vi, November 1952, p. 379 ff.; O. Cullmann, *Peter: Disciple—Apostle—Martyr*, 1953, pp. 146–52. For a recent discussion of the uses of the word τρόπαιον in Christian Latin, see Appendix C, p. 267.

19. Ed. Duchesne, i, p. 54 (text as in the Cononian summary of the first edition). For an alternative interpretation of this passage, relating it to the phase preceding the construction of the Aedicula, see Appendix B.

20. E. Kirschbaum, *Stimmen der Zeit*, August 1952, p. 331.

21. Marrou, *op. cit.* (Note 4), col. 3344.

22. *Ann.*, xv. 44.

23. Even if we assume that the property was sold by Vespasian as a measure of economy, it is difficult to envisage so rapid a decline in its fortunes.

24. The later settlement of the Red Wall (p. 162) is the direct result of the weakening both of the foundations and of the wall itself immediately behind the south-east angle of Tomb Q. The awkward relation of the Aedicula to the buildings behind has been used by von Gerkan (*loc. cit.*) and others to argue that, despite the structural evidence to the contrary, it must be a later insertion. But what is difficult to explain as a part of the original structure becomes doubly so when considered as a later addition, when the builders would have been free to choose a more convenient spot only a few feet away, and to build their shrine up against rather than into the body of the Red Wall.

25. The same objections can be raised to the theory that the Aedicula represents the localization of a very early tradition that St. Peter was buried somewhere on this part of the Vatican Hill (E. Peterson, *Schweitzer Rundschau*, lii, September 1952, p. 326 ff.).

26. In *Report*, i, Fig. 90, the bottom of the footings of the Red Wall (*i.e.* at this point the crown of the arched recess) are shown as about 85 centimetres below the floor of N^2. At the north corner of N^1 they are stated (p. 120) to be 'just over a metre' below the same point. To the north of the Aedicula they are said (p. 120) to be 'much deeper'. Immediately to the south of the Aedicula they are over 2 metres below the same point.

27. V. Capocci, 'Notae: gli scavi del Vaticano alla ricerca del sepolcro di S. Pietro e alcune note di diritto funerario romano' (*Studia et Documenta Historiae et Iuris*, xviii, 1952, p. 209). The *Report* produces no evidence of animal-sacrifices in this cemetery.

28. *Report*, i, pp. 113, 115.

29. Calza, Fig. 30 and p. 80. This little tomb, built up against No. 55, affords a significant contrast to the trouble to which the builders of the Vatican Aedicula went to incorporate their structure into the body of the Red Wall.

30. Possible uses of this slab are as a table for offerings or as a practical means of protecting from the elements the sealing-slab below. It is too high from the ground to have served as an altar (which it otherwise resembles), even if the ascription of such a function to so early a date were not (so far as we know) an anachronism.

31. As found, this buttress had settled slightly away from the wall-face, but the deep foundations clearly indicate its purpose. Marrou's suggestion (*op. cit.*, col. 3339) that it was built to protect the Aedicula from the accumulation of earth washed down the hillside ignores the fact that the Aedicula was enclosed within a level precinct, the north wall of which lay over 3 metres away to the north, and that in any case a protecting-wall would hardly have been so sited as to curtail the monument it was designed to safeguard.

32. *Report*, i, pp. 129–30.

33. R. P. Ferrua, *Civiltà Cattolica*, ciii. 1, January 1952, Fig. 3 on p. 25 and p. 26 (reading ΠΕΤΡ ΕΝΙ; for Πέτρ(ος) ἐν (ε)ἰ(ρήνη)?); E. Kirschbaum, *Stimmen der Zeit*, August 1952, p. 330; J. Carcopino, *Études d'histoire chrétienne*, 1953, pp. 281–2 (citing Josi for the reading Πέτρ(ε) χαῖρε). This *graffito* will presumably be published together with the main group by Professor Guarducci.

34. As Carcopino, *op. cit.*, pp. 188–93, 281–2.

35. Kirschbaum, *loc. cit.*

36. The facts are given, without discussion, in *Report*, i, p. 162.

37. A. Ferrua, 'A la recherche du tombeau de Saint Pierre' (*Études*, January 1952, pp. 35–47), pp. 44–5.

38. G. Lugli, 'Scavi di un sepolcreto romano presso la Basilica di S. Paolo' (*Notizie degli Scavi*, 1919, pp. 285–354).

39. Sketches made by the architect Vespignani during the course of the work undertaken in 1838 and 1850 in and around the high altar show a wall of *opus reticulatum* with brick quoins, as in Tomb D of the Vatican cemetery (p. 64); R. Lanciani, *Nuovo Bullettino di Archeologia Cristiana*, xxiii, 1917, Fig. 3 and p. 14; M. Armellini, *Le chiese di Roma*, 2nd ed., 1942, ii, p. 1151.

40. *Liber Pontificalis*, i, p. 178: eodem tempore fecit Augustus Constantinus basilicam beato Paulo apostolo ex suggestione Silvestri episcopi, cuius corpus ita recondit in aere et conclusit sicut beati Petri ('At the same time the Emperor Constantine built, at Pope Silvester's suggestion, a basilica in honour of the blessed Apostle Paul, whose body he protected with bronze and sealed up, as he had done in the case of the body of blessed Peter').

41. The tomb appears to have stood on a side-road opening obliquely off the main Via Ostiensis; and, to judge from the position of the Constantinian apse

(seen in 1850), the original, westward-orientated church had to be fitted into the relatively narrow space between this side-road and the main road. The problem was solved by Valentinian II, Theodosius I, and Arcadius (who ordered the construction of the new church in 386, in a letter to the Prefect of Rome, Sallustius, the text of which is preserved) by diverting the side-road (described as the old road, 'iter vetus') farther to the west and by reversing the orientation of the church. E. Stevenson, *Nuovo Bullettino di Archeologia Cristiana*, iii, 1897, pp. 287–321; Lanciani, *op. cit.*, pp. 18–27; Armellini, *op. cit.*, p. 1153.

There is no contemporary evidence for the building by Constantine of a basilica in honour of St. Paul. But in their letter to Sallustius (C. Baronius, *Annales Ecclesiastici*, v, 1739, pp. 607–8, No. 40), the three emperors express their desire 'antiquitus iam sacratam basilicam Pauli apostoli pro sanctimonia religionis ornare, pro quantitate conventus amplificare, et pro studio devotionis attollere' ('to adorn, enlarge, and dignify the basilica of the Apostle Paul, consecrated long ago, in a manner worthy of our holy religion, of the crowds of the faithful that flock to the church, and of the eager devotion that it inspires'). This clearly indicates the existence of an earlier basilica on the same site.

42. H. Grisar, *Analecta Romana*, i, 1899, pp. 259–73, Pl. 7; Armellini, *op. cit.*, p. 1152. The inscription is in fourth-century lettering, but the slab has been recomposed in its present position, perhaps even as late as the ninth century, when Benedict III 'adorned [sic] the tomb, which had been destroyed by the Saracens' (*Liber Pontificalis*, ii, p. 145: sepulchrum quod a Sarracenis destructum fuerat perornavit, *i.e.* in 855).

43. The significance of the name 'Catacumbas' (a transliteration of the Greek κατὰ κύμβας is disputed. It may refer to the configuration of the ground ('the Hollows'), or it may be derived from some specific local landmark (Schneider, see Note 44, suggests 'the Prows', from a grave-monument decorated with ships). What is certain is that it was in origin a proper name denoting this particular locality; only much later did it come to be applied in the wider sense with which we are now familiar, as a generic name ('catacombs') for the underground cemeteries of the early Church.

44. The literature dealing with this very controversial subject has assumed formidable dimensions. For a useful account of the work conducted on the site since the late-nineteenth century, including references to most of the principal books and articles published before the end of 1952 (among which special mention may be made here of A. Prandi, *La Memoria Apostolorum in Catacumbas*, 1936), the reader may be referred to the most recent large-scale study of the problem, F. Tolotti, *Memorie degli Apostoli in Catacumbas: rilievo critico della Basilica Apostolorum al III miglio della Via Appia* (Collezione 'Amici delle Catacombe', xix), 1953 (cited hereafter as 'Tolotti'); the author's thesis of a continuous Christian cult in this place since Apostolic times is untenable (pp. 176–7),

but his description of the site is very thorough and in detail acute, and it supersedes all accounts written before the excavations of 1928–9. That of A. von Gerkan, in H. Lietzmann, *Petrus und Paulus in Rom*, 1927, pp. 248–301, now requires substantial modification. Among recent articles two are of especial importance—A. M. Schneider, 'Die Memoria Apostolorum an der Via Appia' (*Nachrichten der Akademie der Wissenschaften in Göttingen, I, Phil.-hist. Klasse*, 1951, No. 3, p. 1 ff.); and L. K. Mohlberg, 'Historisch-kritische Bemerkungen zum Ursprung der sogenannten "Memoria Apostolorum" an der Appischen Strasse' in *Colligere Fragmenta : Festschrift Alban Dold zum 70. Geburtstag am 7.7.1952*, p. 52 ff.

45. For the full text of the inscription, which is recorded in several of the early-medieval collections based on pilgrim-itineraries, including the *Sylloge Einsidlense* (p. 229, Note 1), see E. Diehl, *Inscriptiones Latinae Christianae Veteres*, i, 1925, No. 951 = G. B. De Rossi, *Inscriptiones Christianae Urbis Romae*, ii, 1888, p. 32, No. 77 = *Anthologiae Latinae Suppl. i*, 1895, No. 26. Part of a thirteenth-century copy survives on the site. The inscription was probably cut on the marble slab placed in the church on what, by the sixth century at any rate, was believed to be the site of the grave: *Liber Pontificalis*, i, p. 212: et in Catacumbas ubi iacuerunt corpora sanctorum apostolorum Petri et Pauli, in quo loco platoman ipsam ubi iacuerunt corpora sancta versibus exornavit ('. . . the Catacombs, where lay the bodies of the holy Apostles Peter and Paul, in which place he adorned with verses the *platoma* itself, where lay the holy bodies'). For the position of the *platoma* see Duchesne, *Atti della Pontificia Accademia Romana di Archeologia*, ser. III, *Memorie*, i, 1923, p. 5. In the later Middle Ages, by which time the *platoma* had been removed from its original site, the word passed into medieval legend as the 'Platonia' (*cf.* Tolotti, p. 8).

The other use by Damasus of the word *habitare* to indicate 'dwelling' in death is in an inscription placed on the tomb of the martyr Gorgonius by the Via Labicana: invenies vicina in sede habitare beatos (De Rossi, *op. cit.*, ii, p. 64, No. 13; p. 197, No. 52).

46. Migne, *Patrologia Latina*, xvii, cols. 1215, 1216; ed. H. Lietzmann, *Lateinische altkirchliche Poesie*, 1910, p. 14, No. 15.

47. Migne, *Patrologia Latina*, lxxvii, col. 703.

48. *Liber Pontificalis*, i, p. 150. The attribution of such an event to the pontificate of Pope Cornelius (251–3) is clearly mistaken; see A. S. Barnes, *The Martyrdom of St. Peter and St. Paul*, 1933, p. 89.

49. Postea pervenies via Appia ad S. Sebastianum martyrem cuius corpus iacet in inferiore loco, et ibi sunt sepulcra apostolorum Petri et Pauli in quibus XL annorum requiescebant, et in occidentali parte ecclesiae per gradus descendis ubi S. Cyrinus papa et martyr pausat. For the text of this 'Itinerary', see G. B. De Rossi, *La Roma sotterranea cristiana*, i, 1864, p. 138 ff.

50. Ed. Mommsen, *Monumenta Germaniae Historica, Auctores Antiquissimi*, ix, 1891, pp. 70–1; *Liber Pontificalis*, i, pp. 10–12.

51. The version in the Hieronymian Martyrology (for which see *Acta Sanctorum*, November, ii. 1, 1894, p. [84] (G. B. De Rossi and L. Duchesne); November, ii. 2, 1931, pp. 342–3 (H. Delehaye and H. Quentin), reads: III Kal. Iul. Romae via Aurelia natale sanctorum apostolorum Petri et Pauli, Petri in Vaticano, Pauli vero in Ostiensi, utrumque (for utriusque?) in Catacumbas, passi sub Nerone, Basso et Tusco consulibus. As Duchesne points out (*Atti della Pontificia Accademia Romana di Archeologia*, ser. III, Memorie, i, 1923, pp. 1–2), the words 'via Aurelia' (an obvious reference to the location of the shrine of St. Peter near the Via Aurelia Nova, see p. 19, Note 22) and 'passi sub Nerone' are just the sort of additions to be expected from the eighth-century French editor, from whose edition all the surviving manuscripts are derived. The rest of the passage must, however, derive from some early source closely related to the *Depositio Martyrum*.

52. *Liber Pontificalis*, i, pp. civ ff.

53. P. Styger, (i) *Römische Quartalschrift*, xxix, 1915, p. 73 ff.; (ii) *Dissertazioni della Pontificia Accademia Romana di Archeologia*, ser. II, xiii, 1918, p. 3 ff.

54. F. Wirth, *Römische Wandmalerei*, 1934, Pl. 21.

55. The purpose of the small chamber, furnished with cooking-bench and refuse-bin, opening off the north-east corner of the Triclia, is abundantly clear, if one compares it with the domestic kitchens of Ostia and the funerary kitchens of Isola Sacra (*e.g.* Calza, p. 294: No. 16). It has often been misinterpreted, however, owing to the fact that it occupies the place of an earlier feature (the entrance to the original precinct?).

55a. As suggested by E. Josi in an unpublished communication to the Pontifical Academy on 16 January 1936.

56. Cabrol–Leclerq–Marrou, *op. cit.*, xiv. 2, 1948, *s.v.* 'Refrigerium', col. 2179 ff. The Christian uses of the term quoted here are: (1) material refreshment in non-funerary contexts; (2) pecuniary aid; (3) spiritual refreshment in a general sense; (4) celestial bliss—by far the most common significance *cf.* 'locum refrigerii, lucis, et pacis' in the Canon of the Mass; (5) a ceremonial meal—a sense stated to be peculiar to the San Sebastiano *graffiti*. Of the numerous instances of *refrigerium* and *refrigerare* quoted by Diehl (*op. cit.*, iii, 1931, p. 396), additional to those from San Sebastiano, only one (*op. cit.*, i, 1925, 1565A), from the Catacomb of S. Priscilla, may be a genuinely Christian parallel to these *graffiti*: dulcissimo Antistheni coniugi suo refrigerium (fecit? promisit?) ('... partook of (?) a refreshment-meal for Antisthenes, her sweetest husband'). Diehl, 1565B may be pagan, 1571 is more likely to be pagan than Christian (it has the D.M.S. formula); and *CIL*, xi. 2, 6222 by no means certainly relates to a Christian. The closest parallels to the use of the terms in the *graffiti* are definitely pagan (*e.g.* *Notizie degli Scavi*, 1907, p. 432: Feltre; *CIL*, xiv. 3323:

Praeneste). This Christian *refrigerium*, in the sense of a ceremonial meal, appears to have been in many ways analogous, externally, to the well-known *agape* ('love-feast'), which was a social feast and reunion of a group or community of Christians, in origin non-funerary and associated with (while being distinct from) the Eucharist, but in the third and fourth centuries held on the occasion of the anniversaries of relatives and martyrs, and sometimes degenerating into debauchery (St. Augustine, *Epist.*, xxii. 3 = Migne, *Patrologia Latina*, xxxiii, col. 91: comessationes et ebrietates ita concessae et licitae putantur ut in honorem etiam beatissimorum martyrum non solum per dies solemnes . . . sed etiam quotidie celebrentur ('debauchery and drunkenness are held to be so right and proper, that they are indulged in even in honour of the blessed martyrs, not only on feast-days . . . but daily')). Large rooms for funerary banquets, presumably owned by members of Christian confraternities and sometimes equipped with wells and *agape*-tables, are known in the Roman catacombs and in North African Christian cemeteries (Cabrol, *Dictionnaire*, etc., i, 1903, *s.v.* 'Agape', col. 808 ff.). Communal feasts of this type are mentioned frequently in the writings of the Fathers and others. One passage (Migne, *Patrologia Graeca*, xvii, col. 517), describing these feasts in a Christian community (probably of the fourth century) in commemoration of the dead (ut fiat festivitas nostra in memoriam requiei defunctis animabus, quarum memoriam celebramus ('that our festivity may be in memory of the repose of the souls of the departed whom we commemorate')), in which rich and poor, clergy and laity, all partake, is particularly noteworthy. For it contains a sentence which brings out the distinction normally made between *refrigerium* in the sense of heavenly bliss and the commemorative meal, to which that term is not applied: devote memoriam agimus, tam illorum refrigerio gaudentes, quam etiam nobis piam consumationem in fide postulantes ('we commemorate [the dead] devoutly, both rejoicing in their refreshment and praying in faith for a holy consummation for ourselves'). Only one fragmentary *graffito* from San Sebastiano seems to contain an instance of the normal Christian usage of *refrigerium*: . . .] sinum (the end of a proper name?) in r[ef]ri[g]erium (Styger (ii), p. 68, No. 42). In fact, the *refrigeria* held in the Triclia at San Sebastiano would appear to be, both in nomenclature and character, a distinctive and unusual variety of the Christian commemorative feast. Here the meals, recorded by individuals instead of by communities, seem to have been, not merely accompaniments to commemorations or foretastes of Heaven for the banqueters, but in themselves an honour, almost an offering, to the dead, something that might even benefit them. This thought, if we interpret the phraseology aright, is definitely tinged with paganism. The notion that a funerary or commemorative feast (as distinct from the Eucharist) could in any way affect or help the dead was clean contrary to official Christian teaching.

57. Mancini, pp. 46–75, Pls. 9–16.

58. Tolotti, pp. 115–21. The close connection between courtyard and precinct is established beyond reasonable doubt by the fact that the southern and western walls are of one build.

59. The Sigma is often ascribed to the period following the suppression of the oval courtyard, as proposed by von Gerkan (*op. cit.*, p. 264), who believed that the 'attics' over the pediments of the three mausolea were later than the pediments, and that the Sigma must be later again, since the rough projection of the tile seating for this, above the attic, is too carelessly finished to have been ever visible. This argument can no longer be maintained in the face of the fresh evidence presented by Tolotti (p. 123 ff.) for the continuation of the floor of the Sigma beneath (and earlier than) the barrel-vaulted chamber to the west, and the demonstration that the pediments can never have been free-standing. The attics (although not necessarily the paintings on them) must be an original feature. The Sigma may be later than the building of the tombs (this would help to explain the rough workmanship; *cf.* the later wooden porches). It had, however, itself already been suppressed long before the construction of the Memoria, to make way for a transverse terracing-wall, designed to keep clear the windows of the partly sunken barrel-vaulted chamber. Tolotti (p. 158 ff.) ascribes this wall to a hypothetical transitional phase of the Memoria, after the filling-in of the oval courtyard and the building of the Triclia, but before the paving of the upper courtyard and the suppression of the barrel-vaulted chamber; but the evidence for this is very slender. The interrelation of these structures has an important bearing on the chronology, since, if it could be shown that the Sigma is later than the filling-in of the oval courtyard, then the Memoria could hardly have been established in its final form before the beginning of the fourth century—as von Gerkan maintained.

60. *Journal of Roman Studies*, xxxix, 1949, pp. 20–2, Pls. 3, 4.

61. This group of graves, with typically crypto-Christian formulae, was buried by the first raising of the level of the courtyard, *i.e.* in the first half of the third century. *E.g.* Mancini, p. 48: Greek epitaph of Ankotia Irene, described as φιλόθεος ('God-loving') and φιλοχήρα ('kind to widows'), accompanied by drawings of a fish and an anchor; p. 66: Greek epitaph of Julia Crispa, described as θεοφιλεστάτη ('most God-loving'). A. Ferrua, however, rejects (*Rivista di Archeologia Cristiana*, xxi, 1944–5 p. 204, with Fig. 7) the Christian interpretation of the second epitaph on the score of its formula Θ Δ (=Θ(εοῖς) δ(αίμοσι) ?, 'to the god-spirits'): but like the equivalent *dis manibus*, which is well attested in Christian inscriptions, such a formula would not be wholly impossible in a crypto-Christian inscription.

62. Mancini, pp. 52–3, Pl. 10; H. Lietzmann, *Petrus und Paulus in Rom*, 1927, pp. 301–3, Pl. 9; Wirth, *op. cit.*, pp. 191–4, Fig. 101. Since the attic and the tomb are now shown to have been contemporary, we have no proof that the Christian paintings on the former were appreciably later than some, at least,

of the paintings within the latter. On the ceiling of the recess opposite the entrance, and added when the interior of the tomb was remodelled and re-decorated, are three figure-scenes in roundels, executed in a sketchy 'impressionistic' style: (i) a man holding a wand, extending one hand, and floating heavenwards, without means of support, above the heads of a crowd of very elongated onlookers; (ii) a group including a seated figure with a figure stand-ing in front of it, suggesting an episode of some kind or a religious ceremony; (iii) a funeral-scene with mourners surrounding a corpse laid out on a bier (Mancini, pp. 58–9, Pl. 14, 1–3; Lietzmann, *op. cit.*, pp. 303–4, Pl. 10; Wirth, *op. cit.*, pp. 190–1, Pls. 50, 49, *b*, *c*). As Wirth points out (*op. cit.*, p. 190), the form of (i) is rare among scenes of pagan apotheosis (where, moreover, the dead person is normally carried skywards either in a chariot, or on the back of an eagle, or on the back, or in the arms, of some personification, or on a shield); and he suggests that we may have here a crypto-Christian version of Christ's Ascension. Such an interpretation cannot be proved (and the large scale of the floating figure, as compared with that of the other figures, would be equally appropriate to a scene of pagan apotheosis), but it cannot be wholly excluded. For the two companion-scenes, (ii) and (iii), if not specifically Christian, are not unequivocally pagan; and we have before us the example of the crypto-Christian painting in the Hypogeum of the Aurelii on the Viale Manzoni in Rome. This painting depicts the Triumphal Entry into Jerusalem, in which Christ appears in the guise of a Roman emperor or general on horseback and Jerusalem in that of Rome, with the Tiber flowing through it, while an ass in a stall just outside the city-gate betrays to the initiated the true implications of the scene (*Monumenti Antichi*, xxviii, 1922, Pl. 10, *b*).

63. R. Lanciani, *Dissertazioni della Pontificia Accademia Romana di Archeologia*, ser. II, xiv, 1920, pp. 57–109.

64. See p. 187, Note 44.

65. *E.g.* the tomb-chamber of the imperial slave Elpisius: Mancini, Fig. 21 and pp. 66–7; Tolotti, pp. 98–100. This tomb is built up against, and later than, the footings of the back-wall of one of the first-century *columbaria*, but is itself earlier than the masonry substructures of the 'Tomb of the Innocentii', into which it was incorporated.

66. A tomb-inscription bearing this date was discovered *in situ* in a mausoleum built on the south side of the church after the latter had been erected (Tolotti, pp. 232–3). A stone sill, on which is cut the name 'Constantinus' in monogram, was found *in situ* between the Via Appia and the church and has been plausibly connected with the latter (*ibid.*, Fig. 60 and p. 252).

66a. A recent interpretation of one of the *graffiti* (Appendix C, p. 268), if correct, would prove the Memoria to have been in use already in 260.

67. See p. 188, Note 44.

68. The original name is found as late as the eighth century, see *Liber Ponti-*

ficalis, i, p. 508 (Pope Hadrian, 772–95): ecclesiam Apostolorum foris porta Appia, miliario tertio, in loco qui appellatur Catacumbas, ubi corpus beati Sebastiani martyris cum aliis quiescit, in ruinis praeventam noviter restauravit ('the church of the Apostles at the third milestone beyond the Appian gate, at the spot called Catacumbas, where the body of the blessed Sebastian rests beside the remains of others [Hadrian], found in ruins and completely restored').

69. The authors are grateful to Fr. Cuthbert King, S.J., for bringing these points to their notice.

70. Eusebius, *HE*, vii. 10–12. For discussions of the Valerianic persecution, see *Cambridge Ancient History*, xii, 1939, pp. 205–6; H. Grégoire, *Les persécutions dans l'empire romain*, 1951, pp. 46–54.

71. H. Dessau, *Inscriptiones Latinae Selectae*, 2216, 2222.

72. Capocci, *op. cit.* (Note 27), p. 204.

73. The anti-Christian decrees of Valerian were aimed primarily at the clergy and high-ranking laity. The former were forbidden to hold services in the Christian cemeteries; but it should be noted that there is no suggestion in the evidence of any ban on private devotions, whether at home or at tombs (see the references given above, Note 70).

74. F. Grossi Gondi, *Dissertazioni della Pontificia Accademia Romana di Archeologia*, ser. II, xiv, 1920, pp. 263–77. In particular, the text 'ad Paulum et Petrum refrigeravi' (p. 171) seems to imply the close physical presence of some bodily relics of the Apostles. There is, of course, no question that from the fourth century onwards the phrase is used in contexts that demand the presence of *brandea* (p. 209), rather than of corporeal relics. For instance, an epitaph from Castellum Tingitanum (Orléansville) in Algeria records that parents had erected a memoria to their child 'aput/[sancto]s apostolos Petru(m) et/[Paulu(m)]' (*Mémoires de l'Académie des Inscriptions et Belles Lettres de l'Institut de France*, xii, 1908, p. 324, No. 332). This obviously refers to objects that had touched the shrines of the Apostles in Rome. If the Via Appia shrine was schismatical, this particular *graffito* would have to be explained as alluding to the presence there of similar objects—to a foreshadowing, in the late-third century, of fourth-century and later practice.

75. This practice was certainly not yet current in Rome and the West in the sixth century. When the Byzantine Empress Constantina asked Gregory the Great to send her 'caput eiusdem sancti Pauli, aut aliud quid de corpore ipsius' ('the head of the holy Paul, or some other bodily relic'), the Pope refused, telling her that she must be content with *brandea*: in Romanis namque vel totius Occidentis partibus omnino intolerabile est atque sacrilegum, si sanctorum corpora tangere quisquam fortasse voluerit. quod si praesumpserit, certum est quia haec temeritas impunita nullo modo remanebit. pro qua re de Graecorum consuetudine, qui ossa levare sanctorum se asserunt, vehementer miramur, et

vix credimus ('For among the Romans and everywhere in the West it is considered shocking and sacrilegious to desire to touch the bodies of the saints. Should anyone presume to do this, it is certain that his rashness will not go unpunished. Hence I am filled with surprise and incredulity, when I hear of the practice, said to be current among the Greeks, of moving the bones of saints'). *Epist.* iv. 30 = Migne, *Patrologia Latina*, lxxvii, cols. 701-2.

7

CONSTANTINE'S CHURCH

(a) The Original Building

THE decision to build a great church over the shrine on the Vatican hillside was one that cannot have been taken lightly. As we have already seen (pp. 12–17), it involved the dismantlement of a flourishing pagan cemetery, an event which must, at the very least, have caused much hard feeling among the families concerned and among the pagan community generally; and it involved the builders in terracing-operations comparable in scale to those of such great imperial enterprises as the Flavian Palace or the Baths of Trajan, but carried out on far more difficult, shifting ground. Whatever may have been the precise original purpose of the Petrine shrine, and whatever may have been its history during the persecutions of the second half of the third century, we cannot doubt that, in undertaking this work, Constantine believed, as for many centuries thereafter was universally believed, that he was honouring the actual resting-place of the remains of St. Peter.

Contemporary literature is strangely silent about this great enterprise. During the latter half, in particular, of Constantine's reign attention was directed elsewhere, towards Constantine's new capital, Constantinople, and towards his great new foundations in the Holy Land, with which Eusebius, bishop of Caesarea, our chief contemporary authority, was naturally more concerned than with events in the distant capital of the West. The earliest explicit reference to the construction of the church is probably that contained in the mosaic that once adorned the triumphal arch (the arch between nave and transept) of the old church. It showed Constantine presenting the church to Christ, accompanied by St. Peter, and bore the metrical inscription:

> quod duce te mundus surrexit in astra triumphans
> hanc Constantinus victor tibi condidit aula(m)[1]

('because under Thy leadership the world rose up triumphant to the skies, Constantine, himself victorious, has founded this hall in Thy honour'). From this text we learn that Constantine himself was responsible for the foundation; and it suggests that, even if the building was not completed during his lifetime, it had, at any rate, been carried well forward and possibly consecrated before his death. On the other hand, to judge from the list of properties with which it was endowed, it cannot have been begun very early in his reign.[2] In contrast to the Church of St. John Lateran, the cathedral-church of Rome and surely the first of Constantine's great ecclesiastical foundations, the endowments of which lay exclusively in Italy, the properties settled upon St. Peter's and upon the companion-foundation of St. Paul's, beside the Via Ostiensis, all lay in the eastern provinces of the Empire, which only fell to Constantine after the defeat of Licinius in 324.

Of recent attempts to establish more precisely the date at which the church was begun, two deserve brief mention. The one is based upon what is interpreted as a significant break in the series of dedicatory inscriptions from the Phrygianum, the Vatican shrine of Cybele (p. 6).[3] The nine dated inscriptions found in this area range from 305 to 390, with a long gap before 350 (specifically between April 319 and April 350, if CIL, vi. 1, 508, the find-spot of which is not recorded, may be taken to refer to the same shrine); and it is suggested that this interval should be brought into relation with the Greek text of a marble altar found in 1919 below the Palazzo dei Convertendi (between the Piazza San Pietro and the river), which records, unfortunately without giving a precise date, the restoration of the rites of *taurobolium* and *criobolium* (the sacrifice to Cybele of an ox and of a ram) after an interval of twenty-eight years,[4] an interval which may be explained as due to the disturbance caused by Constantine's building-operations in the immediate vicinity. The argument is ingenious and perfectly consistent with the evidence: the Greek lettering is that found in inscriptions of the middle of the fourth century; the 'night' to which this text refers might well be an allusion to the triumph of Christian 'atheism'; and the brief reign of the usurper Magnentius (350–3) suggests an occasion when the solemn reinstitution of the ceremonial in honour of Cybele would have been particularly appropriate. On the other hand, the evidence is by no means conclusive;[5] and it would presuppose that work started on the site of the church at least two, and possibly five, years before the eastern provinces, from which it was endowed, came under Constantine's control.

An alternative suggestion, put forward by M. W. Seston, notes that in 349 the Emperor Constans passed a law severely punishing *violatio sepulcri*, the provisions of which were made retrospective to cover the past sixteen years.[6] The reason for this, it is suggested, is that 333 was the year of whatever formal enactment or pronouncement was made by Constantine to cover the necessary work of destruction in the Vatican cemetery (pp. 12–17); and that his subjects had taken such flagrant advantage of its terms, by plundering tombs wholesale for building-materials, that drastic steps had now to be taken to check the abuse. But the period between 333 and Constantine's death in 337 is far too short for the building to have reached the relatively advanced state indicated by the mosaic of the triumphal arch. Actually, Mommsen and P. Krüger, in their respective editions of the *Codex Theodosianus* and *Codex Justinianus*, ascribe the law to Constantius, Caesar in 324. This may be an error (not commented on by Seston). In any case, the further hypothesis of Marrou,[7] that 333 was chosen as marking the beginning of the personal responsibility of Constans, Caesar in that year, has little bearing on the date at which work on St. Peter's was first undertaken.

The excavations have, unfortunately, made no direct contribution to the problem, beyond showing that the practical difficulties were indeed many, and that the work must have taken a long time to complete. In order to create a flat surface within the church at the level of the existing shrine, it was necessary to build an enormous artificial platform, of which a part, to the north and west, was scarped into the hillside, and the rest, by far the greater part, had to be built up on massive foundations to a height which, at the south-east corner, was at least 35 feet above the natural ground-level.[8] Within the limits of this platform, which involved the dumping of well over a million cubic feet of earth, the main lines of the church and of its interior colonnades were laid out in massive foundations of concrete masonry, built free-standing and faced partly with carefully coursed brick and partly with alternate courses of tufa and brick. Of the three southern foundations of the nave, the innermost measured 2·06 metres at the foot and 1·96 at pavement-level, which was 7 metres above natural ground-level; the two outermost, which were not fully excavated, measured 2·68 metres. Those parts of the cemetery that did not lie on the direct line of these great foundations were left standing, to help stabilize the mass of dumped earth which made up the body of the platform, and which was to carry the heavy marble floor of the church; and, wherever necessary, the existing structures were heightened or supplemented with partition-walls, so as to break the whole area into compartments of manageable size (Fig. 2).

This work was carried out in stages. First, the clearance of the site and the removal of the debris from the demolitions. Next, the building of the main foundations and of the partition-walls, with provision in both cases for the free movement of workmen from one part of the site to another (the arch by which one now enters the excavations is a workman's passage built into one of the main foundations of the nave). When this was done, the sarcophagi and any other fittings that had had to be moved were stacked in tombs and corridors; and finally the whole platform was brought up to the new level by dumping earth, stage by stage, within the individual compartments. For the greater part of the time many of the tombs remained accessible. Thus, a gap was left in the Constantinian partition-wall sealing off Tombs M, N, and O, and it was not until the first earth was dumped within the tombs and into the area immediately in front of them that this gap was finally closed. An arch was built into the partition-wall against the face of Tomb G, so as to leave the doorway free; and the rough steps down into the forecourt of Tomb B (p. 40) were built, presumably to give access to the inner tomb, when the level of the street in front had already been raised to the height of the original forecourt-façade as a preliminary to carrying this same façade up to the same height as those of the adjoining tombs. In Tomb H, as in many other parts of the excavations, sarcophagi were found stacked against the walls, and one of the secondary partition-walls was added when the tomb was already partly filled with earth;[9] and it was assuredly during the earlier stages of the dismantlement of the same tomb that Christian workmen scribbled on its walls the portraits and invocations described in chapter 1 (pp. 14–17). All of this work throughout the cemetery must have taken a long time, a time to be measured in years rather than in months; and we shall not go far wrong in ascribing the beginning of

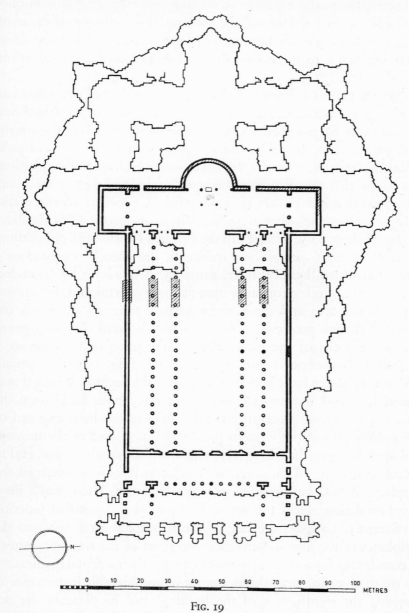

FIG. 19

The Constantinian Basilica, shown in relation to the present church. Remains exposed during the recent excavations are shown shaded.

the enterprise to the 'twenties of the fourth century, possibly but not certainly as early as 322; and the substantial completion of the main structure, although not necessarily of the ornament or of the subsidiary buildings, to the period shortly before Constantine's death in 337.

Old St. Peter's is known to us from a number of drawings and plans that were made before or during the course of its demolition to make way for the present church. The most detailed of these is the plan prepared by Tiberio Alfarano in or soon after 1571 and published in 1589–90;[10] and a very welcome result of the excavations is to show that this plan, made when a substantial part of the structures recorded had already been demolished, is nevertheless remarkably accurate; and what is more, that in its broad lines the late-medieval church was in fact still the original Constantinian building. As laid out by Constantine's architects, the church consisted of a lofty, five-aisled, basilical nave, some 85 metres long by 64 metres wide, with a single projecting apse at the west end and, interposed between the apse and the nave, a narrow transept, of which the terminal chapels projected a short distance beyond the outer north and south walls of the nave; beyond the nave to the east lay a rectangular colonnaded forecourt, or *atrium* (Fig. 19). This *atrium*, which may never have been completed in the form in which it was planned,[11] and the eastern part of the nave both lie beyond the limits of the recent excavations; but sufficient has been exposed of the foundations of the western part of the nave, and of the transept and apse, to show that these were all part of the original plan, and to reveal something of the internal lay-out. It has also confirmed the emphatic distinction between nave and transept. There was a massive foundation across the whole building at the point of junction between the two, on the line of the triumphal arch, whereas the stylobates of the nave-colonnades stop short of the transept, instead of continuing across it, as in so many other early transeptal basilicas.[12] As we shall see (p. 207), this is a point of considerable importance in assessing the significance of the building and its place in the development of contemporary architectural thought.

So far, these discoveries, welcome though they are as confirming the substantial accuracy of the Renaissance accounts, do not add much to what was already known about Constantine's church. What is new, and quite unexpected, is the discovery that the tomb was not at first buried beneath the altar of the new church, as has hitherto been generally assumed, but that, encased in precious marble, the primitive shrine continued to stand above the pavement, and was, indeed, the architectural focus of the whole building. At this point, the pavement of the new church was barely 30 centimetres above that of the pre-Constantinian shrine, and everything except the Aedicula and the short section of the Red Wall containing it had to be demolished down to this level. The Aedicula itself was left standing, enclosed within a small box-like edifice of marble, with pilaster-like panels of porphyry at the angles, and in the middle of the east face there was an arched opening corresponding to the upper part of Niche N^2 and the lower part of N^3. This little marble shrine, which measured barely 2·70 by 1·70 metres, stood near the west end of a low platform, approximately 9 metres square, which was enclosed within a low railing and raised one step above the floor of the rest of the church; and over it stood a monumental canopy, carried on four curiously shaped and elaborately carved marble columns. Church, platform, and shrine were so sited that the two rear-columns of the canopy and the shrine itself stood on the chord of the apse and, together with two more identical columns, formed a curtained screen dividing the apse from the transept. From this screen the platform projected forward into the transept, setting apart for special veneration the area immediately in front of the shrine; and over the middle of it, from the crown of the canopy, there hung a golden lamp (Fig. 20).[13]

Little enough of all this remains to be seen today. All trace of the two outer columns of the screen and of the two front-columns of the canopy was destroyed by the builders of the Covered Confessio (p. 216) and of the Open Confessio (p. 225) respectively. All that now remains in position is a part of the marble casing of the shrine and two substantial patches of the original marble paving immediately to the north and to the south of it, in which can be seen the sockets for the posts and chancel-slabs of the north-west and south-west angles of the enclosure-railing, and the impressions of the two rear (western)-columns of the canopy. Of the north and south faces of the shrine itself, only the base-moulding and some of the masonry backing survive (Fig. 16); but the rear-wall (which was nothing more than the surviving fragment of the Red Wall with an added marble facing) is still largely intact, and a part of this marble facing

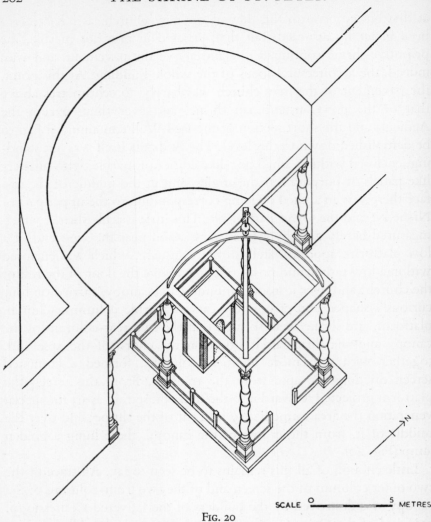

SCALE $\underset{0}{\rule{0pt}{0pt}}$ ▬▬▬▬▬ $\underset{5}{\rule{0pt}{0pt}}$ METRES

FIG. 20

Restoration of the fourth-century shrine, based on the surviving remains and on the Pola casket. There should be gates in the opening in the balustrade between the two front columns. (*Drawing by S. Rizzello*; reproduced from *Journal of Roman Studies*, xlii.)

is exposed and can be seen today, as Constantine built it, at the east end of the Cappella Clementina, beyond the altar of the Confessio (Fig. 25).[14] Within the shrine, the floor of the recess below the travertine slab (N² of the pre-Constantinian Aedicula) was at first about 35 centimetres below that of the pavement without, and consisted of an inscribed marble slab, taken from the tomb of a certain Publius Aelius Isidorus (probably from Tomb E of the Vatican cemetery) and reused face downwards, with its outer edge resting on the travertine sill of the Aedicula.[15] At first there does not seem to have been any provision made for access to the part of the shrine that was below ground (the original N^1); but at some quite early date the floor of N^2 was raised 16 centimetres by the insertion of a second marble slab, and this slab had a rectangular opening, measuring 25 by 19 centimetres, in the middle and, to match it, a similar opening was cut in the slab of Aelius Isidorus beneath. Later, but still before the raising of the presbytery at the end of the sixth century, the floor of the niche was raised again some 16 centimetres by the addition of a thick bed of fine mortar capped by three fine sheets of lead, which once extended up the side walls, presumably as a backing for an overlay of precious metal, but which were cut off at the new floor-level when N^2 was converted into the Niche of the Pallia (p. 223). The central hole was carefully maintained, and this hole, which now formed a shaft over 30 centimetres deep from the top of the lead sheeting to the bottom of the slab of Aelius Isidorus, was the hole through which, as Gregory of Tours so graphically describes (pp. 212–13), generations of pilgrims were able to lower small objects to be sanctified by contact with the holy relic below. At first the inner wall-faces were of marble; but at least as early as the second of the three phases described above, this was covered in thin silver, traces of which were found by the excavators, sealed in place by the later mortar. In the sixth century we can picture N^2, below the travertine slab, as a cupboard-like recess, approximately 1·25 metres wide by 1 metre deep and 1·15 metres high, with a small square hole in the middle of the floor, closed towards the east by doors, and richly ornamented within by precious metal-work. N^3, above the travertine slab, must have been similarly enriched; but of this no trace now survives.[16]

Fortunately, we can supplement the picture presented by the surviving remains from two other sources. One of these is the *Liber Pontificalis*; the other a fifth-century ivory casket, which was found in 1906 at Salmagher, near Pola in Istria, and is now in the museum at Pola (Fig. 21).[17] If one allows for the conventional perspective and the disproportionate scale of the worshipping figures, this casket gives a remarkably clear picture of the shrine as Constantine built it. Beneath the canopy two small figures stand in front of the shrine itself, of which the arched opening, the angle-pilasters, and

FIG. 21

The fourth-century shrine, as it appears on the Pola casket. (*Drawing by D. Black.*)

the carved cornice are clearly shown. Within the arched opening a cross stands on a horizontal shelf, which must represent the original travertine slab dividing N^2 from N^3, and the space below the slab (N^2) is closed by what appear to be a pair of doors. The object below the right-hand figure is a part of the railing enclosing the platform. The upper part of the canopy consists of four ribs, possibly of wood cased in metal, arched towards the centre, and the circular object hanging from it must be the lamp, in the shape of a crown, which is listed by the *Liber Pontificalis* among the gifts of Constantine, and is said to have hung in front of the tomb.[18]

The early chapters of the *Liber Pontificalis*, the official chronicle of the bishops of Rome, were not, until the sixth century, compiled in anything like the form in which they have come down to us; and the story that Constantine buried St. Peter's body in a massive coffin of solid bronze (a story that has exercised the ingenuity of generations of scholars) can now be seen to be no more than a pious legend.[19] It does, nevertheless, contain a great deal of valuable information about the early history of the Roman Church, and one such item is the record that the six carved marble columns, which are such a singular feature of the shrine as it is shown on the Pola casket, were a gift from Constantine, brought 'from Greece'.[20] These columns, all of which still survive, reused in pairs by Bernini to adorn three of the galleries (those of Saints Helena, Veronica, and Andrew) in the dome of the present church, measured nearly 5 metres in height and were cut to a gentle spiral like an old-fashioned stick of barley-sugar, and carved with alternate bands of spiral fluting and of vine-scroll, with naked, winged Cupids playing among the foliage. Both the shape, which is unique in the monumental architecture of its period, and the very distinctive ornament confirm the record in the *Liber Pontificalis*. They must have been carved somewhere about the turn of the second and third centuries A.D.; and they were taken almost certainly from some building in or near the northern Aegean, perhaps from Constantinople itself or from its immediate neighbourhood. As we shall see (pp. 247–51), this was only the beginning of a long and strangely varied history.

To see St. Peter's shrine and the great church that housed it with the eyes of Constantine's contemporaries, we have to remember how new and strange must have seemed the whole idea of a great official sanctuary such as this. Christianity had just emerged from its last and bitterest struggle for official recognition by the Roman State; and although the trend of recent research is to show that the periods of actual persecution were brief and often local in their impact, and that for very considerable periods of the third century the Christian community was able to prosper and to go its own way unmolested, nevertheless it had been at best a precarious prosperity, not one to encourage the building of great monuments or the parade of sacred relics. At the beginning of the fourth century, in Rome as elsewhere, the ordinary Christian meeting-place was still the house-church (*domus ecclesiae*), akin to that of which the Mesopotamian frontier-city of Dura-Europos has now at last yielded an actual example, dating from the middle of the third century.[21] This was a building indistinguishable externally from its neighbours, and modified within only so far as was necessary to serve the varied purposes of the local community—a large hall, consisting of two rooms run together, for the celebration of the Eucharist, and smaller rooms for such purposes as the administration of Baptism and the instruction of those awaiting Baptism, for the lodging of the priest, and for the partaking of common meals. No doubt the churches in the larger towns were larger and more elaborate, and some of them may well have been built expressly for the purpose; but they probably followed traditional models. Today, after more than half a century of intensive search through the Mediterranean world, there is nothing whatever to suggest that prior to Constantine the Church had made any attempt to develop a monumental architecture of its own.

One of the many problems, therefore, that faced the Christians after the Edict of Milan in 312 was nothing less than the creation of an architecture worthy of the status and dignity of the newly enfranchized Christian religion; and in default of a specifically Christian tradition of monumental architecture, it was almost inevitable that they should turn to the models of pagan Antiquity. How far this was the result of deliberate policy, and what exactly were the models chosen, are questions upon which there is as yet no general agreement. But there can be little doubt that one of the most important factors, perhaps the deciding factor, in determining the pattern of the future development of Christian architecture was the policy adopted by the Emperor himself with regard to his own great ecclesiastical foundations. It is against such a background that we have to view Constantine's Church of St. Peter.[22]

As an architectural type, the basilica—that is to say, the hall subdivided by internal colonnades and lit by means of a clerestory over the colonnades of the central nave—had a long history, which goes back in Roman use at least to the beginning of the second century B.C., and which, with the passage of the centuries, came to serve an ever-increasing variety of purposes. Whether or not it owes to Constantine its adoption by the Church as the standard form of hall for the celebration of the Eucharist (the question is controversial, but there is good reason to believe that this may, in fact, be the case), it is a significant fact that a number of the most important of Constantine's ecclesiastical foundations were, in whole or in part, basilical buildings. Almost certainly the earliest of these was the Church of St. John Lateran, the cathedral-church of the bishop of Rome; and the excavations undertaken by Josi between 1934 and 1938 beneath the pavement of the present church have shown that this was probably at first an early-Christian basilica of normal type, with five aisles and a single, western apse; the transept, hitherto assumed to be a feature of the original Constantinian building, now appears to be an addition, dating possibly from the substantial restoration of the church undertaken by Pope Sergius III (904–11).[23] The Church of the Nativity at Bethlehem and the Church of the Holy Sepulchre at Jerusalem, both founded after Constantine's acquisition of the eastern provinces in 324, belong to a rather different category of building, which may conveniently be referred to, by the name that they often receive in contemporary literature as *martyria* (μαρτύρια); that is to say, buildings put up to house and honour objects or places that were tangible 'witnesses' to the Christian faith. These might be the bodies or relics of martyrs, or they might be, particularly in the Holy Land, places associated by tradition with outstanding events in the story of the Old and New Testaments; and the difference in function between such *martyria* and the ordinary churches of everyday congregational use frequently found expression in the adoption of architectural types very different from those of the ordinary basilica.[24]

The main lines of the Constantinian Church of the Nativity were recovered by excavations undertaken in 1933–4, which showed it to have consisted of three distinct elements: a rectangular colonnaded forecourt opening onto a five-aisled basilical nave, and at the far (east) end of the nave, over the Grotto of the Nativity, an octagonal structure, the *martyrium* proper.[25] The form of the original Church of the Holy Sepulchre is much discussed. Very little survives of the original building, and contemporary accounts, such as that of Eusebius, which are the chief source for our knowledge of its appearance, are variously interpreted. There can, however, be very little doubt that it, too, consisted of the same three elements: a short colonnaded forecourt, a five-aisled basilical nave, and (this time at the west end) the *martyrium* proper, which was later a domed circular building, but was probably at the outset an open colonnaded court framing a small, richly ornamented monument on the site of the actual Tomb.[26]

St. Peter's, built to house the traditional site of the Apostle's grave, had a function analogous to that of the Churches of the Nativity and of the Holy Sepulchre; and it belongs, as we have seen (p. 196), to the same later phase of Constantine's building-activity. It is no surprise, therefore, to find that, like them, it consists of three axially disposed elements: a colonnaded forecourt opening onto a basilical nave, and at the opposite end of the nave a structure housing and displaying the object of veneration. The distinction between basilical nave and *martyrium* transept is architecturally less marked than it is at Bethlehem and at Jerusalem. But there may well have been a screen dividing nave from transept (there can be no proof of this, since at this point the Constantinian floor-level has been wholly destroyed); and in any case the fact that, under the influence of this very church, transepts came later to be a commonplace of Western basilical architecture (p. 246), has softened the impact on modern eyes of a distinction which must have been far more clearly felt by observers familiar with the plain basilical halls of pagan Antiquity. It was not until two and a half centuries later (p. 216) that the altar was moved to its present position directly over the tomb, obliterating a distinction between the two halves of the building which, to Constantine's architects, must still have seemed perfectly clear.

Where was the altar in Constantine's church? It has been suggested that the original travertine slab of the Aedicula, which is still clearly visible on the Pola casket, incorporated within the Constantinian shrine, now served as the altar.[27] But, apart from the improbability of the altar being tucked away within a low arched opening, barely 80 centimetres wide, this suggestion ignores the explicit statement in the *Liber Pontificalis* that Gregory the Great (590–604) made it possible to celebrate Mass over the body of St. Peter, a statement which clearly implies that previously this had not been possible. More plausible is the suggestion[28] that the altar was still at this early date a portable object (there is no evidence of fixed altars in Rome before the fifth century), and that for the celebration of Mass it was placed within the reserved space in front of the shrine, immediately below the centre of the canopy. A third possibility is that Mass was not at first celebrated within the *martyrium* at all, but in the body of the basilical nave. This was certainly the practice in the Church of the Holy Sepulchre as late as the end of the fourth century; and both in North Africa and in the northern Adriatic coastlands, the two areas of the Empire from which we have relatively full information on this point, the altar seems regularly to have been in the body of the nave at this early date.[29] It is not at all impossible, therefore, that, in the original plan for the church, Mass (which, it must be remembered, was not a daily office in these memorial-churches, but was limited to certain fixed anniversaries) was meant to be celebrated in the nave, very possibly at a portable altar, and that the transept was reserved for the more personal devotions of visiting pilgrims.

One cannot fail to be struck by the resemblance to such later medieval centres of pilgrimage as the shrines of St. Thomas at Canterbury or of St. Swithin at Winchester; and we have the words of St. Augustine—'every day there are cases of drunken brawling in the church of the blessed Peter, the Apostle'[30]—to remind us that the fourth century was no more free of abuse than the fourteenth.

The fourth-century pilgrim to the shrine of St. Peter on the Vatican Hill ate his meal within the church, as his predecessor a generation earlier had done at the shrine on the Via Appia (p. 172); and, if he were poor, he might profit by the munificence of some such wealthy fellow-Christian as Pammachius, who fed all the poor of Rome within St. Peter's as an act of almsgiving on the occasion of his wife's death—'I seem to see them', writes his friend, Paulinus of Nola, in his letter of condolence, 'pouring into the great Basilica of the glorious Peter . . . in such throngs that all the space is filled, both within the church and before the doors of the *atrium* and before the steps leading down to the open space without.'[31] In another letter[32] Paulinus appears to indicate that the *atrium* was the normal setting for such deeds of charity; but evidently on occasion the nave of the church would also serve. By the end of the fourth century the abuses of which St. Augustine speaks were such that St. Ambrose in Milan and others elsewhere were moved to suppress these meals; and with the assimilation of the *martyria* to the normal cult and the development of an organized system of poor-relief, the practice was gradually dropped.[33]

Within the transept the visitor was presumably free to circulate and to pray at the railings around the shrine, as today the pilgrim prays at the railings of the Open Confessio. The surviving patches of Constantinian paving immediately adjoining the shrine are significantly worn, and needed patching at least once during the two and a half centuries that this pavement was in use; and there are sockets for movable wooden barriers at the entrance to the apse, just as there are sockets in the pavement of the present church for barriers to control the crowds on special occasions.[34] If the visitor were specially privileged, he might be allowed to pass within the railings of the shrine and to have the doors of the shrine itself unlocked. There, as we learn from the graphic description given by Gregory of Tours, he would thrust his head and shoulders into the space below the travertine slab (*i.e.* into what had been N²) and lower fragments of cloth (*brandea*) through the hole in the floor, to be sanctified by contact with the tomb of the saint (pp. 212–13.[35]

This idea of sanctification through contact or proximity was typical of the age, and it found further expression in St. Peter's in the desire for burial as near as possible to the body of the Apostle. The builders of the Renaissance and the recent excavators alike found the levels immediately below the floor of the Constantinian church stacked with the graves of those who had been rich or influential enough to secure the privilege of burial beneath the same roof. One such, consisting of a carved marble sarcophagus, can be seen, as the excavators found it, trenched down through the walls of Tomb R on the left-hand side of the Clivus (Pl. I). No less than five more were found within the area of what had been the courtyard, P, in front of the pre-Constantinian shrine (Fig. 11, Graves α, β, δ, ε, μ). All these consist of slabs of marble (one of the slabs of ε is none other than the epitaph of Gaius Valerius Herma, the builder of Tomb H), and, except perhaps for β, all are contemporary with, or later than, the building of the Constantinian Basilica[36]. Another chance find concerns the finest of all the Roman Christian sarcophagi, that of Junius Bassus, who was City Prefect and died in 359. He was buried within the apse, just behind the shrine, and his sarcophagus was found and the lid destroyed in 1597, when the floor of the central passage of the covered Confessio was lowered to make the Cappella Clementina. The greater part of the inscription has now been recovered, found built into the wall of the chapel.[37]

When we turn from the buildings housing the shrine to the shrine itself, we find that here, too, Constantine's architects were working to a consistent plan. As at Bethlehem, and still more clearly in the Church of the Holy Sepulchre, we see the same combination of respect for the sacred relic and utter disregard for its surroundings and historical associations. The attitude of mind that could cut away the rock surrounding the Tomb of Christ so as to leave it upstanding, cased in gold and precious marble, seems strange to us; but it is one that the Renaissance would have understood and applauded. When the papal architects destroyed Constantine's Basilica to make way for the present church, they did no more and no less than Constantine himself had done in destroying the Vatican cemetery, pagan and Christian tombs alike, and levelling all but the heart of the pre-existing shrine. These were the acts of ages more self-assured than our own; and in this respect, as in the relation of the completed shrine to the architectural complex as a whole, the little marble edifice enclosing the Vatican Aedicula and the canopy above it correspond very closely to the grave-monument that housed the actual Tomb-chamber of the Holy Sepulchre.

Where the age of Constantine differed from the Renaissance was that, however revolutionary its ideas, the language used to express them was the language of tradition. Men might marvel at the form and workmanship of the columns of the canopy; but the canopy itself spoke a language that was familiar to all. As an attribute of divinity it had many centuries of history behind it, at first in the ancient East and later in the Hellenistic world, whence it passed, quite early in the Empire, into the repertory of Roman imperial symbolism.[38] Whether as early as the beginning of the fourth century an actual canopy was already in use in the throne-room of the living emperor, as it certainly was not long after, we cannot say. But we find it established on the coinage at least as early as the second century as a symbol of imperial authority; and the surviving remains of just such a canopy, dating from the end of the third century, have recently been identified in the chapel of the imperial cult in the legionary camp at Luxor.[39] From the imperial cult it passed to the Church. Just as the Christians of the third century had been prepared to borrow and to 'baptize' the symbolism of their pagan neighbours to express their inner hopes and aspirations (chapter 4, *passim*), so in the moment of its triumph the Church turned naturally to the ceremonial of the imperial court for the symbolic expression of divine authority and power. Henceforth, for example, the Apostles wear imperial purple; the empty throne, cushioned and jewelled, that we see in the mosaics of Rome and of Ravenna, is the imperial throne, as we find it on the Roman coinage; and it may very well be that the basilica itself owes its adoption as the standard form of church to the part played by the great basilical audience-halls of the palace in the contemporary ceremonial of the imperial court.[40] As we can see from the pages of Eusebius, Constantine's contemporaries were well aware of the relation. In St. Peter's we can already see these elements taking Christian shape.

(b) The Later History of the Shrine

On Constantine's death, the basilica was already well advanced (p. 196), but it was not yet complete. From the inscription of the mosaic in the semi-dome of the apse, the text of which is recorded in several early collections made between the sixth and the ninth centuries, we learn that the church was the work of Constantine and of his son (presumably Constans, 337–50), who is referred to in terms which clearly show that, when the mosaic was put up, his father was already dead.[41] This mosaic, which may have been damaged in the fifth century, and was certainly restored in the seventh by Pope Severinus (640), was replaced by Innocent III (1198–1216), and this later mosaic was itself demolished by Clement VIII in 1592. But except in such details as the insertion of the figures of Innocent himself and the Roman Church, there is good reason to believe that the thirteenth-century mosaic, of which we possess an official copy made just before its demolition, followed closely the model established by its predecessor; and that, like it, the early-medieval mosaic, which may very well go back substantially to the fourth century, portrayed a central figure of Christ, seated in majesty below the heavenly canopy and flanked by the figures of St. Peter and St. Paul and by two palm-trees; and below, echoing this upper scene, the Agnus Dei flanked by the twelve Apostle-lambs and by the cities of Jerusalem and of Bethlehem, symbolizing the Churches of the Jews and of the Gentiles.[42] The symbolism throughout is that of the fourth century; and it may well be not without significance that precisely the same scenes appear on the face of the Pola casket (pp. 203–4) opposite to that which portrays the Constantinian shrine of St. Peter.

With the later history of the building as a whole we are not here concerned, except in so far as it affects the history of the central shrine; and there is nothing in either the literary or the archaeological record to suggest that the latter underwent any major alterations before the end of the sixth century. Under Sixtus III (432–40) we hear of its enrichment with gifts of precious metal-work;[43] and it may have undergone some minor changes when the church was restored by his successor, Leo the Great (440–61).[44] But it seems to have been still substantially the Constantinian shrine that was seen in or shortly before 590 by the deacon Agiulf, whose impressions are recorded by Gregory of Tours in a passage that deserves quotation in full, if only for the vivid picture that it gives of the tomb and of the practices of those who came to pay their devotions at it:

'St. Peter . . . is buried in the temple formerly called Vaticanum, which has four lines of columns, wonderful to see, ninety-six in number. It also has four *in altare*, making one hundred in all, not counting those which carry the canopy over the tomb. This tomb is placed *sub altare* and is set carefully apart. But whoso wishes to pray, for him the doors (*cancelli*) that give access to the place are unbolted, and he enters the precinct over the tomb, and a small window (*fenestella*) is opened, and placing his head within he asks for whatever he requires; nor is there any delay in granting his request, provided that his prayer is just. And if he wishes to carry away a holy token, a piece of cloth weighed in a scale is hung within; and then, watching and fasting, he makes urgent prayer that the Apostle's virtue further his request. And if his faith prevail, when the cloth is raised from the tomb, wonderful to tell, it is so imbued with holy virtue that it weighs far more than it did before; and then he knows that he has received, along with this sign of grace, a favourable answer to his prayer. . . . There are also snow-white columns of wondrous elegance, four in number, which are said to uphold the canopy over the tomb.'[45]

The figure of ninety-six columns is presumably arrived at by adding to the eighty-eight columns of the nave-colonnades the eight which stood at the west end of the lateral aisles of the nave, where these aisles opened onto the transept.[46] The four *in altare*, a phrase which is used elsewhere by Gregory in the sense of 'in the part of the church that contains the altar',[47] must be the two pairs of columns carrying the partition-walls at the ends of the transept. The *cancelli* are evidently the gates opening into the reserved space beneath the canopy (such gates should be added to the restored drawing of the shrine, Fig. 20); and the *fenestella* is presumably the opening directly over the tomb, beneath the travertine slab. The 'columns of wondrous elegance' are the four vine-scroll columns of the canopy; the other two, set less prominently against the shoulders of the apse, evidently failed to catch the eye of Gregory's informant.

Apart from the vivid picture that Gregory's account gives us of the shrine, it is of value as showing that, wherever the altar may have been in the time of Constantine (p. 208), by the end of the seventh century it was certainly established securely in the transept. One cannot press the words *sub altare* to mean that the altar was now directly over the tomb[48]—the obvious implication of the changes effected by Pope Gregory the Great a few years later (p. 216) is that it was not—but it must have stood somewhere within the central precinct, beneath the canopy. This is in accordance with all that we know of the development of Christian architectural and liturgical practice in the centuries immediately following Constantine. Not only was there a steady tendency to isolate the presbytery and to move it away from the centre of the church towards one end, a tendency which, in the Eastern Church, resulted finally in the development of the iconostasis as a barrier between the celebrant and the congregation; but from the outset there were forces at work tending to merge what had at first been two quite distinct classes of building, the *martyrium* and the ordinary church; and whereas in the East, for a variety of historical reasons, the result was the gradual abandonment of the basilical church in favour of the centralized plans of later Byzantine practice, in the West it took the form of bringing the altar and the holy relic into ever closer association within the framework of the basilical church. Where, as was true in the great majority of cases, the object of veneration was contained in a portable reliquary, it was placed beneath the altar; and, as we can now see in St. Peter's, where the holy relic was itself a fixture, it was the altar that was moved. One of the reasons for this distinction between the two halves of the Christian world is perhaps to be sought in the fact that the Apocalypse—which contains the passage (6: 9): 'I saw under the altar the souls of them that had been slain for the word of God and for the witness they had borne'—was not recognized as canonical by the Eastern Church until a very late date, whereas in the West, not only was it taken into the Canon, but it also exercised a tremendous influence on the development of Christian art and symbolism. Whether or not this is the reason for the change, the fact is clear: in the fifth and sixth centuries we find an ever-increasing emphasis on the association of altar and relic, an association which was to have a profound effect on the subsequent development of western European architecture.[49]

In St. Peter's, we can probably trace the influence of these ideas as early as the beginning of the fifth century. They are already implicit in the words of St. Jerome: 'Is it an evil thing that the bishop of Rome does, when he offers sacrifice to God over what are to us the hallowed bones, to you the miserable dust, of dead men, Peter and Paul, and when he treats their tombs as the altars of Christ?';[50] and it is not unreasonable to conclude that these words are to be taken literally, and that by this date (406) Mass was, in fact, already being celebrated within the precinct of the shrine. Within the Constantinian shrine the natural place for an altar, whether portable or fixed, was beneath the centre of the canopy and the golden lamp,

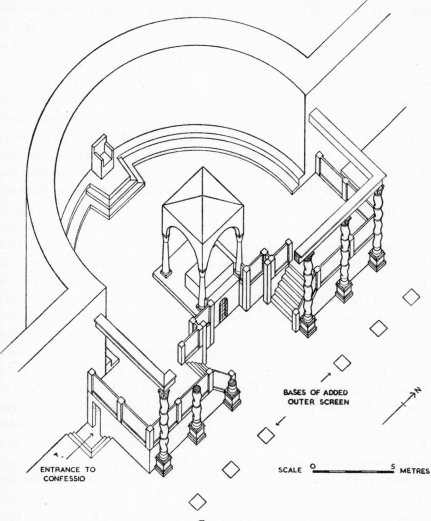

ENTRANCE TO
CONFESSIO

BASES OF ADDED
OUTER SCREEN

SCALE 0 ————————— 5 METRES

FIG. 22

Restoration of the shrine as it appeared after the raising of the presbytery by Gregory the Great, *c.* A.D. 600. The outer line of spiral columns was added in the eighth century. The details of the canopy, of the bishop's throne, and of the balustrade are conjectural. (*Drawing by S. Rizzello*; reproduced from *Journal of Roman Studies*, xlii.)

in front of the tomb; and unless one is prepared to accept the travertine slab in its cupboard-like enclosure as the altar, here or hereabouts it must have stood throughout the fifth and sixth centuries. By the end of the sixth century, however, Constantine's shrine, for all its venerable associations, must long have ceased to represent contemporary practice in a world in which the intimate union of altar and holy relic had long been accepted as the normal rule; and it is not surprising, therefore, that, very soon after it had been seen and described by Gregory of Tours's emissary, it was drastically remodelled to bring it into line with current ideas.

This reconstruction of the shrine (Fig. 22) took the form of raising the whole of the area within the Constantinian apse some 1·45 metres above the old pavement-level to form a new, raised presbytery, and of incorporating within it, below this new floor-level, a crypt, known as the Covered (or Semicircular) Confessio. To allow for steps leading up to the presbytery and down into the crypt, the raised platform had to be carried nearly 6 metres forward into the transept, obliterating all trace of the Constantinian shrine except for the small central edifice, the lower part of which was engulfed in the body of the platform, leaving only the east face exposed between the two flights of steps, while the upper part was incorporated within the new altar, which thus stood almost on the chord of the apse, at the level of the raised presbytery, immediately over the Apostle's tomb. Around the circumference of the apse ran a pair of steps, forming a continuous bench, and, on the axis of the building, the bishop's throne. The Constantinian canopy and screen were dismantled, and the six columns ranged in a row across the front of the presbytery to form a screen. There they were joined in the eighth century by six more, of closely similar form and workmanship, a present to Gregory III (731–41) from the Byzantine Exarch of Ravenna; and these were placed immediately to the east of the original six, to form a second, outer screen.[51]

The crypt, the purpose of which was to provide access to the tomb-shrine beneath the pavement of the raised presbytery, consisted of a semicircular corridor, immediately against the inner face of the Constantinian apse, and an axial passage leading from the head of the apse to the back of the shrine. The semicircular passage, which was entered by two doors in the flanks of the platform of the presbytery, immediately against the west wall of the transept, is still substantially preserved. To provide head-room below the massive ceiling-slabs of marble, which formed the floor of the presbytery, the floor was sunk 64 centimetres below that of the Constantinian church, destroying all trace of the seating of the two outer columns of the Constantinian screen and further damaging the remains of the underlying, pre-Constantinian tombs (e.g. the façade of R). The

masonry, a very roughly coursed, widely jointed brickwork, ranging from 56 to 64 centimetres for ten courses, is altogether cruder
than that of the Constantinian church, and it was hidden from sight
behind slabs of reused marble veneer. The central passage was transformed by Clement VIII into what is now the Cappella Clementina;
but apart from the raising of the ceiling and the addition of two small
lateral chapels, the masonry behind the lavish baroque ornament
appears still to be substantially that of the original crypt. Traces of
the ceiling-slabs were found by the excavators in position against the
west face of the shrine; and a small patch of the floor of coloured
marbles (*verde antico* and red and green porphyry) was found sealed
in place by the masonry of the altar of the Confessio, which still
stands in its original position immediately to the west of the shrine.
This altar, a square, box-like structure of masonry just under 1 metre
high, contained an empty reliquary-recess in the top and a square
opening (*fenestella*) in the middle of the west face.(52) In the twelfth or
thirteenth century it was sheathed in marble, and the west face
decorated with inlaid 'Cosmatesque' mosaic work (one of the
sheathing slabs is part of one of the slabs from the balustrade of the
raised presbytery, reused; another is part of an inscription recording
an assignment of burial-rights in the pagan cemetery);(53) and this in
turn was encased in richer materials by Pius VI in the late-eighteenth
century.

At first, the lower part of the west face of the Constantinian
shrine seems to have been exposed at the east end of the central
passage; and, to cover the gap in the marble facing caused by the
lowering of the floor-level below that of the Constantinian pavement,
the base-moulding along the west face of the shrine was removed
and its place taken by a broad slab of porphyry. Later, a thickness of
masonry was built up against the end-wall of the Confessio. This
added masonry has now been removed (and with it the remaining
fragments of the floor of the raised presbytery) so as to expose the
Constantinian masonry. What the visitor now sees, framed within
the arched vault of the east end of the Cappella Clementina,(54) is the
lower part of the west face of Constantine's shrine, with its two
slabs of Phrygian marble flanking a central vertical strip of porphyry;
below it, the porphyry slab added when the Confessio was built;
above it, the base of the twelfth-century altar. In front, in its later
casing, is the altar of the Confessio; and between the altar and the

shrine can be seen the top steps of the second-century Clivus. It is a glimpse only of the many phases through which the shrine has passed; but it is a very revealing glimpse.

With the construction of the altar of the Confessio we have the first clear trace within St. Peter's of the multiplication of secondary altars that accompanied the increasing fragmentation and dispersal of holy relics throughout the Christian world. The main altar stood above, at the level of the presbytery, immediately over the shrine. Nothing of it can now be seen from the outside; but soundings within the body of the twelfth-century altar have shown that the latter was no more than a casing of Phrygian marble about its predecessor, and that this in turn consisted substantially of the upper part of the Constantinian shrine, adapted to form a rectangular, chest-shaped altar, with a large, central reliquary-recess. The recess, which underwent several modifications of detail, including the blocking of an original square opening (*fenestella*) in the middle of the west face, contained a small marble coffer; and in the coffer were found two small, cylindrical lead caskets, wrapped in fine cloth and sealed, and containing fragments of a still finer cloth. Inscriptions on the caskets and on the cloth-wrappings showed that they contained relics of St. Peter and St. Paul, and of Christ and the Virgin, respectively.[55]

The six columns of the screen stood, three and three, along the outer (eastern) edge of the platform of the presbytery, framing a square re-entrant space immediately in front of the shrine and of the altar; the steps up to the raised presbytery occupied the north and south sides of this space, and in the middle of the west side, in the vertical face below the altar, was a small arched opening, the Niche of the Pallia (p. 223), which was all that now remained visible of the niches of the pre-Constantinian Aedicula and of the open front of the Constantinian shrine. The position of the screen is clearly marked by three of the moulded pedestal-bases of the columns, which are still in position to the north and south of the Open Confessio, together with part of the plinth of the intervening screen-wall, marking the front of the platform of the presbytery. One of the slabs of this plinth is part of an inscription of Petronius Maximus, who was emperor of the West for four months in 455.[56] Of the outer screen, added in the eighth century, no trace remains in position. It was demolished at the beginning of the sixteenth century to make way for the east wall of the structure built by Bramante to protect the shrine and the apse of the old church during the work on the dome above.

That the raising of the floor of the presbytery and the installation of the Covered Confessio are part of one and the same scheme, there can be no doubt whatever; nor can there be much doubt that the main reason, or one of the main reasons, for the change was the desire to move the principal altar of the church to a position directly over the tomb-shrine. All the rest followed logically from this first step. Just as Constantine had to plan the levels of his church so as to bring them into the right relation with the pre-existing tomb-shrine, so now, on a smaller scale, his successors, in order to modify this relation, had once again to adapt the building to the tomb. The placing of the altar over the tomb involved the raising of the floor of the presbytery; and since access to the tomb was an essential part of the cult, the installation of a crypt became a necessary part of the scheme. The form of the crypt was substantially determined by the shape of the apse and by the position of the tomb in relation to it; and the level of the crypt was determined by that of the presbytery above.

It is the logic of the scheme that clearly establishes St. Peter's as the model behind the crypts of a large number of churches in Rome and elsewhere (p. 242), which copied the same form without having the same compelling reason for doing so. The earliest of these is the Church of San Pancrazio, built by Honorius I (625–38); and it follows that the raised presbytery must already have been installed in St. Peter's by that date. At the other end of the scale, the Constantinian shrine was certainly still in use for some time after 407, the date of the inscription found reused in the pavement (p. 232, Note 34), and very possibly after 451, the date of the inscription of Petronius Maximus (p. 218, it is possible however, that this was inserted at a later date, as a repair); and within these broad limits (c. 450–630) there are several aspects of the surviving remains that favour a later rather than an earlier date—the character of the masonry, which may be compared with that of the base of the column erected in the Forum in 608 in honour of the Byzantine Emperor Phocas; and the remains of a large series of chancel-screen panels, which belong very probably to the raised presbytery and are decorated in a style that does not appear to be found in the West before the time of Justinian (527–65).[57] It is, however, the literary record that affords the conclusive argument for the date of the transformation of the shrine. Agiulf, the emissary of Gregory of Tours, left Rome in 590, a few months after the death of Pelagius II and the installation of Gregory the Great; and, as we have seen (pp. 212–13), it is the Constantinian shrine that he describes: of that the reference to the canopy over the tomb, with its columns 'of wondrous elegance', leaves no doubt. That Pelagius had himself in some way embellished the superstructure of the shrine with silver-work we know both from the *Liber Pontificalis*, which records that he 'encased the body [*i.e.* the shrine] of the blessed Peter the Apostle with plates of gilded silver',[58] and in rather greater detail from a letter sent by his successor, Gregory, to the Empress Constantina: the Empress had requested the head of St. Paul, a request which Gregory respectfully refused, on the grounds that he would not dare to touch, let alone disturb, the bodies of St. Paul and St. Peter, so many and terrible are the signs preventing any such disturbance, adding that 'when my predecessor, of blessed memory, was desirous of changing the silver which was over the most sacred body of the blessed Apostle Peter, although at a distance of almost 15 feet from the same body, a sign of no small dreadfulness appeared to him'.[59] It is presumably on the basis of these passages that the excavators assign to Pelagius the construction of the raised presbytery.[60] But in neither passage is there any mention of major structural changes, only of the replacement of some of the silver-work. The raising of the presbytery must surely be the work of Gregory himself who, in the words of the *Liber Pontificalis*, 'made it possible to celebrate Mass over the body of St. Peter'.[61] It must have been begun soon after 594, the probable date of Gregory's letter to Constantina, which makes no mention of such work in a context in which it could hardly have failed to be mentioned; and, since we are also told that Gregory placed a silver canopy over the altar when it was in place,[62] the work must have been substantially complete before his death in 604.

Except for the central corridor of the Covered Confessio which, together with its venerable altar, survives as the Cappella Clementina, the only feature of all this that escaped the zeal of the Renaissance builders was the central recess of the shrine, which from now on may conveniently be referred to by the name that it bears today, the 'Niche of the Pallia'. Beneath a veneer of later ornament, it still retains substantially the form given to it by Gregory's architects on

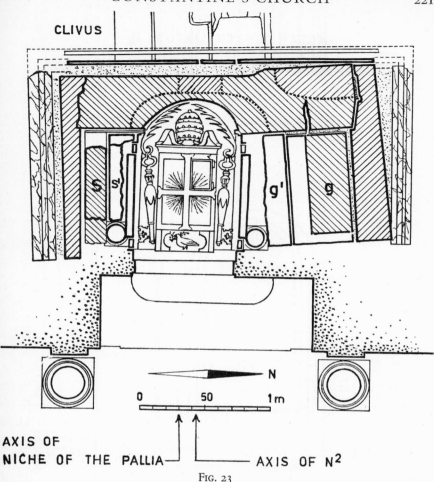

CLIVUS

FIG. 23

Niche of the Pallia, plan. The hatching distinguishes pre-Constantinian (as S and g) from Constantinian masonry. The entrance to the vertical shaft is in the upper right-hand quadrant of the cross.

the occasion of the incorporation of the central edifice of the Constantinian shrine within the structure of the raised presbytery and of its altar (Figs. 23, 24).

Despite the ruthless destruction of its previous setting, the nucleus of the Constantinian shrine had retained the tripartite form of its predecessor, the second-century Aedicula, with a rough niche, N^1, buried from sight below ground, and above ground two more carefully contrived niches, N^2 and N^3, separated from each other by a horizontal travertine slab. The fourth, fifth, and sixth centuries saw the gradual raising of the floor of N^2, to bring it into line with the

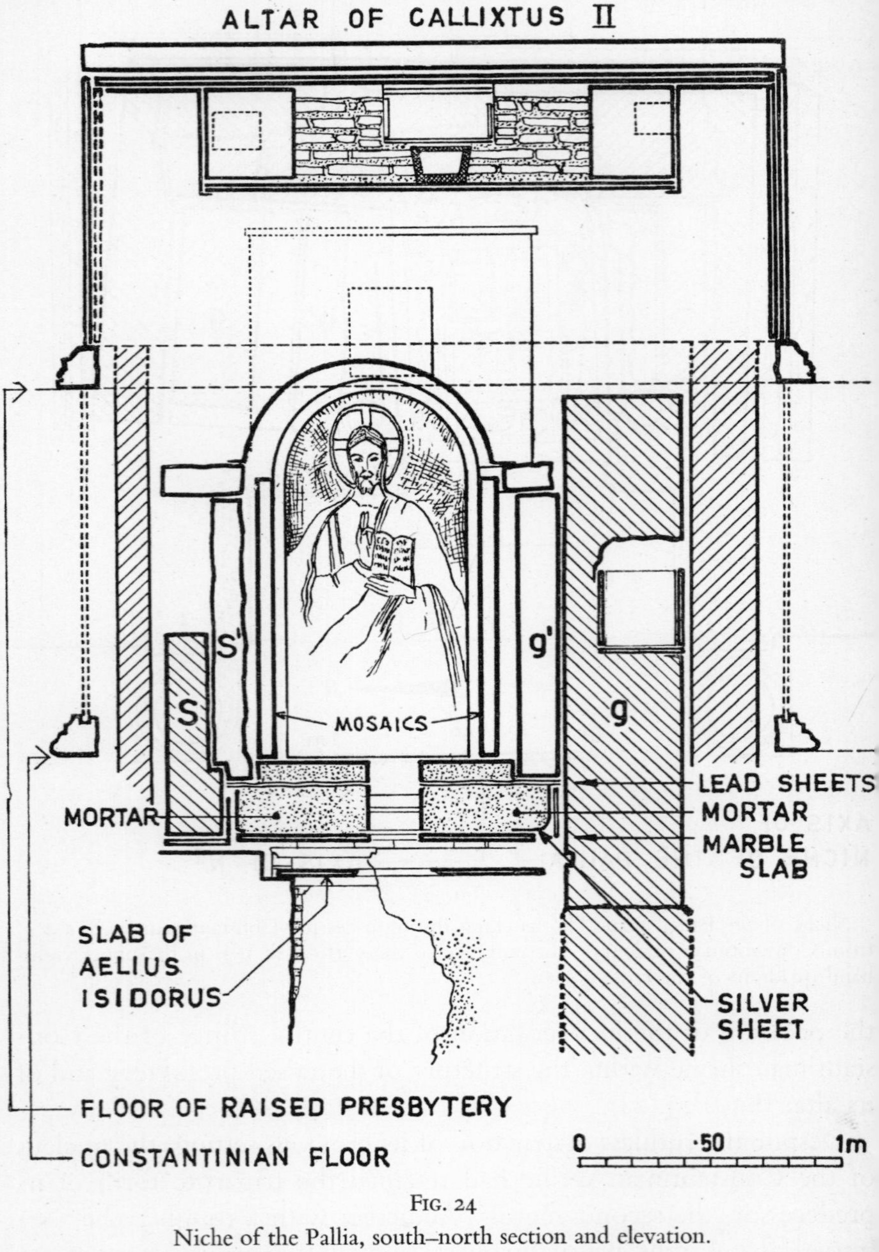

ALTAR OF CALLIXTUS II

MOSAICS

S' g'

S g

MORTAR

LEAD SHEETS
MORTAR
MARBLE
SLAB

SLAB OF
AELIUS
ISIDORUS

SILVER
SHEET

FLOOR OF RAISED PRESBYTERY

CONSTANTINIAN FLOOR

0   ·50   1m

FIG. 24
Niche of the Pallia, south–north section and elevation.

general pavement-level within Constantine's church (p. 203); but, although the shrine as a whole was more and more richly ornamented, it was not until the raising of the presbytery that there was any occasion to change the tripartite arrangement of the interior. It was the placing of the altar directly over the tomb, at the level of the new presbytery, that brought about this change, since the greater part of the upper niche (N^3) lay within the body of the new altar; and to remedy this it was decided to throw what was left of the two niches together, and to create from them a single, central recess, the historic Niche of the Pallia. This new recess was narrower, slightly deeper, and decidedly taller than its predecessor, N^2, and the axis was shifted some 12 to 15 centimetres to the left (*i.e.* to the south).[63] To narrow it, light screen-walls (g^1 and S^1) were built up against the existing north and south inner faces of N^2 (that to the south, S^1, was largely replaced in the Renaissance by a later wall); and it was deepened by cutting back a short distance into the core of the Red Wall. To heighten it, the whole of the central part of the second-century travertine slab had to be cut away, and on the surviving ends of the slab, reaching up into what had been N^3, was built a small barrel-vault, ending towards the west in a semi-dome. The new recess, which for all practical purposes may be regarded as a modification of N^2, suppressing the obsolete N^3, differed chiefly from its predecessor in being taller and deeper than it was broad, being barely 1 metre wide, as against 1·20 metres deep and 1·60 metres high.

This, then, was the Niche of the Pallia, so-called from the time-honoured custom of placing within it the scarf-like vestments (*pallia*) sent by the popes to newly appointed or consecrated archbishops. In the floor, now slightly off axis, there was still the shaft leading down to the grave; and the niche itself was decorated with painting, with mosaic, and with precious metal-work. Of this decoration, many times renewed, we have only tantalizing fragments, and there is no need to describe these in detail.[64] The most substantial surviving relic of the early ornament is the mosaic of the Saviour within the curved western end of the niche, which recalls the type of the Saviour in the ninth-century apse-mosaic of the Church of San Marco, near the Piazza Venezia, but which, as the excavators remark, has been so heavily restored that one cannot be sure that it is not, in fact, considerably later.[65] When Callixtus II (1119–24) restored the altar above, he placed an open-work, gilded bronze screen in front of the niche, the upper part of which still survives; and behind it can be seen the scanty remains of a contemporary scheme of decoration in Limoges enamel, figuring Christ and the twelve Apostles in a setting of arched columns.[66] Clement VIII (1592–1605), in remodelling the whole of the rest of the shrine, did not materially change the central niche. But Urban VIII (1623–44) inserted two flanking panels of mosaic, depicting St. Peter and St. Paul, which were ruthlessly restored by Pius IX (1846–78); and Urban's successor, Innocent X (1644–55), added the plaque of embossed and gilded bronze that now covers the floor of the niche, depicting a cross, flanked by two keys beneath the papal tiara, and, below the cross, his badge, a dove holding an olive-branch. The cross is so contrived that a small door in the upper right-hand panel opens directly onto the vertical shaft; and until the recent excavations this was the only contact that remained with whatever lay below the floor of the church beneath the high altar (Figs. 23, 24).

With the Niche of the Pallia we are carried straight back to the time of Gregory the Great; and although most of the rest of his work was swept away by the architects of the Renaissance, for nearly nine hundred years it provided the setting for such alterations and additions as his successors might care to make. Gregory III in the eighth century might add an outer screen in front of the existing screen (p. 216); Callixtus II, at the beginning of the twelfth, might employ the Roman marble-workers to redecorate the altar (p. 218);[67] and as late as the second half of the fifteenth century we find Sixtus IV (1471–84) adding a canopy over the altar, carried on four porphyry columns.[68] But these were details that did not substantially affect the broad lay-out and functioning of the shrine; and we may fairly say that, with the construction of the raised presbytery by Gregory the Great, about the year 600, Constantine's church and the shrine of St. Peter took on the form that they were to retain throughout the Middle Ages.

The rest is very briefly told. When sentence of death was passed on the old church, the shrine was one of the last things to be touched. The decision to rebuild the church was taken by Nicholas V (1447–55); but on his death work was suspended, and it was not until the beginning of the following century that demolition began in earnest. To protect the shrine during the work, Bramante designed a building which incorporated the whole of the apse of the old church and the projecting part of the presbytery, together with the inner screen of spiral columns. The appearance of this building—which was completed by his successors in charge of the work—is well known from contemporary drawings,[69] and the excavators found substantial remains of the east wall (the base-moulding can be seen in position at the extreme west end of the present lower church) on the line of the outer screen of spiral columns, which was demolished to make way for it. Within it, the presbytery and the apse with its mosaic survived intact until the whole structure, apse and all, was demolished in 1592 to make way for the high altar of the new church. This was completed by Clement VIII (1592–1605) at a level nearly $2\frac{1}{2}$ metres above that of its predecessor. The central passage of the Covered Confessio was transformed into the Cappella Clementina; and work was begun, but never completed, on a scheme to isolate the Niche of the Pallia by means of corridors cut through the body of the raised presbytery immediately to the north and south of the Constantinian shrine, to link up with the Open Confessio. This was a sunken space immediately in front (*i.e.* to the east) of the high altar, giving access to the Niche of the Pallia at a level of some 40 centimetres below that of the Constantinian pavement.[70] It is the Open Confessio, begun by Clement VIII, and completed and possibly enlarged by his successor Paul V, which now covers the greater part of P, the courtyard in front of the original second-century shrine.

Only two other monuments of this late period call for brief mention. The one is the great canopy of bronze erected over the altar by Bernini, on the orders of Urban VIII (1623–44). It is one of the strangest of coincidences that Bernini, for his model, should have chosen the columns which had been used by Constantine's architects for the canopy over the original shrine, dismantled a thousand years before, and that, like its Constantinian predecessor, the canopy itself should have been a bold, and in detail unconventional, openwork structure. The foundations of this canopy were dug right down into the cemetery beneath, destroying substantial parts of Tombs S, R, and Q, and the presumed north-east angle of the Christian enclosure, P.[71] The other monument to add its quota of destruction to the early buildings immediately adjoining the shrine is Canova's statue of Pius VI, which was found by the excavators to be resting on the earthen fill of the south-east angle of Tomb O (Fig. 9).

The object of all the changes that we have been describing was to

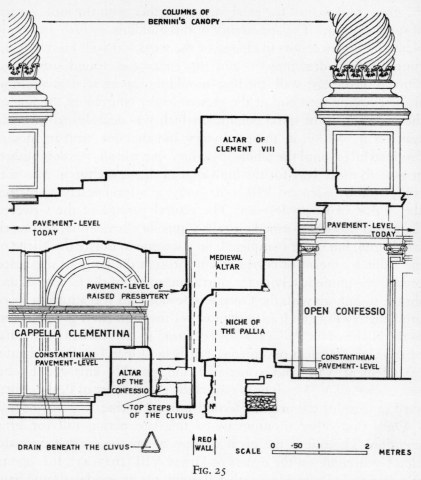

FIG. 25

West–east section of the central complex, showing the relation of the primitive shrine to the present high altar.

do honour to what, at least from the time of Constantine, was universally believed to be the tomb of St. Peter. Not until the Middle Ages were well advanced did anybody think of questioning that St. Peter lay directly beneath the high altar, in the great bronze coffin which the *Liber Pontificalis* describes; and yet, as we have seen in chapter 6, the space below the Niche of the Pallia, corresponding to N[1], was found by the excavators smashed and ransacked, empty save for the coins dropped in by generations of pilgrims and for the enigmatic heap of human bones found tucked away beneath the foundations of the Red Wall. How did this devastation come about?

When, and by whom, was it caused? These are questions to which any account of the shrine must try to give an answer.

We may begin by excluding the idea that the whole great Constantinian building is a deliberate sham, or that it was built to honour an already rifled tomb. Quite apart from the inherent improbability of this idea, the implications of which are considered in chapters 1 and 5, there is clear evidence to show that some of the damage took place well after the time of Constantine, and after the central space had ceased to be accessible from above by any other means than the small shaft in the middle of the slabs that separate it from the upper shrine. Of these slabs, it is almost certain that the earliest, that of Aelius Isidorus, which presumably dates from the reconstruction of the shrine by Constantine, has never been moved; it is quite certain that it has not been touched since it was sealed in place, already damaged, by the marble slab immediately above it.[72] The evidence of the surviving structures is clear and explicit; and it is confirmed by the early growth of legends about the form of St. Peter's tomb: by the time the *Liber Pontificalis* was compiled, in the sixth century, nobody had any clear idea of what lay out of sight beneath the shrine.

It follows that, whoever ransacked the tomb, reached it, not from the floor of the shrine above, but from the pavement immediately in front of it. The thieves have, in fact, left clear traces of their work. To reach the central space, the greater part of Grave η was destroyed and the right-hand end of the travertine sill of the pre-Constantinian Aedicula smashed; and, within it, the sealing-slab of the Aedicula was broken and whatever had supported the right-hand end of it removed; indeed, the entire right-hand half of the space is now little more than a featureless hole. These details carry with them certain clear chronological implications. The smashing of the travertine sill left the right-hand colonnette of the Aedicula suspended in space, supported only by the masonry in which it was incorporated; and the earliest of this masonry belongs to the last phase of the Constantinian shrine as an independent structure; that is to say, to the phase immediately preceding the construction of the raised presbytery and of the Niche of the Pallia. We cannot date the successive raisings of the Constantinian floor (pp. 202–3) more precisely than to the period between c. 330 and 600; but the third and last is hardly likely to have taken place before the middle of the fifth century. We may, therefore, certainly exclude from consideration the sack of Rome by the Goths in 410; and we may probably exclude also that by the Vandals in 455. There are, moreover, other reasons for believing that on both occasions St. Peter's escaped the general devastation. Both the Goths and the Vandals were Christians, although of Arian persuasion, and in 410 we are specifically told that the 'holy places', and in particular the Churches of St. Peter and St. Paul, were treated as places of sanctuary.[73] In 455, the evidence is less explicit; but from the fact that Leo the Great was able to provide sacred vessels for those churches that had been looted by the Vandals by melting down some of the treasure presented by Constantine to the Churches of St. Peter, St. Paul, and St. John Lateran,[74] we may reasonably infer that these three churches at any rate escaped disaster.

It was left to the Saracens, in 846, to occupy and to loot St. Peter's. The text of the *Liber Pontificalis* for Sergius II (844–7) is unfortunately fragmentary, and breaks off after informing us that the marauders 'invaded and occupied the church of the blessed Peter, Prince of the Apostles, committing unspeakable iniquities'.[75] From the annals of Prudentius of Troyes we learn further that they 'sacked the church of the blessed Peter, Prince of the Apostles, and bore off all the ornaments and treasures, together with the very altar which had been placed over the tomb of the said Prince of the Apostles'.[76] Nothing is said in either passage of the looting of the tomb itself; but the letter of Count Adalbert, governor of Tuscany and Corsica, warning the Romans of the approaching Saracen fleet,[77] contains the ominous advice to 'clear the treasures of the churches of the blessed Peter the Apostle and of Paul, and, if possible, to remove the bodies of the Apostles within the walls of Rome'. The advice was disregarded; and it is a reasonable inference from the facts revealed by the excavations that the Saracens, in addition to stripping the shrine, did in fact break into the tomb beneath and steal whatever precious objects lay within.

Whether it was on this and on some other occasion that the tomb was looted, the authorities very understandably said nothing about the loss of the sacred relics. Indeed, it is probable that they had no very clear idea of what exactly had been lost. The space below the shrine had long been inaccessible; and to anyone whose ideas of the tomb of St. Peter were based on the account in the *Liber Pontificalis* (p. 204), it might well seem that, whatever else had been stolen, the tomb itself was still intact. The hole in the pavement was repaired, and the life of the shrine went on as before.

This, or something like it, would seem to be the story of the loss of whatever was preserved below the shrine. If the memory of the exact contents of the grave was already dim in the ninth century, before the sack, still less are we ever likely to learn what exactly the robbers found in the central space. To judge from the dimensions, that space could have contained some sort of casket, dating at least from Constantine's time. Did such a casket hold only valuable offerings? Or did it house human relics, bones found, in Constantine's day or earlier, lying just east of N^1 in the central space and venerated as those of the Apostle? And had those relics been temporarily transferred elsewhere during the third century (pp. 167–82)? Does the pile of bones that was discovered—reburied in the second century and presumably untouched since then—in the recess in the foundations of the Red Wall directly below the Aedicula, represent some portion of a body which the early Roman Church reverenced as that of St. Peter (p. 158)? We must be content to leave all these questions unanswered, and to admit that we cannot today identify with any certainty the Apostle's bones. But, at least since the second century, the belief that his body reposed at that spot has been, and always will be, a well-spring of devotion; and of that devotion the great church remains the living monument.

NOTES

1. First recorded in the *Sylloge Einsidlense*, a collection of inscriptions compiled not later than the ninth century and preserved in the monastery of Einsiedeln; *CIL*, vi. 1, p. x, No. 6 = E. Diehl, *Inscriptiones Latinae Christianae Veteres*, i, 1925, 1752 = G. B. De Rossi, *Inscriptiones Christianae Urbis Romae*, ii, 1888, p. 20, No. 6. The mosaic was still extant, in poor condition, in the middle of the fifteenth century, but had been destroyed before 1525.

2. A. Piganiol, *L'empereur Constantin*, 1932, p. 113.

3. Proposed by Josi, and subsequently elaborated by Guarducci (*Cristo e San Pietro, etc.*, pp. 65–9 and Notes 162–88); *cf.* J. Carcopino, *Études d'histoire chrétienne*, 1953, pp. 129–33.

4. O. Marucchi, *Dissertazioni della Pontificia Accademia Romana di Archeologia*, ser. ii, xv, 1921, pp. 271–8, Pl. 3; P. Fabre, *Mélanges d'Archéologie et d'Histoire*, xl, 1923, pp. 3–18; H. J. Rose, *Journal of Hellenic Studies*, xliii, 1923, pp. 194–6; xlv, 1925, pp. 180–2: 'I bring in this sacrifice the words, thought, action, excellent

life, and all the goodness of Ga[rgiꝫ]lius's understanding. For he offered and brought once more to the Mighty One, who rose again, the bull and ram that are the tokens of happiness. Yea, he scattered the night of eight-and-twenty idle years and kindled again the light.'

5. In particular, the argument for an interval before 350 rests on a series of eleven dated inscriptions, of which no less than eight fall between 370 and 390. Of the other three, two are dated to 305 and 350 respectively; the third, dated 319, is very possibly, but not certainly, from the Vatican.

6. W. Seston, *Cahiers Archéologiques*, ii, 1947, pp. 153–9. The text of this law is in *Cod. Theod.*, IX, 17.2 (ed. T. Mommsen, vol. i, 2, 1905, p. 464).

7. Cabrol–Leclerq–Marrou, *Dictionnaire d'archéologie et de liturgie chétienne*, s.v. 'Vaticanum', col. 3327, Note 3. Carcopino suggests (*op. cit.*, p. 132) that the year 333 marked the conclusion, not the beginning, of the process of filling in the Vatican mausolea, but does not explain why Constantine should have chosen this unlikely moment to act.

8. Traces of the street fronting the cemetery were found at a depth of 11·50 metres below the pavement when trenching for the foundations of the south-east angle of the new church (*Report*, i, p. 27); see also chapter I, p. 7.

9. Clearly visible in Guarducci, Pl. 14.

10. M. Cerrati, *Tiberii Alpharani de Basilicae Vaticanae antiquissima et nova structura*, 1914, Pl. I. For a selection of contemporary drawings, see Hermann Egger, *Römische Veduten* (2nd ed., 1932), i, Pl. 17 ff.

11. H. Egger, 'Quadriporticus Sancti Petri in Vaticano', *Papers of the British School at Rome*, xviii, 1950, pp. 101–3.

12. The foundation across the central nave, which passes through Tomb L, is built of large, irregular lumps of marble bedded in a very hard concrete, a type of construction used also in the Constantinian foundations of St. John Lateran. The return of the stylobate between the lateral aisles of the nave and the transept cannot now be demonstrated, since this part of the early Church is buried beneath the gigantic eastern angle-piers of the Renaissance dome; but it can safely be inferred, not only from the exposed footings of the west wall of the transept, which show no traces of any prolongation of the nave-stylobates, but also from the fact that drawings made during the demolition of the old church show pairs of columns placed screen-wise across the end of each of the side-aisles, at the point of junction with the transept (see Note 46); this detail is incorrectly shown by Alfarano.

13. For a detailed account of the surviving remains, see *Report*, i, pp. 161–72.

14. *Report*, ii, Pl. 68.

15. *Report*, i, p. 196: D(is) M(anibus) S(acrum)/P(ublio) Aelio Isidoro seniori/parenti benemerenti fili e/ius fecerun[t]/liberti(s) liber[tabus] posteris/que eo[rum]. This slab can be seen, photographed from beneath, in *Report*, i,

Fig. 149, and ii, Pl. 77, *a*. It seems certain that it was already in position when the hole was cut, and the workmen cracked the slab when cutting it (see Note 72).

16. These alterations are described in detail in *Report*, i, pp. 195–8. There are frequent references in the *Liber Pontificalis* to the adornment of the shrine with works of gold and silver.

17. A. Gnirs, *Atti e Memorie della Società Istriana di Archeologia e Storia Patria*, 1908, pp. 19–48. See also Peirce and Tyler, *L'art byzantin*, 1932, i, Pl. 113; *Report*, i, Fig. 122 and pp. 169–72; *Journal of Roman Studies*, xlii, 1952, Pl. 1, i.

18. i, p. 176: coronam auream ante corpus qui est farus cantharus, cum delfinos L, qui pens. lib. xxxv ('a golden crown (set) before the body, which is a lamp in the shape of a cup (?) with 50 dolphins, weighing 35 pounds').

19. An ingenious, but in detail unconvincing, explanation of the legend by Ruysschaert (pp. 51–5) may contain an element of truth, in that the legend was very possibly inspired by the misunderstanding of some superficial feature of the shrine, of which we no longer have any trace.

20. i, p. 176: et exornavit supra columnis purphyreticis et alias columnas vitineas quas de Grecias perduxit ('and he adorned it (*i.e.* the tomb) above with columns of porphyry and other columns decorated with vine-scroll, which he brought from Greece'). For a full discussion of these vine-scroll columns and their subsequent history, see *Journal of Roman Studies*, xlii, 1952, pp. 21–33. For the porphyry columns, see p. 237, Note 69.

21. *The Excavations at Dura-Europos*, v, 1934, pp. 238–88.

22. J. B. Ward Perkins, 'Constantine and the origin of the Christian basilica', *Papers of the British School at Rome*, xxii, 1954, pp. 69–90.

23. For a brief account of the excavations, which await detailed publication, see A. M. Colini, 'Storia e topografia del Celio nell'antichità' (*Atti della Pontificia Accademia Romana di Archeologia*, ser. III: *Memorie*, vii, 1944, pp. 344–59); their significance is discussed by Ward Perkins, *op. cit.*, pp. 84–7.

24. A Grabar, *Martyrium*, 1946, *passim*. Grabar's account of St. Peter's was written before the results of the recent excavations were known; and he follows the traditional view of the Holy Sepulchre as incorporating from the outset the familiar domed structure of later times (but see Note 26).

25. E. T. Richmond, *Quarterly of the Department of Antiquities of Palestine*, v, 1936, pp. 75–81; W. and J. H. Harvey, *Archaeologia*, lxxxvii, 1938, pp. 7–17.

26. Most recently and convincingly discussed by E. Wistrand, *Konstantins Kirche am Heiligen Grab in Jerusalem nach den ältesten literarischen Zeugnissen* (Göteborgs Högskolas Årsskrift, lviii, 1952, 1). The precise form of the Constantinian *martyrium* is of less importance to the present discussion than its relative position, which is not in dispute.

27. So Ruysschaert, p. 47.

28. E. Kirschbaum, *Stimmen der Zeit*, August 1952, p. 324.

29. North Africa: *Archaeologia*, xcv, 1953, pp. 64–6. Northern Adriatic: M.

Mirabella Roberti, *Rivista di Archeologia Cristiana*, xxvi, 1950, pp. 181–94 (see, however, criticism by G. Brusin in *Festschrift für Rudolf Egger*, 1952, i, pp. 212–35).

30. *Epist.*, xxix. 10 = Migne, *Patrologia Latina*, xxxiii, col. 119: de basilica beati apostoli Petri cotidianae vinolentiae proferebantur exempla. Compare St. Jerome's letter of thanks to Eustochius for a gift of fruit and pastries on St. Peter's feast-day (*Epist.*, xxxi. 2, 3 = Migne, *Patrologia Latina*, xxii, cols. 445–6): festus est dies et natalis beati Petri . . . unde nobis sollicitius providendum est ut solemnem diem, non tam ciborum abundantia, quam spiritus exultatione celebremus. quia valde absurdum est nimia saturitate velle honorare martyrem quem scias Deo placuisse ieiuniis ('we must take more care to observe this solemn day, not with abundance of food but with exultation of spirit; for it is manifestly absurd to seek to honour with indulgence the martyr whom thou knowst to have pleased God by fasting').

31. *Epist.*, xiii, 11 = Migne, *Patrologia Latina*, lxi, col. 213: videre enim mihi videor . . . tantis influere penitus agminibus in amplissimam gloriosi Petri basilicam . . . ut tota et intra basilicam, et pro ianuis atrii, et pro gradibus campi spatia coarctentur.

32. *Epist.*, xxxiv. 2 = Migne, *Patrologia Latina*, lxi, col. 343: mensa . . . proposita . . . in atriis domus Domini ('the table set out in the *atria* of the house of God').

33. H. Grisar, *Roma alla fine del mondo antico*, 1908, pp. 787–8.

34. One such socket can be seen in *Report*, ii, Pl. 70, *b*, against the imprint of the base of the south-west column of the canopy. Included among the material reused in the later patching is the metrical epitaph of a magistrate from the city of Vienne in southern Gaul, who died in 407 (*Report*, i, p. 172; ii, Pl. 71).

35. See p. 212 and Note 45.

36. See chapter 3, Note 59 and Appendix B, p. 264.

37. *Report*, i, Fig. 171 and pp. 220–2.

38. E. Baldwin Smith, *The Dome*, 1950, *passim*; K. Lehmann, *Art Bulletin*, xxvii, 1945, pp. 1–27.

39. For the canopy in imperial symbolism and ceremonial, see A. Alföldi, *Mitteilungen des Deutschen Archäologischen Instituts: Römische Abteilung*, l, 1935, pp. 127–32; for the legionary shrine at Luxor, U. Monneret de Villard, *Archaeologia*, xcv, 1953, pp. 85–105.

40. Alföldi, *op. cit.* For the possible derivation of the Christian basilica from the palatine basilica, E. Langlotz, *Festschrift für Hans Jantzen*, 1951, pp. 30–6; J. B. Ward Perkins, *Papers of the British School at Rome*, xxii, 1954, pp. 87–8. As regards the smaller basilical churches, we must not overlook their possible debt to basilical Jewish synagogues of imperial times (see the work cited in Note 43 to chapter 4), and to such apsed and colonnaded basilical pagan

mystery-shrines as the Underground Basilica near the Porta Maggiore (p. 100 and Note 54) and the Mithraeum recently excavated in London.

41. G. B. de Rossi, *Inscriptiones Christianae Urbis Romae*, ii, pp. 21, 55, 145, 156:

> iustitiae sedes fidei domus aula pudoris
> haec est quam cernis, pietas quam possidet omnis;
> quae patris et filii virtutibus inclyta gaudet
> auctoremque suum genitoris laudibus aequat.

'The seat of justice, the house of faith, the hall of modesty, such is (the church) that you see, the abode of all piety. It proclaims its joy and pride in the merits both of father and of son, for both alike it honours as its founders.' This inscription was still in position in 794, when we find the first line cited by Pope Hadrian I in a letter to Charlemagne (J. D. Mansi, *Sacrorum Conciliorum nova et amplissima collectio*, 1902, xiii. 774), but it seems to have perished before the twelfth century.

42. J. Wilpert, *Die römischen Mosaiken und Malereien*, 1917, i, Fig. 114, and pp. 361–7. For the repairs by Severinus, see *Liber Pontificalis*, I, p. 329: hic renovavit absidem beati Petri apostoli ex musibo. The reference to a previous restoration of the apse by Leo I (440–61) is questioned by Duchesne (*ibid.*, i, pp. 239–40). Innocent III's inscription (Wilpert, *loc. cit.*) reads:

> summa Petri sedes est h(a)ec sacra principis aedes,
> mater cunctar(um) decor et decus ecclesiar(um).
> Devotus $\overline{\text{XPO}}$ qui templo servit in isto
> flores virtutis capiet fructusq(ue) salutis.

'This sacred shrine of the Prince of the Apostles is the chief dwelling-place of Peter, the mother, the ornament, the glory of all churches. Whoso serve Christ devoutly in this temple shall receive the flower of virtue and the fruit of salvation.' Line 2 is an obvious allusion to the rival claim of St. John Lateran to be the mother-church of Rome.

The apse with its mosaic was still standing, within Bramante's protecting structure, when Giulio Romano painted Old St. Peter's in the Raphael Rooms in the Vatican (*Journal of Roman Studies*, xlii, 1952, Pl. 1, iii and p. 24). By an oversight, the restored drawing of the Constantinian shrine and apse given in the *Report* [i, Pl. H] illustrates the mosaic in its thirteenth-century form.

43. *Liber Pontificalis*, i, p. 233: 'he [Sixtus] adorned the Confessio of the blessed Peter with silver weighing 400 pounds; and he secured from the Emperor Valentinian the gift of a golden image (*imago*), with twelve gates and figures of the twelve Apostles and the Saviour, and adorned with precious jewels, which he placed over the Confessio of the blessed Peter, the Apostle'. This *imago* was still extant in the time of Pope Hadrian I (772–95), but disappeared soon afterwards, presumably when the church was sacked by the Saracens in 846.

44. *Liber Pontificalis*, i, p. 239: 'he [Leo] restored the basilica of the blessed Peter, the Apostle, also the semi-dome of the apse (cameram)'. The words 'et cameram' are bracketed by Duchesne as a probable intrusion into the original text. Leo's repairs were also recorded in a mosaic inscription on the façade of the church, the text of which is preserved in a seventh-century collection of inscriptions relating to St. Peter's (G. B. De Rossi, *Inscriptiones Christianae Urbis Romae*, ii, 1888, p. 55, No. 10); and possibly also in another inscription in the same collection (*ibid.*, No. 7), which was placed 'in the shrine over the body of St. Peter' (in arca sup(ra) corpus s(an) cti Petri) and which recorded a dedication by a high imperial official, Rufius Viventius Gallus. See also Note 56.

45. *De gloria martyrum*, xxviii = Migne, *Patrologia Latina*, lxxi, cols. 728–9: sanctus vero Petrus apostolus . . . sepultus est in templo quod vocitabatur antiquitus Vaticanum, quatuor ordines columnarum valde admirabilium numero nonaginta sex habens. habet etiam quatuor in altari, quae sunt simul centum, praeter illas quae ciborium sepulcri sustentant. hoc enim sepulcrum sub altari collocatum valde rarum habetur. sed qui orare desiderat, reseratis cancellis quibus locus ille ambitur, accedit super sepulcrum; et sic fenestella parvula patefacta, immisso introrsum capite, quae necessitas promit efflagitat. nec moratur effectus, si petitionis tantum iusta proferatur oratio. quod si beata auferre desiderat pignora, palliolum aliquod momentana [*i.e.* statera] pensatum facit intrinsecus, deinde vigilans ac ieiunans, devotissime deprecatur, ut devotioni suae virtus apostolica suffragetur. mirum dictu! si fides hominis prevaluerit, a tumulo palliolum elevatum ita imbuitur divina virtute, ut multo amplius quam prius pensaverat ponderet; et tunc scit qui levaverit, cum eius gratia sumpsisse quod petiit . . . sunt ibi et columnae mirae elegantiae candore niveo, quatuor numero, quae ciborium sepulcri sustinere dicuntur. The passage is discussed at length by Ruysschaert, pp. 40–9.

46. R. Krautheimer, *Art Bulletin*, xxxi, 1949, pp. 211–13, reproducing and discussing a drawing of the transept made during its demolition, in the 'thirties of the sixteenth century, possibly by Marten van Heemskerck.

47. *Cf.* his description of the Church of St. Martin at Tours (*Historia Francorum*, ii. 14 = Migne, *Patrologia Latina*, lxxi, col. 213): habet . . . fenestras in altario triginta duas, in capso viginti ('it has . . . thirty-two windows in the presbytery, twenty in the nave').

48. As does Ruysschaert, p. 47.

49. Grabar, *op. cit., passim*. For an English summary of this part of his thesis, see *Archaeology*, ii, 1949, pp. 95–104.

50. *Contra Vigilantium*, 8 = Migne, *Patrologia Latina*, xxiii, col. 346: male facit ergo Romanus episcopus, qui super mortuorum hominum Petri et Pauli, secundum nos ossa veneranda, secundum te vilem pulvisculum, offert Domino sacrificia, et tumulos eorum Christi arbitratur altaria?

51. For a detailed account of the raised presbytery see *Report*, i, pp. 173–93.

The addition of six columns is recorded in *Liber Pontificalis*, i. 417: hic [Gregorius] concessas sibi columnas VI onichinas volutiles ab Eutychio exarcho, duxit eas in ecclesiam beati Petri apostoli, quas statuit erga presbiterium, ante confessionem, tres a dextris et tres a sinistris, iuxta alias antiquas sex filopares. Super quas posuit trabes et vestivit eas argento mundissimo ('the six spirally shaped columns which he had received as a gift from the Exarch Eutychius, he brought to the Church of St. Peter the Apostle, and he placed them towards the presbytery in front of the Confessio, three to the right and three to the left, alongside six others of the same sort that were already there. Upon them he placed an architrave and covered it with pure silver'). For these columns, see article cited in Note 20.

52. The excavators (*Report*, i, p. 180) suggest that the present altar is later than the Confessio-passage, fragments of the floor of which are sealed in place by the masonry of the altar. If so, the spreading footings, which rest on the north-east angle of the courtyard of Tomb R and on a part of the stairs of the Clivus, and which certainly antedate the same fragments of flooring, show that it replaces an earlier altar on the same site.

53. The marble slab, with a Latin cross in shallow relief on a plain disc within a moulded frame (*Report*, i, Fig. 131), belongs to a type current in Rome during the sixth and seventh centuries. For the inscription, see chapter 4, Note 6.

54. *Report*, ii, Pl. 68.

55. *Report*, i, pp. 189–90: 'sancti Petri et sancti Pauli' and 'Salvatori(s) et Sanctae Mariae'.

56. *Report*, i, p. 185; ii, Pl. 76, *b*: . . . [ornatum Petronius Max(imus)] . . . It may perhaps be connected with the restoration of the church by Leo the Great (Note 44).

57. The size and uniformity of the series, many fragments of which are preserved near the entrance to the excavations, suggests that it must have been made expressly for the new presbytery. The type derives from that still extant in the upper Church of San Clemente, the panels of which are of Proconnesian marble, imported from Constantinople, and bear the monogram of Pope John II (533–5); *cf.* also G. B. Giovenale, *La basilica di Santa Maria in Cosmedin*, 1927, Fig. 107. There is no trace of the interlace ornament characteristic of the eighth century and later.

58. *Liber Pontificalis*, i. 309: investivit corpus beati Petri apostoli tabulis argenteis deauratis.

59. *Epist.*, iv. 30 = Migne, *Patrologia Latina*, 77, col. 701: denique dum beatae recordationis decessor meus, quia argentum, quod supra sacratissimum corpus beati Petri apostoli erat, longe tamen ab eodem corpore fere quindecim pedibus mutare voluit, signum ei non parvi terroris apparuit. The letter goes on to refer to structural work undertaken by Gregory near the tomb of Saint Paul; *cf.* Note 61.

60. *Report*, i, p. 193.

61. *Liber Pontificalis*, i. 312: hic [Gregorius] fecit ut super corpus beati Petri missas celebrarentur. The passage continues: item et in ecclesiam beati Pauli apostoli eadem fecit ('and he did the same also in the church of the blessed Paul the Apostle').

62. *Ibid.*, p. 312: hic [Gregorius] fecit beato Petri apostolo cyburium cum columnis suis IIII, ex argento puro ('he made for the blessed Peter the Apostle a canopy together with its four columns, of pure silver'). Gregory's canopy was transferred to Santa Maria Maggiore by Leo III (795–816), who replaced it with another, also of silver (*Liber Pontificalis*, ii. 27).

63. For the details of its construction and of its subsequent modifications, see *Report*, i, pp. 195–203. The change of axis was a result of the asymmetry of the shrine ever since the building of the buttress, *g*, and the resultant shift of the right-hand column some 20 centimetres southwards. Now that no part of the original surface of N^2 was visible (the curved rear-wall of the new niche was cut out of the masonry of the Red Wall, with a pronounced shift to the left: all that now survives of the original surface of N^2 is that part which lay below the sixth-century floor-level within the shrine), it was more convenient to site the new niche with reference to the surviving pair of columns.

64. See *Report*, i, Pl. K and pp. 202–3; ii, Pls. 78–80. The earliest surviving remains are those of painted ornament in blue and gold on the vault. This was followed by a figured scheme in red and black, contemporary with which are tiny patches of red mosaic in the angles of the vault. This in turn was followed by a further painted scheme in yellowish-white and blue.

65. *Report*, i, p. 203; ii, Pl. 81; G. B. De Rossi, *Mosaici cristiani e saggi dei pavimenti delle chiese di Roma anteriori al secolo XV*, 1899, Pl. 28. For the apse-mosaic of San Marco, the work of Gregory IV (827–43), see M. van Berchem and E. Clouzot, *Mosaïques chrétiennes du IV au X siècle*, 1924, pp. 251–3 and Fig. 314.

66. A. Sarti and I. Settele, *Ad Philippi Laurentii Dionysii opus de Vaticani cryptis appendix*, 1840, pp. 22–3, Pl. 3; the right half is illustrated in *Report*, i, Fig. 152. The metrical inscription along the upper border reads:

  + sic cum discipulis bis sex XPS residebit
   cum reddet populis cunctis quod quisque merebit.
  + tercius hoc munus dans Innocentius, unus
   sit comes in vita tibi Petre cohisraelita.

('Thus, with six disciples on either hand, shall Christ sit when He gives to all the peoples their just deserts. This is the gift made by the third Innocent; may he be one in life with thee, Peter, fellow-Israelite'—a reference presumably to Matthew 19: 28). For the screen and for the enamels behind it, the scheme of which recalls the *imago* presented by the Emperor Valentinian III (Note 43), see G. Wilpert,

Rivista di Archeologia Cristiana, vi, 1929, pp. 65–8, Figs. 4, 5; F. Stohlman, *Gli smalti del Museo Sacro Vaticano*, 1939, Figs. 10–11.

67. This is the altar recorded in the *Liber Anniversariorum Basilicae Vaticanae* (ed. Egidi, p. 290), under 25 March: consecratio alt(aris) maioris bas(ilicae) b(eati) Petri facta a Callisto P(a)p(a) II cum universo concilio anno eius V ind(ictione) I ('consecration of the high altar of the basilica of the blessed Peter the Apostle by Pope Callixtus II together with all the council in the fifth year of his pontificate, in the first indiction', *i.e.* in 1124). According to Grimaldi, describing the work of Clement VIII (Vat. MS., *Barberinus Latinus* 2733, i, f. 166, cited in *Report*, i, p. 192); it is inscribed 'Callixtus II Papa'; but this inscription, if it still survives, is hidden by the vault of the Cappella Clementina. For later work by the *marmorari romani*, see the altar of the Confessio (p. 217); also pilasters found by the excavators reused in the Renaissance corridors to the north and south of the shrine, which are part of a scheme begun by Clement VIII but abandoned before completion (p. 225).

68. Ruysschaert, p. 50, Note 1, citing Grimaldi (Vat. MS., *Barberinus Latinus* 2733, i, f. 159ᵛ–160), and rightly pointing out that the four porphyry columns of this canopy have nothing to do with the porphyry columns mentioned in the *Liber Pontificalis* (i. 176) as having been placed in the Basilica by Constantine.

69. The building was complete when Van Heemskerck was in Rome in the early 'thirties (H. Egger, *Römische Veduten* (2nd ed., 1932), i, Pl. 30) and was certainly still standing *c.* 1560 (*ibid.*, Pl. 32; *cf.* also Pl. 31, and Krautheimer, *Art Bulletin*, xxxi, 1949, p. 211, Fig. 1); it is figured and discussed in detail in *Report*, i, Figs. 155–61 and pp. 205–7. The excavations have also revealed substantial remains of the partition-wall built in 1538, on the orders of Paul III, in order to maintain in temporary use the last eleven bays of the old nave (*Report*, i, Figs. 162–8, and pp. 205–16). Incorporated in the structure of this wall are the plinths and bases of two of the columns of the Constantinian nave (*ibid.*, Fig. 115 and pp. 158–60; ii, Pl. 109), still in their original positions; and the sill of a door belonging to the original project of Antonio da Sangallo, later abandoned, of a church of Greek-cross plan, to be built at approximately the level of the Constantinian church (*ibid.*, i, Fig. 167 and pp. 213–14; *cf.* Fig. 168, the exterior base-moulding of one of the outer walls of the same church, incorporated within the footings of Maderno's nave).

70. For the work of Clement VIII, see *Report*, i, pp. 216–20. The abandonment of the project to link the Open Confessio and the Cappella Clementina by means of corridors to north and south of the central shrine can be dated by a *graffito* to the year 1615; these corridors have now been partly reopened to give access to the earlier structures. It is clear that Clement VIII also planned to make use of the semicircular corridor of the Covered Confessio, linking it directly to the Open Confessio; but this project, too, was abandoned in favour of the

present deambulatory passage outside the Constantinian apse, with a passage driven through the head of the apse to reach the Cappella Clementina. All these changes of plan, so characteristic of the work in St. Peter's, have added greatly to the complexity of the surviving remains.

71. Bernini's canopy was dedicated in 1633. The columns are a free version (with the addition of bees, the badge of the Barberini family, to which Urban VIII belonged) of the columns of the Constantinian canopy and of the eighth-century screen, combining the truncated shape of the pair now in the Chapel of the Blessed Sacrament with the ornament of those which Bernini himself used to decorate the four galleries of the dome. To provide metal for this canopy, the porch of the Pantheon was stripped of its gilded bronze tiles—whence the famous pasquinade: quod non fecerunt barbari, fecerunt Barberini ('what the barbarians did not do, the Barberini did').

72. P. 203. From the way in which the hole in the slab of Aelius Isidorus has been cut, it is almost certain that it was cut when the slab was in position, and that the slab was broken in the process (*Report*, i, p. 196). Even allowing for the support afforded by the right-hand half of the pre-Constantinian sealing-slab (destroyed and removed when the central space below was rifled), it was only the pressure of the later structures above that held it in place, and it is hard to believe that it could or would have been replaced in position so damaged.

73. Orosius, *Hist.* 7, 39 (*Corpus Scriptorum Ecclesiasticorum Latinorum*, v, pp. 544–5): adest Alaricus, trepidam Roman obsidet turbat irrumpit, dato tamen praecepto prius ut si qui in sancta loca praecipueque in sanctorum apostolorum Petri et Pauli basilicas confugissent, hos in primis inviolatos securosque esse sinerent ('Alaric approached the trembling city, and besieged it, and forced his way in, after first ordering that any who had fled to the holy places, and particularly to the basilicas of the holy Apostles, Peter and Paul, should be allowed to go free and safe').

74. *Liber Pontificalis*, i, p. 239: hic [Leo I, 440–61] renovavit post cladem Vandalicam omnia ministeria sacrata argentea per omnes titulos, conflatas hydrias VI basilicae Constantinianae, duas basilicae beati Petri apostoli, duas beati Pauli apostoli, quas Constantinus Augustus obtulit ('after the Vandal disaster, he replaced all the sacred silver vessels throughout all the *titulus*-churches, melting down for the purpose six water-vessels from the Constantinian basilica [St. John Lateran], two from the church of the blessed Peter the Apostle, and two from the church of the blessed Paul the Apostle, all of which were the gift of Constantine Augustus'). The *tituli* fulfilled a function akin to that of the later parish churches. Another object known to have survived the Vandal disaster was the rich *imago* presented to the shrine of St. Peter by Valentinian III, which was still extant in the eighth century (Note 43), to be looted by the Saracens in 846.

75. *Liber Pontificalis*, ii, p. 101: ecclesiam beati Petri apostolorum principis nefandissimis iniquitatibus praeoccupantes invaserunt.

76. G. H. Pertz, *Monumenta Germaniae Historica: Scriptorum*, i, 1826, p. 442: mense augusto Sarraceni Maurique Tiberi Roman aggressi, basilicam beati Petri apostolorum principis devastantes, ablatis cum ipso altari quod tumbae memorati apostolorum principis superpositum fuerat omnibus ornamentis atque thesauris. . . .

77. *Liber Pontificalis*, ii, p. 99: . . . ut certarent liberare beati Petri apostoli et Pauli thesauros ecclesiarum, et, si fieri potuisset, ipsorum apostolorum corpora intro inferrent Roma . . .

EPILOGUE: ST. PETER'S AND THE ART AND ARCHITECTURE OF WESTERN EUROPE

IT is a familiar story how, in the course of centuries, St. Peter's came to usurp a position, which its founder had never intended, as the centre of Catholic Christendom. The Church of St. John Lateran was, and still is, the seat of the Bishop of Rome; and as late as the twelfth century we find its clergy still waging an animated, but unsuccessful, war against those of St. Peter's, to vindicate its title to supremacy. [1] But historical circumstance, and above all the fact of the transfer of the papal residence from the Lateran Palace to the comparative security of the Vatican Hill, was too strong. By the close of the Middle Ages we find St. Peter's securely established in the position that it occupies today, as the effective, if not the titular, mother-church of the Roman Catholic world. Occupying such a position, St. Peter's was bound to exercise a powerful influence upon the architectural thought of western Europe. And it is the purpose of this final chapter to note one or two of the ways in which that influence has made itself felt, and in particular those aspects of it upon which recent work, and specifically the recent excavations, have thrown fresh light.

Until quite recently it was generally believed that the history of western European church architecture during the early Middle Ages could be represented as an orderly progress from the models established in Rome by Constantine. In particular, it was thought that the type of building represented by St. Peter's, a basilical hall with transepts and a single apse, survived in uninterrupted use in Italy right through to the twelfth century; and that from Italy, from the fifth century onwards, it spread all over Europe, furnishing the models from which, by a long process of development and transformation, was evolved the Romanesque architectural system. This theory we now know to be mistaken; the transept, so far from being a characteristic feature of the early-Christian basilica, was an exception, which must always have been added to serve a specific purpose. We have already seen (pp. 207–8) how the transept of St. Peter's, which later came to seem such a natural, almost inevitable, feature of a great basilical church, in the eyes of fourth-century observers would have seemed something quite distinct from the basilical hall to which it was attached. For three or four centuries it was the basilica without a transept that held the field. During this period, with the important exception of the late-fourth-century Church of St. Paul (p. 167 f.), there is no church, either in Rome or elsewhere, which can certainly be said to be derived from St. Peter's. Even in Rome the basilical churches of the early-fifth century, such as Santa Sabina, Santa Maria Maggiore, and SS. Giovanni e Paolo, lack transepts; and San Pietro in Vincoli (420–50) and San Giovanni a Porta Latina (c. 500) herald the fresh influences from Greece and the Near East that were to play so large a part in the Roman architecture of the following two centuries. Outside Rome, northern Italy went its own way, in contact with Greece and the Near East rather than with Rome; and what little we know of the pre-Carolingian churches of France suggests that here, too, such influence as there was from without came from the Near East, and possibly Spain and North Africa, rather than from Italy. Between the beginning of the fifth century and the closing years of the eighth, there is not one single instance of a church, either in Rome or elsewhere, which can be shown to have been derived from the great fourth-century Basilicas of St. Peter and St. Paul.[2]

In all this, architecture was expressing the facts of contemporary history. Already in the fourth century the centre of gravity in Italian affairs had moved away from Rome to the north, to Milan and Ravenna; and in the troubled times that followed the collapse of central authority in the West, Rome was often little more than a venerable symbol, a link with the historic past rather than a present force. The Roman Church, indeed, retained her pre-eminence as an independent, spiritual power; but the prestige of Old Rome as a city was overshadowed by that of New Rome, by the political and cultural dominance of Constantinople. Furthermore, the Church as a whole was still far less centralized than she became later; and no antithesis was felt as yet to exist between a western and an eastern type of Christianity. Communion with Rome was everywhere the test of Catholicity; but east-Christian ritual and liturgical practices and, above all, the early eastern forms of monasticism, circulated freely in the West—to some extent in Italy and Rome itself, but chiefly in Gaul and, through Gaul, in Ireland. Added to these circumstances were the barbarian incursions, which inevitably loosened the ties between Rome and the Christians of the north-west European lands. In Gaul there was never any break with Rome; but as communications with Italy were rendered more difficult, the Gallican rite tended to accentuate certain originally eastern and distinctive characteristics of its own. In the British Isles the situation after the fifth century was such that links with Rome were virtually severed. Celtic Christianity fell out of step with Roman developments, and its way of life evolved on independent lines. There was no change of doctrine, no formal transference of allegiance. St. Augustine's mission to England in 597, and the acceptance by the British clergy of contemporary Roman discipline at the Synod of Whitby, went far to restore the authority of Rome within the Celtic Christian world. But it was not until the eighth century that the wounds inflicted by the barbarians were everywhere repaired and the leadership of Rome in matters of ecclesiastical art and practice securely re-established in the West.

It is not altogether surprising, therefore, that, quite apart from the limitations imposed by their special purpose, the great fourth-century martyr-shrines of Rome should have been without immediate successors. There were forces at work, however, to change this situation. From the first, the enormous popularity of the shrine of St. Peter must have given it a position of unique prestige and influence. And architectural values were changing. In St. Peter's itself, with the passage of time, the distinction between nave and transept came to lose its early sharpness (p. 213); and with the raising of the presbytery (pp. 216–20) it ceased altogether to have any meaning. At the same time, the multiplication of relics, followed in Rome by the transfer of the remains of the martyrs from the catacombs to the safety of the city, meant that there was no longer a clear differentiation between ordinary churches and those devoted to the commemoration of martyrs. It is easy to see how, to the pilgrim visiting Rome, as indeed to the Roman himself, the great transeptal Churches of St. Peter and St. Paul might come to be regarded as the natural models for lesser buildings to copy.

The first trace of this new attitude is to be seen in the adoption by a large number of churches, both in Rome and elsewhere, of the very distinctive form of raised presbytery that was installed in St. Peter's

by Pope Gregory the Great, about the year 600, in which a semicircular corridor follows the inner contour of the apse to give access
to a small central crypt behind and below the altar (p. 216 f.). The
earliest recorded instance of this in any other building is in the
Church of San Pancrazio (built by Pope Honorius I, 625–38); and
there can be very little doubt that, in this and other churches, it was
directly copied from St. Peter's, where alone this rather specialized
form finds an adequate explanation in the peculiar requirements of
the particular site (p. 219). An interesting and instructive parallel to
this is afforded by the 'Confessio', a sunken space in front of the high
altar, which is today so distinctive (and ugly) a feature of many of
the larger Roman churches; in most of these churches it is function-
ally quite meaningless, and has been installed in direct imitation of
the Open Confessio of St. Peter's, where, by contrast, it is the logical
answer to a given problem—that of giving access to the Niche of
the Pallia, which lies well below the level of the present pavement.

For some time that was all. As a building, St. Peter's continued to
remain without successors; and as late as the end of the eighth century we find even such sturdy champions of western tradition and
influence as Pope Adrian I (772–95) and Leo III (795–817) following
models from the Near East, as their predecessors had done, for such
Roman churches as Santa Maria in Cosmedin, Santa Susanna, and
SS. Nereo ed Achilleo. It was, however, the same Leo III who, early
in his pontificate, transformed the ancient cruciform Church of Sant'
Anastasia into something closely resembling one of the fourth-
century Roman transeptal basilicas; and one of his later buildings,
the Church of Santo Stefano degli Abissini, just behind St. Peter's, is
an unmistakable copy in miniature of its distinguished neighbour.
Even more striking is the resemblance to St. Peter's shown by the
Church of Santa Prassede, built by Leo's successor, Paschal I (817–
24). With its transept, its semicircular crypt, its flat architraves, and
its *atrium*, all copied directly from St. Peter's, the whole built on a
scale and in a quality of masonry that far more closely resembles that
of late Antiquity than any of its predecessors for the last three centuries, Santa Prassede is still today one of the most handsome of the
Roman churches, and an eloquent witness to the force and sincerity
of this return to early-Christian models.[3]

Once again we have only to glance for a moment at the facts of
contemporary history to see why this architectural revival should

have taken place just when it did. After the centuries of disintegra-
tion that followed the collapse of the Roman Empire in the West,
the eighth century was a period of rebuilding and of reconstruction;
and the vision that inspired the whole movement was nothing less
than the re-creation of the western Roman Empire, not always, it
may be, in a form that Antiquity would itself have recognized. The
papal curia, for example, was mainly concerned to create a moral
and legal justification for the claims of the Church to secular
authority in Italy and in the West; and one of the chief instruments
of this policy was the notorious 'Donation of Constantine'. This
famous forgery was probably composed in the chancery of Paul I,
about 760; and it claimed that, when Constantine transferred his
capital to Constantinople, he bestowed on the pope the territorial
rule over Rome and the West. Its purpose was to re-establish a state
of affairs which (it alleged) had existed in late Antiquity, at the very
moment when Rome and Christianity had been merged; and by its
terms the pope could consider himself the rightful ruler of western
Europe, with the power to delegate that right to anybody he might
choose.

The Frankish emperors, too, were deeply concerned to re-create
certain aspects of the Roman past, and to reassert the prestige
and independence of Old Rome as against Constantinople. The
coronation of Charlemagne in St. Peter's on Christmas Eve of the
year 800 was the culminating point of a fifty-year-old collaboration
between the Frankish kingdom and the Papacy. Charlemagne
already controlled a large part of what had been the western Roman
Empire; and by his coronation he laid claim to be the legitimate
successor of the Roman emperors of Antiquity. Once again it was
the Rome of Constantine, rather than the Rome of Augustus and
Trajan, that dominated the vision. Not that anyone in the eighth
century would have made the distinction in such terms. Pagan
Antiquity was already beginning to recede into the mists of legend,
significant more for its relation to the faith of which it was the pre-
ordained precursor than for any inherent qualities of its own. True,
we are still far from the credulous nonsense that we find enshrined
in the *Mirabilia* of the later Middle Ages; and in France more than in
any other province of the western Empire there must still have been
a real sense of continuity with the imperial past. In any case, it would
be a mistake to try to define the vision too closely; one can well see

how, in such an age, the idea of re-creating the past might come to cover a whole variety of different notions, ranging from the time-old dreams of a past Golden Age to the shrewdly calculated policies of interested statesmen. But one thing they all have in common—the vision of Christian Rome. Of that vision the twin symbols were the first Christian emperor and the Prince of the Apostles.

Stimulated by this vision, the half-century between the state-visit of Pope Stephen II to Paris in 753 and the coronation of Charlemagne was marked by a great revival of Roman influence and authority north of the Alps. Throughout the Frankish kingdom the Gallican rite and the Irish type of monasticism were gradually eliminated; the Roman Mass replaced the Gallican liturgy; monastic rules were reshaped on the Benedictine model; Roman dedications and Roman relics made their appearance in increasing numbers.[4] As in Rome, architecture was surprisingly slow to follow suit; but when it did so, just after the turn of the century,[5] the impact of the new ideas was all the more decisive. It may fairly be said to mark one of the turning-points in the history of western European architecture.

It is in the great abbey-church of Fulda, as rebuilt by Abbot Ratger between 802 and 807, that we meet for the first time north of the Alps a clear and unequivocal instance of a church modelled on the great early-Christian basilicas of Rome. The present church at Fulda is an eighteenth-century structure; but from ninth-century descriptions, from seventeenth-century reproductions, and from the results of excavation, it is possible to establish a remarkably complete picture not only of the building itself but also of the intentions of its builders. Ratger's building inherited the eastern apse of its predecessor; but for the rest it was a new building, planned on what was, by contemporary standards, an enormous scale (it was approximately the same size as St. John Lateran, very little smaller than St. Peter's), with a basilical nave and a continuous western transept, very tall and narrow, the projecting ends of which were shut off by transverse colonnades; opening off the transept there was a single western apse. That this building was a close and deliberate copy of St. Peter's is established, not only by the remarkable similarities of plan, which have no precedent in early-medieval architecture outside Rome, but also by the comments of contemporary observers, and by the use to which the transept was put. Here, at the junction of apse and transept, was laid the body of St. Boniface, *more Romano* ('according to Roman custom'), as the account of the dedication of the church in 819 puts it. In planning the sanctuary that was to house the remains of St. Boniface, apostle and protomartyr of the German part of the Frankish kingdom, there can be no doubt that the builders of Fulda deliberately set out to establish an image of the venerable shrine that housed the remains of St. Peter, Apostle and protomartyr of Rome.[6]

The example of Fulda was soon followed elsewhere. The church at Seligenstadt, built between 831 and 840 to receive the relics of the Roman martyrs, Saints Peter and Marcellinus, and the Benedictine abbey at Hersfeld (831–50) are two early and well-documented examples of the same derivation, directly or indirectly, from the great fourth-century basilicas of Rome. To follow the influence of this movement farther afield would involve us in the whole complex history of Carolingian and post-Carolingian architecture. Already at Hersfeld we can see in the two tower-like structures flanking the façade the introduction of an element that was new and alien to the Roman concept of basilical architecture. From this point of view, the later history of the Roman type of basilica is one of its gradual fusion with other building-traditions within the larger stream of Carolingian development. But it was a development that was, at the same time, constantly being modified and enriched by fresh reference to the same early-Christian models, sometimes directly, more often at second-hand through earlier derivatives from the same source. What is important, however, in the present context is not the detail of the later development, but the fact that, after nearly four centuries of dependence upon architectural models from the Near East, under Charlemagne and his successors western Europe turned once more to its own architectural heritage. By their deliberate revival of obsolete early-Christian types, the Carolingian architects introduced an element that was thereafter to remain one of the essential constituents of medieval and post-medieval architecture in Europe. 'The fact that the cathedral of Amiens'—or Canterbury or Gloucester—'has nave, aisles, and a transept; that in its elevation arcades, triforium, and clerestory succeed each other; that the walls seem to consist of transparent screens: all this would seem to be rooted in the tradition of the fourth-century basilicas, which was revived and made known to the Occident by the architects of the

Carolingian Renaissance.'[7] Of that tradition St. Peter's was at once the fountain-head and the immediate inspiration.

Between 860 and the turn of the millennium there was little or no building of churches in Rome; and the architecture of the following centuries was in the main derivative and, in terms of contemporary architecture elsewhere, provincial. Even where, as in San Crisogono (1123) and in Santa Maria in Trastevere (rebuilt by Innocent II, 1130–43), the inspiration was ultimately that of the early-Christian architecture of Rome itself, it came, not directly, but through the great eleventh-century abbey-church of Monte Cassino, the form of which was almost certainly determined by that of its Carolingian predecessor. It was not until the Renaissance that Rome once more moved back into the main stream of European architectural development. By that time St. Peter's, condemned to destruction by Nicholas V in about 1450, had long become a venerable monument inherited from a quasi-legendary past. Contemporary architecture had passed it by; but as a storehouse of historical associations, and as a museum of the sculpture, painting, mosaic, and precious metal-work of every century since Constantine, much of it from the hands of the greatest masters of their age—Giotto, Arnolfo di Cambio, Jacopo della Quercia—it was unique. As such, it had lost nothing of its power to kindle men's imaginations; and it is fitting that this brief account of the influence of Constantine's church on the art and architecture of succeeding centuries should end with the story of a group of objects which were already old when the church was built, and which have played an active part in the history of architectural taste and ornament from that day to this.

The richly carved spiral columns which upheld the canopy over the shrine of St. Peter in Constantine's church (p. 204, Fig. 20) were part of a set of six sent for the purpose 'from Greece' by the Emperor himself.[8] They are of classical workmanship, dating from about the end of the second century A.D., and they must almost certainly have come from some well-known building in the neighbourhood of Constantinople, on the shores of the Sea of Marmara or in the northern Aegean. After standing for over two and a half centuries in their original position above the tomb, they were moved by Gregory the Great to form a screen in front of the shrine and in front of the new, raised presbytery (p. 215, Fig. 22). There they stood for almost exactly a thousand years; and there they were joined in the eighth

century by a second set of six columns (p. 216), which are so similar
to the first that it seems that they must have come from the same
classical building, although there are slight differences of workmanship throughout and two of them must date from nearly a century
earlier than the rest.

Their shape, that of an old-fashioned stick of barley-sugar, was
unique; and placed as they were, they were bound to attract the
attention and to excite the admiration of every visitor to St. Peter's.
They were copied intermittently throughout the Middle Ages. The
earliest surviving copies are two pairs of miniature columns, the one
pair in the Church of SS. Trinità dei Monti in Rome, the other now
in the Church of San Carlo at Cave di Palestrina, whither they are
said to have been brought from Rome in the sixteenth century.[9]
Both pairs must have belonged to the chancel-screens of which the
early Middle Ages have left so many dismembered fragments in the
churches of central Italy; and although scholars have been very
chary of assigning a date to such singular objects, the most plausible
suggestion would seem to be that they, too, are a product of the
Carolingian Renaissance, the modest counterpart in sculpture of the
'early-Christian' churches that were being built in Rome during the
first half of the ninth century.

If so, they, and the few other pieces that may perhaps be assigned
to the same renewal of interest in ancient models and craftsmanship,
represent little more than a passing gleam in the darkness that
envelops the sculpture and architectural ornament of central Italy
towards the close of the millennium. It was not until the beginning
of the twelfth century that there was a substantial revival, at the
hands of the *marmorari romani*, the Roman marble-workers (often,
although illogically, known as the 'Cosmati'), whose work is so
characteristic and delightful a feature of the medieval churches of
Rome and Latium.[10] The *marmorari* plundered the buildings of ancient Rome for their materials; and they were as ready to copy and to
adapt such of the sculpture of Antiquity as struck their fancy as they
were to draw upon the contemporary craftsmanship of Sicily and of
Campania for the mosaic inlay with which they enriched it. But,
for all their readiness to borrow, they were, above all, men of their
own day and place. The spirit that breathes through their work is
essentially and unmistakably that of the Middle Ages. They were not
content merely to copy, as were the sculptors of the columns in the

Church of SS. Trinità dei Monti and at Cave. In the hands of the *marmorari* the spiral column took on a simpler and more explicitly decorative form. The bands of carved scroll-work were dropped, and in their place the fluting, enriched with gaily coloured mosaic, now ran the whole length of the shaft, following and accenting its bizarre shape.[11] From the great, free-standing Easter-candlesticks, for which it was perhaps first used, the spiral column passed into the general decorative repertory of the *marmorari*, and thence into painting; and painters and sculptors alike carried it far afield, to Umbria and Tuscany, and into northern Italy (where we can see it in Giotto's frescoes in the Arena Chapel in Padua and, transformed but still recognizable, in the Gothic sculpture of Lombardy)—even to England, where it is one of the motifs used by Peter, *civis Romanus* (very probably the same Peter as had carved the tomb of Clement IV, *d.* 1268, in the Church of San Francesco at Viterbo), to adorn that most unexpected of the works of the *marmorari romani*, the tomb of Henry III in Westminster Abbey.[12]

If the *marmorari* were men of their own day in the use which they made of their venerable models in St. Peter's, no less typical of the times is the legend which grew up around the columns during the later Middle Ages.[13] How this legend arose we cannot tell; but by the beginning of the fifteenth century we find them securely established in popular belief as the columns of Solomon's Temple. One of them in particular had been singled out as the column against which Christ leaned when disputing with the doctors, and it had suffered so severely at the hands of the pious, chipping off fragments as relics, that in 1438 Cardinal Orsini had to enclose it within a marble balustrade surmounted by a metal grille to save it from further harm. This is the column that now stands, with its protecting balustrade, in the same chapel as Michelangelo's Pietà.

In 1507 the outer screen was dismantled to make way for the east wall of the building designed by Bramante to protect the shrine and the high altar of the old church during the erection round it of its successor. Within this building the six original columns of the inner screen continued to stand where they had stood since the time of Gregory the Great, and where the excavators found three of the pedestal-bases still in position. They do not seem to have been to the taste of the artists and architects of the high Renaissance; but Giulio Romano saw them there and included them in his picture of Old

St. Peter's in the Raphael Rooms of the Vatican palace; and Pirro Ligorio copied them in one of his fountains at the Villa d'Este. More important, they attracted the fancy of Bernini, who used eight of the survivors to decorate the galleries above the great angle-piers of the dome; and by one of the strangest of coincidences—for he cannot possibly have had any idea of the original Constantinian canopy, dismantled many centuries before—he used them as the model for the columns of the great open-work canopy of bronze which Urban VIII commissioned him to make, and which stands today, as its predecessor did fifteen hundred years ago, sheltering, and drawing all eyes to the site of, the shrine of St. Peter.[14]

It was, however, not so much their intrinsic quality as the belief that they came from Solomon's Temple which secured them a place in the repertory of European art, long after the old church had been destroyed and the columns themselves dispersed. Jean Fouquet had seen and drawn them when he visited Rome in the 'forties of the fifteenth century; and later he reproduced them to illustrate the Temple in the Book of Hours of Etienne Chevalier and in his miniatures for the 'Jewish Antiquities' of Josephus.[15] But they would have attracted little attention outside Italy if it had not been for Raphael. When he was commissioned, in 1515, to prepare a series of cartoons for tapestries to hang in the Sistine Chapel—the cartoons that are now in the Victoria and Albert Museum—he used these columns to illustrate the scene of the Healing of the Lame Man at the Beautiful Gate.[16] The tapestries woven from these cartoons carried representations of the St. Peter's columns all over Europe, and it was these that inspired the countless corkscrew columns and colonnettes that were used in European art from the mid-sixteenth century onwards. Sometimes the pedigree is clear and direct—as at Mantua, in the palace of the Gonzagas, or, nearer home, in Ham House. More often, all that one can say is that the motif is taken from the general fund of contemporary ornament. But in either case, whether directly or indirectly, they are derived ultimately from Raphael's tapestries, and, through them, from the twelve classical columns that once stood over and around the shrine of the Apostle in Old St. Peter's.

Constantinpole, Rome, Anagni, Padua, Westminster Abbey, Richmond: a pagan shrine somewhere in the northern Aegean, Old St. Peter's, the ducal palace at Mantua, the University Church at Oxford; Constantine, Gregory the Great, Charlemagne, the *marmorari romani*, Henry III of England, Jean Fouquet, Pirro Ligorio, Raphael, Bernini; the names read like a pageant of European history. And it is right that they should. In the story of these columns we have, in microcosm, the story of St. Peter's itself—venerable, but ever vital, something which every age has interpreted in its own way, yet which reaches back without a break to the twin roots of our civilization, Classical Antiquity, and Christianity.

NOTES

1. The best-known documents of this historic quarrel are the *Liber de Sanctis Sanctorum* or *Descriptio Lateranensis Ecclesiae* of John the Deacon (*Codice Topografico della Città di Roma*, iii, 1946, pp. 319–73), and the *Descriptio Basilicae Vaticanae* of Petrus Mallius (*ibid.*, pp. 375–442). Both are dedicated to Pope Alexander III (1159–81), and both are unmistakably polemical in intention.

2. The evidence for most of the statements in this and in the following paragraphs will be found discussed and documented in Richard Krautheimer's fundamental article, 'The Carolingian Revival of Early Christian Architecture', in *Art Bulletin*, xxiv, 1942, pp. 1–38. In particular, Krautheimer is concerned to establish the relation between political events and the development of contemporary architecture. For the pre-Carolingian architecture of France, see also Jean Hubert, *L'architecture religieuse du haut moyen âge en France*, 1952.

3. Krautheimer, *op. cit.*, pp. 15–23.

4. The number of altars and churches dedicated to St. Peter within the Frankish kingdom during the eighth century was less only than that of the dedications to Christ and the Virgin; Krautheimer, *op. cit.*, p. 12, citing J. von Schlosser, *Schriftquellen zur Geschichte der karolingischen Kunst*, 1896, index.

5. The suggestion (Krautheimer, *op. cit.*, pp. 3–7) that the Carolingian Church of S. Denis, begun by Pepin and consecrated under Charlemagne in 775, may have been the first church in the West to receive the T-shaped plan of the early-Christian transeptal basilicas in Rome must now be discarded. Recent excavations by M. J. Formigé (to whom the writers are indebted for the information) have shown that in this respect Viollet-le-Duc's plan of his own, earlier, excavations is misleading.

6. *Ibid.*, pp. 7–12. The references in this connection to 'Roman custom' are to be found in Candidus's *Vita Eigilis* (*Monumenta Germaniae Historica: Scriptores*, xv. 1; pp. 221–33) and in its metrical counterpart (*M.G.H.: Poetae Latinae Medii Aevi*, ii, pp. 94–117).

7. Krautheimer, *op. cit.*, p. 29.

8. For a detailed discussion of these columns, see J. B. Ward Perkins, 'The

Shrine of St. Peter and its Twelve Spiral Columns', *Journal of Roman Studies*, xlii, 1952, pp. 21–33.

9. Ward Perkins, *op. cit.*, pp. 31–2, Pl. 7. The models are the columns of the outer (and more accessible) screen, and these copies cannot, therefore, be earlier than the middle of the eighth century.

10. For the *marmorari romani*, see Edward Hutton, *The Cosmati*, 1950. Examples of spiral columns there illustrated are the Easter-candlesticks of Anagni, Ferentino, Terracina (Pls. 21 and 42, 43, 44) and, on a smaller scale, in the Roman churches (Pls. 31–3); smaller, decorative columns on altars, pulpits, bishops' thrones, and chancel-screens in Rome, and at Subiaco and Città Castellana (Pls. 24–6, 29, 30, 34–5, 37, 46–7); and some of the columns in the cloisters of St. John Lateran and St. Paul's-without-the-Walls (Pls. 6, 9, *b*).

11. These 'barley-sugar' columns must be carefully distinguished from such superficially similar forms as the spirally fluted column of ordinary shape, or the composite column consisting of two shafts spirally entwined, both of which are common in contemporary Sicilian and southern French work, and were occasionally borrowed by the *marmorari* themselves for use alongside columns of the St. Peter's shape, *e.g.* in the Lateran cloister (Hutton, *op. cit.*, Pl. 8).

12. *Royal Commission on Historical Monuments (England)*: London, vol. I, *Westminster Abbey*, 1924, frontispiece and Pls. 48, 49; Hutton, *op. cit.*, frontispiece.

13. Petrus Mallius, writing in the third quarter of the twelfth century, ascribes them to the temple of Apollo at Troy (*op. cit.*, p. 384). Presumably the more colourful legend, that they came from Solomon's Temple, was not yet current.

14. The slight difference in the shape of Bernini's bronze columns is due to the fact that his chosen models were two of the columns from the outer screen, which had stood for a while in the Chapel of John VII and had been cut down to fit their new position, losing the upper band of fluting (Ward Perkins, *op. cit.*, p. 26, Pls. 1, 2, and 5, 6). These two columns now flank one of the altars in the Chapel of the Blessed Sacrament.

15. *Les antiquités judaïques et le peintre Jean Foucquet*, 1908, Pls. 14, 15; P. Wescher, *Jean Fouquet et son temps*, 1947, pp. 23–8, Pl. 17.

16. *Victoria and Albert Museum: the Raphael Cartoons*, 1950, with introduction by J. Pope Hennessy.

APPENDICES

APPENDIX A

List of names, recorded in inscriptions, of persons connected with the Vatican cemetery (see also Appendix D)

No.	Name	Tomb	Relationships	Status	Profession, etc.	References to text, etc.
1.	Acestia Hedone (?)	C (now in the museum)	Wife of 83, mother of 84	Free-born (?)		Ch. 2, Note 40; *Bullettino della Commissione Archeologica Comunale di Roma*, lxx, 1942, p. 99, Fig. 4, c.
2.	M. Aebutius Charito	N		Free-born (?)		Ch. 4, Note 2, xvi; *Report*, ii, Pl. 9, a.
3.	Aelia Andria	E	Wife of 7	Freedwoman		Ch. 4, Note 2, vii.
4.	Aelia Saturnina	E		Freedwoman of 6		Ch. 4, Note 2, ix.
5.	Aelia Stratonice	D	Wife of 47			Ch. 4, Note 2, ii.
6.	Aelia Urbana	E	Wife of 80; mother of 81, 85	Freedwoman		Ch. 4, Note 2, viii, ix, x.
7.	T. Aelius Tyrannus	E	Husband of 3	Imperial freedman	*a commentariis provinciae Belgicae*	Ch. 4, Note 2, vii.
8.	Aelius Valerianus	E	Father-in-law of 7			Ch. 4, Note 2, vii.
9.	Aemilia Gorgonia	F			Christian	Ch. 2, p. 47.
10.	Q. Aninius Liberalis	H	Husband of 90			Ch. 4, Note 2, xiii.
11.	M. Aurelius Hieron Euokatus	F	Father of 15			Ch. 2, p. 46.
12.	M. Aurelius Filetus	F	Husband of 22			Ch. 2, Note 19.
13.	Aurelius Gigas	E	Husband of 63			Ch. 4, Note 2, xi.

				man	
15.	M. Aurelius Hieron	F	Son of 11		Ch. 2, p. 46.
16.	Aurelius Primitivus	R	Son of 38, 39	Free-born (?)	Ch. 2, Note 4; CIL, vi, 3, 17985a.
17.	Caesenius Faustinus	H¹	Son of 20; brother of 18, 19		Ch. 3, Note 86.
18.	Caesenius Pompeianus	H¹	Son of 20; brother of 17, 19		Ch. 3, Note 86.
19.	Caesenius Rufinus	H¹	Son of 20; brother of 17, 18		Ch. 3, Note 86.
20.	Caesenius Severianus	H¹	Father of 17, 18, 19		Ch. 3, Note 86.
21.	Caetennia Hygia	L	Daughter of 28; sister of 29	Free-born (?)	Ch. 2, Note 20; Report, ii, Pl. 3.
22.	Caetennia Procla	F	Wife of 12		Ch. 2, Note 19.
23.	M. Caetennius Antigonus I	F	Husband of 74; son-in-law of 73, 79; brother-in-law of 76		Ch. 2, p. 44.
24.	M. Caetennius Antigonus II	F		Freedman of 26	Ch. 2, p. 46.
25.	M. Caetennius Chilo	F		Freedman	Ch. 2, p. 44.
26.	M. Caetennius Chryseros	F		Freedman	Ch. 2, p. 46.
27.	M. Caetennius Ganymedes	F		Freedman	Ch. 2, p. 46.
28.	M. Caetennius Hymnus	L	Father of 21, 29	Free-born (?)	Ch. 2, Note 20; Report, ii, Pl. 3.

APPENDIX A—*continued*

No.	Name	Tomb	Relationships	Status	Profession, etc.	References to text, etc.
29.	M. Caetennius Proculus	L	Son of 28; brother of 21	Free-born (?)		Ch. 2, Note 20; *Report*, ii, Pl. 3.
30.	M. Caetennius Secundus	F		Freedman		Ch. 2, p. 46.
31.	M. Caetennius Tertius	F		Freedman		Ch. 2, p. 44.
32.	C. Clodius Romanus	N	Son of 99, 100	Free-born (?)		Ch. 4, Note 2, xvi; *Report*, ii, Pl. 9, *a*.
33.	Cornelia Ammas	F	Mother of 59			Ch. 2, Note 21.
34.	Dynaten	H	Wife of 93	Freedwoman		Ch. 3, Note 61.
35.	Fadia Maxima	A	Wife of 69	Free-born (?)		Ch. 1, Note 28; De Visscher, *L'Antiquité Classique*, xv, 1946, p. 117 ff.
36.	Fannia Redempta	B	Wife of 14	Freedwoman		Ch. 2, Note 14.
37.	Flavia Olympias	H	Wife of 94; mother of 88, 95	Free-born (?)		Ch. 3, Note 59.
38.	Flavia Primitiva	R	Wife of 39; mother of 16	Free-born (?)		Ch. 2, Note 4; *CIL*, vi, 3, 17985*a*.
39.	Flavius Agricola	R	Husband of 38; father of 16	Free-born (?)		Ch. 2, Note 4; *CIL*, vi, 3, 17985*a*; *Report*, i, p. 88.
40.	Iulia Palatina	M	Wife of 57; mother of 45	Free-born (?)		Ch. 3, Note 23.

No.	Name	Symbol	Relationship	Status	Reference
44.	Iulius Piscianus	D	Son of 30		Ch. 4, Note 2, vi.
45.	Iulius Tarpeianus	M	Son of 40, 57	Free-born (?)	Ch. 3, Note 23.
46.	Iunia Spatale	D	Wife of 42		Ch. 4, Note 2, iv.
47.	Iunius Rufinus	D	Husband of 5		Ch. 4, Note 2, ii, iii.
48.	Marcia Felicitas	Behind X	Sister of 50		Ch. 3, Note 92.
49.	Marcia Thrasonis	D	Wife of 51	Free-born (?)	Ch. 3, Note 79.
50.	Marcia Urbica	Behind X	Sister of 48		Ch. 3, Note 92.
51.	Q. Marcius Hermes		Husband of 49	Free-born (?)	Ch. 3, Note 79.
52.	T. Matuccius Demetrius	O		Freedman	Ch. 4, Note 2, xviii, *Report*, i, p. 49, Note 1.
53.	Matuccius Entimus	O		Freedman of 55 *lintearius*	Ch. 4, Note 2, xvii; *Report*, ii, Pl. 9, *b*.
54.	T. Matuccius Hermaiscus	O		Freedman	Ch. 4, Note 2, xviii; *Report*, i, p. 49.
55.	T. Matuccius Pallas	O		Freedman	Ch. 4, Note 2, xvii; *Report*, ii, Pl. 9, *b*.
56.	Matuccius Zmaragdus	O		Freedman of 55 *lintearius*	Ch. 4, Note 2, xvii; *Report*, ii, Pl. 9, *b*.
57.	Maximus	M	Husband of 40; father of 45	Free-born (?)	Ch. 3, Note 23.
58.	Novia Trophima	A			Ch. 1, Note 28; De Visscher, *L'Antiquité Classique*, xv, 1946, p. 117 ff.

No.	Name	Tomb	Relationships	Status	Profession, etc.	References to text, etc.
59.	L. Octavius Cornelianus	F	Son of 33			Ch. 2, Note 21.
60.	M. M̄. Onesimus	D	Father of 44	Freedman (?)		Ch. 4, Note 2, vi.
61.	Ostoria Chelidon	Behind Z	Daughter of 62; wife of 97	Free-born		Ch. 4, Note 2, xx.
62.	Ostorius Euhodianus	Behind Z	Father of 60; father-in-law of 97	Free-born	Senator	Ch. 4, Note 2, xx.
63.	Papiria Profutura	E	Wife of 13			Ch. 4, Note 2, xi.
64.	Passullena Secundina	C				Ch. 4, Note 2, i.
65.	Pompeia Maritima	H¹	Mother of 66	Free-born (?)		Ch. 4, Note 2, xv.
66.	T. Pompeius Proculus Successus	H¹	Son of 65	Free-born (?)		Ch. 4, Note 2, xv.
67.	T. Pompeius Successus I	H	Father of 68	Free-born (?)		Ch. 4, Note 2, xiv.
68.	T. Pompeius Successus II	H	Son of 67	Free-born (?)		Ch. 4, Note 2, xiv.
69.	C. Popilius Heracla	A	Husband of 35	Free-born (?)		Ch. 1, Note 28; De Visscher, *L'Antiquité Classique*, xv, 1946, p. 117 ff.
70.	Restitutus	E		Freedman		Ch. 4, Note 2, vii.
71.	Statia Kara	E	Daughter of 41			Ch. 4, Note 2, xii.

No.	Name		Relationship	Status	Reference
74.	Tullia Secunda	C	Daughter of 73, 79; sister of 76; wife of 23	Free-born (?)	Ch. 2, p. 44 and Note 22; ch. 4, Note 2, i.
75.	Tullia Tr . . .	F			Ch. 2, Note 21.
76.	T. Tullius Athenaeus	C	Son of 73, 79; brother of 74; brother-in-law of 23	Free-born (?)	Ch. 2, Note 22; ch. 4, Note 2, i.
77.	L. Tullius Hermadion I	F	Father of 78	Free-born (?)	Ch. 2, p. 46.
78.	L. Tullius Hermadion II	F	Son of 77	Free-born (?)	Ch. 2, p. 46.
79.	L. Tullius Zethus	C	Husband of 73; father of 74, 76; father-in-law of 23	Free-born (?)	Ch. 2, Note 22.
80.	Tyrannus I	E	Husband of 6; father of 81, 85	Imperial freedman	Ch. 4, Note 2, viii.
81.	Tyrannus II	E	Son of 6, 80; brother of 85	Freedman (?)	Ch. 4, Note 2, x.
82.	Ulpius Narcissus	A			Ch. 1, Note 28; De Visscher, L'Antiquité Classique, xv, 1946, p. 117 ff.
83.	M. Ulpius Pusinnio	C (now in the museum)	Husband of 1; father of 84	Free-born (?)	Ch. 2, p. 57, Note 40; Bullettino della Commissione Archeologica Comunale di Roma, lxx, 1942, p. 99, Fig. 4, c.
84.	M. Ulpius Pusinnio Cupitianus	C (now in Z)	Son of 1, 83	Free-born (?)	Ch. 2, p. 57.

APPENDIX A—*continued*

No.	Name	Tomb	Relationship	Status	Profession, etc.	Reference to text, etc.
85.	Urbanus	E	Son of 6, 80; brother of 81	Imperial slave	*adiutor tabulariorum rationis patrimoni*	Ch. 4, Note 2, viii.
86.	Valeria Galatia	H	Wife, or sister, of 96 (?)			Ch. 4, Note 2, xiv.
87.	Valeria Florentia	H	Wife of 91		Christian (?)	Ch. 3, p. 91.
88.	Valeria Maxima	H	Daughter of 37, 94; sister of 95	Free-born (?)		Ch. 3, Note 59.
89.	Valeria Taccina	T	Daughter of 72			Ch. 4, Note 2, xix; *Report*, ii, Pl. 16, *a*.
90.	Valeria Theonice	H	Wife of 10			Ch. 4, Note 2, xiii.
91.	Valerinus Vasatulus	H	Husband of 87		Christian (?)	Ch. 3, p. 91.
92.	A. Valeri[nus?]	F				Ch. 2, Note 21.
93.	C. Valerius Eutychas	H	Husband of 34	Freedman of 94		Ch. 3, Note 61.
94.	C. Valerius Herma	H	Husband of 37; father of 88, 95	Free-born (?)		Ch. 3, Notes 59, 60, 61
95.	C. Valerius Olympianus	H	Son of 37, 94; brother of 88	Free-born (?)		Ch. 3, Notes 59, 60
96.	Valerius Philumenus	H	Husband, or brother, of 86 (?)			Ch. 4, Note 2, xiv.
97.	Vibius Iolaus	Behind Z	Husband of 60; son-in-law of 62	Free-born (?)	*a memoria imperatoris Augusti*	Ch. 4, Note 2, xx.

100.	L. Volusius Successus	N	Husband of 99; father of 32	Free-born (?)		Ch. 4, Note 2, xvi; *Report*, ii, Pl. 9, *a*.

Fragmentary inscriptions of uncertain content

101.	Berenice	H¹	Wife of 104	Free-born (?)		Appendix D
102.	Coelia Mascellina	T (not in original position)	Daughter of 103	Free-born (?)		Ch. 4, Note 6.
103.	Cn. Coelius Masculus	T (not in original position)	Father of 102	Free-born (?)	Husband of woman (name lost) who traded in olive-oil and wine from Spanish province of Baetica	Ch. 4, Note 6.
104.	Diodorus?	H¹	Husband of 101	Free-born (?)		Appendix D

Inscription of uncertain provenance

105.	P. Aelius Isidorus	E (?) (now below the Niche of the Pallia)		Free-born (?)		• Ch. 7, pp. 202–3, Note 15.

APPENDIX B

The 'Memoria Petri' of Pope Anacletus

In his most useful and penetrating analysis of the literary and archaeological evidence regarding the early history of the Vatican shrine, and of the discussion of this evidence occasioned by the publication of the official *Report*, Ruysschaert[1] puts forward an ingenious theory of his own (pp. 21–37) to account for the facts revealed by the excavations. This is based on a passage in the biography of Pope Anacletus in the *Liber Pontificalis* (i, p. 125), which reads: 'hic memoriam beati Petri construxit et conposuit, dum presbiter factus fuisset a beato Petro, seu alia loca ubi episcopi reconderentur sepulturae; ubi tamen et ipse sepultus est iuxta corpus beati Petri, III Id. Iulias', a passage which, shorn of what may reasonably be regarded as later editorial interpolations, probably stood in the first edition as: 'hic memoriam beati Petri construxit et conposuit, dum presbiter factus fuisset a beato Petro, ubi episcopi reconderentur; et ipse sepultus est III Id. Iulias' ('He built and put in order a *memoria* of the blessed Peter, since he had himself been ordained priest by Peter, in order that the bishops (*sc.* of Rome) might be buried there; and he was himself buried on the 13th of July'). Pope Anacletus, who figures fifth in the *Liber Pontificalis* under the name 'Aneclitus', is usually regarded as a doublet of Cletus, who figures third; and if we regard the phrase 'dum presbiter factus fuisset a beato Petro' as a characteristic editorial comment, inserted to explain the attribution to the fifth bishop of Rome of an event that might more naturally have been attributed to the third, under whom the problem of the burial of St. Peter's successors first became actual, we are left with the probability that the sources available to the original sixth-century compiler of the *Liber Pontificalis* included, in addition to two or more variant lists of the earliest bishops of Rome, a tradition that attributed to one of them, Anacletus, the establishment of a *memoria* (a term which would have covered any form of grave-monument or memorial building) of St. Peter, which was intended to serve also as a cemetery for St. Peter's successors.[2]

This passage has been variously interpreted. The one interpretation is that proposed by Kirschbaum (*Stimmen der Zeit*, August 1952, p. 331) and followed by the present writers in chapter 6 (p. 155), which regards the passage as misplaced by the compiler of the *Liber Pontificalis* as a result of confusion in his sources between the very similar names of Anacletus and Anicetus; the latter was bishop of Rome *c.* 160, and the event recorded in this passage is the establishment of the second-century shrine. Another recent interpretation is that of

Carcopino (*Études d'histoire chretienne*, pp. 179–83), who maintains that it was not until the time of Cletus-Anacletus, a couple of decades after St. Peter's death, that such scanty remains of his body as had been salvaged from the place of execution finally received burial in a casket on the site of what later became the second-century shrine. In so far as this hypothesis can be objectively discussed, it may be held to have been covered by implication in chapter 6, where the writers have set out their reasons for believing that the event that occasioned the construction of the second-century shrine was the disturbance of an actual body, which the contemporary Church identified as that of St. Peter.

The clause 'ubi episcopi reconderentur' has, tacitly at any rate, been regarded by nearly all commentators (including Carcopino) as an accretion to the original tradition. Ruysschaert, on the other hand, not only accepts whole-heartedly the view contained in the *Report*, that the central space beneath the second-century shrine marks the original resting-place of St. Peter's body, venerated continuously as such ever since his martyrdom and burial, but maintains that the record of the establishment of an episcopal cemetery by Cletus-Anacletus derives from an authentic tradition of the early Church, and that the excavations have furnished evidence which, although falling short of proof, nevertheless justifies the acceptance of the tradition as a working hypothesis for the interpretation of the remains uncovered. The hypothesis is put forward with reservations: the compiler of the *Liber Pontificalis* or his sources may well have attributed to such an episcopal cemetery burials of which there was no precise record, and neither was the courtyard (P) containing the shrine completely excavated, nor have the contents of the individual graves within it been recorded in detail. Since, however, despite these reservations, Ruysschaert himself does not hesitate to test the practical application of his own proposals by a detailed re-examination of the chronology of those individual graves that have been excavated, and to conclude therefrom that these proposals are well founded, it is legitimate for others to apply the same touchstone. And, so far as concerns the archaeological evidence at present available, his conclusions are, in the writers' opinion, demonstrably unsound.

Ruysschaert's theory hinges on the reinterpretation of the chronology of two groups of graves: (*a*) Graves ι, $\varkappa$, and λ; and (*b*) Graves α, β, δ, ε, and μ. The former group is held to be earlier than, and respected by, the Red Wall, which at this point forms the east wall of Q; the latter group is interpreted as earlier than or contemporary with the construction of the Constantinian Basilica. On the basis of this reinterpretation, Ruysschaert proposes (p. 33, Note 2) the following provisional correlation between the excavated graves and the names of the bishops of Rome who are recorded in the *Liber Pontificalis* as buried near St. Peter (the list and dates are those given by A. Mercati in the current *Annuario Pontificio*, and by A. P. Frutaz, article 'Papa', in *Enciclopedia Cattolica*, ix, p. 759):

Linus (67–76) θ
Cletus-Anacletus (76–88) ι
Evaristus (97–105) ζ (earlier than η, Ruysschaert, p. 104)
Xystus (115–25) η
Telesphorus (125–36) $\varkappa$
Hyginus (136–40) λ
Pius (140–55) β
Anicetus (155–66) ⎤ a, δ, ε, μ, reburials at the time of the construc-
Soter (166–75)   ⎥   tion of the Constantinian Basilica. For the
Eleutherius (175–89) ⎟   burial-place of Anicetus and of Soter, see
Victor (189–99) ⎦   *Liber Pontificalis*, i, p. lxi.

In the case of the second group (a, β, δ, ε, μ), Ruysschaert's chronological observations may be substantially correct. Grave μ is sealed beneath the Constantinian monument, and ε makes use of an inscribed marble slab taken from the Tomb of the Valerii during the construction of the Constantinian Basilica. Grave β, which is certainly the earliest of the group, can hardly antedate the construction of the Red Wall; but the excavators themselves (*Report*, i, pp. 116–17) admit the possibility that it belongs to the pre-Constantinian phase of the shrine, and on the archaeological evidence it could in fact be of any date after the establishment of the ground-level within P at the level marked by the mosaic pavement. It is, on the other hand, very hard to accept Ruysschaert's interpretation of ι, and to believe that the builders of Q, even had they known the exact position of this deeply buried grave, would have been able to dig the foundations of the Red Wall in such a way as not to disturb the flimsy covering of horizontal tiles which was the only protection of the body beneath. The dating of ι carries with it that of $\varkappa$ and λ; and, even if we were to accept Ruysschaert's proposed chronology for these tombs (and on the archaeological evidence as presented in the *Report* it is difficult to exclude it absolutely, however improbable), there would remain serious difficulties. The present writers find it hard to share Ruysschaert's airy dismissal (p. 35) of the level of the footing of the individual walls as an indication of ground-level at the time of construction. It was normal building-practice (the Vatican cemetery itself furnishes a number of examples) to limit the more expensive brickwork facing very strictly to exposed surfaces;[3] and, if this evidence is valid, it is impossible to accept the chronology proposed for ζ and η (both dug after the construction of Tomb S, see p. 147) without drastically modifying the chronology of the whole Vatican cemetery. There remains, in any case, the difficulty that the coincidence between those eleven graves and the figure of eleven bishops of Rome recorded in the *Liber Pontificalis* as buried near St. Peter may be, indeed probably is, quite without significance. The probability that other graves await excavation in the part of P that is still to be explored is such that the identifications proposed, even if they could be made to square more convincingly with the archaeological results, would have little probative value.

The idea of a cemetery established in Flavian times for the exclusive use of the bishops of Rome does not, in the present writers' view, find that support in the archaeological evidence which its author claims for it; and in the absence of independent evidence for what, on the face of it, would seem to be a somewhat unlikely institution at so early a date (it would seem to be more in keeping with what we know of Christianity in this earliest phase that the bishops of Rome should have been buried in the tombs of Christian families, or perhaps, if they were martyrs, near the scenes of their martyrdom), we are probably justified in regarding the attribution of such a project to Anacletus as an interpolation into the tradition recorded in the *Liber Pontificalis*, rather than an authentic record of first-century events. If the entry in the *Liber Pontificalis* has any basis in fact, it must surely be, as Kirschbaum suggests, a misplaced record of the institution of the mid-second-century shrine by Anicetus (155–66). Whether, in that case, Q is or is not a Christian monument (chapter 6, p. 148) is a matter that must be discussed on its own merits. In the present context, it is enough to note that Ruysschaert's reassessment of the chronology put forward in the *Report* for Graves α, β, δ, ε, and μ may be accepted quite independently of the function of Q, since there is nothing to show that these are reburials, rather than the graves of influential Christians who died before (β) or during (ε, μ, and—possibly but not certainly—α and δ) the building of the Basilica; any more than it can be shown that privileged burials such as $\varkappa$ and λ (made after the institution of the shrine) are those of private individuals rather than of Anicetus and his immediate successors. This is a point that could perhaps be established by a fuller account of the condition in which these graves were found when first opened. In itself, the use of sarcophagus-like chests, made up of marble slabs and each of a size to take an extended body, hardly suggests the translation of the remains of bodies buried elsewhere more than a century earlier. But on this, as on other points, Ruysschaert has done a valuable service in insisting on the incompleteness of the evidence at present available. The full story of P cannot be written until that part of it which lies under the Open Confessio has been fully examined.

NOTES

1. See Bibliographical Note, p. x.

2. For the probable relation between the text of the *Liber Pontificalis* and that of the hypothetical first edition, known from two later summaries, see Duchesne, *Liber Pontificalis*, i, pp. xlix–lxvii; and for the probable identity of Cletus and Anacletus, *ibid.*, pp. lxix–lxx.

3. A very clear case in point is Tomb O, of which the outer face to the north is heavily waterproofed (*Report*, p. 49), whereas the whole of the upper part of

the outer face to the west, above the foundation-offset, was built to a good *opus reticulatum* facing—a distinction which can only mean that, whereas the former was built against earth, the latter was built to be seen. It would be very useful to know (and the *Report* does not make it clear) whether in this case the line of the footings was horizontal, or whether (as seems far more probable) it sloped upwards from south to north. It should be added that, quite apart from the evidence of foundation-offsets and wall-surfaces, the relation of ζ to O is clear both from the construction of the grave, with its tiles leaning against the wall of O, and from its absolute level, which is more than two metres above that of the floor immediately to the east of the same wall, and of all the related surface-levels in the adjoining tombs.

APPENDIX C

Other recent publications relating to the Vatican excavations

CHRISTINE MOHRMANN, 'A propos de deux mots controversés de la latinité chrétienne: Tropaeum-Nomen', *Vigiliae Christianae*, viii, 1954, pp. 154–73.

FROM a detailed analysis of the uses of the word 'tropaeum' (=τρόπαιον) in Christian Latin, the writer concludes that Gaius (chapter 5, p. 128 f.) cannot have used it to indicate 'place of martyrdom', since such a usage is not attested in any other document; and she claims that the passage in Eusebius, read in the light of contemporary usage, shows that Eusebius, and presumably also Gaius, had in mind the actual relics of the martyred Apostles (a usage first securely attested elsewhere in the late-fourth century) rather than the funerary monuments that marked their resting-place (a usage for which it is hard to find any parallel).

The word 'nomina', which figures in the second line of the enigmatic epigram of Pope Damasus (chapter 6, p. 168), has recently been claimed (J. Carcopino, *Études d'histoire chrétienne*, 1953, p. 261) as proof that the word 'habitasse' in the first line of the same epigram refers to the sojourn of the Apostles' relics *ad Catacumbas*, rather than to their earthly habitation. Miss Mohrmann points out that the evidence is very far from conclusive. Although 'nomina martyrum' is found, in the sense of 'relics', in North-African inscriptions, of which one at least is as early as Damasus, it is not so attested in Rome and Italy. There can be no certainty that 'nomina . . . Petri pariter Paulique' is more than a common poetic periphrasis for 'Petrum Paulumque'.

In so far as concerns the word 'tropaeum' and the passage in Eusebius, Miss Mohrmann's interpretation has been criticized by Josi in a paper delivered before the Académie des Inscriptions et Belles-Lettres on 25 September 1954 (due for publication in the *Comptes rendus* of the Academy). He points out that at this date the word κοιμητήρια, used by Eusebius in the passage under discussion, means 'tombs' not 'cemeteries', and that Rufinus has been wrongly criticized by Miss Mohrmann (pp. 165–6) for translating it as 'monumenta'. Whatever Gaius may have meant by the word 'tropaea', Eusebius understood him to refer to actual grave-monuments, since he quotes him as describing the τρόπαια as objects that could be 'shown to' and 'found by' visitors to Rome (p. 129). Such phraseology is not applicable to buried relics, and the identification of the Vatican Aedicula with Gaius's 'trophy' holds.

ROBERT MARICHAL, 'Les dates des *graffiti* de Saint-Sebastien', *Académie des Inscriptions et Belles-Lettres: Comptes rendus*, 1953, pp. 60–8.

A proposed new reading of one of the *graffiti* (P. Styger, *Dissertazioni della Pontificia Accademia Romana di Archeologia*, ser. II, xiii, 1918, p. 68, No. 44, Pl. XI) from the walls of the Triclia (chapter 6, p. 171). The reading proposed:

CELERI[NUS]
V IDUS AUG[USTAS]
SACCUL[ARI II]   (*sic*)
ET DONAT[O II COS]

if accepted, proves that the Memoria was already in active use on 9 August 260.

HJALMAR TORP, 'The Vatican excavations and the cult of St. Peter', *Acta Archaeologica*, xxiv, 1953, pp. 27–66.

The purpose of this article is to prove that the excavations have been fundamentally misinterpreted, mainly as a result of dating the entire Vatican cemetery at least half a century too early. The earliest tomb, I, should be dated *c.* 180–90, the latest, Q, *c.* 230. The Aedicula, which is not Christian at all, but is either the tomb of a child or a cult-niche associated with Grave η, dates from *c.* 230–50. The first evidence of Christian interest in the site is the collection of graffiti on Wall *g*, datable *c.* 320. The Aedicula cannot be the τρόπαιον seen by Gaius (who meant no more by his use of this word than the place of the Apostle's martyrdom). The cult of St. Peter must have originated *ad Catacumbas*, where some form of 'invention' took place *c.* 230, to support the pretensions of the Roman Church. For some time after Constantine, the Basilica Apostolorum continued to be the repository of the relics of St. Peter. The Vatican Basilica was not built in the first place to house relics but to commemorate the scene of St. Peter's martyrdom. It was not perhaps until the sixth century that his remains were finally brought from the Via Appia to the Vatican and housed in the marble-lined loculus in Wall *g*.

All of this depends in the last resort on the writer's reassessment of the archaeological evidence, a reassessment which in turn depends for its absolute chronology mainly on the evidence afforded by the types of masonry used in the individual tombs. It is particularly unfortunate, therefore, that he appears to be familiar neither with the site (which would have saved him from some quite unnecessary blunders) nor with certain elementary principles governing the use of masonry techniques as an indication of date. It should not be necessary at this date to point out that the chronological criteria stated by Miss Van Deman (*American Journal of Archaeology*, xvi, 1912, pp. 230–51, 387–432), although still broadly speaking applicable, with certain reservations, to public monuments in the capital, cannot be used indiscriminately to date private monuments like the mausolea of the Vatican cemetery. There are, moreover, regularly two and often three qualities of masonry employed in a single tomb: the fine brickwork of the façade, usually tinted and carefully pointed; a poorer, more widely jointed brickwork, used on the secondary faces and bonded into the finer masonry of the façade by stepped, quoin-like joints at the angles; and an even coarser, internal facing, either of irregular, widely jointed brickwork or of alternate courses of brick and tufa, which served as a basis for the stucco and painted plaster of the interior. Failure to distinguish these factors (*e.g.* Torp, pp. 40–1, Fig. 13), where the date of Q, claimed as the corner-stone of his chronology, is deduced from the masonry of the inner face of one of the grave-recesses, is to invite disaster. To these functional differences must be added differences of local practice. Not only do we find variations of building-practice between sites so closely related as Ostia and Rome (see I. Gismondi in G. Calza, *Scavi di Ostia*, i, 1953, pp. 195–211), but even within the capital individual cemeteries had their own local characteristics. Thus, in the Vatican cemetery, the proximity of the Vatican brickyards (curiously cited by Torp, p. 41, note 62, to show that the brick-stamps in the drain under the Clivus are reused) and even the preferences of individual building-contractors played their part. One can, for example, distinguish two recurrent qualities of brick: a reddish brick, used in Tombs A–G, N, O, Φ, X, and a yellowish brick, used in H, L, V, Q, R, and Ψ. The significance of such factors is not easy to assess. What cannot be gainsaid is the worthlessness of a chronology based on the application of rule-of-thumb methods to a class of monument to which they are fundamentally inapplicable. The last word has not yet been said on the chronology of the Vatican cemetery; but the problem is not to be solved by such methods.

In view of the use that has been made of the evidence of building-materials and technique, it may be useful to append a summary of this evidence tomb by tomb. Unless otherwise stated, the masonry is *opus testaceum, i.e.* concrete faced with thin bricks, and the larger of the two figures given represents an average for 10 courses of bricks and 10 mortar joints, the smaller (in brackets) the average thickness in centimetres of the individual bricks. The latter figure in particular is approximate only, since there was a considerable variety even within the bricks of a single batch, but the average figure is fairly reliable.

Tomb A: Façade, 37 (bricks, 3–3·3); flank, 44. Interior not excavated.

Tomb B: Façade, 35 (bricks, 3–3·2); flank, nowhere free-standing. Interior, coarse brickwork, 49; blocking of inner arch (added in second period), alternate courses of brick and tufa.

Tomb C: Façade, 35 (bricks, 3–3·2); flank, coarser brickwork (not readily measurable). Interior, alternate courses of brick and tufa.

Tomb D: Façade, 34 (bricks, 3); flank, nowhere free-standing. Interior, coarse brickwork, 50 (inner face of façade), and panels of tufa reticulate in a framework of brick.

Tomb E: Façade, 34 (bricks, 3–3·2); flank, coarser brickwork (not readily measurable). Interior, alternate courses of brick and tufa.

Tomb F: Façade, 32 (bricks, 3); flank, nowhere free-standing. Interior (including stairs), alternate courses of brick and tufa.

Tomb G: Façade, 31 (bricks, 3); flank, 47. Interior (including stairs), coarse brickwork, 50.

Tomb H: Façade (including pilasters), 30 (bricks, 2·8–3); flank, nowhere free-standing. Interior (including stairs), coarse brickwork, 52. Walls of forecourt, 31.

Tomb I: Façade, 33; flank, 47 (bricks, 3·2). Interior, alternate courses of brick and tufa.

Tomb L: Façade, 31 (bricks, 2·8–3); flank, 46. Interior, inaccessible.

Tomb M: Façade, destroyed; flank, nowhere free-standing. Interior, coarse brickwork, 48.

Tomb N: Façade, 32; flank, 48. Interior, not excavated.

Tomb O: Façade, 36; flank, 48. Interior, coarse brickwork, c. 50. Forecourt: brick, 36, and panels of tufa reticulate in a framework of brick.

Tomb Q: Outer face, inaccessible. Interior, coarse brickwork, 57.

Tomb R: East flank, towards Clivus, 36. Interior, coarse brickwork, 51.

Tomb S: Façade, 35; flank, 45. Interior, not accessible.

Tomb T: Façade, 31; angle-pilasters and flank, 40. Interior, alternate courses of brick and tufa.

Tomb U: Façade not preserved, but presumably as T; flank, 41. Interior, alternate courses of brick and tufa.

Tomb V: Back and west flank only exposed, 28 (bricks, 2·7–2·8). Interior, not excavated.

Tomb Z: Façade destroyed; flank and back, irregular brickwork, 47–49. Interior, alternate courses of brick and tufa.

Tomb Φ: Façade, sides, and back, all 34 (bricks 3–3·2); angle-pilasters, 39, of finer, more widely jointed masonry (bricks, 3). Interior, alternate courses of brick and tufa.

Tomb X: Façade destroyed; back and sides, 34 (bricks, 3), with angle-pilasters, 42, of finer, more widely jointed masonry, with pointing (bricks, 3–3·5). Interior, not excavated.

Tomb Ψ: Back only excavated, 47 (bricks, 3), with 'quoin' of finer brick-work, 40 (bricks, 3–3·5).

HUGH LAST, *Journal of Roman Studies*, xliv, 1954, pp. 114–16. Review of Carcopiano's *Études d'histoire chrétienne*.

Last comments on the significance of the *graffiti* on Wall *g* and at San Sebastiano, and on the question as to whether St. Peter's body is likely to have been recovered after his martyrdom.

APPENDIX D

New finds of inscriptions in Tomb H

AFTER passing the first proofs of this book, the writers learnt of restorations undertaken recently in the Tomb of the Valerii (Tomb H), in the course of which several further inscriptions have come to light. These inscriptions record, among others, Aurelia Charite and her father Aurelius Psittacus; Aurelius Helius and his wife Satria Ianuaria; and Flavius Statilius Olympius, a Christian, whose delightfully illiterate epitaph incorporates the Chi-Rho monogram. The inscription recording Flavius Diodorus and his wife Selenia Berenice, previously known only in a fragmentary state (Appendix A, Nos. 104 and 101), is now complete; the phrase *comparaverunt libertis libertabusque posterisque eorum,* which it contains, may refer to the purchase either of a whole tomb or of a burial-site within a tomb. A second inscription of Flavius Diodorus and Selenia Berenice records their infant grandson Flavius Velenius Diodorus, and alludes to the purchase (?) mentioned in the first inscription.

INDEX

The writers are greatly indebted to Mrs. Ann Morley, sometime Scholar of Newnham College, Cambridge, for compiling this Index)